# The Webbs and Soviet Communism

BOLSHEVISM AND
THE BRITISH LEFT

*Part Two*

---

# The Webbs and Soviet Communism

Kevin Morgan

Lawrence & Wishart
LONDON 2006

British Library Cataloguing in Publication Data.
A catalogue record for this book is available from the British Library

Typeset by e-type, Liverpool
Printed in Great Britain by Biddles, Kings Lynn

ISBN 1 905007 26 4

# Contents

# Preface and acknowledgements

While the study which follows can stand on in its own as a reappraisal of the Webbs, it also forms the second instalment of a three-part study collectively entitled *Bolshevism and the British Left*. The first volume, *Labour Legends and Russian Gold*, is published simultaneously with this one. A third, centring on the militant trade unionist A.A. Purcell, is still in progress. Chronologically, the study ranges from before the Russian revolution to the onset of the Cold War. Particularly in the course of the third volume, one of the themes it traces is thus the development by this later period of a mainstream Labour anti-communism. Nevertheless, for the intervening period probably the central research problem addressed is the combination in Britain of a largely marginal communist party and a sense of sympathy, solidarity and sometimes identification with Soviet Russia extending far beyond the communists' ranks. The overall rationale for the project, outlined in an introduction to the first volume, is that this is likely to offer insights into the wider character of the British left, not only in respect of ideas and political culture, but as regards its organisational forms and institutional narratives. Through the relatively late arrival and limited reach of national party organisation, the argument is put forward here that it was only over the course of the 1930s and 1940s that a primary cleavage was established between communism, in both its British and Soviet variants, and British social democracy. Persisting much longer than is sometimes imagined, multiple lines of differentiation – political, industrial, functional, generational – continued to offset the sense of a basic Labour-communist divide, at least insofar as this was expressed in attitudes to Russia.

The Webbs, from this point of view, provide a less idiosyncratic case than is sometimes imagined. In pursuing the couple's interconnections with wider milieux on the left, the account presented here makes no attempt to provide a conventional biographical treatment. Given the excellent studies that have been devoted to aspects of the couple's early lives and thought, these are revisited here only to the extent that they help to illuminate the later turnings which they took. Instead, the main narrative picks up the story with what I call the 'Edwardian' Webbs, when both the biographical literature and, in due course, the published editions of Beatrice's diaries become much patchier in coverage. Even for this later period, I have not adopted a consistent biographical focus.

On the one hand, separate chapters on the 'roads to Russia' of Fabian technocrats, militant co-operators and revolutionary elitists serve to locate the Webbs within a set of wider traditions, some more familiar than others. On the other hand, key aspects of the Webbs' own careers, notably Sidney's advancement within the Labour Party, are passed over in relatively cursory fashion. The focus instead on Beatrice is due not only to the fact that the sources are richer, or because I find her more interesting than her husband (though it is useless to deny this), but because the evidence suggests that she was the key partner in embracing communism, and did so for reasons going far beyond the Fabians' proverbial 'state socialism exclusively'. If Beatrice could never have written *Soviet Communism* without Sidney, Sidney would never have wanted to without Beatrice. This, in any case, is the interpretation presented here.

Responsibility for this and all other judgements expressed is mine alone. Compared with the more sociable nature of my interests in communist history, this has been a somewhat isolated enterprise, and intellectually my main debts are to scholars with whom I have not discussed these issues and from whose interpretations of the Webbs and their contemporaries I sometimes found myself dissenting. It is therefore only the more necessary to point out that an account like this would hardly have been possible without the pioneering scholarship of writers and editors like Peter Beilharz, Eric Hobsbawm, Alan McBriar, Norman and Jeanne Mackenzie, Deborah Epstein Nord, Tony Wright, Eileen Yeo and the late Marcel Liebman. I am rather more critical, as will be seen, of the way in which Margaret Cole edited Beatrice Webb's diaries and the way in which this influenced subsequent accounts of some key socialist debates. A special word is necessary in relation to the Webbs' official biographer, Royden Harrison, who died when I was completing my final draft. I have thought it best to leave my references to Harrison's work substantially unaltered, and it will be clear that I was by no means at one with him regarding his assessment of Beatrice Webb. His treatment of Sidney Webb, on the other hand, was in many respects authoritative, and the completion of Harrison's biography would no doubt have provided an important further context for the study presented here.

Among my other debts, I must thank my Manchester colleagues in Government (now Politics) for the internal research assistance scheme which allowed me to supplement a half-year sabbatical on the project in 1997-8. The bulk of the work on Beatrice's diaries and other materials in the Passfield papers was carried out at this time, and I particularly wish to thank the archivists at the BLPES for their assistance in this period. I again want to acknowledge the assistance of the late Noreen Branson, in allowing me access to the LRD archives; and I want to thank Gillian Lonerghan of the Co-operative Union library in Manchester, where I carried out much of the research for chapter nine.

I should also like to thank Serge Wolikow and Jean Vigreux for the opportunity to visit the University of Burgundy, where I was able to follow up the French references used in the same chapter. Thanks also to Sally Davison for her continued editorial support.

Though a draft of the manuscript was completed in 1999, work on the final version had to wait until 2002, when the anticipated arrival of Jane Morgan imposed a final and absolute deadline. Like every other one I missed it, and I want to thank Julie and Sam for this further extended call on their help and forbearance. Janey, we never for a moment thought of calling you Beatrice. Now you're three, we're not so sure. Long may you too decide on your own stereotypes.

Kevin Morgan
November 2005

## Abbreviations used in text and notes

| | |
|---|---|
| Arcos | All-Russian Co-operative Society |
| BLPES | British Library of Political and Economic Science |
| BSP | British Socialist Party |
| BWD | Beatrice Webb diaries |
| CP(GB) | Communist Party (of Great Britain) |
| CPSU | Communist Party of the Soviet Union |
| CU | Co-operative Union |
| CWS | Co-operative Wholesale Society |
| *DLB* | *Dictionary of Labour Biography*, vols 1-10, ed. Joyce M. Bellamy and John Saville, 1972-2000; vols 11-12, ed. Keith Gildart, David Howell and Neville Kirk, 2003-4 |
| ECCI | Executive Committee of the Communist International |
| FRD | Fabian Research Department |
| GFTU | General Federation of Trade Unions |
| GPU | Soviet secret police |
| ICA | International Co-operative Alliance |
| IFTU | International Federation of Trade Unions |
| IISH | International Institute for Social History |
| ILP | Independent Labour Party |
| LCC | London County Council |
| LHASC | Labour History Archive and Study Centre |
| LRD | Labour Research Department |
| LSI | Labour and Socialist International |
| MRC | Modern Records Centre, University of Warwick |
| NAFTA | National Amalgamated Furnishing Trades Association |
| NFRB | New Fabian Research Bureau |
| NCPD | National Campaign for the Prevention of Destitution |
| NEP | New Economic Policy |
| NGL | National Guilds League |
| PCF | Party Communist Français (French Communist Party) |
| PCI | Italian Communist Party |
| RACS | Royal Arsenal Co-operative Society |
| RGASPI | Russian State Archive of Socio-Political History |
| RILU | Red International of Labour Unions or Profintern |
| RSDLP | Russian Social Democratic and Labour Party |
| SDF | Social Democratic Federation |
| SPD | German Social Democratic Party |
| SWML | South Wales Miners' Library, University College, Swansea |
| TGWU | Transport and General Workers' Union |
| TUC | Trades Union Congress |
| WCG | Women's Co-operative Guild |
| WEWNC | War Emergency Workers' National Committee |
| WCML | Working Class Movement Library |
| WIR | Workers' International Relief |

**Major works cited of Sidney and Beatrice Webb**

| | |
|---|---|
| *CCM* | S. & B. Webb, *The Consumers' Co-operative Movement*, Longmans, 1921 |
| *CMGB* | B. Potter (Webb), *The Co-operative Movement in Great Britain*, Allen & Unwin, 1930 edn |
| *CSCGB* | S.& B. Webb, *A Constitution for the Socialist Commonwealth of Great Britain*, Longmans, 1920 |
| *DCC* | S. &. B. Webb, *The Decay of Capitalist Civilisation*, Fabian Society and Allen & Unwin, 1923 (written c. 1919-20) |
| *EPLP* | S. &. B. Webb, *English Poor Law Policy*, Longmans, 3 vols, 1927-9 |
| *HTU* | S. &. B. Webb, *The History of Trade Unionism 1866-1920*, Longmans, 1920 edn |
| *ID* | S. &. B. Webb, *Industrial Democracy*, Longmans, 1920 ed |
| *MA* | B. Webb, *My Apprenticeship*, Longmans, 2nd edn |
| *OP* | B. Webb, *Our Partnership*, Longmans, 1948 |
| *PD* | S. & B. Webb, *The Prevention of Destitution*, Longmans, 1911 |
| *SCANC* | S. & B. Webb, *Soviet Communism. A new civilisation*, Longmans, 2nd edn, 1937 |
| *TASR* | S. & B. Webb, *The Truth about Soviet Russia*, Longmans, 2nd edn, 1944 |
| *WMT* | S. Webb, *The Works Manager Today. An address prepared for a series of private gatherings of works managers*, Longmans, 1917 |

## *Chapter one*

# The Webbs as metaphor

'On any showing, I think, *Soviet Communism* is a great book.' That, at least, was the considered verdict of Harold Laski in 1947.[1] The book thus canonised was Sidney and Beatrice Webb's *Soviet Communism: a new civilisation?*, originally published in 1935 and famously divested of its question mark for a second edition two years later.[2] 'It had a wide circulation', Laski further noted, 'not least in the Labour Movement, and there, in a special degree, among trade union officials, especially of the younger generation'. Through cheap trade union editions, indefatigably organised by Sidney Webb, and through the machinery of the Left Book Club, this leviathan of fellow-travelling did indeed become something of a best-seller. Nearly 40,000 copies were sold by the time of the war, and Beatrice Webb could scarcely contain her delight to find even a London cabbie spending two hours a night on the book. 'When the taxi drivers of London take to reading about the USSR, to the extent of 1100 pages', she enthused, 'the revolution can hardly be far off'.[3] For the young Eric Heffer, who borrowed from an older workmate one of the bulk-order copies bought by the Woodworkers' union, if not the revolution, then joining the British communist party was indeed not far off once he had read the book from cover to cover.[4] Nor were well-disposed intellectuals any less susceptible to its fascination. Laski, who on its publication found it 'a grand book – ample, judicious, with a sense of the significance of the adventure that sweeps one along', also described for the Webbs the still more extraordinary absorption of the Liberal politician Sir Ernest Simon. 'He said he had taken it up with him last week when he intended to walk in the Lakes', Laski wrote. 'Instead he had got so wrapped up in the book that he did no walking at all.' Three days later there came effusive confirmation from Simon himself. 'Thirty years ago you started me on my public career by the [Poor Law] Minority Report', he rhapsodised. 'I don't know yet what you have done to me this time! But it is certainly the most exciting, stimulating and important book I ever read.'[5]

Readers today will not recapture that sense of excitement. Tirelessly applied to Stalin's plans and purges, the leaden prolixity of Sidney Webb's prose, likened by Margaret Cole to 'the slow passing of an infinitely long, laden freight train', has a peculiarly depressing effect. To reel under a Webbian 'heavy artillery of fact' is hard enough without the novel presence of a Fifth Column of palpable untruths and distortions.[6] The book's more imaginative flights, usually Beatrice Webb's but occasionally added at proof stage by Bernard Shaw, are far from being a compensation. The liberal use of exclamation marks, a constant breezy 'fancy that!', bears in retrospect a ghoulish irony. Nobody now thinks this a great book, and, as David Caute has demonstrated, for displaying our wits at the expense of past follies there is no softer target.[7] Even among sympathetic contemporaries, the Webbs' hardiness of commitment stands out from all but the communists and their closest associates. Harold Laski, who from the start had had reservations about the Russians' lack of intellectual freedom, was stung by the trials and purges into a far more critical assessment of the book's second edition.[8] Ernest Simon, so fired by the Webbs as to make his own Moscow pilgrimage, could not help drawing comparisons with Britain that were not always flattering to the Soviets. How much more humane, in his special field of housing, were Simon's own municipal schemes at Wythenshawe compared with Stalin's megalomaniac diversion of building resources to the Palace of the Soviets.[9]

While such concerns signalled the defection of the 'left intellectuals', by 1939 even taxi drivers had stopped buying the book; as Beatrice admitted, the stock of the USSR had fallen almost so low as to discourage 'even fanatics like ourselves'.[10] Almost, though, but not quite; and one is left with the formidable puzzle of this septuagenarian fanaticism, bending but never giving way to circumstance. We are not, after all, dealing here with a clerical oddity like the 'Red' Dean of Canterbury, Hewlett Johnson, or a professional casuist like the lawyer D.N. Pritt. Distinctive in a European context, the Webbs' case seems altogether more challenging and problematic than the average 1930s' fellow-traveller's. Long-acclaimed as scrupulous and pioneering social investigators, they were also co-inspirers of what the Labour leader Clement Attlee described as the 'characteristically British political movement' of Fabianism.[11] With his unheroic gospel of the 'inevitability of gradualness', Sidney Webb remained until 1931 the most cautious and uncomplaining of Ramsay MacDonald's colleagues on the Labour front benches. Even in death, he and Beatrice rest, honoured and complaisant, in the characteristically British pantheon of Westminster Abbey. Amidst their literary and institutional remains, from the Labour Party constitution and London School of Economics, to classic works on English local government and the co-operative movement, their vast apologia for Stalinism sits uneasily. No wonder that successive scholars have felt impelled to untangle the problem.

Most of them have concluded that the riddle is not such a riddle after all. Even before the Webbs had returned from their two-month sojourn in the USSR, G.D.H. Cole was arguing for the 'essential commonality of aim' as between hosts and visitors, and this affinity, variously interpreted, has since then acquired the force of a veritable orthodoxy. 'For wide as are the differences between ... Lenin and Stalin and the Fabian Socialism with which the Webbs are inseparably associated', Cole wrote that early summer of 1932, 'the points of identity go far deeper and are far more important ...'[12] This, said the Belgian historian Marcel Liebman, was less a case of conversion than of discovery, and that itself in large part self-discovery.[13]

For Cole, whose own ambivalence regarding both Stalinism and the Webbs will be noted in due course, a key point of identity was the planned socialist economy, of which he believed Sidney Webb might be regarded as the outstanding prophet. Subsequent commentators, while not contesting that link, have emphasised not just the logic of planning but the hegemony of the planners. A key reference point has been the identification of Fabianism with the *nouvelle couche sociale* of late Victorian Britain: the emerging class of specialists and bureaucrats, personified by Sidney Webb, whose own emancipation seemed bound up with collectivism. 'Talented, educated, ambitious and propertyless', noted Norman Mackenzie, the editor of the Webbs' correspondence, 'they had to find some means of inserting themselves into positions of influence and some convincing rationale for bureaucratic manipulation of the system'. Drawing on potent images of Fabianism as an ideology of social control, Webbian authorities like Mackenzie have stressed the 'elitist and authoritarian bias' that pervaded the Fabian conception of the good society. 'All through their lives', Mackenzie went on, 'the Webbs had believed in a middle-class, quasi-scientific, technocratic or managerial form of collectivism very different from the ambiguities of social democracy, or the realities of the working-class movement'. Another account likens them to Plato's Guardians, revelling in 'the orderly arrangement of the masses by a dedicated and capable elite'.[14] It was not, in consequence, popular upheaval that attracted them but purposive construction; not the exiled Cassandra Trotsky but the great helmsman Stalin. 'The Webbs', Cole accurately predicted, 'would have been fishes out of water in the Russia of 1920; they are likely to find themselves thoroughly at home in the Russia of 1932'.[15]

Those aspects of the double closure argument that postulate an underlying affinity between communism and collectivism thus seem to find their most striking confirmation in the Webbs. Beneath the surface tensions of tactics and vocabulary, the rival forms of state socialism, reformist and revolutionary, evidently shared a more fundamental unity of purpose making such transitions possible. Cole, whose guild socialism is normally seen as a casualty of this consensus of polarities, again set the tone for later accounts. 'The differences', he wrote, 'concern mainly the means of getting Socialism, and not its character when the Socialists have attained to power'.[16] This only seemed to confirm the Webbs' own position on what Sidney once inimitably called 'revolution of a revolutionary kind': that they conceded it nothing in earnestness or extremity of intent, but only 'sadly and sorrowfully' believed it impracticable.[17] Moreover, if Cole suggested that it was the Bolsheviks who had been won over to the Webbs' conceptions at least as much as the reverse, this was no more than the Webbs themselves believed. As Beatrice noted on the return from Russia of Bernard Shaw, their precursor on the trip by a year, 'Russian revolution was pure Fabianism – Lenin and Stalin had recognised the "inevitability of gradualness"!'[18] As early as 1921, at this stage to Beatrice's indignation, the pro-Bolshevik journalist M. Philips Price had seen in Lenin's New Economic Policy a forced resemblance to the Fabians.[19] Even earlier, in July 1918, H.G. Wells had described Lenin as a Russian Sidney Webb, 'a rotten little incessant egotistical intriguer'. That of course was pure invective, though such comments later came to give inordinate pleasure to the Webbs themselves. 'When the commoner type of Tory comes in ... he sees the sinister figure of an English Lenin who is bringing about Communism, not by force, but by underground manipulation of the democratic machine', Beatrice wrote in 1928. 'Not an altogether unpleasant reputation', she added, and the alleged commonality of purpose seems confirmed.[20]

Whatever the political and economic shocks that put paid to the Webbs' earlier anti-Bolshevism, the emphatic endorsement they gave Stalin's regime would be quite inexplicable without a sense of these deep-lying affinities. Moreover, if the language of 'conversion' is indeed inadequate, this is not least because there was never the wholesale repudiation of the couple's earlier beliefs that this would normally suggest. Even so, the parable of the aged Webbs, tidy and clear-cut as they themselves would have wished it, finally rests on a narrative that is both partial and unhistorical. In an illuminating essay, Peter Beilharz has well described how the Fabians, the Webbs in particular, have been 'incredibly influential and yet rarely taken seriously'. Fabianism, as Beilharz puts it, 'has been mocked, caricatured to death, syncretised and homogenised ... All Fabian cats have become apparently grey ...'[21] The Webbs, in other words, have been reduced to a socialist metaphor, all but flattened out by the referential burden they have been made to bear. 'Fabian-Webbism', despite his own rather cavalier use of the term, is the perfect example of the sort of label or 'ism' that Stephen Yeo sees as being used by the labeller-historian to bring what is complex and problematic neatly under control.[22] The deficiencies of such presentations are threefold: first, that the Webbs are inadequately differentiated from their fellow Fabians, and the distinctive inflexions of their thinking often lost sight of; secondly, and perhaps more justifiably given their fondness for the first person plural, that the separate individualities of the self-styled 'firm of Webb' are too easily underplayed; and finally, that the contingencies and adaptations of their several decades of political activity are lost in the frozen postures of a *tableau vivant*.

It is with fitting irony that one of the very worst examples of such oversimplification, stomping over historical niceties for crudely teleological ends, should be entitled *The Pursuit of Certainty*.[23]

It is the last of these deficiencies that the present account is especially concerned to remedy. It recognises the particularities of the Webbs' thinking, and through their close colleague Shaw shows how various were the possible routes from the *Fabian Essays* of the 1880s to the Five Year Plans.[24] The Webbs themselves, where possible and appropriate, will also be disaggregated, for historians have far too readily followed Shaw in assuming that theirs was a 'perfect' and practically indivisible collaboration.[25] If it is true, as their first biographer Mollie Hamilton put it, that it is impossible to think of the Webbs except as a couple, this does not mean that their very thinking was a 'joint process', or that in their writings 'no one can detach what belongs to one from what belongs to the other'.[26] The emphasis placed in this account on Beatrice's contribution is due not just to the vivid body of evidence provided by her diaries, but because the impulsion towards Soviet Russia was, as Cole recognised, initially and more powerfully hers. This, moreover, was not fortuitous but represented a reconfiguration of elements in the Webbs' outlook with which Beatrice in particular can be identified. The tendency of both these distinctions is to temper notions of Fabian state collectivism, seen as leading inexorably to their apotheosis in Soviet Russia, with the Webbian concept of a 'multiform democracy' of state and social institutions alike. As Cole also appreciated, this and not the monolithic state was the 'pure Fabianism' which the couple so erroneously sought for under Stalin.[27]

It is nevertheless the sense of historical volition which it is above all necessary to restore to this narrative; a recognition that it was out of the stresses and controversies of the years that directly preceded it that the Webbs came belatedly in 1932 to discover their new civilisation. No proposal could be more banal and pedestrian, and if it offers new perspectives on a well-worn subject, this merely indicates how neglected this intervening phase of the Webbs' career has been. When one thinks of 'Fabian-Webbism', late Victorian and Edwardian Britain almost invariably comes to mind rather than this later period. Conflicting images loom up of the great unrest and the servile state, with the Webbs emphatically associated with the latter: their methods manipulative, their associations undemocratic and their goals bleakly hygienic and authoritarian. According to Kenneth Morgan's collage of rather sweeping stereotypes, their Fabian keywords were efficiency and order, with a 'creed of Germanic discipline and rigour ... alien to the warm, chapel-reared radicalism from which the ILP derived much of its vitality'.[28] More explicitly and intriguingly, Eric Hobsbawm, whose Cambridge doctoral thesis was on the Fabians, roundly declares them to have had 'no place in the British political tradition' – at first sight, a strangely conservative and exclusive notion.[29] Ramsay

MacDonald, then at the heart of the socialist variant of that tradition, also reflected on the Fabians' 'curious aloofness' from it. 'The movement has listened to the Society', he acknowledged in 1916, 'but in a critical and sceptical frame of mind, and in its great national activities and attitudes it has not been influenced in the very least by the Fabian Society or by one of its leaders'. Two years later, Sidney Webb had the main hand in writing the Labour Party constitution. As Noel Thompson shows, not only was this document very much Fabian-inspired; the dominant economic discourse of the emerging Labour Party was also cast in the same Fabian mould.[30]

The extensive literature on pre-1914 Fabianism is not at issue here. What is at question is the mechanical projection of these Edwardian likenesses some twenty tempestuous years into the future. It is precisely thus that Mackenzie skates over this period to arrive with a bump at *Soviet Communism*. In an essay culminating in the same work, Royden Harrison likewise dwelt on its distant origins without any serious consideration of the Webbs' thinking after 1910.[31] Commentators as diverse as Peter Clarke, W.H. Greenleaf, even Mollie Hamilton, look forward from the Edwardian period to find in the Webbs' communism a seemingly logical and transparent sequel. 'They remained true to the convictions of forty years', Clarke noted, citing the Liberal *Nation* in 1908: '"the will of the people" ... is for them ... only as so much fuel to be utilised by the superior wills of a virtually self-appointed aristocracy of talent'.[32]

In this regard, these leading Webbian authorities fairly represent a literature that has had astonishingly little to say of the partnership's advanced years. Perhaps, as Hobsbawm suggests, the inter-war Fabians simply lost all separate interest and identity in the Labour Party, ill though that accords with their alleged foreignness to British politics. Perhaps, the uneven availability of sources has also played a part. Not only did the long-used Cole edition of the Webb diaries end in 1932, on grounds of their supposed diminished interest thereafter, but it gave a notably partial and circumspect picture of the Webbs' relations with younger socialists like the Coles themselves. Meanwhile, the more searching Fabian historiography of recent years has, albeit with salutary effect, again focused predominantly on the earlier period.[33] So too did the meticulous scholarship of Alan McBriar, while Royden Harrison's long-awaited biography of the Webbs takes the story only as far as 1905.[34] Marcel Liebman's important assessment, fully available only in French, is so far the only attempt to locate in any sort of detail the Webbs' pro-Sovietism in its inter-war context.

It is in the spirit of these less mythologised accounts – significantly, almost all of them approaching the subject from outside the set contours of British labour history[35] – that an evaluation is attempted here of the Webbs' complex evolution following their reorientation to labour movement agencies from the early 1910s. As Liebman's account shows very effectively, this is likely to have a far greater explanatory power simply from the point of view of the Webbs themselves. Far from being the rigid or immobile thinkers that more static accounts either state or imply, the couple were extraordinarily receptive to the changing intellectual currents that repeatedly threatened to pass them by. Certainly, less volatile contemporaries did not fail to observe how the Webbs' oracular status was counterbalanced by extreme impressionability. R.H. Tawney, whose consistency as a thinker was more impressive, conceded their basic continuity of purpose, but also noted their profound accommodations 'both to criticism and to the teaching of events'. Specifically with respect to Beatrice, who was, as we shall see, the more volatile element in the partnership, Tawney wrote of the 'inexhaustible dynamic which swept her through a number of careers', throwing herself into each unreservedly until it paved the way for the next.[36] William Beveridge, an altogether more methodical reformer, also referred to their 'passion for new ideas because they were new', which may be thought a dangerous quality in any but a much wiser epoch.[37] Accounts like Greenleaf's, stressing the couple's ruthless single-mindedness and dogmatism on the basis of partial and overworked citations, tell us more about the ready-made construction of such images than they do about the Webbs themselves.[38] At a purely biographical level, a recognition of the couple's several accommodations, culminating in the grand denouement of *Soviet Communism*, is indispensable to a real historical understanding of the Webbs.

There is moreover a broader and more compelling argument for disinterring these later relationships and debates. No doubt, as Harrison observes in this connection, 'there was a correspondence between the value system of certain late-Victorian professional people and the "strange syndrome of Soviet Marxism under Stalin"'.[39] What is nevertheless more striking is the far more extensive 'correspondence' with Soviet marxism of diverse and even antagonistic sections of the early twentieth-century British left. It was not, to state the obvious, the Webbs' *fin-de-siècle* contacts who were keenest to travel out on 1930s Intourist packages, but those with whom they had much more recently crossed swords or buried hatchets. Moreover, if we do nevertheless isolate the Webbs' nearest contemporaries, these 'certain' late Victorians – Tom Mann, George Lansbury, Eden Paul, Margaret Llewellyn Davies – turn out to have the 'value system' which, without dissimulation, can be referred to as socialism, albeit taking forms, promiscuously combined, as various as syndicalism, co-operation, ethical or Christian socialism and Wellsian eugenics.[40] All these and later figures help to illuminate the path to *Soviet Communism*, and the Webbs' eleventh-hour transmutation needs to be understood within the British labour movement context in which it actually occurred. Only thus can we capture something of the real fractures and commonalities of the Bolshevik-era left.

In part, what is presented here is therefore a relativisation of an episode usually presented either in idiosyncratic terms or as a leftover from a bygone age. Lost in such emphases is the sense that, however distinctive, the Webbs were quite self-consciously part of a very considerable movement of opinion.[41] If they embody deep affinities between Fabianism and Stalinism, what then of the comparable affinities of so many of their guild socialist adversaries, of syndicalists like Tom Mann and A.A. Purcell, of Christian socialists like Lansbury, or of countless forgotten co-operators and trade unionists? The very knottedness and unpredictability of these lines of causation subverts the easy classifications which, like the Webbs themselves, Webbian scholars have so often found irresistible. Moreover, if, like Hobsbawm's communist party, these ill-shaped Webbs cannot be fitted into the British political tradition, that only shows how arbitrary that Procrustean artifice really is. The parallel is perhaps especially apposite, for in its pursuit and interrogation of such easy certainties, the more nuanced Fabian historiography of recent years is strangely akin to the analogous unravellings of communist party history. 'Setting up dichotomies', writes Ian Britain, who also cites the good sense spoken in this connection by Rodney Barker, 'is a neat and plausible way of ... clarifying the rifts within various political, social, intellectual or artistic movements. But are these dichotomies too neat to be true?'[42] It is not the choice of subject but that of historical method that will determine one's reply.

If Morgan's chapels and *verboten* signs suggest one of these dichotomies, a more significant polarity for the years of war and revolution has been that between collectivists and guild socialists: in a word, between the Webbs and the Coles, principally G.D.H. Cole. Providing, in Tony Wright's words, 'a moment of genuine theoretical debate' unsurpassed in a British context, these exchanges have figured prominently in histories of British socialist thought.[43] If in most accounts the Coles have the punchlines and the Webbs the dousings in pails of water, this is due as much as anything to the somewhat less than disinterested literary endeavours of Margaret Cole, who in later years had so far mended bridges with the Webbs as to be appointed one of their trustees. Largely of her own volition, she rapidly expanded the commission to that of chief literary executor and memorialist. Indeed, it was the judgement of such eminent associates as Laski, Tawney and Leonard Woolf that she virtually took personal custody of the Webb legacy; if not, as Laski alleged, as a 'permanent source of income', at least as a long-term security against alternative readings of events.[44] Both Tawney and Woolf withdrew as prospective Webb biographers as a consequence, and half a century later the Webbs' authorised life – eventually entrusted to a former PhD student of Cole's, Royden Harrison – has still to be completed.[45] The result was that, rather than 'not being able to see the Webbs ... for the Coles' , as Woolf commented acidly of Mrs Cole's *Story of Fabian Socialism*, it sometimes seemed impossible – even reading Beatrice's own diaries – to see the Webbs *except* through the Coles.[46] Where there are no victors, history gets written by the survivors; and even Tony Wright, in what remain the outstanding academic commentaries on these events, employs a highly stylised version of the Webbs as little more than a foil for his real heroes.[47]

Revisited here in some detail, a new perspective on these debates helps make sense of what is otherwise inexplicable in the Webbs' own biography, and provides a hitherto neglected context for the Soviet enthusiasms which they came to share with so many of their erstwhile sparring partners. There are also chapters devoted to the 'roads to Russia' of socialist planners and revolutionary elitists, and a re-evaluation of the largely neglected co-operative strand in the couple's work, which hardly figures even in their own official biography. To begin with, however, we need, if we are to make sense of these ramifications, an inkling of how it was that the unflappable Webbs provoked such fury and derision in their detractors, and why it was that the latter should have included so many fellow-socialists and labour historians. The scene is set in Grosvenor Road, Westminster, with not a hobnailed boot in sight.

## NOTES

1. Laski, *The Webbs and Soviet Communism* (Webb Memorial Lecture), Fabian Society, 1947, pp. 5-8.
2. Sidney and Beatrice Webb, *Soviet Communism: a new civilisation* (henceforth *SCANC*), Longmans, 1937 edn for all citations below. A third edition with a new preface was published in 1941.
3. BWD 29 September 1936*. Of the first edition of 20,000 copies, 10,000 were to be distributed in a five-shilling edition through trade unions and other working-class organisations. Of the second (1937) edition, 15,000 went to the Left Book Club, 3,000 to trade unionists and 200 to the normal, thirty-five-shilling trade edition; see BWD 10 May 1936*, 1 October 1937; MRC, UCATT deposit, 78/ASW/3/2/262, Sidney Webb to Frank Wolstencroft, Amalgamated Society of Woodworkers' secretary, 14 January and 11 April 1936 and 10 August 1937.
4. Eric Heffer, *Never a Yes Man*, Verso, 1991, p. 17.
5. Passfield papers 2/4/J/4, Laski to the Webbs, 7 December 1935, Simon to SW, 10 December 1935.
6. Margaret Cole, *The Story of Fabian Socialism*, Mercury Books edn, 1963, p. 53; *OP*, p. 399 for the artillery metaphor.
7. See David Caute, *The Fellow Travellers: a postscript to the enlightenment*, Weidenfeld & Nicolson, 1973, a stimulating account vitiated by easy point-scoring.
8. *Political Quarterly*, January-March 1938, pp. 103-3; see also Michael Newman, *Harold Laski: a political biography*, Macmillan, 1993, pp. 192-5. For Laski's earlier reservations see Passfield papers, Laski to BW, 9 March 1935. Beatrice's claimed that by September 1938, Laski had become 'completely convinced that the Soviet trials and executions were at once

justified in fact and necessary to save the revolution' (BWD 1 September 1938). If this was really the case, the sentiments do not appear to have been expressed in public.

9. BWD 15 February 1936*, 27 August 1937*; Simon papers, Simon to Sidney Webb, 13 April 1937, 'Britain's housing achievement', typescript lecture or broadcast, 19 December 1939. See also Simon et al., *Moscow in the Making*, Longmans, 1937; and, for the Place of the Soviets, Jean-Louis Cohen, *Le Corbusier and the Mystique of the USSR. Theories and projects for Moscow 1928-1936*, Princeton, N.J.: Princeton University Press, 1992, ch. 7.
10. BWD 5 January 1938, 3 January 1939, 15 April 1939.
11. In his review of Margaret Cole's *Story of Fabian Socialism* in the *Sunday Times*.
12. G.D.H. Cole papers A1/2/14, typescript article 'Sidney and Beatrice Webb – socialist forerunners', c. June-July 1932 (article appearing in *Current History*, November 1932).
13. Marcel Liebman, 'Fabianisme et communisme; les Webb et L'Union Soviétique', *International Review of Social History*, vol. 5, 1960, pp. 400-23 and vol. 6, 1961, pp. 49-73.
14. Norman Mackenzie, *Socialism and Society: a new view of the Webb partnership*, London School of Economics, 1978, pp. 17-25; Bill Jones, *The Russia Complex. The British Labour Party and the Soviet Union*, Manchester: MUP, 1977, p. 21.
15. Cole, 'Sidney and Beatrice Webb'.
16. Cole, 'Sidney and Beatrice Webb'.
17. Passfield papers G/73, Sidney Webb, 'The employer of tomorrow; being some of the implications of trade unionism and industrial democracy", typesript lecture, Manchester College of Technology, c. 1920; Webb, *Socialism: true and false*, Fabian Society, 1894, p. 3.
18. BWD 8 August 1931.
19. M. Philips Price, *My Reminiscences of the Russian Revolution* (1921) reviewed by Beatrice Webb, *Fabian News*, June 1921, p. 28. For Price see *Bolshevism and the British Left*, vol. 1, chs 4-5.
20. Wells cited Joseph Freeman, *An American Testament*, Gollancz, 1938, p. 136; BWD 12 July 1934* and 29 November 1928.
21. Peter Beilharz, *Labour's Utopias. Bolshevism, Fabianism, Social Democracy*, Routledge, 1992, p.51.
22. Stephen Yeo, 'Notes on three socialisms – collectivism, statism and associationism – mainly in late-nineteenth- and early-twentieth-century Britain' in Carl Levy, ed., *Socialism and the Intelligentsia 1880-1914*, Routledge & Kegan Paul, 1987, pp. 239, 245.
23. Shirley Robin Letwin, *The Pursuit of Certainty*, Cambridge: CUP, 1965, pp. 342-78.
24. Published in 1889, with Shaw as editor and Sidney Webb as a fellow contributor, *Fabian Essays in Socialism* may be regarded as the founding text of Fabianism.
25. G.B. Shaw, 'Early days' in Margaret Cole, ed., *The Webbs and their Work*, Frederick Muller, 1949, p. 13.
26. Mary Agnes Hamilton, *Sidney and Beatrice Webb. A study in contemporary biography*, Sampson Low, Marston & co, nd, p. 1.

27. Cole, 'Sidney and Beatrice Webb'.
28. Kenneth O. Morgan, 'The Webbs' in *Labour People. Leaders and lieutenants from Hardie to Kinnock*, Oxford: OUP, 1987, pp. 54-63.
29. E.J. Hobsbawm, 'The Fabians reconsidered' in *Labouring Men. Studies in the history of Labour*, Weidenfeld & Nicolson, 1968 edn, p. 252.
30. J.R. MacDonald, review of Pease's *History of the Fabian Society*, *Socialist Review*, August-September 1916, p. 250; Noel Thompson, *Political Economy and the Labour Party. The economics of democratic socialism, 1884-1995*, UCL Press, ch. 7. For a balanced assessment of the Webbs' contribution in this period, see also J.M. Winter, *Socialism and the Challenge of War. Ideas and politics in Britain 1912-1918*, Routledge & Kegan Paul, 1974, e.g. pp. 270 ff.
31. Royden Harrison, 'Sidney and Beatrice Webb' in Levy, *Socialism and the Intelligentsia*, pp. 35-89. Harrison also produced a useful article on Sidney Webb's wartime activities, though without any particular insights for the longer term development of Webbian thinking; see R. Harrison, 'The War Emergency Workers' National Committee, 1914-1920' in Asa Briggs and John Saville, *Essays in Labour History 1886-1923*, Macmillan, 1971, pp. 211-59.
32. Hobsbawm, 'Fabians reconsidered', pp. 254-5; Mary Agnes Hamilton, *Remembering My Good Friends*, Cape, 1944, pp. 258-60; W.H. Greenleaf, *The British Political Tradition. Volume two: the ideological heritage*, Methuen, 1983, ch. 11; Peter Clarke, *Liberals and Social Democrats*, Cambridge: CUP, 1978, p. 262, citing L.T. Hobhouse.
33. Especially suggestive accounts include Ian Britain, *Fabianism and Culture. A study in British socialism and the arts c. 1884-1918*, Cambridge: CUP, 1982; Deborah Epstein Nord, *The Apprenticeship of Beatrice Webb*, Macmillan, 1986; also the essays collected in Peter Beilharz and Chris Nyland, *The Webbs, Fabianism and Feminism*, Aldershot: Ashgate, 1994.
34. A. M. McBriar, *Fabian Socialism and English Politics 1884-1914*, Cambridge: CUP, 1962 and *An Edwardian Mixed Doubles. The Bosanquets versus the Webbs. A study in British social policy 1890-1929*, Oxford: OUP, 1987; Royden Harrison, *The Life and Times of Sidney and Beatrice Webb. 1858-1905: the formative years*, Basingstoke: Palgrave, 2000.
35. Nord is American and Liebman was Belgian. McBriar, Britain and Beilharz are Australian, as is Barbara Caine, author of the important study *Destined to be Wives. The sisters of Beatrice Webb*, Oxford: OUP, 1988.
36. R.H. Tawney, *The Webbs and their Work*, Fabian Society, 1945, p. 14; Tawney papers, 20/4, typescript lecture on Beatrice Webb, mid-1940s.
37. Margaret Cole papers G2/1/4, William Beveridge, 'Centenary of the Webbs. The Webbs' achievement', c.1958-9.
38. See for example Greenleaf, *British Political Tradition. Volume two*, pp. 390-1.
39. Harrison, 'Sidney and Beatrice Webb', p. 37.
40. The first three, like the Webbs, were all born between 1856 and 1859, and Paul a few years later in 1865. All figure in the subplots which follow.
41. It is a virtue of an account like that of Williams's *Labour and Russia*, set in the broader context of the period, that it conveys this point much more effectively; see Andrew Williams, *Labour and Russia. The attitude of the*

*Labour Party to the USSR, 1924-34*, Manchester: MUP, 1989, ch. 13.
42. Britain, *Fabianism and Culture*, pp. 4-5, 229.
43. A.W. Wright, 'Fabianism and guild socialism: two views of democracy', *International Review of Social History*, 23, 1978, pp. 224-41.
44. For the Cole view, see e.g. Margaret Cole, 'Labour Research' in Cole, *The Webbs and their Work*, pp. 147-66; Margaret Cole, 'Guild Socialism and the Labour Research Department' in Asa Briggs and John Saville, eds, *Essays in Labour History 1886-1923*, Macmillan, 1971, 260-83.
45. Tawney papers, 24/1, Tawney to A. Carr-Saunders, 21 April 1949 and 24/2, M. Cole to Tawney, 2 June 1949; Tawney to M. Cole, 6 June 1949; Laski to Tawney, 24 May and 23 September 1949. Woolf papers III, Woolf to A. Carr-Saunders, 11 July and 21 July 1949. Though his objections were less clear cut, Woolf like Tawney referred to a cessation of work on the diaries as a condition of his acting as biographer.
46. Woolf, *Political Quarterly*, vol. 33, 1962, pp. 228-9.
47. A.W. Wright, *G.D.H. Cole and Socialist Democracy*, Oxford: OUP, 1979, pp. 51-2 and passim. The Webbs perform a similar role in Wright's 'Tawneyism revisited: equality, welfare and socialism' in Ben Pimlott, ed., *Fabian Essays in Socialist Thought*, Heinemann, 1984, pp. 81-100.

# *Chapter two*

# Victor and Altiora Bailey

## I

The Edwardian Webbs, if we can use that for shorthand, are not an attractive pairing. H.G. Wells, smarting from his own failed bid to 'make the Fabian Society into an order of the Samurai', cruelly satirised them in his 1911 novel *The New Machiavelli*.[1] For anyone acquainted with the couple, his fictional contrivance of Victor and Altiora Bailey provided not even the thinnest of disguises. Alike in fiction and reality, their centre of operations was a 'hard little house' a stone's throw from Parliament and the rising imperial piles of Whitehall. Here there came to dinner, in juxtapositions that were never accidental, those and those alone who promised utility and influence. 'And what am I here for tonight?' asks a former Prime Minister, not in this case in Wells's parody but in one of Beatrice's diary entries.[2] Frugal suppers, legendary among the habitually overfed, had their compensation in an unstinting disposition to inform, advise, connect and – never quite gently enough to pass unnoticed – steer their guests a little in a collectivist direction. 'At the Baileys' one always seemed to be getting one's hands on the very strings that guided the world', Wells wrote; 'you felt you were in a sort of signal-box with levers all about you, and the world outside ... running on its lines in ready obedience ...' Like an industrious spider at the centre of the web – the metaphor this time is Virginia Woolf's – was Beatrice-Altiora herself. Hers the great scheme evidently was, and even her husband, a brilliant but unassuming gradgrind, seemed chosen not for sloppy or carnal reasons but as its most formidable instrument: 'P.B.P., she boasted, was engraved inside their wedding rings, Pro Bono Publico, and she meant it to be no idle threat.'[3] A good Wellsian, indeed, her beneficent jurisdiction looked beyond mere governance to nature itself. 'If they had the universe in hand, I know they would take down all the trees and put up stamped tin green shades and sunlight accumulators', Wells's narrator observed. 'Altiora thought trees hopelessly irregular and sea cliffs a great mistake ...'

Wells, himself not the most attractive of Edwardians, had a special aptitude for nursing grievances. Moreover, his political tangle with the Fabians had a sharper personal sequel in his liaison with young, emancipated and vulnerable Amber Reeves. Wells's own revealed 'blackguardism' – publicly defying conventional sexual codes in his *Ann Veronica*, even as Amber bore their child – had met with Beatrice's particular indignation.[4] Nevertheless, if he scored such a memorable hit with his caricature of the Baileys, it was because it conveyed what by then had become a prevailing impression of the Webbs. With their friends seemingly found anywhere but on the left, it was clear that, whatever the theories then emerging of the transition to socialism, the Webbian version was not going to arrive by acclaim. Substantially that reflected the revolt against a bureaucratic collectivism personified for the young as 'Webbism'.[5] Nevertheless, the intensity of feeling is best diagnosed as a form of arachnophobia. Already in 1903, Beatrice had written of a 'slump in Webbs' among their own supporters, and ten years later was left speculating as to 'why the Webbs are so hated – all the more so because we are so "damned sure" of our conclusions'. With notable complacency, she ascribed this to the repulsion which fanatics and sentimentalists felt for their qualities of patience, discipline and tolerance.[6] More to the point was a thumbnail sketch by A.G. Gardiner, radical editor of the Liberal *Daily News*, who drew attention to the 'sleuth-like pursuit of their purpose' which made them at once so powerful and so distrusted.

> There is nothing that men dislike so much as being 'managed'. And Mr and Mrs Webb are always 'managing' you. They sit behind the scenes, touching buttons, pulling wires, making the figures on the stage dance to their rhythms. To their modest table come the great and powerful to learn their lessons, and to be coached up in their facts ... A mere suspicion that they are prompting behind the curtain is enough to make them damn the most perfect play.

It says something of their declining stock that Beatrice was to recall this as a 'kindly characterisation'.[7] Relatively, perhaps, it was: Virginia Woolf, when not fixated by Beatrice's 'shark like teeth', likened her to a moulting eagle with a bloodstained beak.[8] As Beatrice stoically observed: 'We are extraordinarily unpopular today – more disliked, by a larger body of persons, than ever before.'[9]

It was Webbian permeation which more than anything had brought them to this pass: an ironical comment indeed on this most ingratiating of strategies, aimed at stealing a collectivist proclivity into broader movements almost without their knowing it. As an explicit alternative to independent labour politics, permeation in its earlier guises had nonetheless fitted comfortably enough into the confused patchwork of late Victorian radicalism. Inseparably identified with Sidney Webb, the Fabians' 'municipal socialism' had as its main vehicle the radical or 'Progressive' majority on the London County Council (LCC), and it is plausibly presented as a regional vernacular well-suited to the Fabian Society's metropolitan habitat. Its accents, no doubt, were middle-class; but the dockers' leader Ben Tillett also took to it as a Fabian-Progressive alderman, nor did that prevent his simultaneous emergence as the voice of independent Labour in *its* northern stronghold of Bradford. Sidney Webb, significantly, gave Tillett his endorsement in both of these roles.[10] Prosaic rather than threatening, municipal collectivism was entirely compatible with Labour's early campaigning enthusiasms, and in 1899 this common purpose was confirmed when the Fabians established a Local Government Information Bureau with the ILP. 'The LCC', as Beatrice put it, 'is a far better platform from which to bring about collectivism than Parliament'; and the equable Sidney accordingly made no exertion to attain the grander stage of Westminster. As the SDF leader H.M. Hyndman acknowledged, this suggested a formidable immunity to the trappings of money and power, for Sidney was nothing if not a potential cabinet minister.[11] Throughout the Webbs' careers, their personal disinterestedness was one thing that was never in doubt.

With that disinterestedness, there was mixed from the start a curious disregard for conventional political mores. In the serpentine pursuit of ends that they took as read, the Webbs were no more concerned about others' sensibilities than they were about their own. 'The truth is that *we want the things done* and we don't much care what persons or which party gets the credit', Beatrice wrote early in Sidney's LCC career. That formula covered not only the settled alignments of London progressivism but whatever shifting agencies and coalitions seemed serviceable for more specific ends. Thus it was that 'Wily Webb', a key figure in the Progressive majority, earned his singular soubriquet through incessant 'colloguing' with Moderates, 'with a view to getting them to agree to things *in detail* which they could hardly accept in bulk'. This indifference to party ties would in due course bring about Sidney's isolation. For around a decade, though, his command of committee work, his broad agreement with his colleagues and the very effectiveness of his colloguing meant that his idiosyncrasies were broadly tolerated.[12]

His chief contribution was in the field of education, notably at the LCC's Technical Education Board.[13] He could not therefore remain unaffected when both the national and metropolitan educational frameworks came under review after the 1900 Conservative election victory. Indeed, it was from the wrangles preceding the 1902-3 Education Acts that Beatrice was later to date the casting off of by the Webbs of their old progressive moorings.[14] Partly this was a matter of policies, particularly that of state support for church schools, over which the couple found themselves out of sympathy with traditional radical agendas. More profoundly, with education at the centre of national politics, it was to this more exalted level, to bishops, ministers and press magnates, that the Webbs now turned their penchant for intrigue. On grounds of their parliamentary majority, they showed if anything a particular attentiveness to the Tories, while Beatrice dismissed the average London Progressive as a bounder, fanatic or 'mere piece of putty'. Together they even schemed against their own side in the 1904 LCC elections, and Sidney's influence on the council was from this time gradually extinguished.[15]

Instead there opened up what for Sidney at least was new territory. This was a world of 'brilliant little parties, and interesting folk versed in great affairs', glimpsed from the pavement and naturally inviting hostile comment. For the Webbs, and there is no need to doubt their word, the pleasures of this society were incidental to their deeper resolve. 'In England, all power to establish new undertakings rests on your influence over the various ruling cliques', Beatrice confided to her diary in 1900. 'The more cliques you are in touch with the easier it is to lay broad foundations.'[16] Nothing could have led more surely into a political cul-de-sac than this seeming manoeuvrability. Amongst their many contacts, the Webbs did, it is true, establish particular intimacies with the Liberal Imperialists, or Limps, and the circle around the Conservative prime minister A.J. Balfour. Their biggest help in this, and according to Beatrice the creator of 'the Webb myth', was the arch-Limp R.B. Haldane, who made no secret of his spiritual affinity with Wilhelmine Germany.[17] Exercising their minds at this time were fashionable obsessions with 'Imperial Efficiency', chewed over at a cross-party dining club established by the Webbs and called the Coefficients.[18]

To that extent, the Webbs exerted a subterranean pull on some very key political actors and opinion-formers. Nevertheless, in a world of tribalism and even principle, the pursuit of every clique and counter-clique meant, in the end, not the broadening of influence but its dissipation. It ensured, ironically, that Britain's Edwardian heyday of progressivism found these over-subtle Fabian prophets without any real political anchorage. Very much less frequent than she had anticipated were the dinners with ministers to which Beatrice had looked forward after the 1906 Liberal landslide. 'The Liberal leaders have always taken us up when they are in opposition and ... dropped us when they are in office', she commented sourly afterwards.[19] The cutting of party ties, it was becoming clearer, worked both ways; and even Beatrice came to see the drawbacks of this 'perpetual transit from camp to camp'. Perhaps it was this that made the couple seem like a foreign presence within the body politic. As Beatrice put it already in 1903, it was 'perilously near becoming both a spy and a traitor – or rather, being considered such by the camp to which we officially belong'. This was a lesson that would have to be learnt before the slump in Webbs – an appropriately plutocratic metaphor – could begin to bottom out.[20]

## II

Neglected as it is, an evaluation of the different roles and resources which the Webbs brought to their famous partnership is indispensable if we are to make sense of its diverse manifestations over time. To contemporaries, it was Sidney who, through the masculine world of public affairs, was at this time the most active and visible of the couple. In accounts like Joseph Clayton's *Rise and Decline of Socialism in Great Britain* (1924), it is he alone who figures, as the 'master-mind' of the Fabian Society and chief prophet of gradualism.[21] Retrospectively, however, this is counterbalanced by a notably asymmetrical evidential legacy: on the one hand, arguably the finest and fullest political diary of its time; on the other, no diary, no real memoir, and, in Sidney's *ne plus ultra* of self-effacement, 'no inside'. Moreover, the dominant voice provided by the diaries only confirmed what had become the prevailing domestic image of the Webbs, in which an unassuming and somewhat browbeaten Sidney had been 'got hold of' by Beatrice.[22] A memorable image that can stand for many is provided by their closest friend over many years, George Bernard Shaw. The setting is Sussex in January, 'a splendid day for walking', says Beatrice, who has their itinerary planned, though thick grey cloud hangs at twenty feet. Fortified by the one poached egg and one cigarette allowed him, Sidney takes up the rear as they set off. Like Shaw's, his beard is soon piled up with large masses of ice, and his nose grotesquely extended in icicles. On the previous day's excursion, turning purple and speechless in the cold, he had been made by his wife to lie down in the breeze until he recovered ('he says half an hour', Shaw reported). There was, then, to be no respite. 'Beatrice called our attention to the fact that it was really very cold', Shaw grumbled later, 'and put on a spurt as we breasted the first hill'.[23]

This effect, of an inversion of conventional sexual roles, informs innumerable private images of the Webbs, reinforced by further animal metaphors in which Sidney figures not as an eagle but as a beetle or cockatoo.[24] As if in compensation, Royden Harrison as the Webbs' official biographer sought to recover Sidney from the perception that even intellectually Beatrice was the more dynamic of the two, and in the process significantly depreciated her contribution to their thinking.[25] He even attempted a correlation of Beatrice's periods and the content of her diary entries that may charitably be described as speculative.[26] Despite such questionable judgements, Harrison was at least sensitive to the individuality of the Webbs and the complexity of the relationship between them. Within their partnership, as in his committee work, Sidney's prolific drafting skills gave him a leverage over their published output which he could not have avoided using even had he wanted to. As Jose Harris comments, in these voluminous, co-authored works Beatrice's 'bold, intuitive, imaginative style of thinking and writing' was usually submerged: 'Sidney's painstaking, clear but somewhat pedestrian manner is nearly always to the fore'.[27]

On the other hand, what was submerged surfaced in a variety of other ways, whether in the conception and 'architectonics' of major works; in occasional writings of Beatrice's own or ones in which she took the major hand; in non-literary forms of influence and activity; and, as a more or less continuous private subtext, in Beatrice's diaries. In the same way, Sidney also gave his own lectures, and had his own political career, and by the differentiation of these distinct and highly gendered identities it is not difficult to arrive at a more nuanced understanding of the partnership itself. At the risk of being over-schematic, periods may be identified in which Sidney provided its crucial ballast, as through the LCC and later the Labour Party he pursued what in other circumstances might have been the landmarks of a relatively conventional political career. Interspersed with these, however, were moments of unsettlement, innovation and neophilia when Beatrice took the partnership into unfamiliar territories. Among such territories were Soviet communism and the control of industry, and it is here that her early interest in the labour and co-operative movements was significant. In method at least, the society Webbs of the early 1900s also reflected Beatrice's willingness to pursue a less conventional political trajectory – which, at the same time, was available to her on at least equal terms with Sidney.

The latter, it is true, had long ago calculated that 'nothing in England is done without the consent of a small intellectual yet practical class in London not 2000 in number'. 'Foxy' now as he had once been wily, Sidney remained by his very nature what the Belgian socialist Camille Huysmans later called 'son eminence grise'.[28] Moreover, in his gradualist conception of collectivism, legislative enactment from above figured far prominently than it had in Beatrice's thinking. There was therefore nothing alien to him in the social philosophy of the Limps, which merely extended to the international plane that exaltation of 'the great social machine' for which Sidney was notorious. As early as the Fabian *Essays*, he had described the struggle of the nations in openly Darwinian terms, with the relative 'efficiency' of their social organisation being tested in the crucible of war.[29] Moreover, Shaw, whom Sidney retained after his marriage as a second and longer-standing alter ego, was the cleverest and most incorrigible proponent of Fabian elitism. With the Liberals in disarray over the South African War, it was directly at Shaw's instigation that in 1901 Sidney emphatically reaffirmed his own deep affinities with social imperialism and the politics of 'national efficiency'. Gladstonianism, with its connotations of Little Englandism and 'administrative Nihilism', he consigned without regret to the dustbin of the nineteenth century. Conservatism, though riding the crest of an imperial wave, was seen as but the temporary beneficiary of Liberalism's discomfiture. Socialism, one was left to infer, did not even figure in the equation. Instead Sidney looked to a 'Party of National Efficiency', as new as the dawning century in its programme and aspirations. Whether it called itself the Liberal Party, 'or any other name that may be convenient', was of entirely secondary importance.[30]

There was therefore nothing in elite permeation at all foreign to Sidney. On the other hand, he had quietly combined his tactical resourcefulness with ambitions for a conventional political career –

something which only the steadier attachments of party seemed likely to fulfil, and whose abrogation in the early 1900s cost him far more than it did his wife.[31] No doubt, like his frozen whiskers, the sacrifice of such hopes went without demur; but there is every indication that this indifference to parliament and its codes of entry was Beatrice's foible and not his. 'Don't talk of "when I am Prime Minister", it jars on sensitive ears', she admonished him during their courtship, and in due course she succeeded in refining both his manner and ambitions alike. 'I sometimes wonder whether I am right in inclining Sidney *not* to go into Parliament', she commented of his routine rejection of Liberal nominations in the 1890s; but she persisted in her preference for 'intellectual leadership', generally exercised from behind the scenes. It was indeed in exactly this guise that Sidney was preserved for posterity in the portrait which Beatrice provided at the beginning of *Our Partnership*.[32] Where Sidney's paean to national efficiency can be interpreted as a rather effective overture to the Limps, writing himself into a new political alignment, Beatrice preferred to visualise him as a permanent free agent. 'If Sidney has a political future it will be as a colleague of these men', she conceded at the end of 1901; but in a revealing diary entry two years later reflected on the 'power, nowadays ... wielded by a non-party expert who is free to throw himself on one side or the other, and who is widely known to be personally disinterested'. Such a position, she went on, 'is the sort of thing I aim at for Sidney'.[33]

What that entry left unsaid was that it was only through that abjuration of the male world of party that Beatrice herself could perform something other than a mere supporting role, such as she had already baulked at even for dashing Joe Chamberlain.[34] It was this period that saw Beatrice's first real emergence as a national political figure, with the drift of permeation from Sidney's natural milieux of the lecture hall and committee room to the salon and dining club for which the young Beatrice Potter had seemed destined. With her bourgeois background, hosting for her father and 'coming out' in the London Season, Beatrice found herself at a decided advantage in their new surroundings. 'Skill in social intercourse was my special gift', she wrote in *Our Partnership*, a boast combining considerable self-delusion with the tremendous self-assurance that was one of its consequences. As Shaw put it to Sidney, invoking a former Liberal prime minister: 'You are married to the only woman in England who dare ask Rosebery to dinner & ask him whether he will take beer or whiskey.'[35] For some years already she had gravitated towards the well-heeled to raise funds for the London School of Economics, and she appears to have had a distinct preference for this over more conventional Fabian activities.[36] Perhaps there was even a half-admitted hankering for pleasures since renounced for Sidney and her social goals: the clash, so fundamental to understanding Beatrice, between 'the ego that affirms and the ego that denies'.[37] It is to Beatrice in any case that we should attribute what she called 'the "setting" I have given [Sidney] of simple fare and distinguished friends', always remembering that the setting was as much hers as her husband's. H.G. Wells, whose closest acquaintance with the Webbs was at this time, recalled that it was she who had the idea of the Coefficients and who excelled in their discussions through a method he described as 'experimental dogmatism'. 'Beatrice', he explained in his autobiography, 'had (and has) a delightful way that is all her own, of throwing out bold general propositions about things in the most aggressive manner possible'. Resistance was met with 'unscrupulous candour and invincible good temper', and a new and invigorating dimension added to the Webb armoury. 'Sidney is not nearly so exploratory', Wells added; 'his convictions are less vivid and plastic; his aim is rather persuasion than truth, he is politic rather than philosophical'.[38]

It was therefore predictable as well as ironic that it should have been Beatrice's first formal recognition as a public figure, and apparent vindication of her society manoeuvres, that came to mean the beginning of the end for permeation. In December 1905 she was appointed by the outgoing Balfour government to the Royal Commission on the Poor Laws, the first comprehensive review since the enactment of the New Poor Law in 1834. Such commissions, once one got a foot in the door, were a permeator's dream. Unconstrained by party whips and attentive to experts and practitioners, as a gesture towards representativeness they also tended to include a token labour or collectivist presence at least proportionate to that found in the House of Commons. Twice in the preceding decade, in commissions on Labour and the Aged Poor, the Webbs had worked with and through these socialistic nominees to chip away at majority opinion and crystallise their own alternative in the form of minority reports. 'Another chicken hatched here', Beatrice had boasted of Tom Mann's Labour Commission report of 1894. 'Certainly persons with brains and independent means may have a rare good time in the part of permeator or fly on the wheel.'[39]

Except that their 'behind the scenes intellectual leadership' moved centre stage, the Webbs took the same approach to the Poor Law Commission.[40] Primarily the subject was Sidney's, who fifteen years earlier had first advanced proposals for its reform and now had the main hand in drafting a 'hugely cumbrous' minority report.[41] Nevertheless, it was to Beatrice that there fell the responsibility of winning round her commission colleagues, a task for which she had little of the tact and guile that Sidney brought to such work. The situation demanded persuasion rather than truth, and unscrupulous candour in a hostile environment proved singularly incapable of charming away the Poor Law. Beatrice herself, moreover, was disinclined to compromise on anything less.[42] If the majority report, even after three years' sittings, bore much less of a Webbian impress than she had hoped, that may reveal less about Beatrice's tactical shortcomings than the inadequacy of permeation itself when it came to sweeping and controversial reforms. Its authors as yet undaunted, the Webbs' minority report, baldly proposing the break-up of the Poor Law, was nevertheless devised very much within a cross-party context. Published at last in February 1909, it was described by Beatrice as 'a clear consistent scheme which can be worked out by any sensible and well-intentioned body of administrators'. The Conservatives, whom she distrusted less, 'are, for this purpose, quite as good as the Liberals and we have as much influence over them'.[43]

What finally put paid to such reveries was the reception accorded the two reports. Although it only gradually became clear that neither Balfour's Tories, still less the ruling Liberals, had any intention of acting upon the Webb proposals, what instantly registered was the marked preference of the national press for the majority report.[44] With only the long neglected partisans of the left acclaiming the Webbs' alternative, an elementary political lesson was now drawn as the Webbs concluded that only an energetic public campaign could give force to their efforts. The influence in this respect of George Lansbury, a Poplar Poor Law guardian and fellow signatory to the minority report, should not be underestimated. Thus was created the National Committee for the Break-Up of the Poor Law, at Lansbury's suggestion renamed the National Committee for the Prevention of Destitution [NCPD], whose monthly magazine also bore the Lansbury-like title of *The Crusade*. The campaign, which was strikingly effective in organisational terms, was very much a cross-party affair, and the young Ernest Simon was just one of thousands of supporters it drew from the older parties, local government and the professions. For its finances, too, the campaign drew on a respectable constituency that was far from being consciously socialistic.[45] Nevertheless, it soon became apparent that a crusading, activist permeation from below and an insidious, after-dinner permeation from above were largely incompatible – or at any rate, could not be carried out by the same persons. As Beatrice later put it, 'you cannot at one and the same time exercise behind-the-scenes influence over statesmen, civil servants and newspaper editors, while you yourself engage in public propaganda of projects which these eminent ones may view with hostility or suspicion'.[46] One may even conjecture that the lessons Beatrice now took in voice production, though indispensable to her new public career, were positively counter-productive when it came to dinner-table colloguing or the tête-à-tête. In any event, with an agreeable sensation that was itself no disincentive to future radicalism, Beatrice now found herself 'rather in disgrace with the great folk!'[47]

## III

In retrospect this may be seen one of the key turning points in the couple's career. At the level of agency, it marked something of a conversion, or reconversion, to the ideas of socialism. Towards the end of 1908, with the minority report nearing completion, Beatrice had expressed the quintessentially permeationist hope that the Liberals would adumbrate her scheme, and the Tories then carry it out. 'Which', she added, 'I should prefer in many ways – there would be no nonsense about democracy!'[48] If one compares this with her exegesis of the report for the ILP just a year or so later, there seems little doubt of her susceptibility to associates like Lansbury, who had himself just been elected to the ILP's governing National Administrative Council. Making up the commission majority, Beatrice now wrote, had been the state officials, the well-born, the representatives of bourgeois philanthropy – 'all the great people of the land'. Pitted against them were the 'poor, humble folk': a socialist, a trade unionist and – audaciously enough – Beatrice herself, 'a mere woman!' 'But may I remind you', she told her new ILP readership, 'that looking back on the history of the world, it has sometimes been a small minority of very humble folk who have proved to be right?'[49] Though this might merely have been the old Fabian chameleon adapting to its surroundings, in fact it proved far more than that. By 1910, Beatrice was writing of her 'despair' at the atmosphere in which her erstwhile dining partners lived.

> Their lives are so rounded off by culture and charm, comfort and power, that the misery of the destitute is as far off as the savagery of central Africa ... We may have, in the end, to establish a real Socialist Party if we want rapid progress. [50]

Though this was hardly by this time a very original analysis, it did perhaps mark the first real step on the road ending up at *Soviet Communism*.

That was twenty years ahead, however, and it is central to the argument advanced here that there can be no tidy elision of the two periods. On the contrary, the intervening dramas, so often passed over, involved in many respects a profound rethinking by the Webbs of the agencies, the processes, the character and even the very purpose of social change. At the same time, there were always evident in their later thinking layers of sediment deposited at different times throughout their lives. One of the fascinations of *Soviet Communism* is to trace the survival or recovery of these older formations which in some cases had seemed half-forgotten and in others overlain by more recent deposits. In this complex geological formation, the residues of the post-Gladstonian collectivism of the Edwardian period, though not alone sufficient for the transformation, were far from negligible. Three features were of particular relevance to the long-term development of the Webbs' thought: their abhorrence of social parasitism; the casting of human history in terms of civilisations; and the elitist cult of the expert, which in this period they identified with a strong and intrusive state. Each is worth brief consideration as providing motifs that would be evident again in the embrace of Stalinism.

Revulsion for the economically or socially parasitic or 'functionless' was fundamental to the Webbs' *Weltanschauung*.[51] This was rooted in the philosophy, not of rights but of obligations, which was to underlie all of the partnership's various political peregrinations. 'I ... regard life as a series of obligations', Beatrice wrote in 1906 in connection with her earlier anti-suffragism; 'obligations of the individual to the community and of the community to the individual'.[52] It is in the varying correlation between these obligations that the eddies in the couple's thinking can to some extent be understood, with the Edwardian Webbs leaning heavily on the collective side of the bargain: 'each individual', as Beatrice bleakly put it, 'to serve the state, in return getting maintenance; to serve the state not merely by making commodities and fulfilling services, but by being healthy, intelligent and loving'.[53] To fathom the significance for Beatrice of this gospel of service, one need only read in *My Apprenticeship* of how perdurably her own character was shaped in struggling against the nullity of purpose to which her sex and 'a masculine capitalism' had seemingly consigned her. It was with obvious feeling on her part that the Webbs insisted on the economic activity of all women, including under that head properly remunerated childcare responsibilities. 'There is no more shameful incident of our present "civilisation" than the irresponsibility, the painful emptiness, and the dishonourable futility of the lives of the great majority of those women of the upper middle classes who are free from personal service in housework and the care of children', they wrote. 'These unoccupied women, married or unmarried, are a drag on the civilisation of the race, insidiously lowering ... its sanity, its public spirit, its intelligence, and even its good manners'. How much happier and more dignified, Beatrice had previously reflected in her diary, was the life of the 'hard-working daughter of the middle-class farmer or shopkeeper'.[54]

It was with the useful and industrious classes – the 'quiet intermediate area of respectable working-class, middle-class and professional life' – that the Webbs therefore identified.[55] Sidney, more particularly, was the product and epitome of these middling strata, having made his way before his marriage through the new meritocratic examination processes introduced in the civil service. Against such varied forms of service, whether waged, salaried or unremunerated, the Webbs set the parasitism, willing or unwilling, of both upper and lower extremities of the social order. The superfluity of the rich was of course a basic socialist tenet, and their 'irresponsible consumption', setting up virtual 'endowments for idleness', had been a major factor in Sidney's conversion to socialism in the mid-1880s.[56] Nor did even the Edwardian Webbs drift quite so smoothly through society as to forget this basic truth. Even as they schemed away at the Poor Law as guests of the parvenu diamond magnate Sir Julius Wernher, Beatrice described the sheer waste of human effort involved in the maintenance of Wernher's barely used country house at Luton Hoo. Even in its owner's absence, the machinery of opulence ground on, with gardeners, electricians, servants and labourers, all toiling for no human benefit, while house and park stood deserted, 'no one coming or going except the retinue of servants, the only noises the perpetual whirring and calling of the thousands of pheasants, ducks and other game that were fattening already for the autumn slaughter'. Meanwhile, just half a mile away lay the crowded mean streets of Luton itself, drunk, sensual, disorderly, and with 'a terrific infant mortality'.[57] It was a memorable and repugnant image of the Edwardian plutocracy, revealing a Ruskinian strand of contempt for 'illth' and idleness. From their post-war socialist *Constitution* to *Soviet Communism* itself, the Webbs were to envisage the appropriation of such estates as amenities for the 'urban toilers' beyond their fastened gates.[58]

What nevertheless dominated their thinking in this period was not the problem of the rich but that of the unproductive but able-bodied poor. Prior to the Poor Law Commission, Sidney had written blandly of the salutary effects in such cases of the semi-penal workhouse or even 'a term of servitude in an educational Labor colony'.[59] The same idea survived into their later scheme of 'training establishments', supposedly quite optional but on such conditions – attendance from 6 a.m. to 7 p.m., with a 'continuous and properly varied programme of physical and mental work' – as presupposed effective powers of compulsion. 'The unemployed man', they conceded with doubtful liberality, 'need not accept the offer if he can manage to live without sponging off the public'; experience even suggested that there would be 'an eager scrambling to hear the daily messages from the Labour Exchange' to escape such an environment.[60] Formally their minority report did acknowledge that unemployment was not a personal disorder, as such training or deterrence schemes implied, but a social malaise, 'mainly due to defects in industrial organisation'. Nevertheless, the Webbs remained resistant to ideas of unconditional rights to benefit and rejected insurance schemes, such as that enacted by the Liberals in 1911, precisely because they carried such an entitlement. What they feared was 'the growth of malingering and the right to money independently of the obligation to good conduct', as insidiously lowering to the race as the cosseting of the similarly blameless daughters of the rich.[61]

Destitution thus connoted idleness as much as deprivation, that 'freedom to loaf' which not even the Webbs themselves were sure of always resisting and against whose temptations their every reforming instinct had to guard itself. Fabian preoccupations with efficiency, if one reads their *Prevention of Destitution*, are less directly in evidence than a tremendous abhorrence for sloth and dependency, the cause along with poverty of a 'moral malaria' in the great cities, and their corresponding elevation of the ideal of a 'self-supporting citizen life'.[62]

In the Webbian language of mutual responsibilities was thus concealed an older moralising diagnosis, its prescription one of 'treatment' and not of 'relief', and its aim of 'prevention' directed not least at the victim's own worst instincts. The guiding assumption on which alone this made sense was that of the basic tractability of the unemployment problem, and the Webbs themselves advanced a series of counter-cyclical proposals of whose efficacy at this time they admitted no doubt.[63] The years of post-war depression were to leave such a programme in tatters. Convinced as they were of the corrosive effects of doles, the Webbs would then see in the mass unemployment that then seemed uncontrollable the decay of Western civilisation itself.

Their disposition to think in such terms was itself prefigured in the earlier period, and this was the second of its lasting legacies. If the nineteenth century thought 'in individuals', as Sidney put it, the twentieth-century Webbs thought not just, as he said, 'in communities', but in civilisations.[64] At a time of sharpening national rivalries, such patterns of thinking were almost hegemonic; and not even socialists – least of all them, it sometimes seems – were immune to the eugenicist and even racist notions which often accompanied them. As we have seen, Sidney was quick to latch on to the Social Darwinian ideas expounded from within the Fabian Society by the philosopher D.G. Ritchie.[65] In 1896, responding as Ritchie had to the 'difficulties of individualism', Sidney wrote of the prevailing 'race struggle – that competition between communities ... which is perhaps now becoming the main field of natural selection'.[66] The decline of the birth-rate – subject a decade later of articles by Sidney in the *Times* as well as one of his Fabian tracts – was long to remain a Webbian preoccupation. Constructive if not restrictive eugenicist notions were also implicit in their support for the 'endowment of motherhood' as that campaign gathered momentum in the same period.[67]

The Webbs' susceptibility to prevailing gusts of opinion was here demonstrated in an unfortunate fashion. Sidney even referred to the 'wrong production, both of commodities and human beings' and 'the breeding of degenerate hordes of a demoralised "residuum" unfit for social life'.[68] In an exposition of the couple's Poor Law proposals addressed to eugenicists, he strongly emphasised the negative eugenic effects of the current Poor Law, while continuing to stress the decisive role of environment.[69] Often there were unpleasant racial overtones to such arguments, as the Webbs slipped effortlessly into a racist discourse of savage Africa and the 'non-adult races'. Moreover, virulent images of the slum, the very crux of social imperialist anxieties, were deeply embedded in the Webbs' politics of respectability. 'How can we build up an effective commonwealth', Sidney asked, 'how, even, can we get an efficient army – out of the stunted, anaemic, demoralised denizens of the slum tenements of our great cities?'[70] Redundancy of function, that other great Webbian concern, informed his similar image of the 'horde of semi-barbarians, whose unskilled labour is neither required in our present complex industrial organism, nor capable of earning a maintenance there'.[71] To these sentiments, it was probably Beatrice who added a more moralistic vocabulary of drunkenness, sensuality and disorder, the never quite relinquished legacy of her early East End social work.[72]

Eugenics has such dire associations nowadays that it is important not to over-generalise. Unlike socialist eugenicists like Eden Paul, the sometime ILPer, Plebs Leaguer and communist with whom Beatrice had shared her experiences in East London, the Webbs at least did conceive both social ills and their remedies in predominantly environmental and not eugenic or racial terms.[73] This, in a domestic context, was a major theme of their book *The Prevention of Destitution*, where the unfit breeding grounds of the slums were addressed as social and not biological phemonena. The 'congenitally feeble-minded' were an ill-defined exception, for whom eugenicist measures of segregation and limitation were proposed, but the prevailing emphasis was on the social causes, and hence the preventability, of destitution.[74] Their paternalist imperialism, founded on the maintenance of a multi-racial commonwealth, also set itself against the ethnic or racial demarcations that posed possible threats to the empire's administrative cohesion.[75] Even their categorisation of non-adult races was, ostensibly at least, a question of political immaturity and not of innate incapacity. Applied to a country like India, their logic was of memorable fatuity. 'Whereas it used to be only seven years old, it is now fourteen', they conceded. 'Are we to try to prevent it from attaining manhood?'[76]

The life-cycle metaphor was a significant one, for with its connotations of infancy and maturity went the gloomier corollaries of senility and decay. Here the Webbs went beyond prevailing concerns with inter-European rivalries to set them in a starker panoptical perspective. Even should those rivalries lead to war, the couple's concerns were less with specific national outcomes than with the inevitable weakening and brutalisation of European civilisation itself. While they rarely pronounced on foreign affairs, a reticence usually vindicated by their comments when they did so, Beatrice in particular was prone to brood on the ebb and flow of race and culture. Prompted by the Russo-Japanese war of 1904-5, she pondered the 'effect of the "Rising Sun" on our Western civilisation' in a way strangely premonitory of later compulsions:

> ... I watch in myself and others a growing national shamefacedness at the superiority of the Japanese over our noble selves in capacity, courage, self-control, in benevolence as well as in all that makes up good manners! They shame our Christianity, they shame our administrative capacity, they shame our inventiveness, they shame our leadership, and alas! they shame our 'average sensual man' ... They seem both more scientific and

more religious than ourselves – a nobler purpose and more ably contrived processes wherewith to carry out this purpose.[77]

Though often the Fabians are regarded as latter-day utilitarians, what is noteworthy here is how very far Beatrice was from employing a utilitarian calculus as her comparative yardstick. 'We altogether reject the "happiness of the greatest number"', she had earlier written in filial repudiation, both of her own mentor Herbert Spencer and of the Jeremy Bentham whom she thought Sidney's 'intellectual godfather'. Even Sidney, one suspects, looked as much to Ruskin, or to the younger Mill who upheld a sense of value in the pursuit of happiness, distinguishing it from mere 'content' by the differentiation of higher faculties of pleasure 'more desirable and more valuable than others'.[78] Beatrice, more emphatically, looked beyond the Greatest Happiness Principle for a sense of moral conduct, beauty and intellectual endeavour, even a capitalised sense of Purpose, that a mean utilitarian ethics could little comprehend.[79] The appeals of Soviet communism were to prove similarly complex.

Stirring to life already was an outlook more expansive than the Fabians' proverbial gas-and-water concerns. For some years it would remain dormant while the Webbs grappled with the Poor Law. Nevertheless, at their first opportunity, in 1911-12, they took off on a tour very different in its objects from their earlier busman's holiday around the civic assemblies of the USA and Australasia.[80] Travelling initially to Japan, their prejudice in its favour was first confirmed and then redoubled by their hostile impressions as they proceeded through China. Again their criteria were not simply ones of efficiency but emphasised moral and spiritual values, a combination making for more than usually complicated responses when they visited India. Sweeping cultural prejudices were tempered by a fitful instinct that even the Chinese, whom they roundly disparaged, formed 'a nation, on a par with European nations, having a civilisation of its own and entitled to equality of consideration and treatment'.[81] What was evidently reinforced was the tendency to think 'in civilisations', which, when combined on their return with racial pessimism and the apprehension of a European war, produced a lurid scenario:

Into this dark picture there comes what is perhaps the gravest feature of all, the rapidly diminishing birth-rate in the 'higher' races among all but the lowest strata of their populations ... Into the scarcity thus created ... there rush in the offspring of the less thrifty, the less intellectual, the less foreseeing races or classes – the unskilled casual labourers of our great cities, the races of Eastern or Southern Europe, the negroes, the Chinese ... If anything like this happens, it is difficult to avoid the melancholy conclusion that, in some cataclysm that it is impossible for us to foresee, the civilisation characteristic of the West European races may go the way

> of the half a dozen civilisations that have within historic times preceded it; to be succeeded by a new social order developed by one or other of the coloured races, the negro, the Kaffir, or the Chinese!

At that very moment in Germany, Oswald Spengler was completing the first draft of his *Decline of the West*, with its own 'morphological' alternative to a bland planetary progressivism. The Webbs' rendition of such themes was itself presented to *New Statesman* readers as 'the answer of pessimism', to which a week later they provided their own Panglossian rejoinder. Significantly, though, the latter was situated wholly within an untroubled domestic context, essentially updating the 'Historic' section which Sidney had contributed to the *Fabian Essays*.[82] Together, the articles read almost like a symbolic dialogue between Beatrice, with her more imaginative forebodings, and the constitutional nil desperandum of her husband. International events were to break in, however, as the bleaker prognosis had anticipated; and if Sidney remained unflappable, Beatrice was to resume her Spenglerian musings and brood again on both 'the answer of pessimism' and the possibilities of a new civilisation.

Where Japan did not excel over the West was in either the form or spirit of democracy. Even as the Webbs planned their trip, the murder and imprisonment of Japanese socialists had met with unanimous condemnation at that year's Labour Party conference. While grudgingly conceding such blemishes, the Webbs' willingness to be seduced by the country's prospects betrayed the elitist and bureaucratic cast to their thinking that was a third dominant characteristic in this period, and which may no doubt be detected in their later enthusiasm for Stalinism.[83] In this regard, too, they were nothing if not abreast of current thinking. Key Edwardian texts were H.G. Wells's *Anticipations*, acclaimed by Beatrice as the 'most remarkable book' of 1901, and its sequel of 1905, *A Modern Utopia*. Wells at this time was at the height of his influence, prophet of a modernity shaped not by numbers but by science. Guiding his utopian conceits was a 'new social Hercules' of ruling technocrats, conceived successively as a Platonic New Republic and – again a sign of the influence of the Russo-Japanese war – a 'voluntary nobility' of samurai. A Fabian and Coefficient, Wells acknowledged his debt to Webbian notions of a disinterested bureaucratic order, 'laughingly' telling Beatrice that his samurai were going to pander to their worst instincts.[84] *Japonaiserie* was in the air; and when during the Poor Law Commission Beatrice visited a Salvation Army camp for the unemployed, it came to her almost without thinking to liken its officers to a '*Samurai* caste', possessed as if with 'some weird faith belonging to another civilisation'.[85]

This samurai conception, often mentioned in the context of *Soviet Communism*, should not be overplayed. While Wells certainly believed in the 'genetic connection' between his thinking and Lenin's contemporaneous invention of the communist party, the Webbs accorded the samurai only a short footnote in their own vast treatise on the subject.[86] They had, in any case, entirely changed their minds about Japan, by the 1930s regarding it as reactionary, militaristic and generally 'an evil influence in the world'.[87] What the samurai fad nevertheless symbolised was a cast of mind that worked from the top down and privileged the exertions of the directing minority. 'If you are inside the clique you help to rule', wrote Beatrice; 'if you are outside you cry in the wilderness'.[88] Countervailing movements from below were, for the time being at least, neither theorised nor recognised in practice. Labour movement agencies, a preoccupation until the mid-1890s, were effectively ignored. The Fabian heartland of local government was also increasingly left to others, and quietly in 1910 Sidney retired from the LCC. Even the minimal controls of a popular franchise were defended only backhandedly as providing 'a "foolometer" for the expert'.[89] The expert, indeed, was the Webbs' social Hercules, as demonstrated by their diverting a Fabian legacy into the establishment of the London School of Economics. '*Hard thinking*' and not 'shouting' was what was required; not the organisation of the '*un*thinking' into socialist societies but the winning over of the '*thinking*' through the advancement of social science. 'Above all', Beatrice had reflected, 'we want the ordinary citizen to feel that reforming society is no light matter, and must be undertaken by experts specially trained for the purpose'.[90]

## IV

It is little wonder that 'Webbism' in this period should have become synonymous with bureaucratic collectivism. The best government, Sidney had urged in the 1890s, was 'that which can safely and successfully administer most'.[91] Already over the Balfour Education Act of 1902, the Webbs had preferred the efficiency of county education departments to the vaunted democracy of the school boards.[92] That now had an echo during the Poor Law campaign, when some socialists defended local guardians on grounds of accountability and many perceived the Webbs' proposals as the last word in administrative Prussianism. As a mood of revolt took hold of younger rebels, the Webbs seemed all too clearly to regard the poor, not as a class to be roused, but as an abscess to be lanced. As organised labour raised its sights, the expert computation of a 'National Minimum' now began to look like little more than a sop.

Even on the left, there had always been dissenters from the shibboleths of collectivism. The difference after 1910 was that they seemed to be rearing their heads everywhere: on picket lines and demonstrations, in union offices and Oxford colleges, hurling their points of order even within the Fabian Society. Not laissez-faire but the servile state was the radicals' anathema; not poverty but slavery, and not permeation but collision was their favoured tactic. It was during the Webbs' year abroad in 1911-12 that the 'great unrest', later characterised by Beatrice as a 'proletarian distemper', really took hold in labour circles. Immediately on their return Sidney spoke of 'a new England', transformed by the awakened insurgency of labour and its new breadth of aspiration. Press and public alike seemed possessed by once revolutionary nostrums. 'Even the House of Commons, which is about the last place for facts or ideas to penetrate, seems at one moment to have realised ... the depths of its own ignorance, and the impotence to which it had actually come'.[93]

What Sidney failed to see was that, amongst the 'Tapers and Tadpoles' thus caught on the hop, the Webbs were in the very first rank. Just before they sailed, Beatrice had pondered whether they should provide the rudderless 'democratic movement' with the benefits of their guidance, and this in effect was what they sought to do on their return.[94] Becoming active for the first time in the Fabian Society executive, Beatrice even joined a branch of the ILP and assisted in the cordial and productive relations it had with the Fabians at that time. She also sought with Sidney to harness Labour's parliamentary representatives for their campaigns, rather doubtfully assisted by her reminding them that they could if necessary work as easily, as effectively and more enjoyably through their Liberal and Tory counterparts.[95] This, however, was little more than bombast. Dropped by their society friends and neglected by ruling politicians, the Webbs were now almost as suspect to the left, and had no personal relations with either trade unionists or co-operators. 'We were in fact neutralised and of no account', Beatrice later reflected, and proposed entitling the relevant chapter of her memoirs 'the eclipse of the Webbs'.[96] That their influence recovered at all was due, on Sidney's part, to an increasing involvement in the wartime remaking of the Labour Party; and, on Beatrice's, to a sustained engagement with the intellectual challenge posed by their younger detractors. The first of these was of greater immediate significance and has received the careful attention of historians.[97] The second, relatively neglected as far as the Webbs' side of it goes, may seem rather more arcane. It provides, even so, the more crucial context for understanding *Soviet Communism*.

## NOTES

1. H.G. Wells, *Experiment in Autobiography*, Gollancz and Cresset Press, 2 vols, 1934, p. 735; Wells, *The New Machiavelli*, Penguin edn, 1966, pp. 155-66.
2. BWD, 10 February 1908, *MA*, p. 401. The visitor is A.J. Balfour.
3. See Eileen Janes Yeo, *The Contest for Social Science. Relations and representations of gender and class*, Rivers Oram Press, 1996, p. 211, where the ring is described as an historical fact; also Anne Olivier Bell, ed., *The Diary of Virginia Woolf. Volume 1: 1915-1919*, Hogarth Press, 1977, p. 26 (entry for 23 January 1915).

4. BWD 27 September 1909, Mackenzie edn, vol. 3, p. 125. The daughter of prominent Fabians, Amber bore their child in 1909. For a balanced presentation see Norman and Jeanne Mackenzie, *The First Fabians*, Quartet edn, 1979, pp. 370-2; for an absurdly unbalanced one, interesting for its Webb stereotypes, Anthony West, *H.G. Wells. Aspects of a life*, Penguin edn, 1985, pp. 12-22, 302-15.
5. E.g. Rowland Kenney, *Westering*, Dent, 1939, p. 197.
6. BWD 14 March 1903, *OP*, p. 261; BWD 6 December 1913.
7. *OP*, pp. 289-90.
8. Woolf to Vanessa Bell, 28 June 1916, in Nigel Nicolson, ed., *The Question of Things Happening. The letters of Virginia Woolf. Volume 2: 1917-1922*, Hogarth Press, 1976, p.104; Bell, *Diary of Virginia Woolf. Volume 2*, p. 20 (entry for 15 February 1920).
9. BWD 6 December 1913.
10. Jonathan Schneer, *Ben Tillett. Portrait of a Labour leader*, Croom Helm, 1982, ch. 4; David Howell, *British Workers and the Independent Labour Party*, Manchester: MUP, 1983, pp. 181-5; Henry Pelling, *Origins of the Labour Party*, Oxford: OUP edn, 1966, pp. 91-2.
11. BWD December 1894 and 29 December 1894, *OP*, pp. 69, 120-1; M. Cole, *Story*, p. 84; H.M. Hyndman, *Further Reminiscences*, Macmillan, 1912, p. 213.
12. BWD 1 December 1894, *OP*, pp. 67-8.
13. See McBriar, *Fabian Socialism*, ch. 8.
14. *OP*, p. 182; see also BWD May 1904, *OP*, p. 291.
15. BWD 25 February 1903, 14 March 1903, 15 March 1903, 8 July 1903, 17 January and 7 March 1904, all in *OP*, ch. 6; 25 January 1904, 13 February 1904, Mackenzie vol. 2, pp. 313-5.
16. BWD 19 July 1900, *OP*, p. 199.
17. *OP*, pp. 97 ff.
18. See S. Webb to H.G. Wells, 12 September 1902 in Mackenzie, *Letters*, vol. 2, p. 170.
19. BWD 31 January 1918.
20. BWD 6 December 1903, *OP*, p. 277.
21. Joseph Clayton, *The Rise and Decline of Socialism in Great Britain 1884-1924*, Faber & Gwyer, 1924, p. 43 and passim.
22. Morgan, 'The Webbs', p. 61.
23. Shaw to Charlotte Shaw, 24 January 1922, in Dan H. Laurence, ed., *Bernard Shaw: collected letters 1911-1925*, Max Reinhardt, 1985, pp. 760-1.
24. Kitty Muggeridge, 'Introduction: my Aunt Bo' in Muggeridge and Ruth Adam, *Beatrice Webb. A life 1858-1943*, Secker & Warburg, 1967, p. 13; Kingsley Martin, *Editor. A volume of autobiography 1931-1945*, Hutchinson, 1968, p. 77.
25. See for example Harrison's insistence, against the evidence, that Sidney 'converted' his wife to socialism, apparently at their first meeting; Harrison, *Life and Times*, pp. 159-60, 169, 213-14. For a stimulating account presenting this as the culmination of a longer term process, see Nord, *Apprenticeship*, ch. 7.
26. Harrison's object (*Life and Times*, pp. 166-9) was to establish a correlation between the frequency and content of Beatrice's diary entries and her

menstrual cycle, and he did so in the form of a table for the year 1886. A number of his symbols are incomprehensible – for example, 'PpD' for 17 October and 'PmdD' for 11 December – and one may perhaps allow for the table having been edited under pressure. Nevertheless, its underlying method and its rationale remain dubious in the extreme.

By allowing seven days for Beatrice's period and a notional three days either side 'on the assumption of a 3-day span of irregularity' Harrison brought virtually half of Beatrice's existence within the potential influence of her menstrual periods. Moreover, despite the succession of mood changes that might be identified within the period of menstruation, he indiscriminately grouped the whole period of seven or thirteen days as one of 'depression, irritability and lethargy'. Further, by arbitrarily deciding that a sole diary reference to Beatrice's period refers to the third day of the cycle – an impossibly exact calculation, even discounting his three-day span of irregularity – Harrison so disposed of her periods for the year in question as to bear out his own hypothesis. If, for example, this one cited comment – that 'my bad days come on' – is held to refer to the first day of her period, there is no greater incidence of diary entries during her menstrual periods. Indeed, for eleven days either side of this one documented allusion to menstruation (20 August 1886 according to Mackenzie, transcribed in Harrison's table as 21 August) there is no diary entry. Given that in this entry Beatrice describes herself as 'practically incapable of thought' there is no reason to be surprised at this.

The supposed correlation between lethargy and sustained literary activity is, to say the least, problematic. Harrison's supposition was that 'a Victorian lady's diary was likely to be best tended when she had "the curse"'. It seems incredible that a journal of universally recognised literary accomplishment, ranging widely over social, political and philosophical matters, should be described in this manner – though no less surprising, perhaps, than Harrison's interjection of phrases like 'Good try, girl!' into passages from the diaries. Several of the entries which he indicated as exhibiting 'total, or almost total depression, irritability and lethargy' do no such thing. Whether or not a diary entry of 2-3000 words *can* demonstrate total lethargy is questionable. One like that of 10 December 1886, falling on the last day of one of Beatrice's presumed periods, refers to ten days' 'hard work' at Marx in French that will have taken up virtually the whole of this period (Beatrice had indicated her intention of getting back to intellectual work on 1 December). The entry also offers Beatrice's detailed considerations on an article on multiple personality in one of the contemporary 'thick' reviews. An incomprehensible symbol ('PmdD'), wrongly attached to the following day, 11 December, means that one is uncertain as to how exactly Harrison wished to characterise this entry. Few readers would describe it as one of 'total, or almost total' irritability, and fewer writers as one of lethargy. Harrison conceded that the exercise was conjectural and subjective; it certainly awaits a better demonstration.

27. Jose Harris, *Beatrice Webb. The ambivalent feminist*, LSE, 1984, p. 11.
28. SW to Pease, October 1886; cited Mackenzie, *The First Fabians*, p. 62; BWD 19 April 1904, *OP*, p. 289; *OP*, p. 7.
29. SW, 'Historic' in Shaw, *Fabian Essays*, p. 58. Sidney referred to D.G.

Ritchie's *Darwinism and Politics*, published the same year, and the example of the Franco-Prussian War of 1870.

30. Sidney's original article, 'Lord Rosebery's escape from Houndsditch', was published in the *Nineteenth Century* for September 1901. Extracts are cited in *OP*, pp. 220-4. Shaw's letters to SW, 26 July 1901, and BW, 30 July 1901, are in Dan H. Laurence, ed., *Bernard Shaw: collected letters 1898-1910*, Max Reinhardt, 1972, pp. 229-35. At Beatrice's suggestion, the 'constructive' parts of the article were then worked up – Harrison's phrase (*Life and Times*, p. 326) is 'tarted up' – into a Fabian Society lecture, published as *Twentieth Century Politics: a policy of national efficiency*, Fabian Society, 1901, from which quotations here are taken.
31. See R.C.K. Ensor, 'Permeation' in M. Cole, *The Webbs*, pp. 60-3.
32. BW to SW, 11 August 1890 in Mackenzie, *Letters*, vol. 1, p. 166; BWD 10 March and 10 July 1894, Mackenzie vol. 2, pp. 26-7, 49-50; 'The other one', *OP*, pp. 1-11. The abandonment of Sidney's parliamentary ambitions is clearly traceable in the couple's correspondence, e.g. Beatrice to Sidney. 21 (?) September 1891 in *Letters*, vol. 1, p. 307: 'I do hope you will not stand for a bye-election. Think of all the expense – £800 thrown away! And I want you at least till the general election to help me.' At the same time, it was Beatrice's income that would have made the expenditure of £800 possible.
33. BWD 9 December 1901, Mackenzie vol. 2, p. 226; BWD 20 December 1903, *OP*, p. 279. Writing at a crucial moment in Sidney's relations with the Progressives, Beatrice had in mind the example of her one-time mentor Charles Booth.
34. For Beatrice's 'short-lived and idiosyncratic' courtship with Chamberlain, see Nord, *Apprenticeship*, pp. 96-103; Harrison, *Life and Times*, pp. 109-26.
35. Shaw to SW, 26 July 1901.
36. See M. Cole, *Story of Fabian Socialism*, pp. 79-80.
37. See *MA*, pp. xi-xii.
38. BWD 22 March 1901, Mackenzie vol. 2, p. 204; Wells, *Experiment*, pp. 600-1, 761.
39. BWD 25 December 1893 and 12 March 1894, Mackenzie, vol. 2, pp. 41, 45-6. The minority report on the Aged Poor was drafted by the Webbs for Henry Broadhurst, former TUC secretary.
40. For a detailed account of this episode see McBriar, *Edwardian Mixed Doubles*.
41. See SW to BW, 14 May 1890, Mackenzie, *Letters*, vol. 1, pp. 134-5, where the 'break up' of the Poor Law and disapproval of promiscuous relief are already indicated. Sidney's Fabian Tract, *The Reform of the Poor Law*, 1890 offers more modest proposals which do not deal with what was to become the Webbs' central preoccupation with the able-bodied unemployed. For the minority report, see SW to J.L. Garvin, 31 January 1909, Mackenzie, *Letters*, vol. 2, pp. 322-3.
42. McBriar, *Edwardian Mixed Doubles*, pp. 236-42.
43. BWD 25 April 1909, Mackenzie vol. 3, pp. 109-10; also SW to Garvin, 31 January 1909.
44. See McBriar, *An Edwardian Mixed Doubles*, ch. 11.
45. See BWD 24 May 1910, *OP*, pp. 451-3.

46. *OP*, p. 423.
47. BW to Mary Playne, July (?) 1909, Mackenzie, *Letters*, vol. 2, p. 331; BWD, 18 June 1909, *OP*, pp. 429.
48. BWD 15 November 1908, *OP*, p. 418.
49. BW, *The New Crusade against Destitution: being an exposition of the Minority Report of the Poor Law Commission*, ILP, 1910, pp. 3-4.
50. BWD 9 October 1910, *OP*, p. 462.
51. A utilitarian-sounding formulation used by the Webbs after the war, e.g. *A Constitution for the Socialist Commonwealth of Great Britain*, Longmans, 1920 (henceforth *CSC*), p. xii.
52. *OP*, 362.
53. BWD 19 July 1907, *OP*, p. 385.
54. SBW, 'Freedom for the woman', *New Statesman*, 5 July 1913, 397-8; BWD May 1904, *OP*, pp. 290-1.
55. BWD 13 March 1910, *OP*, pp. 447-8.
56. See Willard Wolfe, *From Radicalism to Socialism: men and ideas in the formation of Fabian socialist doctrines 1881-1889*, New Haven: Yale University Press, 1975, pp. 198-203
57. BWD 27 July 1908, *OP*, pp. 412-13.
58. *CSC*, pp. 265-6; *SCANC*, pp. 881-2.
59. SW, *Twentieth Century Politics*, p.12; *Socialism: true and false*, Fabian Society, 1894, p. 12.
60. SBW, *The Prevention of Destitution*, Longmans, 1911 [henceforth *PD*], pp. 140 ff.
61. *PD*, p. 168.
62. *PD*, pp. 1-2, 81-2.
63. See *PD*, pp. 105 ff.
64. *Twentieth Century Politics*, pp. 3-5.
65. See D.G. Ritchie, *Darwinism and Politics* (1889), Swan Sonnenschein, 1891 edn, a volume based on lectures given to the Fabian Society in 1888.
66. SW, *The Difficulties of Individualism*, Fabian Society, 1896, p. 6.
67. SW, *The Decline of the Birth Rate*, Fabian Society, 1907; Sidney and Beatrice Webb, 'Freedom for the woman'; BWD July 1894, *OP*, pp. 83-4.
68. SW, *Difficulties*, p. 6.
69. SW, 'Eugenics and the Minority Report', *The Crusade*, June 1910, pp. 51-2. Among the beneficial effects of their proposals, Sidney listed the segregation of defective persons, the discouragement of marriage among those unable or unwilling to conform to a high standard of parenthood and the ending of 'the continuance at large of persons of either sex who are unable or unwilling to come up to the Minimum Standard of Life'.
70. SW, *Twentieth Century Politics*, p. 9.
71. SW, *Difficulties*, pp. 11-12.
72. *PD*, pp. 1-2; *OP*, pp. 442-3.
73. For Paul see ch. 7 below; also his *Socialism and Eugenics*, ILP, 1911.
74. *PD*, ch. 3 and passim; also the Webbs' minority report, cited McBriar, *Edwardian*, p. 301. This somewhat contradicts the well-known presentation of Gareth Stedman Jones, *Outcast London*, Penguin edn, 1984, p. 336, where it is suggested that they attributed pauperism to 'some deviant mutation' or 'some hereditary "taint"'.
75. SW, *Twentieth Century Politics*, p. 5.

76. SBW, 'The guardianship of the non-adult races', *New Statesman*, 2 August 1913, p. 526. For the wider purchase of such conceptions, see Bernard Porter, *Critics of Empire. British radical attitudes to colonialism in Africa 1895-1914*, Macmillan, 1968, pp. 50-2.
77. BWD 22 December 1904, *OP*, p. 299.
78. J.S. Mill, *Utilitarianism* (1863), Everyman edn, 1910, pp. 7-11.
79. BWD 25 January 1901, *OP*, p. 210; 8-9 December 1903, *MA*, p. 33.
80. The earlier trip is summarised in Mackenzie vol. 2, pp. 137-49.
81. See Mackenzie vol. 3, pp. 163-77 for a summary of the tour.
82. SBW, 'The great alternative. (1) The answer of pessimism' and 'The great alternative. (2) The optimist view', *New Statesman*, 30 August and 6 September 1913, pp. 653-4, 686-7; see also H. Stuart Hughes, *Oswald Spengler: a critical estimate*, New York: Scribners, 1952, pp. 6-7.
83. Sidney refused to add his voice to the initial protests and warned against the assumption of an automatic solidarity with 'people *called* Socialists (or even people who call themselves Socialists)': SW to Pease, 5 January 1911, Mackenzie, *Letters*, vol. 2, p. 365.
84. Wells, *Experiment*, pp. 610, 652-3; Wells, *A Modern Utopia*, Nelsons edn, nd, p. 251; BWD December 1901 and 17 May 1905, *OP*, pp. 226, 305.
85. BWD 2 February 1908, *OP*, pp. 400-1.
86. Wells, *Experiment*, pp. 661-3; *SCANC*, p. 1131.
87. BWD 7 September 1937.
88. BWD 1 January 1901, Mackenzie vol. 2, p. 194.
89. BWD 28 February 1902, Mackenzie vol. 2, p. 240
90. BWD 21 September 1894 and 18 April 1896, Mackenzie vol. 2, pp. 56-7, 94.
91. *Difficulties*, p. 6; *Socialism: true and false*, p. 8.
92. For these issues see Logie Barrow and Ian Bullock, *Democratic Ideas and the British Labour Movement 1880-1914*, Cambridge: CUP, 1996.
93. National Conference on the Prevention of Destitution, *Reports and Proceedings* of second conference, June 1912, pp. 392-3.
94. BWD 12 March 1911, 11 October 1912.
95. BWD 25 December 1912; M. Cole, *Story*, pp. 131-2; Winter, *Socialism*, pp. 52-9.
96. BWD 5 June 1937*, 25 November 1938*.
97. Harrison, 'War Emergency Workers' National Committee'; Winter, *Socialism and the Challenge of War*, pp. 184-233.

*Chapter three*

# 'In a motherly sort of way': Fabians and guild socialists 1912-21

In that age of eminent couplings, the Woolfs, dining with the Coles, could not help but think of the Webbs. As Virginia Woolf noted in her diary in May 1920: 'The Coles are Webbs in embryo – with differences of course'.[1] The differences, at the time of writing, were a matter of notoriety. The young Douglas Cole, high theorist of guild socialism, had choked and spluttered on the very word 'Fabian', storming from the society and its 'bloody fools' of an old guard only five years earlier. For the Webbs themselves – the 'Sir and Lady Oracle of the Socialist movement' – he had a special contempt, and a seeming guiding mission to loosen their grip on British socialism.[2] Even so, Woolf's judgement proved a prescient one. Twenty years later, with Sidney and Beatrice beaming like indulgent godparents, the Coles stepped into their shoes as the presiding spirits of the Fabian Society. Margaret Cole, though she would hardly have said so in 1920, now described Beatrice as the greatest woman she had ever known. Cole himself, not usually accused of being unctuous, wrote to Sidney of how much the Webbs' 'incomparable partnership' had meant to those like himself 'who have tried to follow in your footsteps'. If tributes of this type were partly for form's sake, the Webbs at least had looked forward to such a succession even at the height of the Coles' earlier antagonism. What they saw from the start were deep affinities, of cultural formation, intellectual function, ideology and even temperament, that now seem at least as significant as the couples' earlier and more voluble differences.[3]

It is nevertheless the latter that have predominated in a literature investing heavily in the distinctiveness of Cole and his thinking. For a post-1956 'new' left, as Peter Sedgwick put it, Cole's refusal of both communism and social democracy as centralising creeds provided a banner for a new generation to rally to.[4] New editions of his guild socialist writings began to appear: not, it was said, to 'celebrate the past' but 'to snatch a vision of the future'.[5] Writing in the late 1970s, Tony Wright described his appeal as that of a 'sort of permanent opposition to the main tradition of British socialism', calling out to be recovered as that tradition reached an impasse.[6] In Wright's own incisive commentaries, themes of democracy, community, participation and socialist pluralism were set against a stark state collectivist backdrop, whose proponents seem as intolerant of the rude vigour of the guild socialists as they notoriously were of the 'average sensual man' and systems that pandered to him. Cole himself lived long enough to play his own part in the reconstruction. Tellingly, it is from *after* the disillusionment of the Cold War, indeed after the rise of the New Left itself, that there dates Cole's categorical assertion of never having been a communist or social democrat 'because I regard both as creeds of centralisation and bureaucracy'.[7] The permanency of his opposition stood as a sort of mirror image to the similar consistency for baser ends of the Webbs themselves.

In such presentations there is more than a hint of mythologising. Not only was there a much denser pattern of personal, political and generational interaction than accounts like Wright's acknowledge, but the intellectual exchanges were far more even and reciprocal too. It is not just that Cole came to adopt such bleakly 'Webbian' positions as dismayed even Beatrice herself; nor that the Webbs for their part were provoked into developing the democratic and participatory facets of their own thinking. More significantly in the present context, it was precisely what the Webbs had in common with guild socialism that proved to be one of the main currents feeding into their later Stalinism. This is hardly surprising, for many of Cole's closest associates were to find their way briefly or irrevocably into the newly formed communist party, while Cole himself was a supporter of Soviet Russia who only very belatedly condemned Stalinism, and at the cost of 'much personal distress'.[8] There were other ways than the Webbs' of getting to Soviet Communism, and none was more congested than that of the guild socialists.

Organisationally and perhaps ideologically, the whole revolt took place largely within a Fabian context.[9] Born in 1889, Cole was one of a new generation of student Fabians which blossomed in the period of the Poor Law campaign, and which reflected Fabianism's growing acceptance within an older and more privileged *couche sociale* than that which had launched the society at around the time of his birth. Very slightly older than Cole, there had first emerged a brilliant group of Cambridge Fabians including Hugh Dalton and Rupert Brooke. Beatrice had thought them 'quite the most remarkable [set] the Fabian Society has hitherto attracted'. Nevertheless, the group posed little overt challenge to a culture of permeation that was seemingly designed for such brilliant futures as theirs.[10] Cole, on the other hand, headed in a different direction. Though he also cut his teeth in the Poor Law campaign, and at first subscribed wholeheartedly to conventional Fabian tenets, within a year of his graduating from Balliol in 1912 he had all but abandoned collectivism.[11] Boisterous, beery and less conspicuously self-regarding than their Cambridge contemporaries, it was the 'Oxford boys' more generally who predominated among the guild socialists. By March 1913, when the two universities' Fabian societies got together for a joint meeting, 'words rose high over the respective merits of industrial and political action'.[12]

For this different trajectory several possible reasons may be suggested. One was the mere two or three years' age difference which, at a formative moment, confronted Cole with syndicalism, Belloc's *Servile State*, the pre-war labour unrest and the first systematic exposition of guild socialism by another Fabian rebel, S.G. Hobson.[13] In responding to these stimuli as readily as he did, Cole also reflected a distinctive tradition of social idealism within Oxford, identified particularly with his own college of Balliol, with figures like the veteran Oxford Fabian Sidney Ball, and with social initiatives like Toynbee Hall, Ruskin College and the Workers' Educational Association. Retreating from a stint lecturing at the future University of Newcastle as from 'an ordeal in the north', he remained strongly drawn to the Balliol tradition of service which was also a form of leadership. In this respect, Lawrence Goldman has noted how Cole continued to betray the influence of Victorian forbears like T.H. Green and Arnold Toynbee.[14] At a personal level, the influence of William Morris was also critical. It was through reading Morris that Cole described having first become a socialist, and from Morris he derived concerns with the freedom and status of labour that seemed the antithesis of contemporary Fabianism. More than any other of their predecessors, he later wrote, Morris was of the 'same blood' as the guild socialists; and he more than anybody had set him off on his own distinct line of thinking.[15] It was as rebels in the Morris tradition that Cole and his comrades were invoked by Raymond Williams in his *Culture and Society*.[16]

Attracted to the guild ideas then enjoying their first *succès d'estime*, Cole followed Hobson in eschewing the medievalist trappings of their first exponent, the architect Arthur Penty.[17] Instead, he worked them up into a synthesis, or tightrope walk, between syndicalism and collectivism, with a clear emotional leaning towards the former. If he tempered syndicalist notions of workers' control with a continued role for the state as a vehicle for consumer interests, the latter appeared as a counsel of necessity, not desire, and there was no disguising Cole's fervent identification with the 'World of Labour', the title of his first book. Both the ends and means of Cole's guild socialism were thus explicitly defined in opposition to Fabianism, like an echo of Ruskin's revolt against the consumer tyranny at the heart of conventional political economy.[18] The result was a series of exchanges so brusque and boorish that one is amazed to find the contestants sharing the same offices and even working together on the same political projects. Underlying their surface tensions, and as capable of provoking them as subduing them, there was evidently a keen awareness of mutual dependency.

Cole at least did not dissimulate his own motivations. Although in 1915 he left the Fabian Society after a failed attempt to wrench it from its existing leaders, he remained a driving force in the Fabian Research

Department, set up by the Webbs in 1913 to further investigations into the control of industry. Surrounding him was the group of young middle-class activists who between them dominated both the FRD and the National Guilds League, formed as a vehicle for guild socialism in 1915, and who established between the two bodies an almost symbiotic relationship.[19] Educated, metropolitan, unattached and under thirty, these were permeators gone astray to play their part in the authentic labour struggles which were then beginning to offer more dramatic possibilities than the mere prevention of destitution. One of the rebels, Margaret Cole, has vividly recaptured the energy, idealism and sheer high spirits with which they pursued their objectives. Describing themselves as 'the Movement', the phrase just faintly conjures up 'the Party' into which the Movement would largely collapse: not Bolshevised, centralised or even very organised, but still a 'nucleus of "comrades"', rather scornful and superior towards a world beyond not possessed of its secrets.[20] Among the NGL's leading personalities, former guildsman Maurice Reckitt recalled the names of the Coles themselves, Ivor Brown, William Mellor, Raymond Postgate, Monica Ewer, Norman Ewer, A.L. Bacharach, R. Page Arnot, Walter Holmes, Hugo Rathbone and Rose Cohen. All but the Coles and Brown joined the infant CPGB, five of them never to resign, and within the party they at first provided the core of the not dissimilar grouping that became known as the 'nucleus'.[21] Leonard Woolf once noted that the Webbs, despite their absolute disinterestedness, were 'so certain of the rightness of the ends which they were pursuing that they did not worry very much about the means which they used to attain them'.[22] If this was a characteristic shared by Fabians and Bolsheviks, it can also be detected in the 'Movement' that found itself caught somewhere between the two. A supposed 'fundamental antipathy to "Bolshevism"' was less general among them than is often suggested.[23]

What the rebels lacked if they were to advance towards their ends were the material and organisational resources with which to do so. Certainly the NGL was unable to provide them: membership at its peak was barely four hundred, mainly concentrated in London, and its efforts to secure labour movement affiliations were largely unavailing.[24] For Cole and his associates, there thus seemed no choice but to hold onto their corner in the Fabian Society offices. 'G.D.H. Cole told me that they intended to use us "as a platform"', Beatrice noted already in 1914.[25] Even after his resignation from the society itself, the research department continued to provide such a platform, for stamping on as well as elevating himself. 'I cannot write temperately of Fabians', he wrote to Beatrice in 1917, like an like an outraged adolescent angrier still through not being able to get by without his allowance.

> ... I fully realise that only the Fabian element in the Department can find the money to carry on. If, then, I find myself secretary of a 'group of the Fabian Society', it is from the basest financial motives, and without any

> feeling of obligation to or friendship for the Fabian Society, which, to be candid, I detest ... I want to split the Research Department right off from the Fabian Society, as soon as it is strong enough to stand the strain ... The problem is that of getting the money for such a body ... I recognise that we could not keep the Department going for a month, and ... therefore, I don't want to force the issue at the moment ...[26]

Four years later, faced with the same, ongoing financial dilemma, Cole helped push through the Russian deal which not only secured the department's future but detached it at last from the disapproving Webbs.[27] Only then did he discover how unimposing their controls had really been, edging his way back into the Fabian fold with his self-assurance visibly dented.

As to why the Webbs in turn should have borne such insults with equanimity, perhaps that too may be seen in generational terms. Certainly the couple's younger associates liked to cast themselves as brilliant victims of the connivings of old age. To Leonard Woolf, Beatrice's embrace was like being 'ensnared' in a 'spider-web', or, his wife again extending the Webbian bestiary, akin to having the old couple's 'claws fixed in his entrails'.[28] Though fundamentally self-serving, the accusation was not without foundation. With permeation exhausted, and their labour movement contacts neglected, the Webbs had before the war begun self-consciously to look to younger Fabians to push the cause of reform from without. The National Committee for the Prevention of Destitution, Beatrice's 'first attempt at organisation', was thus devised in 1909 as a deliberate experiment in harnessing these youthful energies. With an 'executive committee for consultative purposes', a formulation of which Willi Münzenberg might have been proud, Beatrice ran the campaign through a 'secretariat of young men and women' who directed policy under her own personal guidance. 'What I have got to aim at is make these young people do the work', she wrote, and both the model and the division of labour were subsequently institutionalised in the FRD.[29] With its personnel of rebels just shaking free of middle-class homes, the potential for conflict was obvious. 'I genuinely *like* my fellow mortals', Beatrice had noted ominously of the NCPD, '... I like to interest them, and inspire them, and even to order them, in a motherly sort of way'.[30]

She would, one feels certain, have made a no-nonsense mother. But equally, it is hard not to imagine that more generous maternal instincts, consciously suppressed by Beatrice on her marriage, also found an outlet in her 'avid' attraction to and cultivation of young people – particularly, Margaret Cole suggested, younger men.[31] As early as 1900, she had acknowledged a duty in 'helping forward younger persons, less fortunately placed than oneself, to the pathway of research and investigation'.[32] For a host of them, Woolf among them, the Webbs were not a snare but a springboard, and Webbian heirlooms like the LSE, FRD and *New Statesman* fell to younger hands and careers with only the faintest assertion of their founders' prerogatives. Even as they worked under Beatrice's supposed tutelage, Woolf, Cole and others were offered emoluments, little interference, full accreditation and free use of FRD materials in preparing their own works and careers.[33] 'The new generation must take its own line', Beatrice observed of their successors. 'It is useless for the older generation to cut up rough.'[34]

If that seems an unspiderly way of putting it, part of the explanation lies with Beatrice's increasing intimations of mortality and redundancy during the war years. In mid-1916 she suffered a breakdown which she was to identify with the onset of old age, describing herself as 'packing up so that I may be ready to depart when the day comes'.[35] To Leonard Woolf, who first met her only just before the war, she seemed a mere five years later 'surprisingly old & worn ... talking of retirement & the end'.[36] If such moods encouraged the hunt for successors, they also meant a greater thirst for the youthful elixir of political relevance and engagement. In her account of the wartime breakdown, Deborah Epstein Nord describes its main result as plunging Beatrice back into her diaries, reliving her earlier optimism and discovery of purpose amidst the wreckage of Victorian meliorism. The sequel, reached as usual with the fast-forward button, is the renewal of this sense of purpose in *Soviet Communism*.[37] Though Nord's is a major reappraisal, full of insight, such an emphasis is inadequate, for in reality Beatrice turned to her diaries only intermittently and completed her first volume of memoirs as late as 1925. Meanwhile, during a spell of prodigious productivity even by the Webbs' own prolific standards, the couple produced such major joint works as their *Constitution for the Socialist Commonwealth of Great Britain*, *The Consumers' Co-operative Movement* and an extended version of their *History of Trade Unionism*. That Nord fails even to mention these, though she is generally sensitive to the danger of downplaying Beatrice's 'very remarkable non-artistic achievements', again seems attributable to a primary focus on the earlier decades of her subject's life.[38] Although Beatrice certainly experienced weariness and even nausea for this succession of undertakings, she also remained susceptible to a sense of purpose and discovery as well as duty. Putting aside her diaries for the 'sterner work' that she regarded as her vocation, she even described the writing of their *Constitution* as 'a great lark' – 'I have never enjoyed writing a book so much'.[39] Far from abjuring politics, she engaged strenuously with new currents of thought, meeting them halfway and drawing them much of the other half. In the impact we shall trace upon her of the war, it is important to recognise elements of renewal and radicalisation co-existing with a deeper disillusionment.

It may be that the enlistment in the war effort of the best of the Cambridge Fabians partly forced the Webbs to look elsewhere for their successors.[40] Even prior to this, however, Beatrice at least was showing a far keener engagement with the ideas of those usually presumed to be her antagonists. As early as 1914, she expressed regret at Cole's refusal of a position of equality and mutual tolerance, and the following year claimed that she would gladly have made way for him had he not required the Webbs' 'public execution'. 'Bradlaugh may not know God', she wrote, citing the Christian socialist Stewart Headlam, 'but God knows Bradlaugh'.[41] Sedulously as she sought to modify the rebels' ideas, at the same time she conceded in June 1916 that 'the trend of events is so unfavourable to freedom for the producer that their ideal is valuable as a corrective'. Ignoring the identification of some Fabians with war socialism, including to some extent her husband, the outlook Beatrice expressed was closer temperamentally to that of the rebels.

> The Political State is getting far too much power and this power is far too much in the hands of the capitalist brainworker. Any addition to the efficiency and influence of the manual worker's organisations, any increase of the workman's collective control over the conditions of employment, any raising of his status and standard of life – is all to the good.[42]

With the 'state' subordinated to the ends of violence, she evinced little satisfaction in the pursuit of national efficiency, but on the contrary a *marxisant* awakening to the 'essentially predatory character of the Capitalist State' and the hardening division of society into 'two warring sections'.[43] Largely unfamiliar in a Webbian context, such sentiments reveal a process of ideological convergence and assimilation that requires a fuller examination of the Webbs' own social philosophy to be properly appreciated.

For the moment, it is enough to recognise the instincts of solidarity, almost, in the circumstances, of guardianship, that these shared perspectives encouraged. Sometimes this involved practical as well as moral support, as ideological rebels simultaneously denigrated and exploited older networks and dependencies that transcended political boundaries. Even before the war, William Mellor, Cole's closest abettor as a self-styled herald of revolt, was a beneficiary of these instincts of custodianship. One of a long line of Unitarians, himself intended for the ministry, Mellor had been expelled from the nonconformist Manchester College 'for drinking beer in a place and at an hour which was prohibited', and scraped out of Oxford with a pass degree. Due it seems to a family history of neurotic illness, and Mellor's own reportedly 'peculiar temperament', his future prospects gave rise to some concern, and the Webbs were approached by his college principal bearing a covert stipend to employ him in some improving capacity. It was thus that he was appointed the inaugural secretary of the FRD, where he showed little appreciation of the arrangement and perhaps was not aware of it. '[He] is not an ideal secretary, and yet I see no other means of livelihood open to him', Beatrice noted privately, as Mellor began his career as guildsman and goad to the Webbs while paradoxically beholden to them.[44]

These seem unimposing authority figures indeed; and for those who thought such treatment oppression, the war intruded a new and brutal sense of reality in which the Servile State appeared as anything but a catch-phrase, and metaphors of claws and entrails began to have a more credible application. Conscription, introduced in 1916, provided the most tangible threat, helping foster what began to be called 'the Youth Movement', though in complex ways that were overlain by caste and faction. It was characteristic, for example, that the threatened young men of the NGL did not disdain (or later acknowledge) such privileged connections as were provided for them by the Oxford classicist, internationalist and sometime war propagandist, Gilbert Murray. Cole himself, who according to his wife could not help 'putting his tongue out' at Murray, did not forget to ask him for a testimonial as to his indispensability away from the front. Among those who also enjoyed Murray's advice or assistance were fellow guildsmen R. Palme Dutt – who is said to have tried to enlist at the beginning of the war – Raymond Postgate and Alan Kaye. Murray was especially solicitous about William Mellor, who after two years as secretary had left the FRD for the *Herald*.[45]

Beatrice on the surface was less sympathetic. She disliked the claims to moral and social distinction she detected in exemptionist propaganda and wrote wryly to Murray of how admirably the imprisonment of well-born objectors brought to notice an 'infamous' penal system surviving without protest as long as its victims were the helpless poor. 'I wish we could arrange to have an hundred persons belonging to the upper class – and more especially children of Cabinet Ministers and Permanent Officials – always in prison as hostages for prison reform.'[46] Nevertheless, the Webbs not only supported the case against conscription, but in a practical way, like Murray, they colluded in their critics' efforts to evade the call-up. It was thus with their direct connivance that Cole and his close associate Kaye were exempted through their work for the Amalgamated Society of Engineers and the FRD respectively, while Arnot had unavailing testimonials from both Sidney and the Labour chief Arthur Henderson that his work at the department was of national importance. Walter Holmes, like Arnot a future communist, was another absentee who found temporary refuge in the FRD, and Beatrice noted with justifiable pride the department's role in 'sheltering and sustaining' objectors and absentees. 'We want all of them to get off; we hate compulsion to kill; and we realise that these ardent young men are getting right into the heart of the trade union movement and are creating an intellectual centre for trade unionism', she wrote in March 1916. 'They, and we, are becoming the constant advisers of the labour movement; and the young and the old counsellors do not differ in the advice they give as much as the younger ones imagine.'[47]

Sometimes regarded as the personification of Labour's new managerialist style, 'Uncle' Arthur Henderson's involvement suggests intriguing comparisons with the sharper divisions which were then developing within continental social democracy. Even the avuncular epithet captured a quality of reciprocity which for the time being survived the internecine logic of war and revolution. Henderson not only included the research department within the new national Labour Party in July 1918, but even allowed it a considerable degree of autonomy. Cole, encouraged by the Webbs, was beginning to regard himself as Sidney's 'supercessor' as Henderson's adviser, appointed by him to the National Industrial Conference and overseeing the new Labour advisory committees. It was with some justification that Beatrice lauded Uncle's 'breadth of vision' and their own 'wise magnanimity' in effecting such an arrangement; if, due to what she optimistically called 'temporary prejudices', the compact lasted barely three years, the Webbs themselves can least of all be held responsible. A whole series of entries in Beatrice's diary attest both the warmth and complexity of their relations with the rebels, and the omission of almost every one of these from Margaret Cole's edition of the diary suggests that it was the rebel myth which risked being deflated by the general lack of consternation shown by their elders. In one engaging passage, Beatrice describes with great good humour circulating the rebels with new drafts for the Webbs' *History of Trade Unionism*, only to receive their scornful annotations – '"Wow wow", "How superior", "What execrable manners", "You simply will not understand", etc, etc' – and the suggestion that they had ploughed their furrow long enough and should now make way for their successors. 'We are on excellent terms with these young folk', she wrote, 'there is the most friendly difference of outlook between us'. Only the deal to secure funding for the department from the Russians brought that relationship to an end.[48]

If Fabian cats were not all grey, nor are cats made cats by virtue of their colour. The Webbs were right to see in the rebels kindred spirits and successors, fitted like them for the role of 'clerks' to the labour movement – 'unpaid civil servants of the labour world' – and combining no less awkwardly the notions of service and directive intelligence which this suggested.[49] If the very ideas of the rebels were prescriptive rather than deductive, their functional and social relations with the labour movement also betrayed a note of arrogation as well as identification. 'Trade Unionism', as Cole put it, 'is far too important to be left for Trade Unionists alone to control'.[50] It is not surprising that his scorn and condescension towards trade unionists not quite fit to be left to their own devices should have provoked resentments which are several times referred to in Beatrice's diaries. From the 1915 TUC, a typical entry notes that Cole's disgust with the trade union representatives almost rivalled his contempt for the Fabians, adding: 'There were some nasty references to young men who refused to enlist and preferred to lecture working men from armchairs – a retort to the Cole-Mellor sententious address to Trade Unionists in the *Herald* … telling them exactly what resolutions they ought and ought not to pass'.[51]

Such presumption was partly a matter of youth, partly of having attended the finishing schools in self-regard that were England's older universities. Through class and gender respectively, the Webbs had been spared such an experience, but Beatrice was alert to the 'subtly pervading influence' it could impart to even the most militant of connections.[52] 'Cole is a young Karl Marx', Arnot announced, attesting both collective hubris and the sort of personal claim to leadership which was precisely what was least alien about Bolshevism.[53] According to his Oxford contemporary Louis Golding, Cole had 'the type of mind and the rigid, ruthless personality which inevitably suggests Lenin himself, and yet nobody is more exquisitely possessed of all that is admirable in the Oxford manner'.[54] Virginia Woolf, less admiring, thought him quick, hard and determined, 'covering his Labour sympathies, which I suppose are intellectual, with the sarcasm & sneers of Oxford'.[55] Against that one must set the testimony, not of Margaret Llewellyn Davies but of her maid, who found Cole 'very pleasant-speaking, rather nice-looking – classical-looking': a proper gentleman.[56]

Of course, these were not contradictions at all, for the perceived incongruity of Cole's 'aristocratic' deportment – so both Beatrice and Golding described it – revealed the serpentine persistence of those class distinctions, which, in deference, condescension or masonic complicity, undermined the democratic aspirations of labour. A single snapshot may serve for what must have been countless unrecorded snubs and passwords. The scene was a meeting at the Admiralty to discuss industrial conscription, and the occasion the mistaking of Sidney Webb, with the echo of his dropped aitches, as a common trade union agitator. All seemed lost until the meeting's instigator, J.M. Kenworthy, brought on Cole as a second witness. As if some unseen force was at work – which of course it was – the atmosphere at once miraculously changed. '"G.D.H.", with his Oxford accent, bedside manner, and soothing attitude, got on splendidly with the fiery Post-Captain', Kenworthy recorded, and soon he had won both hearts and minds of his naval interlocutors. Wiliness, in such a context, was no substitute for breeding.[57]

Perhaps it was Cole himself who needed a tongue sticking out at. 'In separate talks about sex and religion, he observed coldly on both occasions, "I am not interested and never have been"', Beatrice recorded a few years later. 'Which I think it true!'[58] He was also, she said, uninterested in other countries, other people and other people's opinions.[59] According even to his wife, Cole had the daunting ability 'to maintain and express continuously his own personal viewpoint', while fellow guildsmen, his supposed peers, were made to feel in his presence their own 'abysmal ignorance'. Margaret Llewellyn Davies was another who commented on Cole's 'abominably conscious intellectual superiority' – 'he rather feels he is going to be an intellectual force behind Labour'.[60] 'With his keen intelligence and aristocratic temperament it is hard to believe that he will remain enamoured with the cruder forms of democracy embodied in the Guild Socialist idealisation of the manual working class', Beatrice added; and it would be easier to dismiss the assessment had it not been proved correct.[61] Only towards his Oxford students does Cole's condescension appear to have relented, and one can only speculate as to what combinations of caste, pedagogical authority and masculine bonding this may be attributed. 'Above all else ... a theorist of community, as an expression of fellowship', Wright describes him. This, however, was the communitarian whose wife described him as deprecating human contact except as a source of information ('and even then I think he would rather they wrote it down and put it in an envelope'), and who, according to Beatrice, 'resent[ed] anyone who is not a follower and has a contempt for all leaders other than himself'. Above all else, it would seem ... a theorist.[62]

The mismatch of precept and reality had a tragic as well as comic side that ill accords with the prelapsarian myth of guild socialism. A figure generally missing from standard accounts is the LRD's assistant secretary Alan Kaye; and yet in 1926, in a more nearly contemporary account of the department, Arnot had paid this tireless but unsung figure his warmest tribute, ascribing to his indefatigable activity the 'largest share of the credit' for the department's wartime achievements.[63] Sadly, this must be read as both epitaph and atonement, for in May 1919 Kaye and the LRD's clerical worker, Sadie Heiser, had killed themselves in particularly unsettling circumstances. Guilt seems to have above all focused on Kaye. Only recently he had had a political falling out with Cole and reportedly had come to hate him. Other factors were no doubt involved: possibly Cole's marriage to Margaret Postgate, or Kaye's torments of conscience 'between extreme revolutionary opinions and Roman Catholic rites'. Whatever the reasons, Cole felt 'desperately miserable' about his own responsibility, while Margaret Cole penned a private valediction, 'Gas', suffused with themes of guilt and betrayal.

> There are other things than girls that break men's hearts,
> Dear gentle hearts, boys' hearts – I can't believe it.
> There is hope & faith & love & trust in men,
> Trust in the cause and in those who have fallen for it;
> And if that breaks, if those one trusted fail one,
> Why not the gaspipe? ...
>
> ... you were only mad in the sense of thinking
> That decent people don't do nasty things. O Kaye, they do!
> They get taken in adultery; they're spiteful.
> They pass by on the other side; they grab their neighbour's

Ox & his ass & anything they can get hold of.
Decent people do, not profiteers or Junkers,
Your friends & mine … And not to know that,
To die for finding it – O Kaye, & I helped to show you!
 Though it's little now serves any of us to wonder
Whose was to blame – 'You killed the hand, I the forehead.'
All's dead; we none of us can say we're sorry …

 O, Kaye! Kaye!
I wish they'd let me see you stuffed in Hampstead.
Maybe you wouldn't haunt me, you lost ghost of the escalator,
With your squashed hat & your bitten nails & your glasses,
Always just round the corner, always looking for Moorgate …
'Moorgate This Way!' – I'm sorry …
 You can't tell a ghost you're sorry.[64]**

Kaye's fate, like that of Rose Cohen, who was to perish in the purges, cast long shadows over these halcyon years. If the one is a reminder of the enormities of Stalinism, the other is a warning not to sentimentalise its predecessors.[65] 'Even the campaign for Guild Socialism – the "movement" to its participants – seemed to offer a foretaste of the vitality and comradeship that would distinguish a Guild society', writes Tony Wright. Perhaps it also prefigured the self-censorship on which experience suggests such a society would have relied to maintain those appearances. 'Don't be too clever, don't be too bloody certain', Margaret Cole had reflected after the tragedy of the deaths of Kaye and Heiser. It is sad that she failed to mention him in her own later accounts of the LRD.[66]

As for the Webbs, one can only marvel as contemporaries did at their seeming lack of rancour or resentment, indeed the positively 'beaming countenances' which they bestowed upon their would-be usurpers.[67] On one occasion Beatrice identified this incapacity for personal hatreds with their lack of moral indignation; on another with a promiscuous kindliness that always stopped short of emotional entanglements. 'Sidney tends to ignore personalities and I study them as specimens', she wrote towards the end of their lives, and the writing of her diary provided her with an outlet for insights into human hurt and frailty which might otherwise have made for more tempestuous relations.[68] What it also reveals is the extraordinary range of contacts and exceptional political mobility that were possible because of this disinclination to invest pride or prejudice in particular projects or allegiances. Towards the end of the war, Beatrice remarked on how they would one day be entertaining a Conservative peer like Lord Salisbury and the next the Clydeside firebrand and deportee Arthur MacManus. 'The good temper of the English people, their readiness to tolerate and work with one another, whatever their opinions, is amazing', she wrote; and if this was indeed a singular characteristic of the British left, it was pre-eminently one of the equable Webbs themselves.[69] Ideologically as well as politically, the journey that took them to Stalin's Russia must consequently be traced through a series of usually overlapping relationships embracing Fabians, revolutionaries, co-operators and disparate other varieties of British socialist, of whom the most significant in this connection were the guild socialists. But at the same time, these sometimes unexpected affinities can only be explained if we take a fresh look at the basic social theory of the Webbs themselves.

**NOTES**

1. Anne Oliver Bell, ed., *The Diary of Virginia Woolf. Volume 2: 1920-1924*, Hogarth Press, 1978, entry for 20 May 1920. While neither of the Webbs can have pre-eminence over the other, it seems reasonable if in this context 'Cole', where not otherwise indicated, refer to G.D.H. (Douglas) Cole.
2. Cole, *Self-Government*, pp. 44-5.
3. Margaret Cole, *Beatrice Webb*, Longmans, 1945, p. 5 and passim; Cole cited Betty D. Vernon, *Margaret Cole 1893-1980. A political biography*, Croom Helm, 1986, p. 109.
4. Cited Wright, *G.D.H. Cole and Socialist Democracy*, p. 282.
5. John Corina, preface to Cole, *Self-Government*, p. x.
6. Wright, 'Fabianism and guild socialism', p. 225.
7. Wright, *G.D.H. Cole and Socialist Democracy*, p.228 and passim For similar comments, also dating from the late 1950s, see L.P. Carpenter, *G.D.H. Cole. An intellectual biography*, CUP, 1973, p.94; Wright, 'Fabianism and guild socialism', pp. 224-5 and passim.
8. M. Cole, *Story*, pp. 255-6.
9. Compare for example Greenleaf, *British Political Tradition. Volume two*, p. 426, where it is suggested that Cole and others joined the Fabian Society for instrumental reasons, to 'use it' for their own separate goals.
10. See Ben Pimlott, *Hugh Dalton*, Macmillan edn, 1986, chs 3-5; also BWD 15 September 1908, *OP*, p. 415; Beatrice to Mary Playne, 21 August 1907, Mackenzie, *Letters*, vol. 2, p. 272.
11. See *Bolshevism and the British Left*, vol. 1, ch. 3
12. *University Socialist*, Michaelmas 1913, p.127; see also BWD 31 July 1914 for a vivid portrayal of the Oxford boys.
13. See S.G. Hobson with A.R. Orage (ed.), *National Guilds. An enquiry into the wage system and the way out* (1914), Bell, 1917 edn, based on articles published in the *New Age*, 1912-13.
14. Laurence Goldman, *Dons and Workers. Oxford and adult education since 1850*, Oxford: OUP, 1995, pp. 147-51; also Standish Meacham, *Toynbee Hall and Social Reform 1880-1914*, Yale University Press, 1987, pp. 8-23; Margaret Cole, *The Life of G.D.H. Cole*, Macmillan, 1971, ch. 3.
15. See Cole, *Self-Government*, pp. 49-52
16. Raymond Williams, *Culture and Society 1780-1950*, Harmondsworth: Penguin edn, 1961.
17. For Cole, Wright's studies may be supplemented by Margaret Cole, *The Life of G.D.H. Cole*, Macmillan, 1971 and Carpenter, *G.D.H. Cole*.

18. See J.A. Hobson, *John Ruskin. Social reformer*, Nisbet & Co, 1898, ch. 5.
19. On this, see Margaret Cole, 'Guild socialism and the Labour Research Department' in Asa Briggs and John Saville, eds, *Essays in Labour History 1886-1923*, Macmillan, 1971, pp. 260-83.
20. Margaret Cole, *Growing up into Revolution*, Longmans, 1949, pp. 61-73.
21. Maurice Reckitt, *As it Happened*, Dent, 1941, pp. 146-7.
22. Woolf, 'Political thought and the Webbs' in Cole, *The Webbs and their Work*, p. 258.
23. Greenleaf, *British Political Tradition. Volume two*, pp. 424-5.
24. G.D.H. Cole papers D3/5/1, notes on NGL annual conference, 1920. These give a membership of 277 in London and 143 in groups elsewhere. Only one affiliated society is recorded as voting at this conference.
25. BWD 31 July 1914.
26. Passfield papers 2/4/G/4, Cole to Beatrice Webb, 14 March 1917.
27. See *Bolshevism and the British Left* vol. 1, ch. 3.
28. Duncan Wilson, *Leonard Woolf. A political biography*, Hogarth Press, 1978, pp. 53-4.
29. BWD, 15 May 1909, *OP*, p. 428.
30. BWD 30 December 1909, Mackenzie vol. 3, p. 133.
31. M. Cole, 'Labour Research', p. 159. For Beatrice's thoughts on motherhood see BWD, 25 July 1894, Mackenzie, vol. 2, pp. 51-5.
32. BWD 22 May 1900, *OP*, p. 168.
33. See e.g. Leonard Woolf papers III, Sidney to Woolf, 2 February 1917 re Woolf's work on international questions for the Fabian Society. 'As to method & scope we must leave this to you. It is an adventure & you must conduct as you think fit.' According to Page Arnot's recollection, Woolf for his part was 'desperately anxious to cling to the Webbs' (M. Cole papers, MIC C/1/73, Arnot to Margaret Cole, 12 November 1969).
34. BWD 3 November 1916.
35. BWD 24 June 1916 (note added 1919).
36. Margaret Llewellyn Davies papers, Woolf to Davies, 23 September 1918
37. Nord, *Apprenticeship*, pp. 217 ff and 239 ff. Nord's interpretation is taken up and vulgarised by Carole Seymour-Jones, *Beatrice Webb. Woman of conflict*, Alison & Busby, 1993.
38. Nord, *Apprenticeship*, pp. 12-13.
39. BWD 11 December 1917, 11 May 1920.
40. M. Cole papers, MIC C/1/79, Arnot to Margaret Cole, 3 July 1975.
41. BWD 15 April 1915*; MSS Gilbert Murray 116/86-7, BW to Murray, n.d., c. 1915; 1 July 1918*.
42. BWD 1 June 1916.
43. *CSC*, pp. 274-5.
44. M. Cole, *Growing*, p. 66; BWD, 8 March 1914, 22 August 1927 and vol. 32, 3287, note dated August 1918*; MSS Gilbert Murray 375 Alan Kaye to Murray, 3 May 1917, Stanley Mellor (William's brother) to Murray 12 May 1917.
45. MSS Gilbert Murray 375 has extensive correspondence; also MSS Gilbert Murray 30, Cole to Murray 18 May 1916, M. Cole, *Life*, p. 42. More generally, see Fenner Brockway, *Inside the Left. Thirty years of platform, press, prison and parliament*, Allen & Unwin, 1941, pp. 66 ff; also *Bolshevism and the British Left* vol. 1, ch. 3.

46. MSS Gilbert Murray 375/171, BW to Murray, 2 July 1917; see also BWD 8 April 1916.
47. Beatrice to Betty Balfour, 28 October 1915 and Sidney to Beatrice, 15 November 1916, both in Mackenzie, *Letters*, vol. 3, pp. 63-4, 75; BWD 9 March 1916 and 15 May 1917*.
48. BWD 20 March, 1 July* and 7 November 1918 and 25 December 1919*.
49. BWD 9 September 1915 and 1 June 1916.
50. Cited M. Cole, *Life*, p. 59.
51. BWD 9 September 1915*.
52. *OP*, p. 99.
53. BWD 13 September 1916*.
54. *Co-operative News*, 28 January 1922.
55. Woolf, diary entry, 20 May 1920.
56. Leonard Woolf papers, Margaret Llewellyn Davies to Woolf, n.d..
57. J.M. Kenworthy, *Sailors, Statesmen – and Others. An autobiography*, Rich & Cowan, 1933, pp. 122-3; see also BWD 7 November 1918.
58. BWD 5 July 1938*.
59. BWD 5 September 1926; 11 September 1928*.
60. M. Cole, *Growing*, pp. 78-9; Kenney, *Westering*, p. 204; Leonard Woolf papers, Margaret Llewellyn Davies to Woolf, n.d. c. 1914.
61. BWD 14 February 1915.
62. Wright, *G.D.H. Cole*, p. 35.
63. Arnot, *History*, p. 16.
64. BWD 7 November 1918 and 3 June 1919*; M. Cole papers, MIC/A3/2/8, 'Gas', poem, n.d. but c. June 1919.
65. Eerily, the suicides took place in the flat of Hugo Rathbone, a 'delicate epileptic voluntary worker in the department' (BWD 3 June 1919*) who was soon afterwards to marry Rose Cohen's sister.
66. Wright, *G.D.H. Cole*, p. 101; M. Cole, 'Gas'.
67. Margaret Cole papers, MIC/C/1, Arnot to M. Cole, 28 November 1967; Reckitt, *As It Happened*, p. 125; see also MIC/A/1, cuttings of reviews by J.L. Hammond (*Manchester Guardian*) and M.A. Hamilton (*Sunday Times*), both October 1945
68. BWD 22 February* and 25 May 1934*.
69. BWD, 15 May 1917.

# *Chapter four*

# Science, state and society: the social theory of the Webbs

## I

'Like the respectable section of the movement, they were very strong upon function.' So William Mellor wrote looking back on the guild socialists in 1922. 'Every organisation was to be judged according to the function it performed, and quite arbitrarily they divided the two main functions of man into eating and working – it was the consumer and the producer who were jointly to rule the roost.'[1] The curt note of dismissal reflected Mellor's conversion to communist readings of state and class, along with numerous other guild socialists, including Cole's other close collaborator, R. Page Arnot. No doubt that movement into the CPGB helped stifle what in many ways was a tremendously fertile exchange of views between the respectable Webbs and their younger challengers. Nevertheless, Mellor's terse assessment did embody two great truths about that debate.

The first is that its main terms of reference were, if not exactly working and eating, overwhelmingly the issues of production and consumption. The guild socialist axiom that 'economic power precedes political power' was not, as we shall see, wholly alien to the Webbs, and to some extent it attested the Fabian intellectual formation of the key guild socialist theorists.[2] In both cases this made for a corresponding poverty of analysis where issues were not reducible to such terms. Of the European war that was raging as they developed their ideas, guild socialists made almost no acknowledgement except as an economic phenomenon. Later vulnerabilities to Leninist-Stalinism were to betray the same neglect of any adequate theory of politics.

Mellor's second insight was that, for all the asperity of the debate, its basic framework was common to both guild socialist rebels and the 'respectable' Webbs themselves. For both, the fundamental problem was the harmonisation or resolution of producer and consumer interests, and it was precisely this shared functionalist vocabulary that made so fruitful a dialogue possible. Eventually there were established not only cordial personal relations but a surprising degree of ideological convergence – even, as the Webbs essayed the system-building methods of the guild socialists, comparable forms of envisioning socialism. The terms of this convergence have been open to question, and standard accounts stress the yielding of the Webbs to the timelier as well as more attractive antonyms of the rebels. But this, as we shall see, is because the standard accounts derive substantially from the rebels themselves.

Perhaps we need to work these theories backwards as well as forwards if we are to unearth their hidden affinities. There is no doubt that the Webbs' vulnerability to the backlash against collectivism in the early 1910s was due not so much to their scheming habits as to their perceived social philosophy. What they stood for in a word was the state – what Margaret Cole called the 'extreme state collectivism' of the Webbs – and the connection has ever since then been axiomatic.[3] Given the powers of intrusion, inspection and compulsion for which they campaigned to tackle destitution, it is hardly surprising that such a characterisation should have prevailed over the gas-and-water projections of municipal Fabianism. It was given a ghastly semblance of life in the figure of their proposed public assistance registrar: trampling over local, elected or voluntary agencies, and, if benignly disposed, issuing them with Dickensian 'Certificates of Non-Overlap'. With a flair for inept analogy, the Webbs even likened their central statistical register to a 'new Domesday Book', as if the precedent of conquest and subjugation was one positively to be recommended.[4] So successful were they in conveying such impressions that they became almost symbolic figures, a bureaucratic counterpart to the bucolic 'Chesterbelloc' that was then to the fore in the reaction against the state. 'In these days', as Rebecca West put it in the *Clarion*, 'I am constantly meeting a certain type of self-satisfied young person who … drinks beer in a priggish manner and experiences feelings of sentimental distension on such occasions as sunset, and … has solved the problem of poverty because he dislikes Mr and Mrs Sidney Webb'.[5]

In the literature of revolt one is constantly meeting such people. Whether Cole preferred to drink in beer or sunsets, in his famous claim that not *poverty* but *slavery* was the issue of the hour, it was the ever-regulating Webbs who provided him with his target. 'Hey, dee, hey, dee for Measurement and Publicity', he paraphrased them in song.

> We'll thoroughly regiment everybody,
> And send up the stock of the State, O![6]

In the 'working-class view' of the *littérateur* Stephen Reynolds – a claim not always treated with sufficient circumspection by historians – the machinery of the minority report was likened alternately to a barracks and a human turnip-slicer.[7] The Catholic distributivist Hilaire Belloc, echoing Wells's skit on Altiora Bailey, satirised the collectivist's 'mechanical appetite for regulation', belching officiously at the prospect of a 'vast bureaucracy wherein the whole of life shall be scheduled and appointed to certain simple schemes'.[8] John Burns, writing to Wells, described the 'new helotry' of the 'archivists of the London School of Economics' as 'a grovelling community ruled by uniformed prigs'.[9] Wells himself, recoiling from the 'arrogance and presumption' of the 'District Visitor spirit', preferred the tolerable nuisance of vagrancy to a class of 'State Serfs'; while Max Beerbohm, in a cartoon for Sidney's fifty-fifth birthday, depicted him in his nursery, arranging tin officials into rows, and with a pin-up beauty on the wall captioned 'The State'. 'Fabianism is the special movement of the government official', the SDFer Belfort Bax wrote during the Boer War, and six decades later the same associations led Raymond Williams to describe as 'a Webb world' the Labour settlement of the Attlee years.[10] Even now, the *étatisme* of the Webbs remains proverbial, and accounts adopting a revisionist view of many aspects of Labour's history adopt without a second thought the equation with the state of the Webbs themselves.[11] In histories of British socialism, 'Webbism' has always been identified at least as much by this 'statist' philosophy as by gradualism and the cult of the expert. If this, according to W.H. Greenleaf, was the 'Fabian model', it was in the writings of the Webbs themselves that its starker aspects were most clearly expressed.[12]

This, however, is only part of the story. There is no doubt that the extolling of the state, even Hegelian allusions to its perfectibility, can be traced from the founding *Fabian Essays in Socialism* of 1889. There, in a passage often cited as representing 'classical Fabianism', Shaw's contribution on 'The transition to Social Democracy' invoked the state as guardian, trustee, manager and stakeholder to the people, looking, indeed, 'to gather the whole people into the State, so that the State may be trusted with ... the land, the capital, and the organisation of the national industry'.[13] Seven years later, on the occasion of the International Socialist congress in London, Shaw's anonymous *Report on Fabian Policy* roundly declared that what the society stood for was 'State Socialism exclusively'.[14] Far from abating such claims, Shaw himself revelled in the controversy that he provoked and ridiculed 'universal abolitionists' opposed to the systematisation of power. '*I'll* servile him', he threatened Belloc, and crucially it was Shaw who during the Boer war asserted the basic congruence of Fabianism and imperialism in their shared dignification of State Organisation and the Duties of the Community.[15] By this time, this had become a distinctively Shavian emphasis, mixed up with Nietszchean overtones and the calculated posture of a *frondeur*. Still, for practical purposes Shaw remained as little distinguishable from Sidney politically as he was utterly unlike him physically, spiritually or temperamentally. To his biographer he described himself as 'really a committee of Shaw & Webb', a committee which already at the time of the *Essays* formed the inner core of an unusually close intellectual fraternity – the 'Fabian

Musketeers'.[16] As the other musketeers – Graham Wallas and Sydney Olivier – drifted their different ways, these two remained in apparently indissoluble union at the society's head and together assailed the disparate radicalisms they categorised as 'Gladstonian Liberalism'. Along perhaps with Pease, a fixture as the society's secretary, Shaw and Webb were the oldest, the most indomitable and the most infuriating of the Fabian 'old guard'.[17]

However close and uninterrupted this relationship, there was a third party to it who brought to classical Fabianism a rather different cast of mind. Unknown to the Fabians when they wrote their *Essays*, and virtually inactive in the society for some twenty years thereafter, Beatrice Webb was both of and curiously apart from the Fabian mainstream. Pease, we know, she thought a bore and a nuisance, and Shaw, though she hardly thought him that, suffered what she called 'a current in my mind of depreciation' for his petulant reasoning and lack of accuracy, logic or dignity.[18] Entertained over many years, such misgivings were confirmed and reinforced in the 1920s by Shaw's extravagant support for that self-styled guardian, trustee and manager of the people, *Il Duce* Mussolini. Fortuitously enough, Shaw's withdrawal from active involvement in the Fabian Society before the war had coincided exactly with Beatrice's belated emergence as its leading figure.

More importantly in the present context, Beatrice also had the makings of a social vision which had little or no place in the original Fabian scheme of things. When, in 1919, Sidney penned a retrospective preface to the *Fabian Essays*, he acknowledged three major oversights in its original, one might almost say pre-Beatrice Webb, prospectus for socialism. A concern with the first of these, that of 'practically autonomous Local Governing Bodies' distinct from the central state, was consistent with Sidney's own long preoccupation with municipal socialism and implicit in the essayists' own earliest political efforts. Indeed, in Annie Besant's contribution, the potentialities of local government were scarcely understated even in the *Fabian Essays*. The other new elements, more radical still from the prevailing perspectives of 'State Socialism', cannot be traced to such a Fabian source. These were the voluntary agencies of workers and consumers, the trade unions and co-operatives respectively, whose contribution to the attainment or realisation of socialism had nowhere been indicated either in the *Essays* or any other major Fabian utterances. Together they effected a dramatic shift in Fabian thinking: away, Sidney recalled, from the bogeys of bureaucratic tyranny and 'an all-pervading uniformity of social life', and forward to greater freedom, diversity and 'an indefinitely varied development of human personality'. It all sounded, and by 1919 was meant to sound, very different from the Servile State. Even so, it was this notion of a multiform democracy which the Webbs later projected onto Stalin's Russia.[19]

For both the original conception and its transposition, the main responsibility lay with Beatrice. Already, when she met Sidney in January 1890, she was well-advanced with her researches into the co-operative movement. Sidney, it is true, then helped her with suggestions and a publisher, but the book which Beatrice wrote was like nothing yet bearing a Fabian hallmark.[20] If it was dismissive of producer co-operatives, a tolerably Fabian inflexion, it not only extolled the neglected virtues of consumers' co-operation but signalled the occupational concerns which were already leading Beatrice into parallel investigations into trade unionism. Anticipating countless later debates, she looked even in 1891 to 'the intermarriage of the Co-operative and trade union movements – not the dissolution of one by the other, or even the subordination of one to the other; but the voluntary interdependence, on terms of equality, of two opposite but complementary corporations ...'.[21] Of such concerns, there was not the remotest hint in the *Fabian Essays*. The mere idea of seeking 'levers whereby the working class may secure sovereign power in industry as in politics' was foreign to the volume's Benthamite ambitions, and Sidney's own contribution described the march of socialism exclusively in terms of legislative enactment. In lectures, and even in the *Co-operative News*, he dismissed 'co-operative storekeeping' as leading 'nowhither in the social problem'; and the very month that he met Beatrice published a book on *Socialism in England* which had nothing to say about the unions and set aside as irrelevant the 'huckstering' to which co-operation had in his view descended.[22]

It was not only Beatrice, therefore, who had something to learn from their exogamous courtship. Just four months after meeting her, Sidney accompanied Beatrice to his first Co-operative congress, and there he apologised to co-operators for the 'taunts and sneers' of the London socialists.[23] At her behest, he then abandoned a proposed treatise on political economy and in its place offered his assistance with her own project on the unions.[24] Thus commenced the first of their great joint enterprises, and one that represented a tremendous broadening of the Fabians' horizons. It is curious that in her memoirs Beatrice ascribed to her new acquaintances a less restricted and parochial vision than her own.[25] Much more likely, it needed somebody less absorbed than they in the ways of London radicalism to begin to grasp the significance of these sturdier movements beyond the capital. Even on their metropolitan home territory, it was Besant, another relative outsider, who was the first and only Fabian to make any meaningful connection with the New Unionism. Even she, despite her estimable role in the matchgirls' strike, drew from it no wider conclusions about the unions' possible role in her contribution to the *Fabian Essays* on 'Industry under socialism'. As for other leading Fabians, if, as Harrison avers, the dock strike of 1889 'had already made inconceivable the indifference with which ... [they] had treated the trade unions', it is odd that Sidney's *Socialism in England*, revised and updated in December of that year, showed not the slightest portent of such a change of heart.[26] Indeed, with the sole exception of projects already initiated by Beatrice, it is difficult to find any evidence in Fabian activities and publications that this indifference *had* been overcome. Shaw can be found in December 1891 lecturing on 'The goal of co-operation' to the Socialist Co-operative Federation; his diary records, 'Reading Beatrice Potter's book to get up material for the lecture.'[27] It took until 1900 before a Fabian tract, *How Trade Unions Benefit Workmen*, was devoted to the subject. Tract No. 104, and four pages long, it appeared in a larger typeface than its hundred or so predecessors.[28]

The 'partnership' of the Webbs was thus a genuine meeting of minds, not the dissolution of one by the other.[29] The attunement of these different strains varied over time with the pressure of external events, the extent of Sidney's public duties and the division of labour the couple practised as well as preached. Beatrice tended to think of herself as investigator and Sidney as executant, and it is true that hers was the more spacious and enquiring mind and the greater responsibility for conceiving many of their larger projects. Francis Galton, the couple's secretary in the 1890s, recalled that Beatrice had the 'genius' for devising plans and schemes, though not necessarily for carrying them out; while Cole thought hers the 'quicker and ... more imaginative' intellect and Sidney's the more orderly and systematic. At home, by her own account, she would sit in long brooding silences, while Sidney, incapable of self-absorption, would count the spots on the wallpaper if deprived of something to read. One may imagine that it was in Beatrice's silences that the couple's more adventurous projects had room to gestate.[30]

On the other hand, in engaging herself to Sidney, Beatrice found he brought with him the further formidable intellects of Wallas and Shaw: not so much a partner as the famous Fabian junta, unattached, united by a masculine camaraderie and eager to assist and permeate with their own assumptions her project on the unions. With the additional factor of Beatrice's dependence upon Sidney for the execution, and to that extent the final form, of their larger projects, it is not surprising that a political legacy perceived as more than usually transparent reveals on closer study the distinct ambiguity of its dual origins. Commenting on the abridgement of Fabianism to its merest catchphrases, Eric Hobsbawm has rightly noted how 'few serious writers about society have had their thoughts more consistently neglected than the Webbs'.[31] Nevertheless, Hobsbawm's own penetrating overview draws disproportionately on Sidney's relatively slight solo productions to stress the technocratic or statist thrust to the Webbs' thinking, and in this it prefigures more extended accounts which virtually ignore more considerable and significant works bearing Beatrice's greater imprint.[32] Even in the Webbs' official biography, Harrison barely mentions Beatrice's book on co-operation and shows no appreciation of the distinctive insights which it contained. The omission is still the more remarkable in view of the excellent, expansive commentaries which Harrison provides on the *History of Trade Unionism* and *Industrial Democracy*.[33] It is possible that in some cases these emphases can be justified by the particular preoccupations of the authors in question. In the present context – of the control of industry and *Soviet Communism* – both the works on social movements and their principal instigator are critical.

## II

Generated from outside the academy and virtually creating its own field of study, this corpus of early writings presents several features of consistent or recurrent significance for the Webbs' thinking. Basic to their creed of gradualism was the profoundly inductive character of their method and philosophy. R.H. Tawney even cited Oakeshott's view of ideologies as 'abstracts of some kind of concrete activity' to convey this aspect of the Webbs' work. They conceived of socialism, Tawney said, 'not as a system to be imposed, but as an organic growth', and tried as thinkers 'not to draw designs for imposing new palaces' but 'to reveal the significant features of the transformation under way about them [and] elicit conclusions of general application from the mass of raw experience provided by it'.[34] Though Cole and Tawney himself were also steeped in historical precedent, the very fabric of Webbian thinking was woven of historical materials. It was for this historical sense that Beatrice first sought out Sidney, contributor on this theme to the *Fabian Essays*;[35] it was historically that she then unfolded her own account of co-operation; and it was on a trade union *History* that they jointly ventured before, and only on that basis, attempting their treatise and prospectus *Industrial Democracy*. Even this last volume prefaced its theoretical section with some six hundred pages of historical and descriptive matter. It is true that in this case they began writing their analysis before completing their empirical investigations, and that their histories were actively shaped by the social philosophy that seemed inexorably to emerge from them.[36] Nevertheless, the significance of this approach to the study of society should not be underestimated, and had they applied it to Soviet Russia a good many errors might have been avoided. As Leonard Woolf pointed out, it was not as 'static products of human history' but rather through their 'dynamic principles and causes of ... growth' that the Webbs sought to understand social institutions by methods that were provisional by their very nature.[37] As Sidney himself put it in 1898, 'why, after all, should there *be* any completely rounded and systematically perfect theory of anything whatsoever?'[38]

No doubt the method had something of the naive self-assurance of Victorian positivism. To the study of society it self-consciously brought the disciplines of the 'other' organic sciences, albeit with an acknowledgement of fallibility and political subjectivity that helps explain the couple's readiness for later adaptations. 'Like all scientific theories', they wrote in *Industrial Democracy*, '[ours] will be quickly broken up, part to be rejected as fallacious or distorted, and part to be absorbed in later and larger views ... [and] even those who ... accept our economic theory as scientific, will only agree in our judgement of Trade Unionism ... in so far as they happen to be at one with us in the view of what state of society is desirable...'[39] Like the American pragmatist William James, whom Beatrice came to regard as her favourite philosopher, they turned away from 'abstraction ... fixed principles, closed systems, and pretended absolutes' and towards concreteness, facts, action and power.[40] Theirs moreover were not the pretensions of the engineer, nor even of the laboratory, but of that votary of classification, the Victorian naturalist; or, more augustly, the 'biologist', to whom their own claims to a scientific method were invariably compared.[41] Their fondness for organic metaphors, though less cloudy and superficial than Ramsay MacDonald's, had still more ambiguous implications. On the one hand, they suggested a view of social change that was deeply non-coercive, hardly even needing labour-pains let alone the marxian midwifery of violence; this deep-seated gradualism, spurning any 'violation of the habits and established expectations of large masses of people', was to be immortally associated with Sidney's presiding address to the 1923 Labour Party conference.[42] With gradualism, however, as Sidney famously noted on that occasion, went inevitability, and with it the danger that to its laws of motion all moral critique could be subordinated. Perhaps that helps explain the couple's confessed inability even 'to *feel* moral indignation, either against races, classes or individuals' – though not necessarily against systems, as their post-war *Decay of Capitalist Civilisation* would show.[43] Nevertheless, the couple's social imperialism, Labour reformism and communism all had in common a susceptibility to the march of progress regardless of its particular forms or blemishes. An acquiescence in the movements of history could mean an acquiescence in its brutalities even as they were disavowed as a means of change.

If their method was historical, their subject was not the individual but the collectivity expressed in organised social movements. 'It is a moving multitude of men that I seek to describe', Beatrice wrote of co-operation, and hers was anything but a tale of heroes and hero-worship:

> ... I have failed to discover in the history of Co-operative institutions any one man, or even group of men, who have contributed in an absolutely pre-eminent degree ... [It] is, literally speaking, the *Co-operation*, or joint work of thousands of honest, capable, self-devoted citizens – men standing as a class far above the average in intelligence and practical sagacity, but presenting a high level, rather than peaks and chasms of efficiency, varied ... by examples of self-subordination,

> scrupulous integrity, enthusiastic industry, rising to the heights of moral genius.[44]

For a couple the 'very quintessence of the intellectual in politics', alternately described as platonic guardians and a 'latter-day version of the philosopher-king', the neglect and even condescension they evinced towards intellectuals is arresting.[45] Unlike Cole in the majority of his historical writings, unlike even Sidney in his bachelor efforts, the Webbs wrote histories whose moving forces were only exceptionally thinkers like themselves. Instead, Beatrice took from Herbert Spencer, her initiator into the world of ideas, a profound scepticism as to 'the great-man-theory of History', though without Spencer's concomitant disbelief in the susceptibility of social environments to collective agency.[46] Thus, while Robert Owen figured as the founding father of co-operation, its real genius lay with the Rochdale pioneers and their invention of the 'divi': the brainchild, said the Webbs, not of a professional economist or entrepreneur, but of a 'simple-minded Lancashire weaver'. In a passage hard to identify with this future sorceress of permeation, Beatrice even described how little Owen's ideals were effective until transported from philosophers' bookshelves and the tables of the great to the 'plodding uniformity' of the back street and crowded city.[47]

Conversely, the failed alternative of producer co-operatives was identified, like the later guilds, with the articulacy and forwardness of middle-class idealists. How regrettable it was, Beatrice noted of these well-meaning social redemptionists, that through their 'superior attainments as lawyers, writers and orators' they should have acquired such a hold over the representation of co-operation. To that she added two further notes of demotic Whiggery. The first, adducing the Gallic innovation of national workshops, was to stamp producers' co-operation with its 'foreign' origins. The second, from the perspective of democratic development, was to stress that the consumers' associations alone embodied the critical Webbian principles of 'growth and continuity'.[48] Already spelt out in Beatrice's first book on co-operation, precisely the same arguments were thirty years later to be directed at the 'intellectual philanthropists and world reformers' of the guild socialist period.[49] For a similar capacity for self-government in the world of labour, meanwhile, Beatrice looked not to experimental workshops but to the undemonstrative achievements of trade-union organisation.[50]

At one level this betrayed the institutional fixations so clearly to be displayed in *Soviet Communism*. At another, less familiar but similarly prefiguring that work, it can be seen as a search for community and the values of self-government. What initially drew Beatrice to co-operative milieux was not a problem to be managed, nor a threat to be contained, but a glimpse of unforced social cohesion and advancement. Like others of her caste and sex, she had first encountered working people as an East London charity worker, and like others she found the experience dispiriting and almost physically repellent. This image of the slum, gripping its inhabitants like a sort of 'moral malaria', was to justify policies of human clearance as well as prevention: an even more disturbing consideration if whole peoples – the Russians perhaps – could come to be regarded in the same way.[51] Significantly, among the dirt and drunkenness what Beatrice's diary entries most of all stressed was the absence in the East End of 'combined effort or common interest'. As a society, it was 'an ever increasing and ever decomposing mass'. Even its better qualities of sociability and generosity found a focus only in the drink-sodden parlours of the 'public'. The forging of affective ties took place – 'there is something grotesquely coarse in this' – outside the tenement water-closets.[52]

No doubt these emphases were less distinctive than their corollary: not continued philanthropy and the provision of middle-class social leadership; not the poor-law reforms that already exercised the bachelor Sidney's mind; not even the London social surveys for which Beatrice seemed so suited, but a 'sentimental journey' to her distant family roots in the industrial north. The aim of this journey, she later wrote, was to see for herself, not the people of the abyss, but the ordinary, 'normal' British manual worker. 'How had this class, without administrative training or literary culture, managed to initiate and maintain the network of Nonconformist chapels, the far-flung friendly societies, the much abused Trade Unions, and that queer type of shop, the Co-operative store?', she mused, at least retrospectively – though it seems unlikely that the recognition of working-class virtues can have been quite so clear-sighted even in advance.[53]

Nevertheless, it required a singular curiosity to transport, under cover of an incognito, this socialite *manqué* to the small cotton town of Bacup, north of Rochdale. Unlike George Orwell, that other social excursionist from the south, what Beatrice sought in Bacup was not the extreme of destitution that Orwell found in Wigan, but a respectable self-sufficiency. This she described with the same face-at-the-window quality that Orwell, memorably and perhaps derivatively, was to make his own:

> Sitting by the hands at work, watching the invigorating quickness of the machinery, the pleasant fellowship of men, women, and children, the absence of care and the presence of common interest – the general well-being of well-earned and well-paid work – one was tempted to think that here, indeed, was happiness – unknown to the strained brain-worker, the idle and overfed rich, or the hardly pressed very poor. Young men and women mix freely; they know each other as fellow-workers, members of the same or kindred chapels; they watch each other from childhood upwards, live always in each other's company. They pair naturally, according to well-tested affinity, physical and spiritual. Public opinion –

> which means religiously guided opinion – presses heavily on the misdoer or the non-worker – the outcasting process, the reverse of the attracting force of East End life, is seen clearly in this small community, ridding it of the ne'er-do-well and the habitual out-o'-work.[54]

Almost every line suggests its metropolitan antithesis: not just the slums and spooning in the stairwells but the drawing-room ennui and marriage brokering that was seemingly ordained for Beatrice herself. It was, she wrote in her book on co-operation, in the chapel and the co-op that she discovered both 'the inborn capacity of Englishmen for self-government' and the middling sort of Englishmen – 'that intermediate class neither too poor nor too wealthy for democratic self-government' – who could best give effect to it.[55]

Unevenly as it may have been, the Webbs' elitism was thus counterbalanced from the start by these concerns with an orderly but essentially self-regulated democracy. Although these may seem like scenes of the deserving poor, such values were not alien to British Labour but on the contrary suffused its ethos of collective betterment. In Beatrice, like many other British socialists, they can frequently be found linked with the idea of an essentially religious framework for human relationships. Already she described Bacup as 'the only society I have ever lived in, in which religious faith really guides thought and action, and forms the basis to the whole life of the individual and the community'.[56] The awakening to such a possibility left its traces in many of the later phases of her career, perhaps providing hidden connections between them. Certainly it played its part in the genuine meeting of minds, which some have regarded as incongruous and manipulative, between the Webbs and Arthur Henderson. A north-country lay preacher as well as politician, in Beatrice's estimation Henderson was the 'wisest and most disinterested' Labour leader they had ever encountered.[57] The sequel seems unlikelier still, for the sober dignity which made Henderson one of the defining Labour figures of his generation seemed to her by 1934 to qualify him as 'an excellent member of the political bureau of the CP in the USSR' – should it only adopt his 'undogmatic Christianity'.[58]

However fanciful such a notion, it was not the only such perception of hidden consanguinity. The following month, observing Russian co-operative officials – 'hardworking, simple, well-mannered folk, with missionary Marxist faith' – Beatrice was reminded irresistibly of her 'God-fearing Bacup relatives of 1884'.[59] Perhaps, by extension, the Bacup which she idealised suggests in hindsight not just an ordered but a closed society, almost in its small way a premonition of dystopia. 'Unless a man can work regularly he cannot work at all', Beatrice had written to her father from the town. 'Then a bad character is socially an outcast, the whole social life depending on the chapel and the "Co-op".' Already the example had set her musing about a stronger local government, continuously involving working people in 'the active regulation of their own and their neighbours' lives' and granting them 'considerable power to check individual action'.[60] Comradely courts and the branding of transgressors, the Soviet face of moral as well as social cohesion, seem briefly just a step away. Of course, the Bacup outcast drifted into Manchester, not into labour camps, and chapel-bred moralities no more pointed inexorably to Stalinism than did the *fin-de-siècle* passion for social reform. What the analogies do remind us is how serpentine such paths usually were. The glimpse of a society cleaned of outsiders, and thinking itself all the better for it, enjoins us to sentimentalise the nonconformist conscience as little as we usually do the Webbs themselves.

**III**

Inseparable from this vein of historicism was a second key to the Webbs' philosophy: their ungrudging acceptance of the social textures of industrialism. Whatever significance they accorded the values of community, the idea that these could be restored through simpler or more natural relations of work and society was dismissed by the Webbs as mere nostalgic fantasy. The Beatrice who went to Bacup may at least have felt the pull of a society 'know[ing] nothing of the complexities of modern life'.[61] Sidney, a Londoner through and through, did not even find the fantasy attractive. Like Emile Durkheim, and just a year after the publication of Durkheim's *Division of Labour in Society*, Sidney described as irreversible the 'elaborate differentiation and complication of modern civilisation', and derived from this condition the justification of a bureaucratic controlling mechanism. 'To suppose that the industrial affairs of a complicated industrial state can be run without strict subordination and discipline, without obedience to orders', he wrote with what seems a gratuitous emphasis, 'is to dream, not of Socialism but of Anarchism'.[62] Seven years later, referring again to growing social density, complexity and largeness of scale, he proposed to Wells the inclusion of the administrative expert in his future ruling caste of 'New Republicans'. 'Men', he cheerfully pointed out, were going to need organising quite as much as machines – 'or rather, much more'.[63]

This was not the only possible inflexion, however. Beatrice's first intellectual mentor was Herbert Spencer, an increasingly sad and splenetic figure whose individualist social philosophy eventually failed to convince even such a friend as Beatrice Potter proved to be. Nevertheless, for some years Beatrice counted herself Spencer's 'disciple'. Appointed by Spencer as his literary executor, she was permanently to be influenced by the evolutionary notions of ever-increasing 'heterogeneity' which he accorded the status of a universal law of progress. While casting off individualism as Spencer understood it, she saw the possibilities of human fulfilment in what she once called the 'joy of specialisation – a joy akin to that of the artist and poet'. Already long since experienced by the Webbs themselves, the vocationalism which they embraced can thus be seen as a fitful attempt to generalise a measure of self-development through the acquisition of distinctive skills and responsibilities. Steadied by Spencer's balancing principles of integration and the interdependence of unlike parts, it supported a social vision of 'multiformity' – a word Beatrice must have had from Spencer's own lips – that was systemic and diverse on the pattern of nature itself. Here, then, complexity had different connotations: not the Webbian 'rule of the road', avoiding social collisions through the acceptance of a common authority, but of the flowering of a positive freedom offsetting Benthamite obsessions with human traffic management.[64]

Whatever the particular emphasis, the embrace of complexity and the division of labour was the very cornerstone of Webbian thinking. In Beatrice's *Co-operative Movement* it entailed the rejection, as atavistic as well as unrealisable, of the self-governing community or workshop.[65] In their subsequent trade union studies, the supercession of 'primitive democracy' by mature forms of bureaucratic differentiation and representative authority was likewise presented as progressive and irreversible.[66] Similarly, upholding vertical as well as horizontal differentiation, they preferred occupational to industrial unions, less on grounds of superior rationality than of the deep-seated moral claim to a 'trade'. Against the 'ludicrous' notion of single labouring class, they described the dynamic of trade unionism as 'adopting and strengthening the almost infinite grading of the industrial world into separate classes, each with its own corporate tradition and Standard of Life'.[67] Within the workplace itself, Sidney propounded for any conceivable industrial order a 'specialised and differentiated hierarchy', to handle not matter or machinery but the human will. A works without a manager, he proclaimed in his wartime paean to the genus, was no more imaginable than an orchestra without a conductor. Almost simultaneously, the same image was being deployed in the Bolshevik textbook *The ABC of Communism*, albeit with the unfulfilled proviso that under communism the administrative baton would be passed around and no settled class of conductors tolerated.[68] Both musically and politically, neither Webb nor the textbook's authors, Bukharin and Preobazhensky, could imagine the 'conductorless orchestra' which had its heyday in the Russia of the 1920s.[69]

For the Webbs there was hardly a question of morals or authority that was not susceptible to the same logic. 'We need the expert here as elsewhere', Beatrice wrote of the Anglican church, conceding the benefit to society of professional ministration to 'diseases of the soul'.[70] In the narrower field of politics, never the Webbs' strongest point, the forms of democratic authority were to be subjected to the same administrative logic. Jocularly, Beatrice once remarked that she had no objection to examinations for parliamentary candidates, 'because I know my husband would come out top'.[71] Such engaging self-parody nevertheless concealed a serious issue, for in the Webbs' proposed 'new calling' of 'expert parliamentary representative' problems of social and functional dislocation were glibly surmounted by the assiduity with which the expert would attend to constituency interests. Entirely negated thereby was the suggestion of an inverse proportion between representative legitimacy and professional specialisation which the Webbs had convincingly expounded in a trade-union context.[72]

No less paradoxical was Beatrice's initial anti-feminism. Here, possible derivations may be detected both from Spencer himself and another close family friend, the doyen of English positivists, Frederic Harrison.[73] It was through Harrison that Beatrice came to order the works of Auguste Comte from the London Library, and she continued to reflect their influence even as she came to regret having publicly endorsed Harrison's anti-suffragist platform. If even Annie Besant was 'beguiled' by Comte's view of woman as an angel, Beatrice too, though similarly defying conventional expectations as to her own life's work, proposed a Comtean division of sexual roles which validated the private sphere as it surrendered to men that of public affairs. For active citizenship – for wealth, power and even learning – she believed men were suited by their very 'physical restlessness', just as the periodic lassitude and incapacity of her own sex seemingly 'ordained' it for a gentler nurturing role. 'Surely it is enough to have half the human race straining every nerve to outrun their fellow in the race for subsistence or power?', she wrote, momentarily indulging regrets for her own unborn children. 'Surely we will need some human beings who will watch and pray, who will observe and inspire, and, above all, who will guard and love all who are weak, unfit or distressed?'[74] No doubt a similar concern can be traced in Beatrice's support for gender-specific factory legislation, and her opposition to equal rights feminists 'eager for the Rights of Women to work all hours of day and night with the minimum of space and sanitation'. An argument for domesticity or philanthropy, this could also translate into concerns with the relational and mutualist aspects of socialism, and the 'strong prejudice' against the masculine world of competitive politics was to remain discernible in Beatrice's thinking long after the initial impulse of renunciation had passed.[75]

This specialisation even of politics itself was what most clearly separated the Webbs from what Logie Barrow and Ian Bullock have called 'strong' variants of democratic thinking on the left. In this as in any other field, the 'professional expert' sought from the 'average sensual man' only that 'consciousness of consent' whose minimalism seemed to underline the Webbs' limited expectations of a mass democracy.[76] Legislation, as Sidney once put it, was 'as much a distinct craft as shoemaking', and just as little susceptible to general participation.[77] Though it is true this was not a 'strong' view of democracy, given the Webbs' belief in the inevitable specialisation of administrative power, there was at least consistency in their concern with commensurate powers of scrutiny and control; and in the argument that these too demanded a comparable level of expertise. Moreover, there was something to be said for the claim that forms of mass affirmation could as easily lead to the 'uncontrolled domination' of a dictator or bureaucracy as to the more familiar Webbian bugbears of inefficiency and disintegration. As a possible credo for the activist citizen as well as the enlightened ruler, the Webbian conception of democracy – when they remembered it themselves – was as forcefully opposed to the 'strong' variants of anti-democratic thinking, such as Shaw's, as to more radical movements to their left.[78]

Nevertheless, despite the Webbs' repeated affirmation of Matthew Arnold's dictum to 'choose equality', the extolling of differentiation in what were relationships of power could not but undermine such good intentions. In her memoirs, Beatrice cited as the final cause of her conversion to socialism 'the psychological evils of a community permanently divided into a nation of the rich and a nation of the poor, into a minority always giving orders and a vast majority always obeying orders'.[79] Those basic socialist instincts, though too often overlooked, nevertheless allowed for differences of power and status reflected in other than pecuniary rewards. 'Choose equality and flee greed', Arnold had cited the Athenian Menander, but beyond the baser appetites of which Arnold disapproved were more discriminating pleasures wholly compatible with relative material abstinence.[80] 'The goodwill of a great community, the political power and social influence equitably earned by the able and energetic official of a powerful and growing organisation have proved as efficient a form of remuneration as the unknown gains and lawless expenditure of the capitalist *entrepreneur*', Beatrice had written already of the Co-operative 'brain-worker'.[81] At one level – Matthew Arnold's perhaps – the ethos is that of the Victorian public servant, whose 'unpretentious self-subordinating devotion' was almost a Webbian watchword.[82] At another, it provides an early foretaste of the Vocation of Leadership which Beatrice would later discover in the USSR.

## IV

Another cornerstone of the Webbs' thinking, in all its various inflexions, was the subordination of the producer to the consumer. That too suggested differentiation, and in *The Co-operative Movement in Great Britain* Beatrice had dangled the notion of the trade unionist as 'wage-earning man' and the co-operator as 'housekeeping wife'.[83] Some years later, Percy Redfern, the Tolstoyan historian of the Co-operative Wholesale Society (CWS), was to comment pointedly on how it had taken this 'educated woman' to expound the significance of consumers' co-operation as against the opprobrium or neglect to which masculine producer interests had consigned it.[84] Fundamentally, though, the counterposition of producer and consumer signified not the differentiation of individuals according to function but of functions or attributes commonly combined in the same individuals. This went beyond functionalism per se, for the final case for consumer authority – once again, when the Webbs remembered it – was that this was where the demands of function ceased and the sphere of human possibility opened up. All too easily, however, this could become reduced to the blunter question of efficiency; for it was a Webbian truism that producer associations tended not only to the refusal of innovation, whether of organisation or technique, but to the restriction of output and recruitment for sectional benefit.[85] While a permanent role for trade unionism was already indicated in Beatrice's early co-operative writings, its functions were thus conceived as essentially limited and defensive ones. Against the wider democratic authority of the consumer, they offered a means of redress and guarantee of personal dignity, but only such autonomy as was 'practicable and desirable' subject to that authority.[86] As Beatrice put it in her 1892 paper on the unions and co-operatives: 'Any particular trade exists, not for the benefit of the workers employed in it, but for the whole nation.'[87] The worker, Sidney added two years later, 'is and must be the servant of the community. From that service Socialism offers no escape.'[88]

With such double-edged abstractions, we come to a more contentious proposition: that the Webbs are more usefully regarded as theorists of community, with all its ambiguities, than of the state. To make such a claim is to enter a thicket of semantic syncretism. As Eileen and Stephen Yeo have pointed out, 'community' as a value has lent itself to widely differing interpretations, which they classify as 'mutuality', 'service' and 'state'.[89] The Webbs, as we have seen, have almost invariably been identified with the last of these. For Raymond Williams, whose own antinomies for community were (middle-class) 'service' and (working-class) 'solidarity', they epitomised a statist mentality to which Williams opposed a democratic tradition culminating in guild socialism. What distinguished Cole from Webb, he wrote, was 'the line of thinking which is summed up in the word "community", rather than the word "state"'; the idea, that is, of the 'vital associative life' which Cole discerned, not in the parliamentary fraud of a General Will, but in voluntary associations rooted in 'real collective experience'.[90]

More familiar now than when Williams proposed it in the 1950s, the antithesis will not stand up to a reading wider than Williams's single Fabian source of the *Fabian Essays*. Nor is it adequate to suggest that the sociable overtones of community were simply hijacked by collectivists for distinct and alien purposes. The emphasis on the contestability and multi-referentiality of language, an outstanding feature of Eileen Yeo's work, remains indispensable.[91] On the other hand, too clinical a separation of different meanings and their champions can obscure the extent to which common vocabularies provided scope for dialogue, for the massaging of dissensions and for sudden modulations from one layer of meaning to another.[92] This was true of the Webbs themselves as collaborators, for, if Beatrice was the greater 'mutualist' and Sidney the greater 'statist', the importance to them of community was precisely that it allowed shifting or ambiguous readings to encompass their different accents. The same multivocalism provided the broader movements they inhabited with a means of intercourse, consensus and adaptation, avoiding the suppression or overaccentuation of their rather considerable internal differences. In that sense, the looseness of community fitted perfectly with such heterogeneous strategies as permeation, progressivism, social paternalism, the Labour alliance, or even that no less loosely defined chimera of socialism itself.

It was precisely this slippery usage, and more specifically the conflation of community and state, which in due course led Williams to draw back from a term so loaded with potential betrayals.[93] Particularly when reified as 'the' community – for example, in Cole's invocation of 'that General Will which resides in the community alone' – the meanings seem almost impossible to entangle.[94] In the same spirit, perhaps that refusal of a facile dichotomy between these terms should therefore also be extended to the 'state' itself, a concept hardly so fixed or transparent as more casual usages – Williams's 'capitalist state', for example – might suggest. Certainly, the thinkers in the Fabian tradition with whom we are concerned had no all-embracing definition of the state. Margaret Cole, noting the term's elusive significance for guild socialists, distinguished three distinct meanings, of coercion, territoriality, and 'the spirit of the community'.[95] The Webbs, independently but contemporaneously, arrived at a very similar definition, only substituting the idea of consumption for the territorial principle. In neither case was the inter-relationship between these functions properly clarified, and the Webbs frankly described their entanglement as a 'vicious mixture'.[96] In a world that required distinguishing between rival state forms, the different ways in which the state could be imagined, through community to authority and even terror, were far from incidental to some larger issue of socialist principle. On the other hand, community itself provided a way of not seriously thinking about the state, or of consciously or otherwise dissimulating the realities of state power. Like class, it was not antonymous to the state, but potentially at least its real or pretended modifier. The Webbs were thus entirely of a piece with their syndicalist contemporaries in later reading into the USSR, not so much the triumph of Leviathan, as, in their case, an older vision of community which they did not adequately understand how to distinguish from the state. Indeed, the affinity was profounder still, for 'community' was to prove all the more treacherous in their hands though its further symbiosis with class itself.

The problem, therefore, was not the cult of the state but its indistinctness. If, like the Webbs themselves, we take the state to comprise obligatory forms of association, then the 'Great State' of which contemporaries spoke was almost the least of their concerns.[97] Wright describes theirs as a 'one-dimensional collectivism', reasoning from the centre until alerted by Cole to a 'new group view' of politics, and identifying socialism with the economic power of the state.[98] Certainly the Webbs could not conceive of the individual outside of the social framework and its obligations. In unguarded moments, they were not above describing as 'products' the nation's 'annual output of men and women'; and with wondrous indifference to the effects of their metaphors, they imagined them passing before the reader's eye, 'as an Australian squatter rounds up his uncounted flocks and herds'.[99] The collectivity, however designated, was at the heart of their thinking, and more particularly Sidney's. The 'perfect and fitting development of each individual', he wrote in the *Fabian Essays*, was 'not necessarily the utmost and highest cultivation of his own personality, but the filling, in the best possible way, of his humble function in the great social machine'. The individual was the creation of 'the social organism of which he forms a part'; it was therefore necessary to abandon the 'self-conceit of imagining that we are independent units' and 'bend' jealous minds in 'subjection' to the common end.[100]

Nevertheless, if the centre meant the state, then it was not its centrality, so to speak, but its virtual absence that characterised the bending of independent units which the joint work of the Webbs represented. Instead, their concern was with that ensemble of collectivities which does not seem so far removed from Cole's vaunted 'group theory'. 'We have now been for thirty years investigating and describing democratic institutions, and only in the twenty-ninth year did we publish any volume dealing with the ... Political State', they wrote in 1921:

> We started at the opposite end ... because the other manifestations of Democracy ... seemed actually of greater importance than the Political State itself. For we have always held that it is in the spontaneous undergrowth of social tissue, rather than in a further hypertrophy of the national government, that will be found, for the most part, the institutions destined increasingly to supersede the Capitalist System.[101]

In this they may be contrasted with a genuine state socialist like the Labour leader MacDonald, who not only produced a two-volume exegesis of the state in 1909, but freely ascribed to it such human attributes as will, personality, corporeality and even nutritional requirements.[102] This did not preclude some ugly anxieties on the

Webbs' part as to the quality of this social tissue.[103] Conversely, even their most bossily reformatory impulses were envisaged as promoting a capacity for personal and collective self-government – 'the level of Co-operative citizenship' – as much as the needs of the state.[104] Oscillate though they did between efficiency and democracy, Tawney was undoubtedly right to observe that it was not from such materials as they chose to quarry that 'idolators of the Great Leviathan are wont to build their altars to him'. Theirs was not the ideal of an 'omnicompetent state'.[105]

Less idiosyncratic than they are often imagined to be, the Webbs, as Mellor seemed to intimate, were thus linked to the guilds by a line more of kinship than antagonism. Wright describes as Cole's major contribution to democratic theory his rejection of unitary theories of sovereignty based on the representation of the 'whole' self.[106] While it is true that Cole set out to theorise what the Webbs had held to only implicitly and inconsistently, their role as his immediate progenitors has been far too easily overlooked. When in 1918 Beatrice averred her broad assent to Cole's functionalist version of group theory, it was on the credible basis of having long held such views.[107] Two years later in their *Constitution for a Socialist Commonwealth of Great Britain*, the couple even staked what looks like a tacit claim to paternity. 'This new conception of Democracy sprang ... from observation of the living tissue of society', they wrote. 'While metaphysical philosophers had been debating what was the nature of the State – by which they always meant the sovereign Political State – the sovereignty, and even the moral authority of the State itself, in the sense of the political government, were being, silently and almost unwittingly, undermined by the growth of new forms of Democracy.'[108] It was thus, consistent in their own minds, that the Webbs repudiated the indivisible authority of representative government and emphasised instead the 'manifold character' of their own democratic vision, as they had begun to do since at least as early as 1914.[109]

It was not therefore that the Webbs glorified the state but that they lacked any adequate theory of the parameters or distinctive characteristics of state power. Even Sidney, whose regard for authority was conventionally late-Victorian in character, came to portray the state with a curious naivety simply as the community coming together for certain limited purposes. Such a notion was firmly rooted in the couple's studies of local government institutions, whose origins they traced to the association of private citizens for such common ends as sanitation and the protection of property. Indeed, they were to foresee in the provision by the co-operative movement of libraries, clinics and other public amenities a democratic and welfarist variant of the same process.[110] Possibly the same instinct showed in their controversial endorsement of the public subsidy of existing denominational schools, essentially for expedient reasons but with the positive gloss – at least retrospectively – of allowing 'group autonomy and diversity in democracy'. 'I ... would permit each local community to teach its particular form of "Aspiration" and or "Faith" out of common funds', Beatrice wrote in this connection to Bertrand Russell.[111] Even the couple's most statist prescriptions, notably for the replacement of the Poor Law, posited the virtual interchangeability of public and voluntary agencies and the apportionment of their respective spheres of responsibility without reference to wider principles.[112] Before the realities of power which lay behind 'compulsory' forms of association, the Webbs' powers of cognition and imagination simply wilted.

Not only did they never examine the central state, but their gradualist conception of history all but collapsed before its advance. Contrary to their original intentions, their several histories of local government ground to a halt in the 1830s, precisely at the moment where modern local government began.[113] Tellingly, the only exceptions were their studies of the Poor Law, which alone were less concerned with the evolving institutions of self-government than with the drastic treatment from above of those deemed socially incapacitated by the 'disease' of destitution.[114] Here, as in the colonies and perhaps later in Russia, a positive case for the directive state was predicated upon the absence of independent social volition. In broad terms Sidney had traced the growing regulatory appetite of 'the community' as a form of 'unconscious socialism'. Nevertheless, the meshing of this narrative with one of a broadening civic consciousness proved elusive, at least in modern times. It is telling that in respect of the state alone the Webbs showed a hankering for the 'palace-building' from which Tawney was otherwise to absolve them. Under the stimulus of H.G. Wells, Beatrice even hatched out schemes for 'scientific' local government that were Napoleonic in their disregard for customary ties, even to the extent of metricated electorates.[115] More characteristically, though, such questions were simply left to one side. In contrast to their labour movement surveys, updated to take in the latest developments and their likely sequels, the organic development of the local state and citizen-consumer was arrested some time short of the present. No real attempt was ever made to reconcile the spontaneous growth of local tissue with the reality of growing centralisation.

This reluctance to take cognisance of the state was to culminate in their post-war socialist *Constitution*, when they hit upon the palpable contrivance of dividing its functions between a 'social' parliament and a 'political' one. Alan McBriar has described the first of these as a sort of 'enlarged LCC for all England', in the spirit of the Bradford ILPer Fred Jowett's proposals for the reform of parliament on local government lines. As such, it allowed the decanting onto the 'political' parliament of such war-making and coercive state functions as ill accorded with the Webbs' basic social philosophy.[116] Thus, in defiance of the world around them, the couple maintained intact the illusion of a 'housekeeping state' outgrowing its association with the 'police state', while subjecting the 'political' state itself to only the most cursory and inadequate examination. 'The State has silently changed the character of its authority', they wrote, in a passage it is hard to credit as dating from the end of the First World War. 'What was originally wholly what the Germans call *Verwaltung* and the French *autorité régalienne* or police power, has become increasingly *Wirtschaft*, *gestion*, or administration of public services – in fact, merely housekeeping on a national scale.' Though hardly exalting the state, granting it only the allegiance one would give a 'busy housekeeper', this revealed a staggering complacency rooted in a Victorian sense of security and civic peace. No conception of the state could have been less suited to the study of Stalin's Russia.[117]

And yet the Webbs' confusion was deeply rooted in socialist thought. According to the Belgian social democrat Vandervelde, the differentiation of the 'government-state' and 'administrative-state', with the former ceding place to the latter, was 'the common conception of all the great theorists of Socialism', whether marxists, anarchists or Saint-Simonian technocrats.[118] The Webbs themselves paid tribute to the 'old slogan of Socialists' that distinguished the government of men from the administration of things.[119] More immediately, their vertical bicameralism betrayed a hidden affinity with the guild socialists, who, while distinguishing the state from the guilds, proposed a 'separation of powers' between them, and accorded the guilds what in anybody else's book would be the 'state' powers of sovereignty based on compulsion. 'Where now the State passes a Factory Act, or a Coal Mines Regulation Act, the Guild Congress of the future will pass such Acts, and its power of enforcing them will be the same as that of the State', wrote Cole; and it is hardly surprising that his most avid disciples found what they were looking for in the Soviets.[120] Furiously though they traded functionalist discourtesies, both Cole and the Webbs further posited the essential unity of co-operation and collectivism, Cole describing the state as 'merely a functional association' or 'only all the consumers', and Sidney as 'that greatest of co-operative societies, the state itself'.[121] Others might have said that the state was only 'all the capitalists' or – potentially at least – 'all the workers'. The easy interchange between voluntary and compulsory forms of association was to prove a fatal vulnerability to the attractions of Bolshevism.

## V

In their underlying attitudes to state and society there was thus a great deal to attach the Webbs to a broader current of left-wing opinion. The paradox, in Britain at least, was that it was not usually state socialism that was projected onto the Soviets; rather, it was a vision of progress identified, like the Webbs' histories, with the development of working-class institutions, shot forward as it seemed by the hothouse growth of revolution. It was not Britain's state socialists who sang hosannas to Lenin; not MacDonald, Snowden, Hyndman or the younger Fabian collectivists, but those syndicalists, trade unionists, co-operators and guild socialists who saw in the workers' state the ascendancy of the movements with which they identified, and did not have the critical apparatus to distinguish between the two. There were of course exceptions – Shaw, as always, was one – while on a later generation, itself profoundly influenced by the Soviet example, the imprint of the state was less ambiguous. But for the generations whose formation predated Bolshevism, it is to the continuum between state, class and community, and not their construction as alternatives, that we need to look for an explanation of the widespread tendencies to pro-Sovietism.

This is nowhere truer than of the marriage of group and statist approaches which the Webbs' own partnership represented. 'If any man deserves to be regarded as the prophet of a planned economy', Cole wrote in 1932 as the couple set off for Russia, 'that man is Sidney Webb ... And if anyone deserves to be regarded as the first person to recognise the vital points which Trade Unionism and Co-operation – the two great voluntary movements of the wage-earners – will need to play in the working of a Socialist community, that credit belongs to Beatrice Webb.'[122] Cole, who by this time was on intimate terms with the Webbs, also pointed out that it was to Beatrice that the couple's initial impulse to communism was due. It is the argument presented here that this, however paradoxically, was precisely because of her greater orientation to the 'great voluntary movements of the wage-earners' which in reality were being suppressed by Stalin.

In any case, it is clear that the somewhat volatile political trajectory of the Webbs can neither be understood nor properly contextualised without identifying and where necessary disentangling the different strands they brought to it. Despite the public appearance of consensus, even the most characteristic of their works can betray hidden tensions. *Industrial Democracy* itself, which for many commentators is the last word in Webbian social theory, was in some respects a partial and contested representation of their views. Specifically, this was the case with its longest and most significant chapter, 'The economic characteristics of trade unionism', which approached its subject not from the trade unionist's standpoint, but from that of the 'economist and statesman'.[123] This was precisely the posture that was to be characteristic of the 'Edwardian' Webbs, and already the chapter pursued an 'Edwardian' social agenda. To promote 'the selection of the most efficient factors of production', and hence 'the permanent efficiency of the nation', Darwinian watchwords of the Selection of the Fittest and Functional Adaptation were deployed with repulsive officiousness and inhumanity. If, for example, even the preferment of the older worker to one in the prime of life offended these Webbian canons, how much more so did the toleration by the community of the 'incorrigibly idle', the 'morally deficient' or just the plain 'constitutionally inefficient'. On these the Webbs lavished the full lexicon of degeneracy, disease, contamination and quarantine, favouring labour colonies as an act not of regeneration but of removal. It is on writings such as this that the Webbs' identification with the state depends, and in relation to this whole phase of their career such an identification can hardly be gainsaid.

And yet, even from within the Webb partnership, such an emphasis appears to have given rise to misgivings. It was as if Sidney, having abandoned for Beatrice his intended work on political economy, had now smuggled it back into her own project on the unions. It is certainly significant that Shaw, who was in a position to know, should describe this not as the Webbs' book but Webb singular's: 'thought out by two minds', as Beatrice put it, but written in its entirety by Sidney.[124] More particularly, Beatrice described in her diary how, in relation to the 'economic characteristics' chapter seemingly encapsulating the Webbs' social philosophy, the partnership had simply foundered. 'At last', she wrote, 'we got into such a hopeless state of continuous argument that it was clear that we were wasting energy so he agreed to go on by himself ...'[125] 'By himself' in reality included Shaw, to whom chapters were sent on completion, exactly as Shaw and Wallas had assisted with the earlier *History of Trade Unionism*.[126]

The cause of these disagreements was not indicated, but the likeliest explanation may be gleaned from Beatrice's original plan for her trade union book. In this, no provision at all was made for the 'statesman's' view. Instead, such telling concerns were indicated as 'Personal independence: mutual protection against personal tyranny' and 'Facts with regard to the technical and moral gratifications of the worker as a professional'. As to the economist, the synopsis decidedly preferred the trade unionist's understanding of such questions, on the Ruskinian grounds, far removed from conventional political economy, 'that they – the union leaders – have had the *right object* in view – the making of the Man; whereas the economists and employers have had the making of Commodities'.[127] Unfulfilled in *Industrial Democracy*, in *Soviet Communism* the making, or 'remaking', of man was to have a chapter to itself.

In the most recent biography of the Webbs, the independent development of Beatrice's socialist philosophy is sometimes belittled or disregarded in order to recover a more traditional narrative focused on the male protagonist.[128] As Nord had already commented, women like Beatrice who achieved prominence in tandem with their husbands would typically be imagined 'as "masculine", as emasculating and yet as inseparable and indistinguishable from their male partners'.[129] Inadequate and ill-substantiated in itself, such an interpretation also diminishes the Webbs' collective biography through the banishment to the margins of a dissenting voice, often subdued or suppressed, but subtly and sometimes overtly providing a counterpoint to Sidney's more bureaucratic cast of mind. In her diary for February 1890, immediately prior to Sidney's first appearance there, Beatrice recorded her moment of conversion:

> ... I turn from the luxurious homes of these picked men of the individualist system, and struggle through an East End crowd of the wrecks, the waifs and strays of this civilisation; or I enter a debating society of working men, and listen to the ever-increasing cry of active brains, doomed to the treadmill of manual labour, for a career in which intellectual initiative tells: the bitter cry of the nineteenth-century working man and the nineteenth-century woman. And the whole seems a whirl of contending actions, aspirations and aims, out of which I dimly see the tendency towards a socialist community, in which there will be individual freedom and public property, instead of class slavery and private possession of the means of subsistence of the whole people. At last I am a socialist![130]

There seems more to this than the passion for order and 'apocalyptic' fear 'of being overwhelmed by the lower depths' that Norman Mackenzie refers to.[131] Sentiments such as these linked Beatrice with a much wider ferment of opinion, and, in the same entry, she mentions her sympathetic contacts with both old and new unionists, co-operators of all schools and the metropolitan socialists among who she was about to find her husband. After the long hiatus of drawing-room permeation, it was to the resumption of such contacts that she was to turn again after the collapse of the Poor Law campaign.

**NOTES**

1. William Mellor, 'A critique of guild socialism', *Labour Monthly*, November 1921, p. 401.
2. For example S.G. Hobson, who coined the phrase.
3. M. Cole, *Growing*, p. 64.
4. *PD*, ch. 9.
5. Jane Marcus, ed., *The Young Rebecca. The writings of Rebecca West 1911-17*, Virago, 1992, p. 218.
6. *Fabian News*, November 1914, p. 82; G.D.H. Cole, *Self-Government in Industry* (1917), Hutchinson edn, 1972, pp. 40-2; G.D.H. and Margaret Cole, eds, *The Bolo Book*, Labour Publishing Co. 1921, pp. 52-3.
7. Stephen Reynolds and Bob & Tom Woolley, *Seems So! A working-class view of politics*, Macmillan, 1911, p. 284. This 'working-class view' is taken too much at face value by many historians, e.g. by Yeo, *Contest*, pp. 242-5; Patrick Joyce, *Visions of the People. Industrial England and the question of class 1848-1914*, Cambridge: CUP, 1994 edn, pp. 80-1; Stefan Berger, *The British Labour Party and the German Social Democrats. A comparative study 1900-1931*, Oxford: OUP, 1994, p. 29; Barker, *Political Ideas*, pp. 71-3. Purportedly co-authored with two Sidmouth fishermen, while simultaneously attesting the fashionable literary influences of Henri Bergson, Graham Wallas and the *New Age*, the book's context is manifestly that of pre-war literary London (around whom the fishermen were

paraded) and its 'working-class view' is no less clearly mediated and directed (in this case towards a 'New Toryism or Nationalism') than in any other account. Three years later, by a nice irony, Reynolds acquired the Webbian position of an Inspector of Fisheries! See David Garnett, *The Golden Echo*, Chatto & Windus, 1954, pp. 130-1; and for a sympathetic account, describing the book as 'semi-fictional', Reynolds as 'the directing mind' and the Woolleys as his 'willing objects', E.W. Martin, ed., *The Countryman's Chap-book*, Dennis Dobson, 1949, p. 90.

8. Hilaire Belloc, *The Servile State*, Foulis, 1912, pp. 127-30.
9. Burns cited Jose Harris, *William Beveridge. A biography*, Oxford: OUP, 1997 edn, p. 259.
10. Wells interviewed *Labour Leader*, 17 May 1910; Beerbohm cartoon reproduced in M. Cole, *The Webbs*; Bax, cited Yeo, 'Three socialisms', p. 225; Raymond Williams, *Culture and Society 1780-1950*, Harmondsworth: Penguin edn, 1961., p. 187.
11. E.g. Martin Francis, 'Economics and ethics. The nature of Labour's socialism, 1945-1951', *Twentieth Century British History*, 6, 2, pp. 233-42; Duncan Tanner *Political Change*, p. 39. Both Francis and Tanner identify the Webbs with the 'centralised state', and Tanner further links this 'Statist philosophy' with 'the material interests of producer groups concerned with state intervention'. This is a long way from the Webbs' actual position in this period. This statist reading of Fabianism and the Webbs is also a major theme in Noel Thompson's *Political Economy and the Labour Party*, ch. 2 and part 1 passim, e.g. pp. 51-3, where Tawney's institutional pluralism is counterposed to this Webbian tradition.
12. Greenleaf, *British Political Tradition*, vol. 1, pp. 381 ff.
13. Shaw in *Fabian Essays*, pp. 180-2, cited e.g. Wright, *G.D.H. Cole*, pp. 52-3; also Greenleaf, *British Political Tradition*, p. 175.
14. *Report on Fabian Policy*, Fabian Society, 1896.
15. Shaw to G.K. Chesterton, 27 October 1911 in Laurence, *Letters 1911-1925*, p. 54; McBriar, *Fabian Socialism*, pp. 82-95 and 124-5; Barrow, *Democratic Ideas*, pp. 32-3 and 176.
16. Shaw to Archibald Henderson, 3 January 1905, in Laurence, *Letters 1898-1910*, pp. 488-9; Hamilton, *Sidney and Beatrice Webb*, pp. 14-15.
17. Hubert Bland, though another fixture, combined Tory and marxist influences in a way clearly distinguishing him from the rest of the 'old guard'. For the alliance of Shaw and Webb on the Fabian executive see S.G. Hobson, *Pilgrim to the Left*, Edward Arnold, 1938, pp. 76-8.
18. BWD 16 January 1903, Mackenzie, vol. 2, p. 267; BWD 13 July 1913.
19. Bernard Shaw, ed., *Fabian Essays in Socialism*, Allen & Unwin, 1948 edn, introduction by S. Webb dated November 1919.
20. BWD 27 July 1890, Mackenzie vol. 1, p. 337.
21. Beatrice Potter, *The Co-operative Movement in Great Britain*, Allen & Unwin, 1930 edn (henceforth *CMGB*), p. 193.
22. Passfield papers, 6/35-6: S. Webb, lecture notes on co-operation, c. 1889 and 'The economic limitations of co-operation', *Co-operative News*, 12 January 1889; Sidney Webb, *Socialism in England*, Swan Sonnenschein, 1890, pp. 89-94. For the socialists as the Benthamites of their generation, see Sidney's *Socialism: true and false*, p. 6.
23. BWD 24 May 1890, Mackenzie vol. 1, p. 332.

24. Sidney to Beatrice, 26 August 1890, *Letters*, vol. 1, p. 181.
25. *MA*, pp. 345.
26. Harrison, *Sidney and Beatrice*, p. 221. Harrison's case for Sidney's awakening to the importance of trade unions is that he had solicited contributions for the dockers' strike fund. Regarding co-operation, Pease, *History*, p. 92, does mention talks between Fabians and co-operators during 1889, but their impact on either the *Fabian Essays in Socialism* or *Socialism in England*, which was still in preparation, is imperceptible. Conversely, the impact of readings like Ritchie's *Darwinism and Politics*, published the same year, is very much in evidence.
27. Stanley Weintraub, ed., *Bernard Shaw: the diaries 1885-1897. With early autobiographical notebooks and diaries, and an abortive 1917 diary*, University Park and London: Pennsylvania State University Press, 1986, p. 773, entry for 6 December 1891.
28. It is only fair to add that other Fabian tracts, for example *Sweating: its cause and remedy*, 1895, were also addressed in particular to a trade-union readership. Then again, this was a theme which Beatrice had previously made her own, and the tract itself (by H.W. Macrosty) largely reflected ideas already to be found in her *How to Do Away with the Sweating System*, Co-operative Union, 1892, reprinted in S. & B. Webb, *Problems of Modern Industry*, Longmans, 1898, pp. 139-55.
29. Psychobiographers may care to speculate on Beatrice's use of this metaphor at the time of her courting by Sidney.
30. BWD, 7 July 1891, *MA*, p. 352; Galton, 'Investigating with the Webbs' in M. Cole, *The Webbs*, pp. 29-37; Cole, 'Sidney and Beatrice Webb'; BWD August 1903, *OP*, p. 176; see also W.A. Robson, *Public Administration*, 21, 2, p. 57.
31. Hobsbawm, 'Fabians', p. 255.
32. Both Hobsbawm ('Fabians') and Wright (*G.D.H. Cole*) discuss the wartime lectures published by Sidney as 'A stratified democracy' and *The Works Manager Today* respectively, and in the context of *Soviet Communism*, Harrison makes much of Sidney's 'Rome. A sociological sermon' ('Sidney', p. 57; also Harrison, *Life and Times*, pp. 34-6).
33. Harrison, *Life and Times*, pp. 217-51.
34. Tawney, *The Webbs*, pp. 9-10.
35. BW to Edward Pease, 29 December 1915 in *Letters*, vol. 3, p. 65.
36. BWD 10 August 1894*.
37. Woolf, 'Political thought and the Webbs' in Cole, *Webbs and Their Work*, p. 254; *New Statesman and Nation*, 22 January 1922, p.452.
38. SW to Graham Wallas, 26 October 1898 in *Letters*, vol. 2, p. 88.
39. *ID*, pp. xix-xxiii; see also BWD, 20 February 1900, *OP*, p. 195.
40. James cited Lloyd Morris, *William James. The message of a modern mind*, New York: Sribners, 1950, p. 26.
41. E.g. SW to William Smart, 8 November 1899 (not sent) in Mackenzie, *Letters*, vol. 2, p. 116.
42. *CSC*, pp. 318-19; SW, *The Labour Party on the Threshold*, Fabian Society, 1923.
43. BWD 22 February 1934*.
44. *CMGB*, pp. 90-2. In her later enthusiasm for Japan, she was similarly to note the triumph, not of individual genius, but of the 'intellectual, physi-

cal and moral qualities of the whole people'; BWD 22 December 1904, *OP*, p. 299.

45. Gertrude Himmelfarb, 'The intellectual in politics. The case of the Webbs', *Journal of Contemporary History*, 6, 3, 1971, p. 3; Jones, *Russia Complex*, p. 21.
46. Herbert Spencer, *The Study of Sociology*, Kegan Paul, Trench & Co, 1887 edn, pp. 30 ff.
47. *CCM*, pp. 6, 184; *CMGB*, p. 35.
48. *CMGB*, pp. 41, 116-19, 171-2.
49. *CCM*, pp. 1, 446.
50. BWD September 1889, *OP*, p. 22.
51. *PD*, see pp. 32-3 above.
52. BWD n.d. but 1886, Mackenzie, vol. 1, pp. 185-7.
53. *MA*, pp. 130-1. Sidney's Fabian Tract *Reform of the Poor Law* was published in 1890.
54. BWD, October 1886, *MA*, pp. 141-2. Orwell was familiar with *My Apprenticeship* and was to use the same slightly sentimental, slightly patronising tone in describing the 'peculiar easy completeness' of the better sort of working-class interior. 'I should say that a manual worker, if he is in steady work and drawing good wages ... has a better chance of being happy than an "educated" man. His home life seems to fall more naturally into a sane and comely shape.' Characteristically, Orwell described Beatrice as the archetypal 'high-minded Socialist slum-visitor', forgetting that like himself, and with similar frankness, she had been trying to describe how she *became* a socialist; see *The Road to Wigan Pier*, Gollancz, 1937, pp. 149 and 211-12.
55. *CMGB*, pp. 36, 226-7, 232, 239.
56. BW, letter to father, October 1886, *MA*, p. 143.
57. BWD 11 November 1937. Morgan, 'Webbs', p. 59, describes the relationship as 'unlikely'. Mackenzie, *Socialism and Society*, pp. 22-3, attributes it to simple calculation, as 'Sidney attached himself ... like an able civil servant taking on a new minister'.
58. BWD, 19 August 1934*. For Henderson's representative qualities, see Chris Wrigley, *Arthur Henderson*, Cardiff: GPC Books, 1990; Ross McKibbin, '"Arthur Henderson as Labour leader"' in Ross McKibbin, *The Ideologies of Class. Social relations in Britain 1880-1950*, Oxford: OUP, 1991.
59. BWD 9 September 1934*.
60. BW, letter to her father, October 1886, *MA*, pp. 143-4.
61. BW, letter to her father, October 1886, *MA*, p. 141.
62. SW, *Socialism: true and false*, pp. 10-11, 18.
63. SW to H.G. Wells, 8 December 1901 in Mackenzie, *Letters*, vol. 2, p. 144.
64. Passfield papers 6/79, broadcast talk on Spencer, 27 February 1928; BWD 10 June 1917*. For an encapsulation of Spencer's philosophy, see Herbert Spencer, *An Autobiography*, Williams & Norgate, 1904, vol. 2, chs 34-5.
65. *CMGB*, pp. 167-9.
66. *ID*, chs 1-2 passim and pp. 834-6 and 843-4.
67. *ID*, ch. 4 passim and pp. 514 and 841.
68. *ID*, p. 748 (for Sidney's authorship of this passage see pp. 80-1 below); *WMT*, pp. 4-7, 157; N. Bukharin and E. Preobazhensky, *The ABC of*

*Communism* (1920), Penguin edn, 1969, p. 118. Though he preferred 'quieter' managerial methods than the Americans', Sidney was not perhaps too far removed from them in spirit. Beatrice, on the other hand, candidly described welfare schemes and scientific management as 'anti-trade union movements' which in the context of the war economy represented 'the good and bad features of the "Servile State", not according to the "Webbs" but according to Kitchener'; BWD, 19 May 1915*.

69. Richard Stites, *Revolutionary Dreams. Utopian vision and experimental life in the Russian Revolution*, New York: OUP, 1989, pp. 135-40.
70. BWD 15 January 1901, *OP*, pp. 209-10.
71. Passfield papers 6/83, *Manchester Guardian* cutting, 18 October 1929.
72. Holding that the removal of the workman from his trade would so 'alter his manner of life, his habit of mind, and ... his intellectual atmosphere ... that he gradually loses that vivid appreciation of the feelings of the men at the bench of the forge, which it is his function to express', the Webbs nevertheless recommended a professional class of expert parliamentary representatives such as they sought to counterbalance within the unions by more direct forms of representation; see *ID*, pp. 38 ff, 54-5, 65-7; *CSC*, pp. 219-22.
73. For Harrison see *MA*, pp. 48, 124-5, 302-3; Barbara Caine, *Victorian Feminists*, Oxford: OUP, 1993 edn, pp. 46-50; Martha S. Vogeler, *Frederic Harrison. The vocations of a positivist*, Oxford: OUP, 1984, p. 213 and passim.
74. BWD 25 July and 9 October 1894, Mackenzie, vol. 2, pp. 51-3, 58. See also Anne Taylor; *Annie Besant. A biography*, Oxford: OUP, 1992, p. 91; and for further such sentiments expressed by BW, Passfield 6/53, interview with *British Weekly*, 29 June 1893.
75. BWD 7 July 1889, *MA*, p. 303; see also Chris Nyland and Gabia Ramia, 'The Webbs and the rights of women' in Beilharz and Nyland, eds, *The Webbs, Fabianism and Feminism*, pp. 54-87, citing BW p. 55.
76. Much quoted as a defining statement of the Webbs' philosophy, this remark was made in a diary entry after a crushing defeat for the Progressives in the Westminster vestry elections, showing the slums to be 'as completely Tory as the palaces'. It is a regrettable that diaries attesting so vividly the fluxity and complexity of political commitment have been quarried for a handful of passages to which whole movements and generations can then be reduced. See BWD December 1894, Mackenzie vol. 2, pp. 61-3 and e.g. Wright, 'G.D.H. Cole', p. 55; Clarke, *Liberals and Social Democrats*, p. 44. For 'strong' and 'weak' theories of democracy, depicted without this crushing reductionism, see Barrow, *Democratic Ideas*.
77. Lectures on 'The machinery of democracy' (1896) summarised in McBriar, *Fabian Socialism*, pp. 75-7.
78. *ID*, pp. 36-7, 843-4; BWD 27 October 1929.
79. *MA*, p. 335.
80. Menander's dictum was cited on several occasions, e.g. *WMT*, pp. 155-7; *MA*, p. 335; *DCC*, pp. 38-9; *SCANC*, p. 924.
81. *CMGB*, pp. 214-15.
82. BW to H.G. Wells, October 1908, in Mackenzie, *Letters*, vol. 2, p. 317.
83. *CMGB*, pp. 191-202.

84. LRD archives, P. Redfern, 'The store movement and the wholesale society', FRD conference on the control of industry, 1913.
85. See for example *ID*, p. 819; BW, 'The relationship between co-operation and trade unionism' (1892) in S. & B. Webb, *Problems of Modern Industry*, pp. 202-3.
86. *MA*, p. 336.
87. BW, 'Relationship', p. 202; also *CSC*, pp. 156, 288; *CCM*, p. 466.
88. SW, *Socialism: true and false*, p. 17; see also *ID*, 818 ff.
89. Eileen and Stephen Yeo, 'On the uses of "community": from Owenism to the present' in Stephen Yeo, ed., *New Views of Co-operation*, Routledge, 1988, pp. 229-58.
90. Williams, *Culture*, pp. 182-91; see also e.g. Greenleaf, *British Political Tradition. Volume two*, p. 464.
91. Yeo, *Contest for Social Science*, passim.
92. See Eileen and Stephen Yeo, 'On the uses' for a cruder depiction of language essentially as a tool to be appropriated and manipulated.
93. Raymond Williams, *Politics and Letters. Interviews with New Left Review*, Verso edn, 1981, pp. 118-20.
94. Cole, *Self-Government*, p. 12.
95. G.D. H. Cole papers, D3/10/4, M. Cole, memorandum 'On the state', c. 1919.
96. *CSC*, 75-8. This in fact was a commonplace of contemporary socialist thought. See for example Bertrand Russell, *Principles of Social Reconstruction*, Allen & Unwin, 1916, pp. 102-3: 'The civil functions of the State – legislative, administrative and judicial – have no essential connection with the military functions, and there is no reason why both kinds of function should normally be exercised by the same State.'
97. Woolf papers IIIa, Sidney to L. Woolf, 16 May 1921; Barker, *Political Ideas*, p. 55.
98. Wright, 'Fabianism', p. 236; Wright, *G.D.H. Cole*, p. 54.
99. *PD*, pp. 62-3.
100. Sidney, 'Historic', p. 58.
101. *CCM*, p. v.
102. Ramsay MacDonald, *Socialism and Government*, ILP, 2 vols, 1909, esp. chs 1, 3 and 6.
103. See for example SW to BW, 9 October 1890, *Letters*, vol. 1, p. 203: 'I fear these Co-op societies – even the best of them – are not much use as social tissue.'
104. *CCM*, pp. 320-1.
105. Tawney, *Webbs*, p. 8.
106. Wright, *G.D.H. Cole*, pp. 57-9.
107. BWD, 30 December 1918*.
108. *CSC*, pp. xiii-xviii.
109. BW in *Labour Leader*, 30 April 1914, cited Barrow and Bullock, *Democratic Ideas*, pp. 267-9.
110. *CCM*, pp. 425-9.
111. SW, 'Fabianism justified', *Fabian News*, December 1924, pp. 51-2; SW cited McBriar, *Fabian Socialism*, p. 215; BW to Russell, 16 October 1904, Mackenzie, *Letters*, vol. 2, pp. 208-9, also BWD 11 May 1905, *OP*, p. 308.
112. *PD*, ch. 8.

113. Gertrude Himmelfarb, 'The intellectual in politics', pp. 7-9. Though Himmelfarb rightly notes the circumscription of the Webbs' historical sense, she fails to recognise that this was true only of a certain class of their writings, with consequently more ambiguous implications than Himmelfarb is prepared to entertain.
114. Sidney and Beatrice Webb, *English Poor Law Policy*, Longmans, 1910, p. 1.
115. BWD 2 March and November 1903, *OP*, pp. 175, 177.
116. Alan McBriar, 'Sidney Webb and the LCC' in M. Cole, *The Webbs and their Work*, pp. 95-6. For 'Fred's obsession', or Jowett's proposals for the reform of parliament on local government lines, see Barrow, *Democratic Ideas*, ch. 10; for BW's approval of Jowett's 'constructive' approach to parliamentary questions on their merits, BWD 12 February and 22 April 1914.
117. *CSC*, pp. 13-14, 119; *OP*, p. 149.
118. Emile Vandervelde, *Collectivism and Industrial Revolution*, ILP Socialist Library, 1907, pp. 151 ff.
119. *CSC*, p. 111.
120. Cole, *Self-Government*, pp. 26-9. In a review of Hobson's *National Guilds*, Sidney had already commented on their character as what he saw as a particular form of state socialism; *New Statesman*, 6 June 1914, p. 267.
121. Cole papers, D3/18/2, Cole to Mrs Ellingham (copy), 5 November 1914; SW cited *OP*, 222; SW, *Threshold*, 13-14.
122. Cole, 'Sidney and Beatrice Webb'.
123. *ID*, pp. 703-806.
124. Shaw to A.J. Marriott, 1 May 1899; to John Burns, 11 September 1903, and to Hubert Bland, 19 January 1904, all in Laurence, *Letters 1898-1910*, pp. 89, 372, 400-1; also BW to Frederic Harrison, 28 December 1897, in Mackenzie, *Letters*, vol. 2, p. 59.
125. BWD 27 August 1897.
126. BWD 17 September 1893 and 9 April 1895; Weintraub, *Bernard Shaw: the diaries*, pp, 964-8, entries for 26 August-17 September 1893.
127. BW to SW, 2 September 1891 and 9 (?) December 1891, Mackenzie, *Letters*, vol. 1, pp. 286 and 346. Her other six proposed headings covered facts relating to (1) organisation, administration and representation; (2) the expenditure of the worker; (3) restrictions as to process and labour supply; (4) the attempted organisation of all workers.
128. Harrison, *Life and Times*, pp. 143-60.
129. Nord, *Apprenticeship*, p. 3.
130. BWD 1 February 1890, *MA*, pp. 348-9.
131. Mackenzie, *Socialism and Society*, pp. 17-18.

*Chapter five*

# Fabians and the control of industry: socialist debates before the closure

## I

*Industrial Democracy* is often regarded as the Webbs' greatest literary monument, generalising from their empirical researches and providing, in Eric Hobsbawm's words, 'an entire theory of democracy, the state and the transition to socialism'.[1] The translation of the work by Lenin and Krupskaya and its perceived influence upon Lenin's *What Is To Be Done?* only seems to confirm the elitist cast of mind that united both authors and translators.[2] Five years earlier, the couple's first joint endeavour had been the conclusion to Beatrice's book on co-operation, underlining the movement's limitations and dampening down some of Beatrice's initial enthusiasm.[3] Now, through the 'intellectual communism' of Webb, Shaw and even Wallas, the same concerns with democratic self-government had been annexed to the stronger Fabian currents of efficiency. Shaw once remarked that Annie Besant must have felt like the 'fifth wheel' on the Fabian coach, 'as other women later found'. It is difficult to imagine who else but Beatrice this could have referred to.[4]

She was hardly drawn with the coach against her will, and described herself as simply 'lost in admiration' for the analytical intelligence Sidney brought to their work. Moreover, it was to be the pattern of her career, no doubt partly attributable to Sidney's influence, that bursts of enthusiasm typically gave way to more sober evaluations of the movements that attracted her, sometimes to the point of open disillusionment. Even so, the hybrid persona of the Webbs concealed resources of reason, memory and motivation that eluded easy synthesis. Famously described as two typewriters beating as one, they more closely resembled a pantomime horse, taking turns at being the front half and occasionally moving off in different directions. In the early years of their partnership, and particularly with the completion of *Industrial Democracy*, it was Sidney who took the intellectual lead, as the couple's larger projects centred on his longstanding interests in local government and the Poor Law. An official co-operative history was briefly mooted, but even Beatrice confessed her waning interest in a movement that now appeared as ponderous and unimaginative as it was public-spirited.[5] Not until the pre-war unrest did she again show a hankering for the vision she had initially brought to the partnership. In the meantime, as Cole observed in 1913, their early concerns with the world of organised labour had not been reflected in the work of the Fabian Society, and even Sidney 'seemed, till only the other day, to have forgotten much of the best of his earlier teaching'.[6]

That this 'only the other day' was also the moment of Beatrice's first real emergence into socialist politics was therefore anything but fortuitous. Initially a somewhat retiring Fabian, she was dissuaded from more active involvement both by what she called the 'hidden masculinity of Sidney's views of women'; and perhaps by her own lingering sentiment, initially prompted by seeing Annie Besant speak, that it was 'not womanly to thrust yourself before the world'.[7] The challenge of the Fabian rebels and her notoriety during the Poor Law commission will have done something to encourage her to adopt a more active political role. So too, more conjecturally, will the practical example of the Suffragettes, with whom Beatrice had publicly affirmed her solidarity in 1906.[8] Whatever the impulsion, it was only in 1912 that Beatrice at last joined the society's executive. Rapidly she became what Pease's official Fabian history described as the society's 'dominant personality', bringing a 'fresh and fertile mind' to its councils. 'Her twenty years of membership and intimate private acquaintance with its leaders made her familiar with its possibilities, but she was free from the influence of past failures', Pease recorded in 1916, 'and she was eager to start out on new lines which the almost unconscious traditions of the Society had hitherto barred'. If she was more conciliatory to the youngsters than either Shaw or Pease, that was because they revived as well as challenged some of her own oldest preoccupations. With renewed energy, she assembled and chaired a 'Committee of Enquiry on the Control of Industry', whose broad composition, not excluding leading syndicalists, would otherwise hardly have been entertained.[9]

Judged by Beatrice a roaring success, this committee proved the start of some eight years' involvement with the control of industry, she taking the lead while Sidney cemented relations with the emerging Labour Party. Such indeed was his sense of personal detachment that he later described this period of extraordinary intellectual ferment as one of 'diminished activity' by the Fabians.[10] Brooding day and night 'in the old way', it was Beatrice who was the principal architect both of *The Consumers' Co-operative Movement*, always her special concern, and of their socialist *Constitution*, which she schemed out and drafted, describing it as 'the jointest of our joint efforts'.[11] She also took on from Sidney a new chapter on 'the place of trade unionism in the state' for their updated *History of Trade Unionism*.[12] That the latter was precisely the brief which Sidney had handled from the 'statesman's' perspective in *Industrial Democracy* should not pass unnoticed. Together, the departures from classical Fabianism evident in all these writings suggest not only an evolution in the Webbs' corporate thinking but a reassertion within it of strains identifiable with Beatrice. 'Mrs Webb seems to come more and more over to Cooperation', wrote Leonard Woolf from a pre-Fabian summer school – a noteworthy emphasis in a letter otherwise referring without distinction to 'the Webbs'.[13] Sidney, meanwhile, continued to hold to 'the pure milk of Collectivist Socialism', lecturing on subjects like 'The works manager today' and 'The employer of tomorrow', familiarly addressed in the first person plural and provided with a somewhat humanised version of his old preoccupations with efficiency and 'obedience' – 'ever so much obedience'.[14] Only in 1921 did the balance once more shift, as Beatrice tired of a subject that seemed to bear so little fruit and deferred at last to Sidney's long-postponed career in parliament.

Though the extent to which the Webbs simply tailed after their juniors is often exaggerated, it was unquestionably the audacity and articulacy of these younger critics that forced them to redefine their own philosophy. Only a year or two earlier, noting the new ferment of public opinion, they had congratulated themselves that they alone had knowledge and consistency enough to give direction to it.[15] In reality, they more than anybody were confronted with what the young flatterer Cole called the courage of their obsolescence. Possibly Beatrice recalled the morose old age of Herbert Spencer, a cautionary tale of the prophet outliving his own intellectual moment.[16] Perhaps inviting their fiercest controverters to their Fabian gatherings was a way of pre-empting their likely failure to invite the Webbs to theirs.

Certainly it confronted them with the strength of feeling their philosophy aroused. Noah Ablett, South Wales coalfield activist and co-author of the classic syndicalist text *The Miners' Next Step*, took direct issue with his hosts in proposing to eliminate the very notion of the consumer. Consumption, he said, was merely an 'incident in production': the logic of an industry like coal, defined by class, oblivious to gender, with a predetermined product and a market subject only to quantitative fluctuations. 'If a man consumes food, or bedclothes, its importance lies in the fact that he is then producing energy for future production', Ablett went on. 'If an individual consumes products, its importance lies in the fact that it is a part of the process of production.'[17] In *The Miners' Next Step* itself, the problem of demand was reduced to one of a statistical department for needs and desires, a proto-Sovietist notion later cropping up in *The ABC of Communism* and realised after a fashion in Stalin's Gosplan.[18] Ablett at a Fabian summer school was like a figure from another world, but the challenge he represented to the collectivist will of the consumer was upheld in its essentials by the middle-class rebels who based upon it their own seeming synthesis of guild socialism. Arnot later recalled the 'very big impression' that Ablett's paper made on Cole and Mellor – a paradoxical consequence of Beatrice's open-mindedness – and this influence is manifest in their writings. 'A society which organises its industry on the basis of consumption will be inevitably servile', Cole wrote. If he at least acknowledged the consumer as an 'entity', it was always as a subordinate one.[19]

Further provoking the Webbs was the wartime vogue for industrial partnership, threatening not only the consumer but also the inalienable functions of the unions, through a coalescence of producer interests. As a member of the cabinet's Reconstruction Committee, set up in 1916, Beatrice was alone in subjecting the Whitley proposals for Joint Industrial Councils to what Lloyd George called a 'torrent of destructive criticism'.[20] That Cole had apparently contributed informally to the Whitley scheme, and later served as secretary to Lloyd George's National Industrial Conference, only reinforced her misgivings as to this sinister harnessing of both guild and capitalist sentiments.[21] 'I object to a coalition government of industry with capitalism as the predominant partner', she fulminated, alleging possible conspiracies against the 'public' as well as the undermining of the solidarity of labour by enmeshing the unions in 'an acceptance of the status quo'. With industrial partnership as fashionable as killing Germans, this put Beatrice well to the 'left' of much labour movement opinion and provoked demurrals from pragmatists like John Turner, the anarchist Shop Assistants' official.[22] Even so, while sharing with the syndicalists a commitment to the unions' independence, Beatrice was not about to convert to their larger industrialist vision. On the contrary, cabals of labour and capital only confirmed her worst suspicions concerning producer cohesion, and provided another stimulus to work up an alternative utopia based on consumption.

In returning to the co-operative movement, the Webbs thus sought in the realm of consumption a socialist vision to match that of Cole and Ablett. Partly this was effected by a shift from the state to co-operation as the major vehicle of consumer interests. No longer were the limits of co-operation stressed, but the revolutions it could hope to achieve, recounted, as Leonard Woolf conceded, with 'a freedom and spaciousness of vision' that were unfamiliar in the Webbs.[23] In place of the 'equalitarian state', there emerged as their preferred shorthand for the socialist future the 'co-operative commonwealth', a phrase linked by Stephen Yeo with the 'New Life moment' of British socialism.[24] Woolf himself must have provided one stimulus through his own writings on co-operation.[25] So too did Percy Redfern, who at the Control of Industry conference had presented a strongly feminist case for consumers' co-operation, and whose advice on the subject Beatrice once again sought ought after the war.[26] Another possible influence was the *République coopérative* of Charles Gide and Ernest Poisson, whom the Webbs were to meet in Paris while preparing their own study. In his book of this title, published the year before the Webbs' study, Poisson, though himself an active socialist, depicted the development of consumers' co-operation as an alternative to the 'political economy of production' which he held both capitalism and state socialism to represent.[27] The parallel is particularly instructive in that Poisson, like his mentor Gide, and like the Webbs themselves, was to evince complex and in some respects quite positive reactions to the adaptation of such notions by Soviet co-operators.

Though never regarding this co-operative republic as sufficient unto itself, the Webbs now acknowledged its transformative possibilities within the more eclectic framework of their own Co-operative Commonwealth.[28] No longer did they stress the movement's inevitable limitation to the provision of household requirements. On the contrary, its larger significance lay in the 'substitution for the Capitalist System' of forms of democratic control whose field of encroachment on the profit motive seemed boundless. Anticipating, they said, only 'half a dozen or so' nationalised industries, they looked to the municipalities and co-operative movement, along with producer-based organisations, to provide the 'greater part of the new social order' destined to supersede capitalism.[29] Significantly, this may be contrasted with the more statist or monopolist conceptions still evident in Sidney's lectures, where he continued to describe as 'inevitable' the organisation of industry into 'great national monopolies'.[30] As wartime pressures forced co-operators to look increasingly to their own chains of supply, the Webbs scorned the distinction between production and distribution and prophesied the extension of co-operation to 'the whole of the processes of industry, right back to the earth itself'. In their own version of Direct Action, trade unionists and co-operators would accord each other a superiority of work and conditions respectively; thus, without regard to state action, they would 'transfer trade after trade to the joint control of the democracy of consumers in alliance with the democracy of producers'. Within their variegated commonwealth, co-operation exemplified the principles of voluntarism, local autonomy and federal association, and the Webbs wholly discountenanced talk of a rationalised national movement more nearly integrated with the state.[31]

This vision of the achievement of co-operative ideals, not at the expense of work-based movements but in association with them, seemed more feasible at the close of the war than ever before or since. Closer relations between the co-operative movement and the TUC, initially reflecting common anxieties as to food prices, were formalised in 1917 with the establishment of a joint National United Advisory Committee. In 1919 this proclaimed an 'unequivocal declaration of war against the Capitalist System, as the purpose of both Movements alike', and the sentiment was impressively borne out by the co-operators' unprecedented solidarity during that year's national railway strike and miners' lockout.[32] A further augury closer to home was the affiliation of the Co-operative Union to the LRD in 1918, and the establishment by the department of a flourishing Co-operative Section. With arrangements made for joint affiliation to the LRD and the Co-operative Union Statistical Bureau, co-operative affiliations came flooding in, and numbers soon bore comparison with union and trades council subscriptions.[33]

It is true that militant trade unionists tended to regard co-operation instrumentally, as a commissariat for labour in its battles at the point of production.[34] Nevertheless, its distinctive role in the making of a new social order was beginning to be acknowledged beyond the co-operative movement itself. Even Cole, sometime secretary of the LRD's Co-operative Section, modified his earlier disparagement of the movement. He now accepted that it and not the state provided 'by far the most natural expression of the consumers' point of view' and one whose popular and spontaneous gestation accorded better with guild philosophy.[35] Within the unions themselves figures like Fred Bramley, the new TUC assistant secretary, were far from adopting a purely industrialist perspective. 'Personally', Bramley wrote in July 1921, 'I have much more faith in the process of eliminating capitalism by the alternative of co-operative control of production and distribution than I have in any attempt to make capitalism unprofitable by trade union efforts to increase wages, or political efforts which are not directed to the purpose of securing a change in our economic system'.[36] Significantly, the context for that statement was that of Black Friday, the collapse of the industrial 'Triple Alliance' and the subsequent defeat of the miners. Against this, the unexampled solidarity of the co-operative movement, which Bramley himself had promoted as secretary of a Joint Advisory Committee of Trade Unionists and Co-operators, proved unavailing. Even by 1921, the refusal of co-operative support for Labour's newspaper, the *Daily Herald*, signalled the settling down into older alignments, and comparable levels of support were henceforth to prove unattainable.[37] By 1926, with earlier debts still unsettled, co-operative assistance in the miners' lockout was notably attenuated.[38] Already the immediate post-war years seemed to represent the apogee of a class-based perspective embracing both movements.

Nevertheless it was precisely at this moment of optimism that the Webbs began work on their own long-anticipated study of the co-operative movement.[39] This should be regarded as part of the more general summation of their philosophy that in the previous year had already produced their updated *History of Trade Unionism*, their *Constitution of the Socialist Commonwealth of Great Britain* and a draft version of *The Decay of Capitalist Civilisation*. None of these works has much occupied historians of political theory, and the 'Cole' view of the Webbs particularly dismisses the work on co-operation, to which Cole's own dilatory attentions are implausibly preferred.[40]

Nevertheless, the study is not only critical to the Webbs' own intellectual biography but helps locate it within a wider political conjuncture.

Beginning as customary with long descriptive surveys, Beatrice initially found the task dull and over-familiar, exactly as she tended to once the moment of intellectual discovery had passed.[41] What gradually redeemed the new task, as she reacquainted herself with co-operation's northern heartlands, was the discovery of a genuine vein of idealism that seemed to offer new hopes of advance towards the Co-operative Commonwealth. 'Up and down the country I have met many interesting, public spirited young men', she wrote with a characteristic emphasis, 'and I go back far more hopeful about the advance in the Co-operative Movement and its possible developments'.[42] Those possibilities were the subject of a long concluding section to the book, whose flights and thrusts bore Beatrice's unmistakeable imprint. She, we know, not only planned and researched the volume as her own 'special job', but contributed more than was usual to its 'actual composition'.[43] Shaw once observed that Beatrice alone of the Webbs had any gifts of expression or imagination, and one may perhaps discern in *The Consumers' Co-operative Movement* a hint of suppressed creative yearnings. 'I want to imagine anything I damn well please without regard to facts as they are', she had written during the grinding work on *Industrial Democracy*, dreaming instead of a fictional anticipation of society eighty years into the future. Sick to death then of 'hideous facts, multitudinous details [and] exasperating qualifications', she experienced something of the same mood in the latter months of 1921, again hankering for the more personal forms of composition which were to result in *My Apprenticeship*. Did such personal flights help to relieve the 'task work' for which she felt such distaste while writing the book on co-operation? Certainly, her gilded vision of the CWS Commonwealth was one of those occasions, certainly not the last of them, on which she brought to the craft of the investigator an unavowed penchant for romancing.[44]

The basis of that vision was the banal assertion, familiar from a mass of socialist literature, that only by a reduction in the demands of work could there be secured a real extension of personal fulfilment. Already implicit in Marx's casting of a 'true realm of freedom' apart from that of toil and necessity, this idea informed the thinking of leading marxists of the Second International like Kautsky, Bebel and Lafargue, the last of whose *Right to be Lazy* was disseminated in Britain by both the SDF and the ILP.[45] From a different tradition, more formative for the Webbs, Herbert Spencer had also defined human progress as the means of 'liberating more and more life from mere toil': life, he agreed with the marxists, 'is not for work, but work is for life', and Sidney was to repeat these sentiments almost word for word as his credo for the works manager.[46] The wide purchase of such ideas was confirmed around the end of the century in the campaigns for the eight-hour day which proved so characteristic and universal a socialist demand as to provide the main slogan for the first international celebration of May Day in 1890.

Even within this agitation, however, different motivations can be discerned. For militant trade unionists, shorter working hours were often perceived primarily as an instrument of the class struggle. Sometime syndicalists like Tom Mann and A.A. Purcell, both lifelong advocates of shorter hours, argued that by soaking up unemployment this would increase labour's bargaining power, and by its scope for 'mental and moral training' raise the worker's status and remuneration alike. Both of these inflexions were compatible with, and arguably worked to further, a producer world-view. For a revolutionary gloss, Mann further argued that an expanded working-class intelligence made not for a bovine contentment but for a 'more active discontent' with capitalism.[47] In the context of the communist party activism whose first precondition was the time in which to be active, we have seen that this was indeed a possible though far from universal corollary.[48]

Partly coexisting, partly competing with such arguments, were those identifying the quality of life with increased leisure, exactly as seemed to follow from both Spencer and Marx.[49] Among middle-class or 'reformist' campaigners for shorter hours, such concerns were usually paramount. Sidney was one of the most active of these, and, though never entirely relinquishing the idea, he had little time for 'work fund' notions of a correlation between working hours and employment levels. He even stated categorically that shorter hours did 'nothing whatsoever' to combat unemployment. Instead, his primary concerns were twofold: first, with the 'brighter, fuller life' to be secured outside of work, and secondly with the greater efficiency of the work process itself, a theme underlying the Webbs' broader advocacy of a 'Common Rule' governing working conditions. In the classic Fabian equation, the efficiency achieved was the precondition of the brighter, fuller life, although frequently, it is true, brightness slipped from view, and efficiency was left to appear as an end in itself, or as a means to greater, national goals. For the Webbs themselves, one might fairly describe the whole Edwardian period as a case in point.[50]

This nevertheless was the vision that the couple sought to recapture after the war. What they envisaged in *The Consumers' Co-operative Movement* was a continuously diminishing requirement for social labour, described as 'the price ... to pay for the privilege of living', and the corresponding enlargement of a private and irresponsible sphere of 'the utmost possible freedom'. 'Man does not live in order that he may work', they wrote, like true Spencerians. 'He works merely in order that he may live.' The whole machinery of government and social organisation was thus depicted as the means to private ends beyond all co-optation and commodification. 'They are the priceless gifts of individual genius, above and beyond any social organisation', ran the book's concluding section. 'They are part of the perpetual act of creation, not rendering services which can be paid for by livelihood, but adding new values to humanity's life.'[51]

This was a politics not merely of leisure but of consumption. In Labour folklore, the Webbs have anything but such a reputation, and in Anthony Crosland's *Future of Socialism* (1956) their 'instinctive hostility to higher consumption' on grounds of 'the moral virtues of abstinence' was famously invoked as a sort of incubus to be thrown off by Labour in meeting the post-war challenge of abundance.[52] Crosland, as we shall see, was correct to point out the profound ambivalence of the Webb tradition as to the form which higher consumption should take. Nevertheless, while scornful of conspicuous consumption – the 'licentious pleasures' and 'insolent manners' of the functionless rich – the Webbs now insisted that levels of popular consumption were 'disastrously small' from the standpoint both of personal freedom and collective advancement.[53] Thus they restated the politics of efficiency, not now for the advancement of the 'race', but for the fulfilment of the individual. Even the works manager, in Sidney's inimitable turn of phrase, was 'out for the fullness of life, just as much as the poet'. At once a counterblast to snobbery and the self-satisfaction of cultural elites, the sentiment had something in it of Bolshevism, when even poets wrote of Driving Axles and Cement, and something of the impossible philistinism of Henry Ford.[54]

Explicitly presented as an alternative to the guild socialist ideas then percolating throughout the labour movement, the Webbs' consumptionism can be located within a broader line of reaction to work-centred ideologies. Inevitably, the co-operative movement itself was one major source of alternative ideas. Already at the pre-war Control of Industry conference, Percy Redfern had immediately countered Ablett by asserting the primacy of demand over supply and of the consumer – described as 'mistress' rather than master of industry – over the producer.[55] Though Ramsay MacDonald, as we shall see, wavered on his basically statist prescriptions, an outspoken collectivist response was provided by Philip Snowden as the most 'Fabian' of the ILP leaders and one well-versed in Webbian language and concepts.[56] In 1916, he challenged Cole with a vision of socialist production in which the expert took responsibility and the grateful worker the rewards of leisure and abundance. 'Even under Socialism ... if the remuneration of the workmen is such as to provide for the satisfaction of every reasonable requirement of health and a cultured life, if the workman has abundant leisure, then he will have little desire to be bothered too much about managing the industry, and will find a more congenial sphere for his aspirations and interests in the wider field of enjoyment outside the workshop'. The individual, he concluded, lived 'not to produce but to consume', and as a consumer achieved self-realisation.[57] This was the same social equation as Fordism, and, as the credo variously of state collectivism, consumers' co-operation, business unionism and Americanism, the 'price to pay' encapsulated what its critics meant by servility. Cole, in an essay on Ford, was to liken it to Plato's 'city of swine'.[58]

If this had an obvious Labour sequel it was in the revisionist feeding troughs of the age of affluence. 'If, one believes in socialism ... as a means of increasing personal freedom and the range of choice', Crosland wrote in 1956, 'one does not necessarily want a busy, bustling society in which everyone is politically active ... and feels responsible for all the burdens of the world'.[59] On the other hand, to view the Webbs in this longer perspective underlines how much more they had in common, not with their nominal successors, but with their contemporary critics. Gaitskell and Crosland were nothing if not Fabians, but the Fabian lineage was a convoluted one in which democracies of exertion and acquiescence coexisted without ever being reconciled or even properly disentangled. Disrupting or intersecting with these lines of descent were the distinct mentalities of period and generation, so that the 'price to pay' in its post-First World War Webbian version had more in common with guild socialism than with either Snowden, Gaitskell or that mellowing Cole, more Webbian than the Webbs, who watered with his own hands a seedbed of revisionists. Though warring pamphleteers juggled consumers and producers in ever more bewildering arrangements, they were at one in holding that socialism involved values and power relationships that were utterly distinct from capitalism. They were, in a word, qualitative socialists, concerned with what Sidney's programme for the Labour Party called a New Social Order.[60] Underlying that common aspiration a whole series of further shared assumptions can be detected. Among them were a belief in the independent organisation of workers as workers; a vision of self-governing community; and the lack of any adequate theory of politics or socialist transition. More fundamentally, as we shall see, they shared a vision of a new moral world whose projection onto Soviet Russia, while never universal, defied the conventional boundary markers of socialist historiography.

## II

The first of these commonalities was the emphasis on the need, as much within the new order as within capitalism, for vigorous associations of producers. The differentiation of producer and consumer meant that, unlike some socialist thinkers who subsumed these categories to class, the Webbs had always emphasised the necessity of trade unionism in any democratic social order, even 'the most complete Collectivism'.[61] This indeed had been one of their main objections to the disappearance of the unions in an apparatus of guilds, and they had drawn a similar distinction with the purely state socialism of the marxists. According to the Webbs' own account, the German SPD had even objected to a translation of their trade union history on the grounds that the unions 'had no place in the Socialist State'.[62] Now, however, they went much further than in the 1890s, conceding the 'soulless' preoccupation with efficiency and managerial order that characterised consumers' democracies, and allowing as a safeguard a sort of diluted syndicalism in the shape of works' committees. Moreover, they emphasised that the defence of workers from the arbitrary sanctions of employers was as essential to basic civic rights of religious, cultural and political expression as to the integrity of collective bargaining.[63]

In effect, the Webbs had come to accept Cole's dictum that not poverty but slavery, or what they now described frankly as unequal power relationships, was the fundamental problem with capitalism and the test of whatever was to replace it.[64] In this they were not alone. Because it shaped so little Labour's future work of government, it is sometimes overlooked how pervasively guild socialist concerns had, by the early 1920s, tempered the outlook of the younger socialist politician. In this, the cordial relations established between Cole and Clifford Allen, then emerging as the leading representative of the ILP's younger generation, must have played a significant part.[65] Clement Attlee, then parliamentary private secretary to Ramsay MacDonald, was just one mainstream figure who welcomed the recovery of the Ruskin-Morris tradition as a challenge to Fabian reasoning and the biological conceptions of MacDonald himself.[66] William Graham, the most orthodox of Cole's contemporaries, whom Beatrice characterised as a Fabian of the late 1890s, concluded his book *The Wages of Labour* (1921) with a sort of attenuated guild theory, adding: 'The numbers who now advocate State Socialism are comparatively small.'[67] Even MacDonald himself, proposing a draft constitution for the ILP in the same year, abjured the control of industry by a 'State political bureaucracy' in favour of workers' organisations rooted in the workshop.[68] Embodied more forcefully in the ILP programme of 1922, thanks not only to Allen but to Attlee's vigorous advocacy, guild socialist sensibilities were for a time *de rigueur* for the coming generation.[69]

Where the Webbs' emphasis remained distinct from Cole's was in their preference, at least in the future social order, for vocational over industrial organisation. Having gone so far as to accept the reality of the class war, the Webbs conceded the advantage of the tightest possible cohesion in the revolt against the existing social order. Nevertheless, such 'battle formations' – the martial terminology was borrowed from Cole – could not but prove inadequate to the future challenge of construction: inadequate, that is, 'if the purpose be not fighting but co-operation; not uniform discipline, but diversified freedom; not identity of faculties and desires, but the utmost range in variety ... not repression of individuality in the battle between one herd of human beings and another, but the largest enjoyment ... of the widest possible personal liberty'.[70] This was not a view shared by

Cole, whose forms of self-government were only imaginable at the level of the industry, and thus, if the Webbs were right, limited not only by largeness of scale but the subordination of vocational identities. By the end of 1919, though Cole had come to anticipate the gradual break-up of the 'enormous centralised industrial system' created by capitalism, it was on lines of localism and smaller-scale production rather than craft.[71]

The Webbs' positive vision of vocationalism, now expressed in strikingly egalitarian terms, meant embracing a societal division of labour but not that detailed subdivision already expounded by Adam Smith and afterwards regarded as the hallmark of capitalist efficiency.[72] 'It is plain that no self-respecting Commonwealth will allow such a degradation of its citizens as is implied in the perpetual lifelong repetition of an exclusively mechanical operation', they wrote in their socialist *Constitution*.[73] Seemingly that had radical consequences for some of their own earlier utterances. However, even in *Industrial Democracy* they had recognised the moral significance of 'the right to a trade' and Beatrice from the start had rejected the dehumanising impositions of Scientific Management. 'It is the only justification I have yet read for the policy of Sabotage', she had written of Taylorism in 1912, adding that, whatever its reception among 'the degraded declassed foreign populations of the United States ... [any] individual suggesting it in a British workshop would be kicked out of the place'.[74] Now the Webbs looked beyond the defensive reflexes of the craft unions, or their own concerns for the status of the professional worker.[75] Instead, they proposed the development of a richer and less stratified division of work which would obliterate any 'fundamental cleavage' between the professions and manual worker and do away with the very notion of unskilled labour. 'Every member of the public has, or might have – we should say, ought to have – his own specialisation, in which he should be superior to the outside world', they wrote. 'All occupations call, in different measure, for both muscular dexterity and intellectual skill.' Increasingly the balance in all cases would tilt to the latter.[76]

In the socialist society of the future, the Webbs therefore looked to a 'reorganisation of the Vocational World' and the adoption by all groups of workers of codes of ethics and public service such as they believed characterised existing professional bodies and gave them their far-reaching authority.

> The spirit of corporate freedom that struggled for expression in the medieval guilds of craftsmen ... has always assumed the form of a continuous and an insistent demand, on the parts of groups of persons who feel that they possess a common craft or mystery, a common art or science, that they should be allowed ... to determine the conditions under which they should render their peculiar social service ... It is through the intensification of this tie of a specialised vocation ... that

> man as a producer gains the maximum freedom to express himself in production.

Apparently belying their deep scepticism as to producer innovation, the Webbs even forecast the development of productive technique by workers themselves, 'for pure love of the progress of their several arts'. 'There may then be', they wrote, with more than a foretaste of Stakhanovism, 'in each manual-working vocation, the same emulation, the same zeal for training, the same high proficiency, perhaps even the same sort of friendly contests, as was developed in a Huxley or a Tyndall ...'[77]

As evocative now of the Soviet Plans as of the Victorians, this also spoke to a plebeian discourse of craft unionism whose values it redefined within a project of social transformation. That was unusual though not unique. Although socialist trade unionists for the most part espoused a class or industrial form of organisation, at least one key figure expounded a case similar to the Webbs' and apparently drawing upon it. This was Fred Bramley, the future TUC secretary, whose commitment to co-operation and associations with the Fabians marked him as the most obviously 'Webbian' of trade unionists in the post-Edwardian sense of the word.[78] As Furnishing Trades' organiser Bramley had long since done battle with the National Union of Railwaymen over the organisation of craft workers on the railways.[79] In 1922, by now the TUC's assistant secretary, he sought to generalise the case against industrial unionism. Exactly like the Webbs, he asserted the enduring significance of craft as against the mere expediency of 'a sort of standing industrial army', whose fighting objectives he felt could in any case be secured by the centralised control of trade disputes. To restrict trade unionism to such functions, on the other hand, appeared to take for granted the permanence of capitalism. 'We may, by wiping out all regard for occupational interest and exterminating pride of craft and love of accomplishment, unite the workers ... [for] the destruction of the present system', he acknowledged. But what, he went on to ask, 'shall we require after this task has been accomplished?' His answer was a vision of socialism not usually evoked in a Webbian context, and doubtless expressed in accents more fluent and convincing than theirs.

> If I understand the ideals of Socialism and the aspirations of the best-informed members of our Labour movement rightly, I believe that ... we shall aim at the cultivation of a love of all things which are durable and beautiful. We shall desire the skilled craftsman to develop a real love for the work he is expected to do. We shall no longer assume that the production of commodities in enormous quantities without regard to quality of workmanship, or the development of the worker through his occupation, is the main object of our system of production ... Taking a

> very long view ... craft-consciousness, properly understood, is of more permanent value to society than class-consciousness, and pride of workmanship not less indispensable than hatred of the capitalist exploiter.[80]

In Bramley's case, like Redfern's, the Webbs and their social tissue appear in a genuinely reciprocal relationship. If Bramley by his own account belonged to the movement's 'extreme Right Wing', it was one defined in such a way as to include a clear vision of socialism no less than of international solidarity.[81] Due to his untimely death in 1925, Bramley is caught permanently at this moment of possibility, with responses to Mondism, MacDonaldism and Stalinism all impossible to foretell. Even in his lifetime, his encomiums to craft had become somewhat distinctive, and George Hicks of the Building Trades, a supporter of the building guilds, responded directly to him in terms akin to Cole's. The paradox was that he did so by vaguely disparaging the notion of work as identity which had been Cole's great discovery in Morris.[82]

A second commonality, again marking off both the Webbs and Cole from the minimalist visions of their successors, was the location of the private sphere within a clear vision of community and collective self-government. While noting without satisfaction the low levels of participation in co-operative democracy, the Webbs stressed the effectiveness and still greater potential of its representative institutions, and the provision for the active and motivated co-operator to bring its executive bodies to account. In proposing as a civic duty the exercise of such 'perpetual' vigilance and 'incessant' discussion, the Webbs' ideal of an 'active citizenship' seemed comparable if not identical to Cole's. 'The man or woman who simply accepts, with more or less grumbling, the collective arrangements by which he is surrounded, and does not make these part of his daily thought and personal interests', they wrote, with what in hindsight is an unfortunate turn of phrase, 'is ... unconsciously a traitor to the community'. If they continued to stress the virtues of 'expert' representation, albeit including therein the continuous alertness of the rank-and-file delegate or activist, the Webbs also laid much stress on the encouragement of a broader democratic culture. Bureaucracy, while remaining inevitable and indispensable, for that very reason demanded commensurate safeguards. Nevertheless, democracy was portrayed not just as a mechanism of 'consent', but as a positive value in itself, complementing the private sphere in the 'development of personality, and that enlargement of faculty and desire dependent on the assumption of responsibility and the exercise of will'.[83]

In this depiction of a functioning democracy, the distinction between the state and society was vague and elusive. Simply in the provision of material wants, the Webbs, like any visionary co-operator, anticipated both the extinction of the private trader in basic commodities and the ending of the geographical overlapping between co-operative societies: effectively, that is, a form of association which was all but compulsory. Consumer rights would thus be exercised, not individually, through the market, but through a democratic collectivity tantamount to a public authority. Far from the state 'subsuming' the community, the community organised for consumption took on the semblance of that Webbian 'state within a state', and with ambitions hardly less extensive. With future 'divis' earmarked for social, welfare and cultural purposes, the Webbs seemed briefly to step into a Soviet future. 'Everything fits in, everything (save Art) is dealt with, and every contingency apparently provided against completely and consistently', a Fabian reviewer gently chaffed them. With social clubs, sports clubs, libraries, lectures, communal laundries, communal kitchens, choirs, charabancs, games rooms, rest homes, summer schools, orphanages and Collective Life Assurance, the Webbs caught a glimpse of the future and listed it. Even unto death itself, they looked to the example of the medieval guilds for the burial of every member with full co-operative honours. It was a vision as inclusive as the state but freed of its paternalist associations, so that in this last instance the dignity of co-operation was explicitly counterposed to the humiliating stigma of burial by 'the parish'.[84]

Conceivably the community of consumers was a less restrictive conception than that of its production-based rivals. Obviously it was tendentious to include even the hours of sleep in calculating that already the average working life was given over predominantly to non-work activities. On the other hand, such lines of reasoning did mean embracing those who, through age, incapacity or the sexual division of labour, had a subordinate role in producer ideologies. Paradoxically, it was precisely the 'functionless', or more precisely those whose functions had no recognition in wages, who were enfranchised by consumption; just as the Webbs did not recognise consumption itself as a 'function' but as a sphere beyond the performance of such social roles. Even within the ranks of labour there was a hierarchy of struggle, and Sidney's famous jibe at 'the school for the school-teacher and the sewer for the sewerman' did implicitly raise the question of the specificity of syndicalist-type demands to particular industrial sectors.[85]

At its narrowest, in many of Sidney's utterances, the critique of producerism was that of the 'little man', nestling behind the 'community' for the maintenance of social distance and recognition. Nevertheless, the larger point cannot be dismissed so easily. When Mellor dismissed 'community' as a fraud, he rightly instanced its use to obfuscate the realities of class struggle; but that same conception of struggle, with its attendant military terminology, also consigned working-class women to the passive and stoical role of 'non-combatants', forming the 'weakest link in the chain of Labour' and threatening the workers' defeat 'through the wasting bodies of their wives and children'.[86] Even the contemporaneous example of the suffrage agitation does not appear to have suggested more positive images. Cole in particular, as described by his wife, was a thoroughgoing misogynist whose pastimes, liaisons and social philosophy were, in the broadest sense of the word, somewhat monkish. Women, he apparently believed, were a 'rather low type of being' whose 'main purpose in life ... was to distract man from his proper work, either directly or (if "good" women) by giving him "a stake in the country" which turned him into a "stick-in-the-mud"'.[87] Occasionally gender issues were raised directly, and during the wartime battles over dilution Beatrice noted how Cole spoke of workers' control when what he meant was control by the male workers concerned.[88] The underlying point, however, was a more general one. In contrast to the exclusions on which unions relied to control the labour supply, the Webbs posited not just the universalism of the state-community but the inclusiveness of co-operation, to which each recruit meant but a further step towards the Co-operative Commonwealth.

A third common feature of these social visions was the lack of any proper conception of politics. It is true that the Webbs' *Constitution* posited an elaborate system of checks and balances, both between producers and consumers, and to scrutinise and delimit the inevitable bureaucracy. The notion of a 'general will', which Sidney had casually opposed to 'arithmetical' conceptions of democracy, was now explicitly repudiated, or at least disaggregated, and parliaments based on different suffrages offered as the guarantee of individual freedoms.[89] What was missing, as it had been from all their writings, was anything one might understand by the word 'party'. The strengths the Webbs perceived in co-operative and trade union democracy did not imply leadership changes through 'spasmodic mass votes' – indeed, they rather approved the 'remarkable permanence of tenure' secured through habits of re-election – but the continuous exercise of an effective control of the executive. Even their projected Social Parliament, as we have seen, disdained tumult and faction for constructive committee work, explicitly generalising from Sidney's experiences at the LCC. There was nothing in their constitution about an 'opposition', and rather than proposing cabinet government as a model for the unions, as is sometimes suggested, they consciously looked to these social movements as the basis of an alternative to cabinet government.[90] Elections were thus envisaged, not primarily as providing changes of direction, but as satisfying administrative criteria of consent or accountability, as the fixity of an agreed common purpose was projected onto the wider organisation of society. The device of the referendum was dismissed for precisely the same reason.[91]

As to party, in their whole four hundred-page prospectus for socialism, the Webbs offered little more than the hope and prediction that 'organised political parties as they exist today will pass away'.[92] If that partly reflected the culture of British socialism, where party had arrived late, by the back door of the unions, and was never to attain the scope or authority of its continental counterparts, the absence was also deeply grounded in Webbian social theory. As at once an aggregation and a polarisation of interests, the idea of party cut across the principles of both multiformity and integration. Instead, the Webbs preferred to imagine a flowering of issue-based groups, transient, sporadic and disaggregated, but working within and upon an agreed framework of government. The parliamentary representative, in such a conception, was not a factional figure, but a skilled and 'relatively impartial' sounding board for these campaigns.[93] Beatrice, to whom party personally offered so little, would always feel a 'strong prejudice' against 'political methods' and the 'wasteful' parliamentary game of 'ins and outs'.[94] Sidney, though well practised in the game itself, did not take it at its own estimation. To Wells he once admitted that politics for him meant merely 'state institutional': 'not at all necessarily forming a separate party, or any party, or indeed having anything at all do with elections or electioneering! ... Elections and parties are quite subordinate – even trivial – parts of political action.'[95] The extolling on the one hand of social movements and diversity, and on the other of bureaucratic continuity, coincided in the denigration of party and the ultimate fantasy of a non-party state.

In this respect too the Webbs had much in common with Cole. Cole too thought 'indirect "democracy" ... a form of slavery'. He was also indifferent to the mediating role of party, providing what Wright euphemistically describes as a 'deceptively minimal account of inter-group conflict' in which the necessity of protective organisation was lost in a bewildering sleight of shows of hands.[96] The Webbs did at least allow for 'inter-group' conflict, and thus, as distinct from Cole and Woolf respectively, rejected the future adoption by either unions or co-operatives of parastatal functions. 'We want to preserve as much as we can of voluntary association in the Socialist State', Sidney wrote to Woolf:

> & hence our long continued advocacy, both of the Co-operative Movement and Trade Unionism ... But just as Trade Unions cannot become legal monopolists and State organs without losing their present character of voluntary organs of defence & resistance against the employing community, so it seems to me that Co-operative Societies could not become bodies in which membership was legally obligatory ...[97]

These were principles which were largely to be forgotten in their positive assessments of the Soviet Union. For the moment, though, the Webbs were far removed from any thoughts of dictatorship and sought the resolution of social division by almost any instrument but the state. Where once they had upheld central authority against insupportable industrial actions, they now proposed the spontaneous counter-measures of other vocations. Thus, as they somewhat unimaginatively put it, unwarranted strikers would be deprived of 'spirits, beer, picture-palaces and tobacco'.[98] Such ideas were very much in the air. Among the groups who actually threatened such retribution were Manchester butchers and Brighton doctors. Meanwhile, at theatres in 1921 a dramatisation of such a conflict, *The Right to Strike*, set a stage doctor against his working-class patients, and the proletarian pit against the stalls. The atmosphere, according to the *Co-operative News*, was 'red hot' and 'eloquent of the reality of the class war'.[99]

The absence of politics was closely bound up with the lack of any theory of the transition to a new social order. Economic Power Precedes Political Power, said the guild socialists, and the Webbs in their own way presented the taking hold of the machinery of government as the sequel to the 'irresistible groundswell of British democracy'. Between present conflict and future harmony lay a long transition, whose indeterminacy was easily debunked by Marxists. Against their rival notion of a clean slate, which the Webbs themselves would presently find compelling, they offered only the continuing growth of social 'tissue', now accompanied by the corresponding electoral advance of the Labour Party.[100]

At the same time, both to guide such a process and to compensate for its *longueurs*, they dabbled in the sort of elaborate system-building which Cole so relished. The resulting clash of blueprints has been described by Wright as 'perhaps ... the high water mark of optimistic social engineering in a modern context'.[101] Drawn for the first time from their old myopic concerns with process, the Webbs competed in the representation of a new society uprooted from the habits and survival strategies that the present one demanded. 'The Socialist Party has aroused great expectations as to the construction of a New Social Order', Beatrice had proclaimed at the inception of the FRD. 'Unless we can meet these expectations by carefully drafted and tested specifications, we shall be adjudged ... intellectually bankrupt.'[102] Just as Cole had abandoned the Webbian description of *The World of Labour* for his own recasting of that world's immanent potentialities, so now the Webbs responded with a similar imaginative leap; and whereas reviewers of *The Consumers' Co-operative Movement* noted its characteristic 'feats of legerdemain' by which future possibilities were conjured out of present accomplishments, their resulting *Constitution* was as cardboard a contrivance as a three-tier wedding cake.[103] Beyond all differences of detail, the device of the blueprint, or utopia, meant a profoundly technocratic way of envisioning and peopling the new world, not just as its prophets but as its unacknowledged legislators. In that respect at least, the Webbs' *Constitution* was the direct precursor of the institutional fantasy world of *Soviet Communism*.

A parallel may be drawn with the contemporaneous projections of the founder of Bolshevism, Lenin himself. As A.J. Polan has noted in his interrogation of Lenin's most 'innocent' and utopian work, *The State and Revolution* (1917), the 'central absence' of that work too is that of any adequate theory of politics or political institutions. Superficially representing a refusal of bureaucratic power, according to Polan, Lenin's failure to define the separate spheres and interaction of bureaucracy and politics, or state and civil society, ended by conflating them in a monological state form allowing no space for the articulation of conflicting values. If anything, Polan's argument is strengthened by the analogy with western pro-Bolsheviks. Whereas a large historiography has attributed the decay of Soviet democracy to economic and social circumstances – briefly, the country's underdevelopment – Polan's ascription of a major responsibility to matters of theory and culture is lent credibility by the unforced adhesion to Stalinism of western socialists unaffected by those material factors, or experiencing them primarily as 'texts' and 'ideas'. On the other hand, precisely because of these well-attested affinities, it is difficult to accept Polan's contention that the Soviets' rejection of politics derived 'ab initio' from the 'total nature' of Lenin's reconstruction of socialist theory after 1914.[104]

## III

A still more fundamental issue going to the heart of what socialism represented was that expressed in the Webbs' ideas as the tension between organised consumption and consumption conceived as a 'sphere for individual decision'. The issue seemed straightforward. If consumption, as they suggested, was a form of empowerment, then the 'substantial equality' of income and material circumstances which they proposed implied mass empowerment. Hence it was with its denial of personal forms of property that the Webbs indicted capitalism.[105] Though inseparable from the couple's proverbial philistinism, the restriction of matters of culture, belief and identity to this private sphere may in some respects be regarded as a less intrusive, prescriptive and ultimately claustrophobic utopia than those of Morris or 'guild socialist man'. 'The time and energy thus set free, in every member of the community, for the life and affections of the family, for social intercourse, for the arts and sciences, and generally for the spiritual development of the individual, must necessarily be left at his own disposal', the Webbs wrote. Neither Gaitskell nor Crosland, who also espoused a gospel of efficiency to achieve such a goal, would have demurred. The contrast between Fabian concerns with output and 'liberal socialist' ones with the consumer was, perhaps, a good deal less stark than is often allowed.[106]

On the other hand, the sanctifying of a private realm of personal decision did not even now wholly supplant the horror for merely idle or degrading pleasures with which the Webbs are so often associated. In theory, the Webbs envisaged in their Socialist Commonwealth a proliferation of novel cravings, 'inventive, artistic, emotional, religious': an anticipation, almost, of Spencerian diversity in the field of leisure. Tacitly overlooked, however, were other cravings, not always novel ones, which lacked the improving overtones of the Webbs' list, and contributed nothing to the spiritual development of the individual. As Beatrice put it in a pre-war diary entry, they stood for 'the maximum of personal invention and individual divergence alike in ends and means from the common mean', but with a caveat – 'so long as this divergence is not downward towards the animal in man'.[107] 'Let it never be forgotten', Sidney had stated in an interview with a Christian weekly in 1893, 'that what we are in pursuit of is not the better housing, feeding and clothing of the people except as a means to an end – the development of individual character'. In the same interview, Beatrice had prophesied not just municipal bakeries but municipal dressing establishments, to be attended only after visits to doctor and artist for both orthogenic and aesthetic prescriptions. 'She would not be Mrs John Smith, but type No.16A', the interview went on, 'and would go to a subdivision of that great establishment for the fair-haired, the brunette, the mother, the young collegian, as the case might be.'[108] The underlying issue, though not apparently Beatrice's approach to magazine interviews, was a serious one. Competing with the 'cravings' of the individual, the Webbs can be linked with a tradition of rational consumption, replacing 'anarchic' personal expenditure with 'scientific ascertainment' of social needs. Traceable to the origins of co-operation, it can particularly be identified with the example of Robert Owen, prominently advertised in Beatrice's first book.[109] 'Here and there, even billiard tables and a bowling green', they later conceded of the co-operative future, like a Sunday School outing allowed a rampage on the swings. The single word 'even' conveys a world of meaning.

Nor was it simply Owen the co-operator from whom a line could be drawn, but equally Owen the industrialist and director of labour. Just as they upheld the industrial division of labour, so too the Webbs endorsed the 'time-thrift' of modern industry and the corresponding aversion to 'idleness' which is so powerfully attested throughout their writings. The tension can be traced from the very beginnings of the 'partnership'. In an almost lyrical passage in *Industrial Democracy*, the Webbs conjured up what seems the enviable world of the pre-industrial craft worker. 'Unless he is driven ... to work "all the hours God made" in order to get bare subsistence, he may break off when he likes to gossip with a friend or slip round to the public-house; he may, in the intervals, nurse a sick wife or child; and he can even arrange to spend the morning in his garden, or doing odd jobs about the house.' Here, it seems, was the elusive work-life balance! Apparently enjoying that 'sphere of individual decision' which the Webbs sought to recover through the extension of leisure, the craftsman worked as little or as much as suited him, even taking the odd Monday off 'to recover

... from the "expansion" of the preceding days'. 'No one acquainted with the daily life of the home-working, skilled craftsman, earning "good money", will ignore the large use that such a man makes of his freedom.'[110]

This, however, was precisely the problem: how to be certain that their 'average sensual man' would turn his opportunities to fitter use than mere 'expansion' – or any of the other rumbustious pursuits that exercised the royal commissions and moral reformers of the Victorian era. When they wrote *Industrial Democracy*, itself a late product of that era, the Webbs had little doubt of the 'injurious effect' of this self-regulation of working hours and felt that, both at home and at work, the average worker was better off for the discipline and regularity of the factory.[111] Such indeed was the nub of their case against unemployment, and with a daunting emphasis they wrote that 'for every class of society, the deliberate organisation of leisure is as necessary as the organisation of work'. 'We may foresee a time', they went on, 'when these skilled workmen will be advised and assisted to spend their "idle time" ... partly in holiday excursions, and organised games, and partly in the technical and literary and music classes that the Local Education Authority ought to be providing.'[112]

Prefigured, as Edward Thompson has shown, by a legion of Victorian tracts and sermons, such forebodings of indolence were given a sharper edge by the rise of leisure industries which were readily construable as exploitative, and thus encouraged the shifting of responsibility for misspent hours from individual to systemic factors.[113] Like most socialists, the Webbs were antagonistic to advertising and commercialised pleasures – what they classified as 'pernicious commodities and services' and 'the hypertrophy of selling agencies' – and from their stern disapprobation not even the humble tea-shop was exempt. 'In all the great capitals of the world', they wrote with staggering innuendo, 'millions of pounds are invested ... in dwelling-houses, tea shops, massage establishments, concert rooms, dancing halls, and other convenient covers for the profitable business of first decoying, and then interning girls and boys for the purpose of sexual vice'.[114] The reverse of that base coinage was the unalloyed admiration Beatrice was soon to show for the Reithian BBC: not wholly unaccountable, she stressed, but nevertheless subject to only the discriminating pressures of what seems a Fabian anticipation of the Viewers and Listeners Association. 'Such control as is exercised by the consumers of the service, is not as with the Press exercised by a multitude of individual buyers and individual advertisers; it can only be by individuals deliberately intervening by writing letters of complaint or suggestion, and the common, illiterate or apathetic person cannot write letters or make effective protests.'[115] The same exclusion of all that was 'low' or 'bad' was approvingly remarked upon by hundreds, including the Webbs, on visiting the USSR. Appropriately, Beatrice's own initial impressions of Russia were themselves most widely disseminated with the Reithian imprimatur of the BBC Home Service.

It was this that Crosland had in mind when he counterposed 'liberty and gaiety in private life' with a Webbian 'Fabian tradition'.[116] In the consumers' collectivism of William Graham or the later Cole, it may be detected in discussions of the 'education' or 'redirection' of demand, whether for economic reasons or – through excise on spirits or subsidies to municipal orchestras – political and cultural ones.[117] Beyond that, as Chris Waters has shown, the discourse was common to socialists of the most varied persuasions, not least those described as 'ethical' socialists.[118] Even Lafargue's *Right To Be Lazy* was careful to distinguish between the leisure 'that makes life beautiful' – the 'mother of the arts and noble virtues' – and the leisure whose exploitation made for new forms of servitude.[119] That sounds uncannily like the Webbs themselves when in *Industrial Democracy* they looked to the 'instinct for knowledge and beauty', along with the widening of personal horizons to consider the needs and desires of others, as the ennobling fruits of an increase in free time.[120] Perhaps in the Webbs the filiation of a socialist culture from the 'rational recreation' of Victorian reformers seems especially marked. Nevertheless, it is difficult to see how the good society could even have been imagined, let alone pursued, without some idea of how it was to spend its time.

In this sense, Crosland was no doubt correct to identify within the socialist tradition a strain of censoriousness as to the character of popular leisure and consumption. Nevertheless, there was more to this concern than just the 'puritanism and paternalism' which Crosland alleged, and the issue was more fundamental to the general discourse of socialism than Waters perhaps allows.[121] If Crosland himself, like Samuel Gompers, simply wanted 'more' for those he represented, he was notably unperspicacious in his assessment of the agencies and power relations by which that 'more' was constructed. For those socialists, on the other hand, who wanted not just 'more' but 'different' or 'better', that could not but imply a critique of current cultural or behavioural patterns – not easily separated from current people – as somehow not 'better' and therefore unfulfilled, undeveloped or – though few put it quite like this – simply 'worse'. The specific legacy of rational recreation, though significant in its British context, was not the basic cause or condition of such a problem, and Waters produces no real evidence for his contention that the discourse of improvement was peculiar to British socialists and the cause of their special deficiencies.[122] On the contrary, all recent scholarship suggests that such attitudes were just as clearly attested in the socialist experiments of Red Vienna and Workers' Russia, or the counter-hegemony of the Italian communist party. Certainly they can be found in the example which Waters cites, of the pre-1914 German SPD. Envisaging the *neue*

*Menschen* or 'new Soviet man' involved a moral or moralistic critique of the old and unmade that was common to all qualitative socialisms, and provided a continuous tension with their prevalent notions of working-class agency.[123]

In such a perspective, the dividing line between 'moral' and 'mechanical' reformers loses much of its sharpness. So too, in this functionalist context, does that between the competing utopias of work and leisure, or of production and consumption; and this despite the fact that, for many of those involved, the distinction was crucial to their self-identity. Consciously hearkening to William Morris, A.J. Penty, medievalist, guilds theorist and future fascist, portrayed the Leisure State and Servile State as interdependent.[124] Cole described it as 'the "Selfridge" State' of 'Mr "Callisthenes" Webb'; and if, as Wright suggests, Cole was a 'diagnostician of alienation', then the Webbs' 'price to pay' was the disease itself.[125] Sometimes the antithesis has been represented as a tale of two utopias: on the one hand Edward Bellamy's *Looking Backward*, the American state socialist fantasy that had its British *succès d'estime* simultaneously with that of *Fabian Essays*; and on the other Morris's pastoralist and unpoliced reponse to it, *News from Nowhere*. Morris himself denounced Bellamy's as a 'cockney paradise', doubtless with the cockney Webb and his tram-line Fabians in mind, and rejected a future in which ever increasing 'machinery' brought not pleasure in work but only its diminution. 'Machinery' indeed, both actual and metaphorical, was Morris's defining aversion, and precisely what he most objected to in Webb. A guildsman before his time, he was, in Edward Thompson's coinage, the original 'diagnostician of alienation'.[126]

And yet on closer sight, the polarities of work and leisure, like state and community, melt into each other. Morris did not for a moment imagine that all work would be pleasurable: sewer-cleaning, coal-hewing and midwifery were among his interesting selections as types of 'necessary and usually repellent work' to be performed as a 'social duty'. He did however draw the distinction between this unavoidable 'tribute to the community' – work on which the minimum time and intelligence should be expended, and the maximum efficiency attained – and those creative endeavours of hand and brain, 'now called work', with which he would have filled a leisure more abundant without ever degenerating into 'idleness and aimlessness'. His enemy, like the Webbs', was vacuity, and his ideal not far removed from what they would have called 'character' or 'personality'.[127]

Morris died in 1896 and there is no way of knowing what he would have made of later debates. There were many, however, who claimed to speak on his behalf. Among them was his disciple and self-styled torch-bearer, the ILP propagandist J. Bruce Glasier, who in his book The *Meaning of Socialism* (1919) carried forward this part of Morris's credo to the socialist debates of the post-First World War period. Just like his teacher, for the meaning of socialism Glasier looked beyond the mere limitation of working hours:

> will not both men and women ... be eager to work freely and without regard to length of hours for the enjoyment of exercising their strength and skill and adding to their own comfort and as a free gift to the commonwealth? Will they not wish to give a considerable part of their leisure hours to their gardens, to rebuilding, decorating and furnishing their homes, to building public halls for art and science, to working in municipal craft-workshops and scientific laboratories, or to getting up concerts, plays and other means of education and entertainment? For you do not, I hope, really believe that the citizens in a Socialist community will want to spend one half of the day doing nothing except engaging in idle chatter, loafing at street corners, or watching other people making themselves happy by exercising their energies and abilities at games and other performances – as, alas, so many people do to-day, knowing no better how to pass the time?

With which passage we can compare the post-materialist vision of the Webbs:

> we may expect, in the distant future, whilst the supply of food, clothing and other material things will represent a steadily diminishing proportion of the community's production, there will be a continuous increase in the proportion represented by such common services as education, music, and the theatre, and social intercourse between the peoples of different regions of the earth. The beauty of the landscape may even come to be deemed as important as the wheatfields; the purity of the atmosphere and uninterrupted sunshine as valuable as a multiplication of factories ... More and more of [the unions'] activities will be devoted, not to organising their work in its aspect of constituting the price that they pay for the privilege of living, but to developing that side of it which is beyond money and price – for which they can, indeed, never be paid – when it is an expression of their own creative activity, their own inventive faculty, their own exuberant energy. On this side of the association it will not be a question of government, even of self-government, but of free comradeship ... for the cultivation in common of the free life of the spirit.[128]

In passing, it may be noted that repeatedly featuring among the Webbs' indictments of capitalism was its sole concern with the 'cheapest possible exploitation' of natural resources, without regard to their 'wise conservation' or 'such priceless amenities as pure air, unpolluted streams and unspoilt scenery'.[129] Nevertheless, such incidental affinities with the ecological holism of the Glasiers matter less in this context than the thorough confusion of what then seemed some of the salient categories of socialist debate.[130] With 'real leisure in work', and purposive leisure as a 'direct good to the community', it is difficult indeed to conceive how such passionate debates took place around so slippery and elusive a demarcation. Within work and beyond, socialists stood for both the expansion and fulfilment of opportunity that they referred to as the 'fuller' life, and Morris more particularly as the 'full and reasonable life'. One of the Victorian moralists referred to by Thompson railed at what he called the 'annihilation' of time. Socialists too, albeit from the standpoint of human emancipation and potentiality, were exactly such enemies of vacancy.[131]

Anticipating for a moment, it may be noted that Morris's memory was to be invoked far more often than Bellamy's, let alone Sidney Webb's, when visitors beheld the prospect of busy-ness which was Soviet Russia. Usually it was Morris's ideal of fellowship that was invoked; sometimes it was also the transformation of work. Indeed, while almost everybody laid claim to some aspect of Morris, this element of his teaching was particularly seized upon by Britain's communists. Some of them, perhaps, did so for a reminder of aspirations buried under Stalinist *realpolitik*; more of them on the assumption that Stalinism itself represented the realisation of those aspirations.[132] In 1952, for example, the communist historian A.L. Morton brought his *English Utopia* to fruition not with Bellamy, whom he dismissed as a 'mechanical' bureaucrat, but with the culminating vision of Morris – prefatory to discussing the Stalin plans which were then remaking even the Russian climate.[133]

Conceived in the same spirit was E.P. Thompson's marvellous but similarly blemished monument to Morris, published three years later. Acknowledging as his mentor the former LRD volunteer, Dona Torr, and as his 'masterly' precursor Cole's former sidekick Arnot, Thompson persuaded Cole himself to cast a kindly eye over his conclusions. In these, while conceding that Morris did not foresee the full 'excitement of collective industrial creation', Thompson argued that his deeper ambitions were being realised in the 'great construction projects' of the USSR. As to Morris's 'factory that might be' – the title of one of his most inspirational essays – that factory now existed in Soviet Russia, and Thompson quoted that other great diagnostician of alienation, J.V. Stalin, to capture its achievements in the all-round development of human faculty and transformation of labour from toil into pleasure. Thompson, of course, was also to find in Morris the materials for a searing critique of Stalinism: exactly as, had they lived until 1956, the Webbs might have rediscovered their own more sceptical intelligence. These lineages, in other words, were never static or straightforward, and can never offer more than possible connections. Even so, in explaining the Stalinist attachments that were such a feature of the inter-war decades, the opposition of a Morris-derived guilds tradition to one of Fabian state collectivism offers extraordinarily little in the way of workable correlations.[134]

Instead, we are left with the 'making' of socialists: a shared aspiration which, whether in its environmental or evangelical sense, in Owen's thought or in Morris's, implied the unmaking or replacement of the currently prevalent non-socialists. The Webbs, who in *Soviet Communism* were to describe this process as 'the remaking of man', spelt out its basic rationale as early as 1913 in connection with their own utopian vision of the 'participation in all social power by every adult citizen'.

> ... Socialists are the last to ignore that what they demand is against the present 'human nature' of the majority of the community. Just for this reason is it that the Socialist Movement is valuable and vital. Every reformer – especially every religious reformer – begins by being against the 'human nature' of his time and place. The whole process of civilisation has been one of raising 'human nature' to higher planes of moral purpose and practical achievement.[135]

Cole believed that his own optimistic reading of human nature was fundamentally at odds with the 'Fabian heresy of distrust'.[136] In reality, both he and the Webbs were at one in holding, first, that human nature was socially constructed and therefore malleable; secondly, that a socialist human nature would therefore transcend the limitations of capitalist humanity; and finally, that this indeed was the whole point of socialism. Cole, if anything, was decidedly the more exacting, for the Webbs, in spite of countless pungent asides, did at least discern in the unions and co-operatives as they existed a capacity for self-government within the future Co-operative Commonwealth. Cole, by contrast, tended to abstract the claims of democracy from its existing institutions, and described even the unions' active personnel – the cadres, one would have thought, of his guild society – as merely 'the residue which Capitalist selection leaves behind'.[137] 'Guild Socialist man chose his ideal and willed its achievement', Wright argues: but 'Guild Socialist man' was that Frankenstein of self-government, Cole himself.[138]

If, as Henry Drucker wryly argues, Tawney's agent of human progress was cast as a schoolteacher, Cole's was a veritable demiurge moulding the future out of human clay. Perhaps this was the 'Bolshevik soul in a Fabian muzzle' for which Cole has been remembered in Maurice Reckitt's epigram. 'The working class is for a Lenin what ore is for a metalworker', Maxim Gorky wrote in 1917, and Cole the same year merely preferred a less plebeian metaphor. 'We', he wrote, 'are the world's builders. We have to hew our statue out of the block of marble, and the material on which we have to work is the modern wage-slave.'[139] Confronted with this 'great inert mass', contented with the prospect of mere material comfort, Cole himself stepped forward as the wage slave's Wilberforce. 'Slavery would never have been ended if we had waited for the slaves to end it, or even to revolt against it in their minds', he wrote a few years later in an essay on Henry Ford.

> A contented slave – even a whole population of contented slaves – is not a sufficient defence of slavery ... If men are as Henry Ford believes they are, is that a reason for acting on their being so, or is it not rather a powerful reason for so acting as to make them different? ... Does it allow them to be men as of good 'quality' as they are capable of being? With John Ruskin and William Morris, I say without hesitation that it does not ... I say that it is bad for the quality of human living.

Perhaps so emphatic a claim was aimed at quelling the 'inner voice' to which Cole was to ascribe his own very considerable apostasy of the late 1920s. 'But to make men, and not cars', he reminded the mere motor manufacturer with messianic emphasis, 'is the supreme task of leadership'.[140] Stalin too had a phrase for it: 'engineers of human souls'.

Obviously, the identification of attitudes which could and often did lead to the idealisation of Bolshevism provides only a partial view of these movements – though not, perhaps, more partial than accounts which pass over them completely. Instead of regarding these as incidental blemishes, an anatomy of socialist politics is required that can accommodate and respond to such embarrassments. A.J. Polan invokes Foucault's proposed reading of marxism in the light of Stalinism: not, he said, to establish the distortions or misunderstandings by which the original theory could thus have been betrayed, but to re-interrogate the theory itself from the standpoint of such a development. 'Rather than searching in those texts for a condemnation in advance of the Gulag', Foucault wrote, 'it is a matter of asking what in those texts could have made the Gulag possible ...'[141]

In reality one needs to do both. Searching out only what made the Gulag possible, and not what might have condemned or prevented it, means ending up with the Gulag – or in this context a predisposition towards the system which produced it – seeming not only possible but inevitable. Moreover, in what truly would be a 'grand narrative' of marxism, those other possibilities are marginalised, not all of them by any means the 'texts' with which Polan is preoccupied, that were also necessary to produce the Gulag. In all the countless possibilities of a text, unless a sense is retained of how some alone are realised, and always incompletely, the end result will be an unabashed teleology. Polan himself, in applying Foucault's dictum, does not avoid this danger, or the treacherous shorthand of 'inevitability', when he moves from textual analysis to the plane of historical explanation.[142]

Certainly, in the case of the Webbs' unusually convoluted trajectory, no teleology will explain how they spent ten years condemning Bolshevism and the next ten extolling it as a new civilisation. Had they only died at sixty, the inevitable would never even have been suspected – as who would suspect it of Morris or Keir Hardie? Had they died instead at seventy, in the mid-1920s, then the dabbling with socialist blueprints would have seemed a mere subplot, and Sidney's decorous parliamentarism a return to the crablike sideways march of Fabian collectivism. Though reflecting longstanding Webbian concerns, the grander vision they had briefly entertained seemed unsustainable beyond that moment of unbridled imagination that followed the armistice. Even Beatrice, when in November 1930 she wrote a new preface to her original book on co-operation, could think of no better peroration on the Co-operative Commonwealth than to invoke the second Labour government – which was, even as she wrote, demonstrating beyond all cavil that it was not the means of achieving it.[143]

The debacle which eventually befell that government, along with the slower discrediting of other agencies of transformation, were to prove critical in precipitating the Webbs onto uncharted paths. Superficially, the transformation was an abrupt one, unheralded by any symptom of radicalisation in the preceding decade; with Sidney in the public eye, it was with 'Sidneywebbicalism' that the couple were once more primarily identified. Only the closer study allowed by Beatrice's diaries reveals an underlying strain of pessimism and emotional leaning to the left that was to help them find their democracy of consumers in its very antithesis

**NOTES**

1. Hobsbawm, 'Fabians', p. 255; Harrison provides a lucid summary of some of the volume's main themes, *Life and Times*, pp. 235-51.
2. M. Cole, *Story*, p. 179; Harrison, *Life and Times*, pp. 258-61.
3. *CMGB*, pp. 232-40 and preface (1930), p. xxi.
4. Shaw cited Taylor, *Annie Besant*, p. 182.
5. BWD 12 June 1895* and 15 June 1903, *OP*, p. 268.
6. Cole, *The World of Labour*, Bell, 1913, p. 8.
7. BW to Pease, 18 April 1893 in Mackenzie, *Letters*, vol. 2, p. 5; BWD 27 November 1887, Mackenzie, vol. 1, pp. 222-3.
8. For the renunciation of her opposition to women's suffrage see *OP*, pp. 360-3.
9. Edward Pease, *The History of the Fabian Society*, A.C. Fifield, 1916, p. 220; BWD, 2 January 1914; Fabian Society annual reports for 1913 and 1914; Passfield papers, 2/4/F/6, BW to Betty Balfour, 22 August 1913.
10. SW, 'Fabianism justified'.
11. 'I designing the separate chapters and dictating a rough draft and re-dictating until it expresses my mind, and then Sidney correcting all of it and re-writing and adding sections to it after discussions with me'; see BWD, 12 March, 5 July 1919 and 11 May 1920 for *CSC*; BWD 1 July 1920, 16 July and 28 August* 1921 for *CCM*.
12. BWD 5 July, 18 November and 1 December 1919.
13. Leonard Woolf papers III, Woolf to Margaret Llewellyn Davies, 27 July 1914.
14. See *WMT*, p. 111 and passim; SW, 'The employer of tomorrow'. For Sidney's collectivism see for example his review of Emil Davies's *The*

*Collectivist State*, *Fabian News*, December 1914 and Margaret Cole's observations in her 'Labour Research', p. 155.

15. BW to SW, 18 or 19 October 1910 in Mackenzie, *Letters*, vol. 2, p. 353.
16. BWD 3 July and 8-9 December 1903, Mackenzie vol. 2, pp. 285-6, 306-8
17. LRD archives, Ablett, 'Syndicalism', FRD conference on the control of industry, 1913.
18. *The Miners' Next Step* cited Barrow, *Democratic Ideas*, p. 246; Bukharin, *ABC*, pp. 118 and 335-6.
19. SWML, Arnot interviewed by Hwyel Francis, 6 March 1973; Cole, cited M. Cole, *Life*, p. 56.
20. David Lloyd George, *War Memoirs*, Odhams edn, 2 vols, nd, pp. 1160-2; see also Paul Barton Johnson, *Land Fit for Heroes. The planning of British reconstruction 1916-1919*, University of Chicago Press, 1968, pp. 48-54.
21. BWD 3 June 1917 with note dated May 1918*; also BWD 3 August 1916. Beatrice called it the 'Greenwood cum Cole Report', alluding to Cole's influence over the committee's secretary, Arthur Greenwood, whom he knew through the WEA. See also Winter, *Socialism*, pp. 135-8 and, for the National Industrial Conference M. Cole, *Life*, pp. 99-100. For Cole's theoretical justification of such arrangements, see *Self-Government*, pp. 91-2, 99-100.
22. BW, lecture on 'Proposed organisation of employers in state-aided associations', *Fabian News*, April 1917, p. 19; also *HTU*, pp. 653-4.
23. *New Statesman and Nation*, 21 January 1922, p. 452
24. Or of course *Socialist* Commonwealth as in the title of their *Constitution*. On 'Co-operative Commonwealth' see Keith Harding, 'The "Co-operative Commonwealth"; Ireland, Larkin and the *Daily Herald*', with editorial note, in Yeo, *New Views*, pp. 88 ff; also Yeo, 'Three socialisms', p. 228. As Yeo points out, the phrase had come to have rather different connotations from those of the 'German' state socialism of Lawrence Gronlund's original *Co-operative Commonwealth* (first British edition, 1886).
25. See e.g. Leonard Woolf, *Co-operation and the Future of Industry*, Allen & Unwin, 1919.
26. Beatrice to Redfern, 22 March 1920, Mackenzie, *Letters*, vol. 2, p. 133.
27. Poisson, *The Co-operative Republic* (1920), Manchester: Co-operative Union, 1925, pp. 84, 87 ff and passim.
28. Though not strictly interchangeable, *la République coopérative* was itself often translated as 'co-operative commonwealth'; see for example Charles Gide, *Consumers' Co-operative Societies*, New York: Alfred A. Knopf, 1922, p. 287.
29. *CSC*, p. 168; *CCM*, pp. vi-vii, 383-4.
30. Passfield papers 6/73, lecture to Manchester College of Technology, c. 1920.
31. *CCM*, pp. 179-81, 272 ff, 350. Compare the more limited conception in *CMGB*, p. 232, on which Harrison's claims in 'Sidney', p. 53, must be based.
32. Sidney Pollard, 'The Foundation of the Co-operative Party' in Briggs and Saville, *Essays*, pp. 201 ff; *CCM*, pp. 275 ff; E.L. Poulton, TUC president, cited *Co-operative News*, 10 September 1921. It is notable that WEWNC in 1914 was established by the TUC, GFTU and Labour Party, but

required the co-option of co-operators; see Harrison, 'War Emergency', pp. 211-15.

33. LRD archives, LRD minutes 18 January, 1 March and 6 September 1918. In six months of these arrangements some 160 co-op. affiliations are recorded and a 'Monthly Circular statement' of May 1921 records a circulation divided fairly evenly between 'general section' (362), co-operative organisations (368) and trades councils or 'Trade Union Survey' (349). It appears (LRD minutes, 5 August 1921) that the arrangement with the CU was terminated following the department's exclusion from the Labour Party.
34. See e.g. S.G. Hobson with A.R. Orage (ed.), *National Guilds. An enquiry into the wage system and the way out* (1914), Bell, 1917 edn, p. 107; John Jagger, 'The co-operative commissariat of Labour', *Labour Monthly*, August 1922, pp. 103-9.
35. Cole papers, D3/10/5-9, draft memorandum c. October 1919 (2nd draft); A1/50/13, lecture on Guild Socialism, 9 February 1921; LRD archives, LRD minutes, 18 October 1918 for Co-op Section. For the 'conflict of principle' between co-operation (except as a distributive mechanism) and the guild idea, see Cole papers D3/18/2, Cole to Mrs Ellingham (copy), 5 November 1914.
36. Bramley, *Co-operative News*, 16 July 1921 and *Why Trade Unionists should be Co-operators*, Manchester: Co-operative Union, 1924.
37. E.L. Poulton, *Co-operative News*, 10 September 1921.
38. Walter Citrine, *Men and Work. An autobiography*, Hutchinsons, 1964, p. 253; Margaret Morris, *The General Strike*, Penguin, 1976, pp. 66-8.
39. A first minor variant took the form of a *New Statesman* supplement, 30 May 1914. In 1916 the Webbs had then agreed to a title on 'The position and prospects of the Co-operative Movement throughout the World' for Allen & Unwin but this never appeared (LRD archives, FRD EC minutes, 31 March 1916).
40. M. Cole, *Life*, pp. 55, 256-7; M. Cole, *Beatrice*, p. 144. Co-operation is omitted entirely from the collection *The Webbs and Their Work*. For the Webbs' *Constitution* there is a brief but compelling commentary by Rodney Barker, 'The Fabian state' in Pimlott, *Fabian Essays*, pp. 27-38.
41. BWD 1 July 1920, 28 August and 7 and 24 December* 1921; see also BWD 2 January 1901 and 21 April 1911, *OP*, pp. 205, 473 for similar comments regarding their work on local government and the Poor Law.
42. BWD 29 January 1921.
43. BWD 16 July 1921.
44. Shaw to W.A. Robson, 3 July 1943, in Dan H. Laurence, *Bernard Shaw. Collected letters 1926-1950*, Viking Penguin, 1988, pp. 671-2; BWD 1 February 1895, Mackenzie vol. 2, pp. 66-7; BWD 24 December 1921* and 17 October 1922.
45. Chris Waters, *British Socialists and the Politics of Popular Culture 1884-1914*, Manchester: MUP, 1990, pp. 1-15 and 43-64; Beilharz, *Labour's Utopias*, pp. 7-10, 94-109, 120-1.
46. Spencer, *Autobiography*, vol. 1, pp. 412-13; *WMT*, p. 11.
47. Dona Torr, *Tom Mann and his Times. Volume one: 1856-1890*, Lawrence & Wishart, 1956, pp. 214-25, Joseph White, *Tom Mann*, Manchester: MUP, 1991, pp. 18-24, 55-62, BWD 19 November 1889, Mackenzie vol. 1,

304; A.A. Purcell, 'The importance of May Day', *Labour Monthly*, April 1926, p. 210, NAFTA *Monthly Report*, January 1919, p. 13; TUC *Report of Proceedings*, 1918.

48. See *Bolshevism and the British Left*, vol. 1, ch. 6.
49. David R. Roediger & Philip S. Foner, *Our Own Time. A history of American Labor and the working day*, Verso edn, 1989, provides an excellent introduction to these issues in an American context.
50. Jose Harris, *Unemployment and Politics. A study in English social policy 1886-1914*, Oxford: OUP, 1972, pp. 58-73; SW, NCPD, *Reports and Proceedings*, 1912, pp. 445-73; *ID*, p. 849; SW, *A Plea for an Eight Hours Bill*, Fabian Society, 1892.
51. *CCM*, pp. 479-87.
52. C.A.R. Crosland, *The Future of Socialism*, Cape, 1956, p. 290.
53. *CSC*, p. xii; *DCC*, pp. 69.
54. *WMT*, pp. 11-12. Gladkov's *Cement* and Ilyenkov's *Driving Axle* were published in English in 1929 and 1933 respectively.
55. Redfern, 'The store movement'.
56. For a good example see Philip Snowden, *Socialism and Syndicalism*, Collins, n.d., 1912?, pp. 185-92.
57. Snowden, 'State socialism and National Guilds', *Socialist Review*, April-June 1916, pp. 120-1. Note also Clifford Allen's diary entry of 22 January 1919 following a conference of ILPers concerning guild socialism: 'Snowden by far the worst. He seems to have very little grip on the industrial side of things.' (Martin Gilbert, *Plough My Own Furrow*, Longman, 1965, p. 128.)
58. Cole papers, A1/1/4, typescript article on Henry Ford, n.d., early 1930s?
59. Crosland, *Future*, p. 341.
60. Though with a slightly different usage, I take the phrase qualitative socialists from Nicholas Ellison, *Egalitarian Thought and Labour Politics. Retreating visions*, Routledge, 1994.
61. *ID*, pp. 823-4.
62. SW, review of Hobson's *National Guilds*, *Fabian News*, July 1914, pp. 61-2; SW, *Socialism: true and false*, p. 14; *HTU*, p. 652.
63. *CSC*, pp. 22-3, 42-3, 176 ff.
64. Indeed, when, even in *Industrial Democracy*, the Webbs indicted the 'anarchic irresponsibility' of the consumer, it was not, at least in this context, in relation to the 'wasteful misallocation of resources', but rather the disregard of the legitimate interests of the producer; see Thompson, *Political Economy*, p18; also *ID*, p. 674, *CSC*, pp. xii-xiii.
65. See Allen's diary entries of 18 and 22 January 1919: 'He [Cole] was more delightful than I could have imagined. Wants to work with me – the very thing I wanted.' (Gilbert, *Plough My Own Furrow*, pp. 127-8.)
66. Attlee, 'Guild v. municipal socialism. A reply', *Socialist Review*, May 1923, pp. 213-15.
67. BWD 10 February 1919; William Graham, *The Wages of Labour* (1921), Cassells, 1924 edn, pp. 145 ff.
68. MacDonald, *Socialist Review*, January-March 1921, pp. 10-11. For MacDonald's earlier elevation of the state over 'apparently more voluntary forms of organisation', see for example his 'The people in power' in Stanton Coit, ed., *Ethical Democracy. Essays in social dynamics*, Grant

Richards, 1900, p. 79.

69. Fenner Brockway, *Inside the Left. Thirty years of platform, press, prison and parliament*, Allen & Unwin, 1942, p. 142; G.D.H. Cole, *A History of the British Labour Party from 1914*, Routledge & Kegan Paul, 1948, pp. 148-50, describing Attlee as a 'prominent figure' in the agitation for workers' control.
70. *CSC*, pp. 50-8, 274-7; *ID*, new introduction (September 1920), pp. xv-xvii; *CCM*, pp. 474-5.
71. Carpenter, *G.D.H. Cole*, p. 83, Cole, *Self-Government*, pp. 58 ff, 176-7 and Cole, *Guild Socialism*, Fabian Society 1920, pp. 15-16.
72. See Krishan Kumar, *Prophecy and Progress. The sociology of industrial and post-industrial society*, Penguin edn, 1978, pp. 83-8.
73. *CSC*, pp. 291-2.
74. *ID*, p. 514; Passfield papers 2/4/F/5, BW to Betty Balfour, 15 October 1912. Henry Pelling, *America and the British Left*, A. &. C. Black, 1956, pp. 95-6, notes the contrast with Sidney's earlier welcome for the Premium Bonus system.
75. See Woolf papers IIIa, BW to Woolf 23 November 1914.
76. *CCM*, p. 336.
77. Or, they went on, though this was certainly a Shavian interpolation, 'as is seen in such a boxing champion as Carpentier'; *CSC*, pp. 51-8, 299-304; for continuing scepticism about producer innovation see however *CCM*, pp. 466-7.
78. For Bramley's Fabian associations see BWD 13 December 1916* and 6 March 1917*, *Fabian News*, November 1916, p. 45.
79. See NAFTA *Monthly Report*, August 1915, p. 13 and Bramley's 'Craft versus industrial unions' in the *Labour Year Book* for 1916.
80. Fred Bramley, 'Trade unionism and the craftsman', *Socialist Review*, October 1922, pp. 163-9.
81. Bramley, *Relations with Russia*, speech to IFTU, 6 February 1925, 'Trade Union Unity', 1925, p. 10.
82. George Hicks, 'Craft or class. The future of trade union organisation', *Labour Magazine*, November 1922, p. 303.
83. *CCM*, pp. 46 ff, 306, 331-8; *CSC*, pp. 99-100.
84. W.A. Robson, *Fabian News*, June 1922, pp. 29-30; *CCM*, pp. 83, 298 ff, 368.
85. *Socialism: true and false*, p. 13.
86. Mellor, *Direct Action*, pp. 91-5, also ch. 4: 'The community'.
87. M. Cole, *Life*, pp. 56, 90-3.
88. BWD, 15 December 1916*.
89. SW to Leonard Courtney, 4 November 1909 in Mackenzie, *Letters*, vol. 2, pp. 336-7; *CSC*, pp. 139-41, 144.
90. For the opposite view see e.g. Barrow, *Democratic Ideas*, p. 34, referring to *ID* and arguably confusing 'model' and analogy.
91. *CSC*, pp. 119-20, 125-6, 134; *CCM*, pp. 118-25.
92. *CSC*, p. 145.
93. *CSC*, pp. 144-5.
94. *MA*, p. 303; BWD 25 February 1930.
95. SW to Wells, 15 June 1907, Mackenzie, *Letters*, vol. 2, pp. 263-5.
96. Cole, *Self-Government*, p. 186; Wright, *G.D.H. Cole*, pp. 57-9.

97. *CCM*, p. 426; Leonard Woolf papers IIIa, Sidney to Woolf, 16 May 1921.
98. *CSC*, pp. 297-8, compared with *ID*, pp. 813-14
99. 'The speeches of the labour orator were vociferously applauded in the pit and gallery; the doctor's heated rejoinders evoked similar applause from the dress circle and stalls; a unique occurrence in our thirty years' experience of the theatre ...' (*Co-operative News*, 9 July 1921). See also Paddy Maguire, 'Co-operation and crisis. Government, co-operation and politics, 1917-1922' in Yeo, *New Views*, p. 193.
100. *CSC*, pp. 168 ff; *CCM*, pp. 383-4.
101. Wright, *G.D.H. Cole*, pp. 51-2.
102. LRD archives, BW, printed memorandum on 'Committee of Inquiry on the Control of Industry', 1913.
103. See the reviews of *CCM* by Robson and Woolf.
104. A.J. Polan, *Lenin and the End of Politics*, Methuen, 1984, pp. 129-30, 152 and passim.
105. *CSC*, pp. 296, 341-2.
106. *CCM*, pp. 480-1; Thompson, *Political Economy*, p. 45.
107. BWD 8 December 1913.
108. *CSC*, pp. 267-8; Passfield papers, 6/53, interview with the *British Weekly*, 29 June 1893.
109. *CMGB*, pp. 24-5.
110. *ID*, p. 326.
111. *ID*, pp. 324-8.
112. *PD*, p. 129.
113. E.P. Thompson, 'Time, work-discipline and industrial capitalism' in his *Customs in Common*, Penguin edn, 1993, pp. 352-403; see also Waters, *British Socialists*.
114. S. & B. Webb, *The Decay of Capitalist Civilisation* (henceforth *DCC*), Fabian Society and Allen & Unwin, 1923, pp. 102-11.
115. BWD 23 December 1925.
116. Crosland, *Future*, pp. 521-4.
117. Graham, *Wages*, pp. 13-15, 56; G.D.H. Cole, *Principles of Economic Planning*, Macmillan, 1935, pp. 224 ff.
118. Waters, *British Socialists*, pp. 2-4 and passim.
119. Lafargue, cited Waters, *British Socialists*, p. 5-6.
120. *ID*, p. 849.
121. Crosland, *Future*, p. 290; Waters, pp. 187-95 for a summation of his views. It will be seen that Waters's positing of a Morris tradition relatively free of this tension is not followed here.
122. Waters, *British Socialists*, p. 4.
123. For some of the same problems confronting even the boldest and most innovative of European socialist movements, see Helmut Gruber, *Red Vienna. Experiment in working-class culture 1919-1934*, New York: OUP, 1991, esp. chs 4-5.
124. Cited Williams, *Culture*, p. 187.
125. Cole, *Self-Government*, p. 51-2; Wright, *G.D.H. Cole*, p. 27.
126. J. Bruce Glasier, *William Morris and the Early Days of the Socialist Movement*, Longman, 1921, p. 150; Morris, reviews of *Looking Backwards* and *Fabian Essays*, reprinted in Nicholas Salmon, ed., *William Morris. Political writings: contributions to Justice and Commonweal 1883-*

*1890*, Bristol: Thoemmes Press, 1994, pp. 419-25 and 457-63.

127. Morris, 'How we live and how we might live' (1887) and 'How I became a socialist' (1894) in A.L. Morton, ed., *Political Writings of William Morris*, Lawrence & Wishart, 1973, pp. 148-54, 239; Ernest Belfort Bax and William Morris, 'Socialism from the root up. Chapter 23: socialism triumphant (1)' (1888) in Salmon, *Political writings*, pp. 611-17.
128. J. Bruce Glasier, *The Meaning of Socialism*, National Labour Press, 1919, pp. 92 ff; *CCM*, pp. 483-6.
129. See also *CSC*, pp. 150-1.
130. For the Glasiers' ecological outlook see Laurence Thompson, *The Enthusiasts*, Gollancz, 1971, p. 75.
131. John Foster (1821) cited Thompson, 'Time', p. 395.
132. See Douglas Hyde, *I Believed*, Heinemann, 1951, pp. 36, 185-6, for the first such case.
133. A.L. Morton, *The English Utopia*, Lawrence & Wishart, 1952, pp. 149-73, 212-13; Lionel Munby, 'William Morris', *Communist Review*, July 1948, pp. 215-20.
134. E.P. Thompson, *William Morris. Romantic to revolutionary*, Lawrence & Wishart, 1955, pp. 743, 760, citing Stalin's *Economic Problems of Socialism in the USSR* (1952). Arnot's *William Morris. A vindication* was published by Martin Lawrence in 1934.
135. *New Statesman*, 3 May 1913, pp. 107-8.
136. Cole, *Self-Government*, p. 166.
137. Cole, *Labour in the Commonwealth*, Headley, 1918, p. 68.
138. Wright, *G.D.H. Cole*, pp. 77 and 86.
139. H.M. Drucker, *Doctrine and Ethos in the Labour Party*, Allen & Unwin, 1979, pp. 52-3; Maxim Gorky, *Untimely Thoughts. Essays on revolution, culture and the Bolsheviks 1917-1918*, Garnstone Press, 1968, p. 89; Cole, *Self-Government*, pp. 155, 207.
140. Cole, *Self-Government*, p. 155; Cole papers, A1/1/4, typescript article on Ford, n.d.; G.D.H. Cole, *The Next Ten Years in British Social and Economic Policy*, Macmillan, 1929, p. viii. For Cole's apostasy, see ch. 8 below.
141. Polan, *Lenin*, p. 183.
142. For example, Polan descibes the 'inevitability' of the Lenin and Stalin cult in extravagant terms: 'According to the culture he had created, he was ... a figure of transcendental significance ... the living embodiment of the identical subject-object. How, then, could one do less than worship him ...?' Polan, *Lenin*, p. 144 and ch. 4 passim. For the classic example of this method and the dangers of teleology, see J.L. Talmon, *The Origins of Totalitarian Democracy* (1952), New York: Norton Library edn, 1970.
143. *CMGB*, new preface, 1930, pp. xxi-xxii.

*Chapter six*

# Cobwebs and decay: the Webbs in the 1920s

**I**

No phrase better encapsulates the Webbs' image in the 1920s than 'the inevitability of gradualness'. Coined by Sidney in his address to the 1923 Labour Party conference, it perfectly captures the post-war recovery of Fabian certainties and their ready identification with the advance of parliamentary socialism. Sidney himself was the very incarnation of Labour's new respectability. Just a few years earlier his role in the drafting of Labour resolutions had, by common consent, not been publicised.[1] Now, as principal author of the party's programme and constitution, he was saluted by Labour's official magazine as 'the maker of British Socialism ... the architect of the Labour Party ... an epitome of the history of the British Labour Movement'. Here at least there was no sense of his peripherality. 'It was Mr Webb who transformed the insurrectionary Socialism of a generation ago into a political programme which appealed to the commonsense of the British working-class movement and brought the Labour Party into existence', the article effused. 'At every stage of its development the Labour Movement has, consciously or unconsciously, been under the influence of Mr Webb ...'[2]

Nor was it only his unmistakeable circumlocutions that he contributed to the party's development. In 1922 he was at last elected MP, for the Durham miners' seat of Seaham, and capped his public career as a cabinet minister in the first two Labour governments. Alike in its composition and in its deference to established expectations, he hailed the first of these governments as the crowning vindication of Fabianism, and as President of the Board of Trade proved moderate and ineffective even by the unexacting standards of the MacDonald era. 'Socialism was not obtained by the creation of Socialists', he declared, which certainly was true of the government in question; it depended on 'gentle persistent pressure and complete absence of shock'. Willingly restrained by the demand of continuous authority and the brake of a mass electorate, Sidney approved the inclusion in the cabinet of Liberals and Tories and took special comfort from Labour's readiness to govern even against its own sectional interests.[3] A committee that he established on the revival of trade was actually boycotted by the TUC, and the civil servant Thomas Jones recorded his disappointment that so prolific a writer of cures for unemployment should know of no other remedy available to the government.[4] Publicly the most loyal, and privately the most supportive of MacDonald's deputies, in 1929 Sidney acquired the uncoveted title of Lord Passfield and sat in the Lords as Labour's colonial secretary. From Ben Tillett, representing a broader body of disaffected trade unionists, his performance in office had already earned the less flattering sobriquet of 'cob-webb'.[5]

In their contemporaries' eyes, these post-war Fabians had not so much lost their identity in the Labour Party as insinuated their defining characteristics upon it. John Strachey, then an up-and-coming Labour politician, was to describe Sidney's double inevitability of social progress and Labour advance as the salient feature of the 'British socialism' of the 1920s, with Sidney himself depicted as the movement's intellectual pilot.[6] In such interpretations, the shipwreck of 1931 was a critical watershed, the inauguration for the British left of the 'red decade' of 'the 1930s', in which the abandonment of Webbism by its progenitors had from the outset a special symbolic resonance.[7] Like Strachey himself, it looked as if the Webbs had staggered overnight from the debacle of reformism to its seeming antithesis. Shaw's return from Russia, pronouncing Stalin the inheritor of Fabianism, added a touch of theatricality that features prominently in most accounts.[8] So dramatic a denouement seems both to confirm the essential compatibility of these rival schools of inevitability, Fabian and Stalinist, while attesting the exhaustion of the first of them through the collapse of the Labour government.

For Sidney, conceivably, such a summary will do service; and with the turn to the masculine world of party politics it was with Sidney that the couple's public profile was once more identified. Indeed, in the *Labour Magazine*'s panegyric, his career was fulsomely described without it at any point being mentioned that he had a collaborator in his life's work. For Beatrice, even regardless of such oversights, the role now allotted her was an uncongenial and frustrating one. As recently as 1917 she had sought to dissuade Sidney from what she slightingly described as 'ostensible leadership', which for her was not even that.[9] A model member's wife, she fired off letters to Sidney's women constituents and conscientiously mingled with Labour's parliamentarians, 'honestly', as she put it, 'try[ing] to show the symptoms of being interested'. But her own hankerings were different ones: for 'the cottage and the writing of books'.[10] The cottage was the retreat at Passfield Corner on the Surrey-Hampshire border, which the couple bought in 1923, moving in properly only five years afterwards on account of Sidney's career. The books were ones in which Beatrice's own intellect might have found expression and recognition, but which again she was unable to write without her husband and helpmate.

In the meantime, her diaries recorded what gradually developed into a profound scepticism as to the future of moral or social progress. Pulled both right and left by instincts for order, morality and social justice, already by the end of the 1920s Beatrice began to exhibit her interest in what was at once the most conservative and most uncompromising of utopias. The demise of the second Labour government thus had for the Webbs a double significance: not just dashing hopes in Labour's new social order, but permitting the last of those shifts from Webb to Webb which had so often marked a realignment in their thinking, while at the same time allowing its expression in a major work of research. *Soviet Communism* would fully bear Sidney's imprint, and may indeed be considered a last attempted resolution of the differing impulses that the couple's entire partnership had been spent in negotiating. Nevertheless, like the co-operative and trade union studies, the enterprise was ultimately the product of Beatrice's more restless imagination. That alone suggests the need for a major re-evaluation of its significance. If the focus is on Sidney and his political career, then the leap in the Webbs' outlook is accentuated, from MacDonaldism to Stalinism in what seems like eighty days. Only in Beatrice's diaries, and in the subtexts of their rare collaborations, is the moodier alter ego to this unsuspected Dr Jekyll of reformism recorded.

## II

The bifurcation can be traced from the war years. Whereas in respect of the control of industry these years involved significant revivals and continuities in the Webbs' thinking, on the broader issues of governance and civilisation supposedly underlying the conflict they marked a more obvious turning point. Sidney, predictably, was the less affected. Whatever his failings, he could not have been described as warlike or vindictive, and in the South African war had even leant towards the pro-Boers while maintaining a studied public neutrality.[11] Probably Shaw was right to suggest that, preoccupied with domestic reconstruction, he simply deferred on such issues to *Monsieur Tout le Monde*.[12] Pacific but unimaginative, he privately sanctioned efforts to stem racial bitterness and promote 'peace and goodwill on earth', while lending his voice to pro-war propaganda and recruiting campaigns. Though generally avoiding the stridency of other social imperialists, even in his own home he came across as 'stolidly patriotic', and with his usual administrative zeal countenanced '*Universal submission* to the National Need', that is, the full Servile State as an emergency war measure.[13] With his renewed prominence as a public figure, it is to Sidney that we owe the Webbs' routine identification with the hyper-collectivism of 'war socialism'.[14]

Beatrice, in a reversal of their respective positions in 1900, accepted the necessity of the war with a heavier heart and hardly a glimmer of conventional patriotism. Even so active an opponent of the war as Fenner Brockway recalled unambiguously her assent to that position.[15] Agnostic and resigned in her better moods, in her worse ones she tended towards a Fabian version of revolutionary defeatism, expressed in catastrophic terms. The very week the war broke out she wished all its participants 'soundly beaten', and two months later, on declining to sign an anti-German manifesto, speculated whether the best outcome to the conflict might not be the 'complete collapse' of all the great powers involved.[16] 'I want a peace in which none of the great belligerents gain anything whatsoever', she wrote at the time of her breakdown. 'I want all of them to feel that the war has been a hideous calamity without any compensating advantages – a gigantic and wicked folly from which no good can come ... I should like the propertied classes ... to be mulcted and the working classes to suffer sufficiently to make them wisely revolutionary'.[17]

Such reactions to the war, described by Kenneth Morgan as 'enthusiastic', had more than a passing significance. Intellectually bewildered by a conflict which defied Fabian categories of analysis, Beatrice formally maintained the posture of the notorious Fabian *Mission* forswearing any public competence except in the society's own 'special business' of practical socialism.[18] Pragmatic considerations of unity were in this case, as Brockway pointed out, an issue not just of wider policy but of preserving the public concord of the Webbs themselves. Nevertheless, the denting of old complacencies was unmistakeable, and it was precisely the incapacity of Fabianism to explain or describe the war that led to its stiffening with a language of struggle, now extended to the sphere of 'practical' socialism as well as world affairs. 'Under the present Dictatorship of the Capitalist, the community is divided into two warring sections', ran a section of the Webbs' *Constitution* with which even Lenin could have agreed.

> This sharp division ... has been immensely emphasised by the Great War. The sudden and awful searchlight thrown on the Capitalist System by the war itself, and by the nature of the peace which has succeeded it, has revealed to the great mass of manual workers the essentially predatory character of the Capitalist State.

In *The Decay of Capitalist Civilisation*, the first of their books to be framed solely as indictment, they reached a fitting climax with 'The capitalist system as a cause of war', meaning, by this time inextricably, both the class war and the 'culminating calamity' of imperialist war.[19]

Beyond this enlarged perception of issues of power, there lay the profound sense of moral and spiritual crisis that contributed to Beatrice's breakdown in 1916. Dissatisfied with utilitarian ethics, Beatrice had long been troubled by the ends and purpose of existence lying beyond the reach of Webbian empiricism. The very relativism of the sociological method intensified this craving for the anchorage of values; and a deep religious impulse, momentarily inclining to Catholicism, Theosophy and even Buddhism, drew Beatrice more consistently to the consolations of Anglican liturgy and private prayer.[20] Around the turn of the century, she discovered the psychologist and philosopher William James, whom she described as 'the truest to me of all metaphysicians', and in James's *Will to Believe* (1897) and *Varieties of Religious Experience* (1902) found afffirmed the validity of a religious instinct going beyond particular dogmas or the proofs and disproofs of science.[21] An earlier formative influence, emotionally towering above the intellectual mentorship of Herbert Spencer, was the humbler figure of the Potters' housekeeper, Martha Jackson, whom Beatrice described with unwonted liberality as a saint. Martha was a Particular Baptist, whose faith Beatrice described as an 'overpowering consciousness of love', but a love 'strangely impersonal': an 'all-inclusive' or 'equalitarian' beneficence 'manifested quite indifferently to all'.[22] Beatrice, who shared that inclusive benevolence and a confessed inability to 'reverence' humanity, was palpably of the same species.[23]

Though drawn to its transcendental forms, she also conceived of religion as a means to worldly ends of better human conduct and feeling; even, more instrumentally, those of a better organisation of society. Though deeply felt, this was a functionalist conception, positing a cosmic division of labour between science and the spirit, and proposing the higher communion of the latter, 'in order', as Beatrice put it, to raise human values and ennoble behaviour. Far from providing a spiritual refuge, the interdependency of faith and human conduct lent a religious intensity to secular afflictions to which Fabian reasoning had no convincing answer. The war was by far the greatest of these afflictions. 'When and where will arise the spirit of love?', she exclaimed in the horror of a world turned against itself. In 'the continuous waking nightmare' that followed she came close to despair.

> Is there no depth of misery or degradation, endured by other persons, which will not be accepted as normal and inevitable? The horrors of peace ... are as much the deliberate choice of those who govern as the horrors of war. Both are the result of imagination, moral as well as intellectual imagination. We don't believe in Love, we believe in force; we insist on knocking the weakest down ... we refuse to share what nature gives to man, we rob and murder in order to get more than our share. In war the murder and robbery is conscious and deliberate so that all may see. In peace it is subconscious and secret ...

Both the 'will to believe' and this search for a right rule of conduct continued to haunt her after the war, as each further correlation of science and barbarism mocked the Fabian equation of moral and material progress. Only at last in Russia was she to find the consummation of the 'secular' and the 'religious', and the systematisation of a regime of equalitarian beneficence.[24]

Of course, the war had another aspect as an engine of reform. To Sidney, whatever its horrors, it would finally prove a 'landmark of progress', and Beatrice too took comfort from the advance of collectivist values.[25] Even despite its sordid ends, the call to arms had brought forth that spirit of public service by which the Fabian set such store, and she found it impossible not to admire the 'moral magnificence' and 'unsensational dutifulness' of the trenches.[26] Moreover, she did not overlook the opportunities for reform. Appointed to Lloyd George's Reconstruction Committee, while quickly perceiving its limitations she remained encouraged by the extension of state control over 'capitalism'.[27] Even so, the advances she most esteemed were not so much ones of efficiency as of status and public morals. While both Beatrice and Sidney dismissed the counterfeit authority of Labour's involvement in government, she yet perceived in the movement's subterranean stirrings a pointer to a new democratic order.[28] 'Never again will the manual workers ... agree to a position of social servility', she wrote in October 1917, as the Bolsheviks prepared their own more practical demonstration of the same lesson. 'Their leaders will fall into all sorts of traps, but the great multitude behind will press forward, stumbling slowly over innumerable obstacles to a world based on social equality.' Two months later, perhaps helped on by the news from the east, she posed a starker choice: on the one hand, ruin; on the other, 'radical revolution' – the greatest opportunity for rapid social advance that the world had ever seen. 'We are at the end of one civilisation', she wrote, 'the question is are we at the beginning of another?'[29]

To that there were two possible answers. Sidney's was to be found in *Labour and the New Social Order*, the Labour Party programme of June 1918, which in his own unmistakeable accents expounded its new commitment to socialism. In its opening section it defined the moment in Webbian terms as 'the end of a civilisation', perhaps even the death of European civilisation itself. Invoking the ominous precedents of Babylon, Rome, Egypt and Carthage, Sidney nevertheless dispelled such anxieties with a programme of constructive reform whose postulates were blandly positivistic. At once inspiring the Labour Party and yet escaping the vagaries of political agency – for no administration, wrote Sidney, could avoid confronting the tasks the document spelt out – the document thrummed already with the inevitability of gradualness, to whose stately rhythms even the destinies of empire were to be subjected.[30]

How very different was Beatrice's answer, as an 'evil' victors' peace confirmed the horror of war, and the 'senseless cruelty' of class and racial domination took the shape of famine and disease as well as violence. Haunted by a sense of impending catastrophe, her diaries of 1919-20 are scattered with epitaphs to a lost world of Fabian meliorism. The peace itself – 'an unclean thing' – the collapse of Wilsonism, the 'savage suppression' of Ireland and the success of Bolshevism, all conspired to mock this benignant world-view. 'Where', she wondered, 'is "the freedom broadening down from precedent to precedent"?'

> Ten years ago one would have left the world feeling that human society was getting steadily more loving and more enlightened. Today it needs a

> robust 'Will to Believe' to avoid the fear that we are sinking back into a barbarism as dark as any endured since the times deemed 'civilised'. One dreads that human life is becoming worse and not better...

Prolific in schemes that looked to the future, and confessedly happy and productive in her personal life, the contrast only sharpened the sense of its unreality. There must, she mused, have been many a Roman administrator, contented, hard-working and conscientious as his world cracked up around him, 'to disappear in the dark ages of brutal disorder, universal poverty, chronic war and creed persecutions'.[31]

The analogy is a revealing one. As Europe squandered its opportunity for renewal, Beatrice, long accustomed to think 'in civilisations', began to turn from an evolutionary view of their development to a cyclical one. Colloquially, this mood, in this period, is usually thought of as Spenglerian. Bombastic and incoherent, Spengler's particular arguments, assuming Beatrice even read them, can have impressed her no more than they did her fellow Fabian Harold Laski, who wrote to her of his 'deep disappointment' when the first instalment of *The Decline of the West* was translated in 1926.[32] What Beatrice nevertheless shared with the Spenglerian mindset was a sweeping racial pessimism more obviously conducive to conservative conclusions than revolutionary ones, or else suggesting possible connections between the two. Like the ongoing concerns with eugenics, which themselves were now shifting from the differential fertility of social classes to that of the white and non-white races, fears and apprehensions of the decline and brutalisation of 'the West' cut across party affiliations and sometimes ran deeper than them.[33] Inaugurated amidst such violence and irrationality, a new age of uncertainty thus already insinuated a sense of discord. For Beatrice, not only her private happiness but also the measured advancement of her public projects seemed suspended like a gossamer pathway over an abyss. This was not a 'Fabian' sensibility, nor even a characteristically socialist one. To the linear histories of these discrete traditions it adds the muddying temporal dimension of a new sensibility, already becoming known as 'post-war' and thus, in the words of the writer and painter Wyndham Lewis, defining even its computations of time.[34]

Incongruous though the allusion to Lewis may appear in such a context, it was not among the balmier barometers of progressive opinion that one finds moods most akin to Beatrice's. Rather, it was among those also moved to despair by the fragility of those pre-war values of order and progress which were now revealed to have been interdependent. In his own way a hybrid of the reactionary and the modern, Lewis too registered the shattering impact of the war as a portent of race suicide and descent into irrationalism. After the 'glorious auto-da-fé' of the 'suicidal White War', he wrote, nothing could impel the further atrocities of war and revolution but a 'general abstract appeal to hatred' pushed beyond the bounds of human reason. At the same time, he also targeted the cultural mores of the jazz age, notably 'male-inversion', primitivism and the shallow hedonism of having a 'good time'. These, he claimed, betrayed an absence of human purpose for which suicide both served as a metaphor and provided the empirical confirmation, through an 'epidemic' of actual suicides.[35] Published in September 1927, one doubts whether Lewis's essay would even have been read by Beatrice. Nevertheless, two months later she wrote in her diary: 'Voluntary withdrawals from life – without any fuss or reproach; without the excuse of special pain or misery – will become more and more common, unless there arises a new faith and a new rule of conduct, or possibly an authoritative physical and mental hygiene ...' Italian fascism, Russian communism and hundred-per-cent Americanism, she went on, all represented reactions from the prevailing 'creedless and purposeless outlook'.[36]

Assuming this was a coincidence, it recalls Lewis's own suggestion of the 'hidden liaison' of phenomena apparently unconnected except in time, overlooked because 'they do not lie obviously together and publish their conjunction explicitly and prominently'.[37] If the internal boundaries of the left were porous, nor should we be surprised if left and right themselves, or the still more amorphous categories of politics and culture, were similarly prone to cross-pollination. Because of the temporary curbing of the Webbs' joint researches, Beatrice at this time was not restricted to the proverbial Fabian blue books, and reading a novel or so a week was moved to dismal apprehension by what she perceived to be a literature of decay. Exactly like Lewis, but also prefiguring the *marxisant* critics of the 1930s, she railed at the futility of Bloomsbury coteries and their 'boresome world of parasitic nonentities'. Characteristically, she ascribed the shallow and promiscuous *bavardage* of Huxley's *Point Counter Point* to the lack of any gainful employment – 'even the typists are present as prospective prostitutes'. Also echoing Lewis even to the very words that she used, her strongest distaste was for the animalistic 'primitivism' of D.H. Lawrence, whose anti-intellectualism and disavowal of any fixity of purpose she regarded as 'deliberately sub-human'. As the reaction towards Soviet communism began to be felt, it was with relief that she turned from Lawrence's mystique of 'blood' and physical impulse to the 'hard hygienic view of sex' she found expressed by the Soviets.[38] Perhaps that too suggests a parallel with Lewis, who at that time was allured by the supposed asceticism of the Nazis as they swept away the decadence and 'inversions' – another animus Lewis shared with Beatrice – that flourished still more conspicuously in Weimar Germany.[39]

Important and neglected as these issues are, such a liaison of left and right was not only hidden but in many respects tenuous and partial. It certainly does not connote a simple equivalence between the appeals of Stalin and Hitler. Even the shared language of race could conceal significant distinctions. For Beatrice, it is true, racial and cultural fears were inextricably confused, and, as any Spenglerian might have, she referred to 'western civilisation' and the 'white race' almost interchangeably. 'The clouds in the East grow steadily darker and the flood of anarchy and barbarism seems to get steadily nearer', she wrote with wild allusiveness just after the war. 'One is conscious of great waves of agony, mental and physical, traversing continents to break on one's imagination, stunning hope and faith in the white race.'[40]

Apparently that could again be compared to Lewis and his shrunken 'White spirit', oppressed by war and threatening cataclysm, 'its very position of world-mastery, racial advantage and prestige ... becom[ing] a mockery and burden to it'.[41] However, unlike Lewis, Mosley, and many others who thought in such categories, Beatrice was not for a moment attracted to fascism or the 'acuter ... race consciousness' it represented.[42] Hitler's accession to power, though she 'devour[ed] books about Germany', struck her only as a symptom of decay. Shaw's boosting of Mussolini as a sort of Fabian action man drew from her only well-deserved epithets such as ignorant, conceited, flippant and a buffoon. Worse even than Shaw's cult of power, she wrote, was 'the absence of any kind of sympathetic appreciation of the agony that the best and wisest Italians are today going through; any appreciation of the mental degradation as implied in the suppression of all liberty of act, of thought and of speech'.[43] Obviously that shows a fellow-feeling for socialists and liberals oppressed by fascism. But it also suggests that for Beatrice western civilisation, despite its racial connotations, was more fundamentally a matter of values; and that of these values, tolerance and rationality, perhaps because of their very vulnerability, were in this period very much to the fore.

Perhaps we should think, as Lewis did, in terms of a racial 'analogy', by which Lewis meant the racial identification of what were really competing systems of ideas.[44] This does not mean that Sidney in particular did not harbour some ugly eugenicist views, which were not in the least bit analogical. In 1923, explaining to Fabians the waning of successive civilisations, he cited almost every factor but the social, be it 'climactic change, or the ravages of disease, or racial poisons, or the effects of sexual perversions, or dysgenic miscegenation (a degenerating fatal inter-marriage between races)'. Nor, to avoid the 'mutual degeneration' of Port Said and the East End of London, was he above proposing the restricting of racial 'mingling' to society's 'higher and more educated elements'.[45] As so often, such sentiments were paraphrastic rather than original. In 1925 Leo Chiozza Money, a fellow Fabian collectivist and recent collaborator with Sidney on the Sankey Commission, published a book, *The Peril of the White*, whose arguments were wholly constructed in such racial terms.[46] The same year, William Beveridge, Sidney's nominee as director of the LSE, was instrumental in establishing a new Department of Social Biology, to whose special fields of demography, heredity and eugenics Beveridge himself attached a large significance. 'The questions now facing us',

Beveridge declared of the declining birth-rate in 1923, 'are how far the fall will go; whether it will bring about a stationary white population long before the white man's world is full; how the varying incidence of restriction among different social classes or creeds will affect the stock; how far the unequal adoption of birth control by different races will leave one race at the mercy of another's growing numbers...'[47]

Beatrice too was moved by what she would call 'the biological factor in the ... decay of capitalist civilisation', and she too would describe the declining birth-rate in the old Edwardian language of 'race suicide'.[48] Nevertheless, despite her racial catastrophism, she regarded such evils as the symptom and product of social ills, not their fundamental cause – a distinction of more than semantic significance. 'If democracy fails Western civilisation goes under', she wrote shortly after the war:

> the white races will steadily decay, alike in numbers and quality of mind. And very naturally we do not see our successors as the coloured races we have always deemed inferior to our own ... But whichever race proves to be united in its purpose – a purpose coinciding with the nature of things – and shows itself capable of pursuing that purpose scientifically, must become the leader, if not the ruler, of the human race – or at any rate, of all other races having no fixed purpose ...[49]

The categories remain those of social imperialism, but the malleability of racial traits did mean that for Beatrice, unlike the Roman, the decline of the west could be imagined as its supercession by a more advanced social order. Conversely, at least the potentiality for such an order could be granted even the hordes at the gate – a position some way removed from Money's concerns with the paramountcy of 'the White'. Nothing showed this better than the reversal of Beatrice's initial judgements on the Japanese and Chinese: the former dismissed by the 1930s as an evil influence, the latter transformed by a new philosophy and providing an exemplar for the peoples of India and Africa.[50] The clouds in the east, when they parted, were to reveal a radiant prospect in which racial determinations were altogether secondary.

## III

Beatrice's diaries can be grouped with a wider literature of unsettlement, which sought in fellow-travelling of left or right – exceptionally, as in Shaw's case, of both – an escape from the stench of decay. Absorbed though she became in current affairs, the latent sense of doom continuously forced its way to the surface at moments of crisis. 'The world is again at war, and at war in a peculiarly horrible way', she wrote during the French occupation of the Ruhr in 1923. 'The trampling on Germany by France is a disgusting vision, making the whole of the sacrifices during and since the War a detestable combination of suicide and murder.' Again, during the General Strike three years' later, she relived the 'nightmare feeling' of the war years: 'I have lost my day dreams, I have only my nightmare left ... that European civilisation is in the course of dissolution'. Even after Soviet communism had come to provide an alternative, when momentarily confidence faltered, she was to ponder not just race but species suicide – that, bereft of a new code of living, 'man ... might even die out like other animals have done'.[51]

Hardly a hint of such concerns will be found in the Webbian public utterances which by now were usually Sidney's. Nothing less like a jeremiad can be imagined than the inevitability of gradualness, and even in the clamour of a partisan House of Commons, Sidney reduced the dramas of state to matters of administrative rationality. The three essentials of socialism, he stated in a Fabian lecture of 1924, were that it should be consistent with the four rules of arithmetic, the Ten Commandments and the Union Jack.[52] Like the Victorian paterfamilias in the George Moore novel, his reaction to untoward events might well have been that it 'would all be the same a hundred years hence'; and repeatedly Beatrice noted his confidence in continuous legislative advance irrespective of party politics, quite as if the old Fabian steamroller had once again emerged from the smoke of war and revolution.[53] This was a new and more categorical version of 'state socialism exclusively', now raised to the very threshold of office. Nevertheless, its exclusion of alternative strategies was also a mark of its underlying fragility. Between the lines of the couple's public utterances, there could be sensed the hollowness of a social vision offering little prospect but the narrow path of permeated Labourism, and no prospect at all should this appear to fail.

Even as Sidney proclaimed the inevitability of gradualism, a curious volume, *The Decay of Capitalist Civilisation*, appeared to qualify or confute its double-edged complacency. Drafted some three to four years earlier,[54] the book offered the Webbs' first sustained indictment of capitalism, sweeping from old concerns like the 'moral miasma' of destitution to what was now described as the greater evil of unequal power relations. Another theme particularly marked in this period was concern with the environmental degradation of capitalism, expressed in what now seem strikingly contemporary terms.[55] Despite its eloquence of denunciation – the young Hugh Gaitskell found himself more powerfully aroused by it than he was by actual human suffering[56] – the Webbs nevertheless failed to achieve a comparable fluency in depicting an alternative to capitalist decay. Little enough hope was given of partial redress, for by this time they had relinquished the headier prospects of 1918-21 without recovering the dynamic of their earlier reformism. Pathetically, the book concluded with 'an attempt, possibly vain' to persuade the directors and beneficiaries of capitalism that only their wise anticipation of social reform – 'intelligently anticipated, planned and guided by the rulers of the people' – could avert the 'Universal Sabotage' of open class war. Its one good augury of change was not the developing labour movement, with its stigmata of 'democratic infantilism', but an honest, efficient and well-instructed 'salariat' – the *nouvelle couche sociale* of bureaucratic Fabianism, once more underpinned by the 'necessary and beneficial subordination' of managerial hierarchy.[57] Significantly, Sidney's is the hand detectable in the book's revisions, assisted by Shaw. It seems a telling reversion to pre-war collaborations and the 'view of the statesman' to whom the volume's final plea was addressed.

Nevertheless, the absence in the volume of democratic agencies of change reflected Beatrice's growing disillusionment as well as Sidney's reversion to type. Wider social movements which, in the most recent version of Webbian doctrine, had preceded, made possible and necessitated similar advances at the level of national government, now seemed to both of them exhausted or irresponsible. Atrophied or neglected, the triple agencies of worker, consumer and citizen were all but marginalised as they looked instead to a Labour government to 'increase the efficiency of industry', and dismissed the active labour movement as 'a turbulent mob, instead of a select body of brain workers'.[58] This return to government, brains and efficiency as the mainsprings of progress was not, as we shall see, an emphasis peculiar to the Webbs; and both the evisceration of their multiform democracy and its strange resurrection in the form of Soviet communism represented a much more general regression to the state.

Most dramatic was the eclipse of the unions. If Beatrice famously described the General Strike as a 'proletarian distemper' that had run its course, so too had her own milder inflammation with industrial democracy dating back to the late 1880s. Though never partisans of direct action, the Webbs in 1920 had comfortably accommodated the notion within the presentation of collective bargaining in their updated trade union *History*. There, while the right to strike was unconditionally reaffirmed, a general strike was described as unimaginable except in the event of such prior 'direct action' by state or employers as to provide it with both legitimacy and mass endorsement.[59] The 'nine days' of May 1926, to their undisguised dismay, met no such condition: unclear in object and without prospect of success, the dispute merely suggested to them the folly and incapacity of that bureaucratic stratum they had once conceived as one of the very sinews of democracy. To his Seaham mining constituents, Sidney offered not even the solidarity of fine words, and Beatrice diplomatically abandoned her constituency letters while the dispute continued. Free of such restraints in her diaries, amidst a dozen similar accolades she described the union leaders as 'mentally deficient', and the miners' officials Herbert Smith and A.J. Cook as an 'honest mule' and 'inspired goose' respectively.[60] Sidney described them as 'somewhat dense' and a 'mad man'.[61]

If 'windbag revolutionary Trade Unionism' had had its nemesis, so, too, had the Webbs' own more modest hopes of a 'sane' trade union movement advancing to its full stature in the affairs of the nation. In tones of finality, Beatrice now forecast the demise of 'Trade Unionism as a Mass proletarian Movement', and, in that surest sign of a Webbian change of tack, abandoned plans for a further update of their *History of Trade Unionism*. 'It is the biggest defeat of Industrial Democracy, moral as well as material, in our life time', Beatrice wrote, as capital and 'community' ground the miners down. 'I am inclined to think that it is the end of an epoch; that some other type of organisation will slowly emerge and supersede the Mass Trade Unionism of the last decade.' Appalled by the 'sectional egotism' of strikers as well as coal-owners, she foresaw for both labour and capital the need for 'discipline' and even 'compulsion' in the interests of the unoffending citizen and consumer.[62] Fixing her hopes more firmly on the 'steady and sensible political action' of the Labour Party, she only wished it shorn of its dependence on the unions and bolstered by the remnants of the Liberals. The unions themselves, by the end of the decade, seemed exhausted of either threat or potential; and a possible book on the subject was again abandoned on the grounds that they had no future. Everywhere, said Beatrice, their capacities seemed in decline 'relatively to other agencies for influencing mankind – such as Governments, Political Parties, Capitalist Trusts, the Press and Broadcasting'.[63]

It will be noted that the other agencies of Webbian democracy did not even figure on Beatrice's list. In that too the Webbs were moving with the times. Co-operation, as one of its left-wing advocates acknowledged in the mid-1920s, was by this time all but overlooked by socialists except as 'a concession to some crank'.[64] In the three-volume *Book of the Labour Party*, published in 1925, it was barely mentioned, and a chapter on the consumer was entrusted to the Fabian collectivist Emil Davies, who ignored it completely.[65] Perhaps deflated by the muted reception given their own book on the subject, the Webbs did not put up much of a rearguard action. Immediately on its publication in December 1921, they had initiated a series of Fabian tracts 'for the instruction of co-operative officials', hoping to emulate the Fabians' successes in the field of local government. They also contributed two of the pamphlets themselves.[66] However, comment on their book in the co-operative press entirely passed over its more visionary passages, while the Co-operative Union declined to produce a cheap edition. Doubtless this owed something to its frank, independent and often critical tone, which elicited a frosty response from CU official Fred Hall in the *Co-operative News*.[67] Subsequently, the Webbs did encourage Percy Redfern in his mission 'to reintegrate the consumer and producer', and Beatrice contributed an essay to Redfern's symposium of the late 1920s, *Self and Society*. For herself, however, there were no more dreams to be spun from 'that most worthy but ugly block of humanity – the Co-operative officials of Great Britain!'.[68]

Nor was their interest in municipal self-government maintained, despite superficial appearances to the contrary. In 1930, Beatrice attracted much comment on proposing the devolution of the functions of their erstwhile 'social parliament' to national assemblies in England, Scotland and Wales.[69] Nevertheless, her object was not the extension of democracy but a more effective and professionalised executive which would 'really set about reorganising British society' through the supercession of local by central authorities and the subordination of the elective principle to that of continuous professional expertise. In candid terms, this meant the 'obsolescence of local government', and it was to 'some such subconscious conclusion' that Beatrice attributed the tacit abandonment of their huge work of investigation into the subject.[70] In both timing and motivation her schemes may be grouped with G.D.H. Cole's simultaneous advocacy of regionalist principles, also with the aim of amassing powers from below rather than decanting them outwards.[71] With the 'irresistible groundswell of democracy' confounded on all three fronts, Beatrice found herself torn between acquiescence in its downfall and a personal confession of faith in democratic government. 'I am even uncertain whether what is known as western political democracy is a necessary basis', she admitted in November 1930. 'Will Soviet Russia's creed autocracy deliver the goods – if all that the average man *really* desires is security for a good livelihood ... combined with the consciousness of social equality?'[72]

While the movements which had prompted a more optimistic conception of socialism seemed on the retreat, the pessimistic scenario of a servile state was revived by the return of mass unemployment. This was a phenomenon so unsettling to the Webbs as to bring forth their one major research project of the 1920s, their *English Poor Law History*. Though apparently this was merely the resumption of unfinished business, the unassimilable fact of involuntary mass unemployment posed the Webbs a moral and social challenge whose contradictions were ultimately insoluble within a framework of gradualism. Jose Harris has rightly noted that the couple had never fully extricated even in their own minds the issue of social and individual responsibility for unemployment.[73] According to their own lights they had never previously had to, for their earlier conviction that the *prevention* of destitution was a feasible goal, and the conquest of involuntary unemployment attainable, had reassured them of the legitimacy of salutary measures against any irremediable residuum of ne'er-do-wells. Thus had they envisaged an equilibrium of responsibility and opportunity, of personal discipline and social justice, whose basic compulsion was the universal obligation of useful work. With post-war unemployment, however, faced with the evident utopianism of proposing such an obligation, the whole equation collapsed and its proponents were confronted with a more difficult choice. George Lansbury, that most prominent socialist adherent and signatory to the Webbs' minority report, made his own decision unambiguously as a champion of the unemployed as victims.[74] Even the Webbs, in *The*

*Decay of Capitalist Civilisation*, conceded the verdict of a mass democracy against compulsion of those unwittingly out of work. Capitalism had lost the 'Whip of Starvation', they admitted, and no democratic case could be made for its restoration.[75] On the other hand, they regarded the corollary of systematic doles as disastrous alike for their recipients and for society as a whole. The reality was that they believed as much in the Whip of Starvation as in the Prevention of Destitution, and it was no small part of their indictment of capitalism that it had neither the means nor the moral authority to enforce it.

Their main attempt to grapple with the problem was the Webbian triple-decker of *English Poor Law History*. As elephantine as *Soviet Communism*, and similarly conceived in its time as their 'last will and testament', the work took up a challenge beyond all powers of ratiocination. 'How can we devise some treatment of the Unemployed which will be "less eligible" than wage labour without being blatantly *inequitable* to the men and their families who are out of work through no fault of their own?', Beatrice mused as they began the work. No such resolution proved possible, and the Webbs, when forced to choose between the two evils, arrived at conclusions that were both intellectually flawed and socially regressive. Formally, they inveighed against 'proletarianism', by which they meant the laxness and humanity we associate with Lansbury's Poplarism. They also looked benignly on the rigours of the current Conservative poor law administration of Neville Chamberlain. 'When we remember how specially exasperating "misdoing on principle" has always been (and always will be) to those in authority', they wrote with undisguised approval, 'it is only human nature if proletarian Boards have found themselves singled out for detailed investigation, public condemnation and exemplary discipline ...' If this was a sorry sequel to Beatrice's initial promise of 'revolutionary doctrine', so too was their rejection for purposes of relief of 'the agency of any Local Authority whatever, which will for this service, be all the more incompetent if it is a popularly elected body'.[76]

Beatrice had misgivings about such judgements and she was right to have had them. While the Webbs approved the 'deterrence' of 'voluntary and intentional pauperism', they could not but concede that such deterrents also punished the transparently blameless without in any way addressing the basic issue of involuntary mass unemployment. Stubbornly they denied the alternatives of 'work or maintenance'; but they secured the link between them, not, as before the war, by the better organisation of work, but by the withdrawal of maintenance and the sheer brute poverty of 'less eligibility'. Even amid the soaring unemployment of the second Labour government, Beatrice could not resist the old, irrelevant complaints of a wilful idleness preferred to work. Nor, on the other hand, could she lightly sanction remedial measures while the grosser profligacy of the 'idle rich' went unchecked. 'Luxury hotels and luxury flats, Bond Street shopping, racing and high living in all its forms to go unchecked; but the babies are not to have milk and the very poor are not to have homes', she wrote of the cuts which brought down the government. Only the eradication of unemployment allowed the social disciplines underpinning Webbian notions of community, but such a prospect seemed inconceivable – at least under capitalism.[77]

Perhaps the greater urgency and panache of the Liberals' employment schemes helps explain the more positive regard which Beatrice – like Lansbury – had for them by this time.[78] But far more persuasive in the end was the 'land without unemployment' where work, maintenance and authority seemed both practically and ethically indivisible, and the radical and conservative responses to destitution equally satisfied. 'What no party and no country as yet realises, except perhaps Russian Communists', Beatrice wrote already in 1930, 'is that the State cannot *guarantee* livelihood except under conditions of a *managed* population – and that this management must start with a complete register of every individual within the community so as to insure that the principle "from each according to their capacity" in return "to every one according to their need" will be enforced'.[79]

**IV**

There was nothing fortuitous in the way the Webbs took up or abandoned their various projects, and their reabsorption in the Poor Law both encouraged and confirmed the return to the administrative grand narratives of fin-de-siecle Fabianism. In the science of living in communities, they concluded their *Poor Law History*, the widening social purpose of the public-spirited citizen required the 'larger and larger measure of foresight, invention and technical efficiency in the specialised groups of brain-workers on whom, for the most part, the execution of this social purpose will necessarily devolve'.[80] Sometimes the technocratic emphasis came with a note of scorn for the 'brainless rivalry' of faction, whose wilder oscillations of policy carried the hidden threat of a countervailing dictatorship. At other times, the clamour of party was seen, if not as a positive good, at least as relatively undisturbing to the processes of good government. Exactly as a Labour government felt itself restrained from impetuosity, Sidney argued, so were Conservative governments prevented from retrogression; and in the critical field of the Poor Law, Liberals and even Conservatives seemed, not for the first time, the more enlightened agents of reform. Beatrice, at the time of the 1929 election, could hardly even discern the difference between them in their espousal of 'socialistic' policies.[81] Common to moods of both optimism and despondency was the ideal of a disinterested governing wisdom. Even in opposition Sidney upheld this by advertising 'the good features of the [Conservative] administration as well as the bad ... in order that we all may be friends in spreading the good news to the people' – the good news being that the state was not indifferent to their well-being.[82] In practice as in theory,

Sidney hardly saw the point of an opposition and was 'bored' by having to form part of one.[83]

Nobody need therefore have been much surprised had Sidney backed MacDonald when in 1931 he deserted his Labour colleagues to form the National Government. 'The General Council are pigs', he grumbled when the TUC refused further concessions in the purported national interest, and a cross-bench arrangement to see through expert measures of economy might have been thought a fitting finale to a life given over to Fabianism. Even conceding the strength of Sidney's belated personal loyalty to the Labour Party, discreet explorations of a middle way were as compatible with that allegiance as communism, and more consistent with the temporising Fabianism which Sidney continued to espouse even in 1931. Indeed, it was that very phrase 'the middle way', marshalling governments of either persuasion, with which Beatrice had associated him as early as 1925, adding that 'in his heart of hearts ... he still believes in Fabian permeation of other parties as a more rapid way than the advent of a distinctly Socialist Government'.[84] When, around 1930, Beatrice began showing a pronounced interest in the new Russia, Sidney at first displayed no more than a flickering and sceptical interest while warning her not to become a monomaniac. 'What I am beginning to doubt is the "inevitability of gradualness", or even the practicability of gradualness, in the transition from a capitalist to an equalitarian civilisation', she reported in February 1931.

> Sidney says 'it will make itself', without an acknowledged plan accepted by one party in the state and denounced by the other. We shall *slip into the equalitarian state* as we did into political democracy – by each party whether nominally socialist or anti-socialist taking steps in [this] direction ...

Beatrice too viewed favourably the prospect of a Lib-Lab rapprochement, and thought progressive Liberals 'more socialistic and more daring in their Fabian proposals' than Labour itself.[85] Even so, interspersed with such reflections, it is in Beatrice alone that the possibility of a private revolution can be detected. 'Beveridge is beginning to think that I am a Bolshevist at heart, and therefore "out of the picture"', she wrote as late as September 1931; 'but he still believes in the good sense and experience of *The Other One*: with his comfortable slogan of the inevitability of gradualness!'[86]

Despite this creeping disillusionment, it was only at the end of the decade that Beatrice began to discover a compensating enthusiasm in Bolshevism. Partly that was down to supply-side factors: both the new pace and purpose of Soviet life and its transmutation into glowing testimonies by writers like H.D. Harben and Maurice Hindus. Harben, the Prudential heir, was an old friend of the Webbs, a former LSE governor and Fabian executive member who visited Russia in 1930 and privately circulated a somewhat superficial catalogue of his impressions. 'One might almost be in Fascist Italy', he wrote of its 'manifold signs of prosperity'. Based on observations which one trusts were not misconstrued, he also judged the well-being of ordinary Russians by the plumpness of the women's legs. ('The horses, too', he added unchivalrously, 'are round and well kept'.)[87]

Though Beatrice found even Harben's 'hopefulness ... catching',[88] Hindus's *Humanity Uprooted*, which she read in June 1930, had a greater resonance. The account of an American journalist of Russian birth, it described Soviet Russia not as a political experiment – in the section on institutions, neither 'state' nor 'party' even figured, though sex, religion and the family did – but as a new civilisation. It had little on the economy and nothing on planning, but a great deal on the Soviets' new secular morality based on social service. This was held to have sublimated the religious instinct and raised the dignity of the ordinary Russian through 'social and intellectual ascent' and what Hindus, in a quintessentially Webbian phrase, called the 'expansion of personality'. Hindus even contrasted the matter-of-fact Soviet view of sex with the very authors Beatrice detested, Lawrence and Huxley, whom he accused of 'toy[ing] around with love as though it were only a putrid appendix to man's psychology, fit to be slashed out and cast into the garbage pail'.[89] Possibly no other single work was so influential in the image that Beatrice was beginning to build up of Soviet Russia.

For Beatrice, if not for Sidney, at least the potential for the abandonment of conventional reformism can therefore be traced well before the end of the 1920s. Nevertheless, if accounts like Hindus's only now made so forcible an impression upon her, it was because of the desperation she had begun to feel regarding the absence of practical alternatives to capitalism. In that sense, the debacle of 1929-31 retains its significance as a catalyst, with decay, now quickening into crisis, breaking at last from its oxymoronic coupling with Fabian optimism. Though sometimes it seemed as if there was no aspect of western civilisation which was not capable of generating woe, two particular themes stand out in Beatrice's diaries for this period. One was that of Labour's record in office, the other its sheer irrelevance to the larger issue of the future of western civilisation. Both themes fuelled the interest in Soviet communism and, as the crisis developed, were increasingly framed in explicit reference to it.

With regard to the MacDonald governments, Beatrice accepted with Sidney that the basic test was of Labour's fitness for office, and she too identified this with political moderation, the maintenance of 'order' and the thwarting of 'little bands of wrecking communists'.[90] On the other hand, she was at one with many Labour activists in also viewing the question of 'fitness' in the more basic sense of Labour's integrity of purpose and conduct. Attitudes to MacDonald himself were a touchstone, and even at the height of his public standing Beatrice evinced a marked distrust both of MacDonald as a leader – at best a 'fine façade' – and of the strategy of 'inverted permeation' by which he had Labour dance to the tune of the 'philistine citizen'.[91] 'On balance, *my* sympathies are with the left', she wrote, emphasising the singular pronoun; 'their leaders are sounder in character and more honest in their sympathies ...' Even despite her scorn for their 'wild and chaotic' schemes, Beatrice did recognise in figures like Lansbury a commitment to the 'common people' that was lacking in other Labour leaders, possibly even including Sidney himself. 'Personally I sympathise with the ILP', she wrote, again with the shifting pronouns whose significance one can only infer; 'we of the Right are too damned comfortable, and we are sinking into a senile complacency with things as they are.'[92]

More than any of its actual policies, what Beatrice most shared with the left were its apprehensions as to Labour's susceptibility to the lures of society. In her own case, such concerns can be traced at least as far back as 1913, when she commented acerbically of MacDonald's sublimation of Lib-Lab rivalries on the golf links. 'Imagine a German Social Democratic leader playing golf with the German Prime Minister!', she had written of what seemed a containment strategy of truly Fabian guilefulness. 'The British governing class is extraordinarily clever in winning over the abler revolutionary elements!' Ironically, Beatrice commended instead the 'tradition of non-intercourse' pioneered by Parnell, though admittedly she did so with no semblance of consistency.[93] Nevertheless, it was precisely to such an analysis that she returned a decade later, as Labour now breached the very citadels of power. More than that, with the complacency of breeding as to its own beneficent influence, she took it upon herself to 'give a lead against participation in London Society', and in 1924 played a major role in establishing both the Parliamentary Labour Club and the notorious 'Half Circle Club' which she organised for Labour members' wives.[94]

Almost invariably, both contemporaries and historians have construed her aims as the polishing up of the under-bred for initiation into a better class of society. 'A school of snobbery', growled the miners' leader Robert Smillie, and the impression has prevailed of a resurgent Altiora Bailey, self-appointed as 'hostess' to socialist Westminster and vying for position with the inveterate social climber Ethel Snowden.[95] Once again, the impression of dramatic discontinuity between the permeating 1920s and fellow-travelling 1930s is created. In reality, however, Beatrice's concern was never really with Labour's presentability so much as its vulnerability to 'social ambition'. Detesting Ethel Snowden, her efforts were not directed at Smillie or Labour's '"kernel" of socialist puritanism', but at those whom she feared too weak to resist the subtle flatteries of position. The Half Circle Club was thus conceived, not as a passage into society, but as its repudiation. Beatrice herself refused invitations to establishment functions and she looked to the club to promote a sufficient 'sense of solidarity and puritanism to keep some of the frailer vessels upstanding against the onslaughts of duchesses and millionaires against their dignity'. More principled and also more astute than many Labour leaders, she appreciated the grand symbolic capitulations involved in court dress and such 'mark[s] of servility' as the curtsey. After the first Labour government she thought it a mistake even to have formed an administration 'too accommodating to the manners and customs of a "Society" they had always denounced'.[96] Of such a verdict, there was, in Sidney's private assessment of the government's record, not a hint.[97]

Precisely the same diagnosis, of 'mental enfeeblement' linked with 'unutterable snobbishness', was repeated in even stronger terms during the second Labour government. Characteristically, when Sidney went to the House of Lords, Beatrice refused the title Lady Passfield, dreaming meanwhile of Chequers as a rest-home for children or hard-up intellectuals.[98] By this time, moreover, such criticisms were beginning to be linked with a sense of possible alternatives. 'Here at last we witnessed the Will and the Way', she recalled of a week spent observing the 'studiously simple and concentrated life' of the Viennese social democrats in 1929.[99] Subsequently she was still more impressed by the rejection of metropolitan 'society' by the new Russian ambassador in London, Grigory Sokolnikov. 'Here proletarianism of a grim character was rampant in all its fanaticism and puritanism', she wrote of the Soviet embassy, though it was at this one alone that she confessed to feeling 'at home'. Sokolnikov himself she found 'studious and ascetic' like a WEA tutor, or the 'best type of young workman in good character in search of knowledge'.[100]

The 'ugly memories' of Labour's corruptions, and the search for a purer socialist faith and rule of conduct, were to play a significant part in the attraction to Soviet communism and the identification of a new 'vocation of leadership' with its ruling communist party.[101] Nevertheless, it was not just the inadequacy of the Labour Party but the futility and irrelevance of British politics as a whole that drove Beatrice towards such radical solutions. Intermittently during the 1920s, she kept returning to the idea that Europe had been reduced to a 'backwater' through 'the redistribution of racial power and influence brought about, or at any rate coinciding with, and intensified by, the Great War'. Like Alexander Herzen after the comparable setbacks of 1848-51, it was on the 'vital world forces' of Russia and America that she rested her hopes and fears of the future, and increasingly she envisaged the outcome as the result of the contest between them. Though they resembled each other both in their violence and in their fixation on material progress, Beatrice saw those vital forces not just as rivals but as alternative 'social experiments', the one in uncontrolled capitalism and the other in 'despotically controlled' communism. Unlike Antonio Gramsci, she did not identify Americanism with puritanism, but with gangsterism, greed, corruption and frivolity; and judging the two endeavours on 'the relative quality of the human nature produced', it was in its honesty and disinterested service to the community that she came to discern the superiority of communism. 'What interests me most ... is not the now familiar tale of the success of the General Plan as a method of wealth production; but the reaction of this success on the scale of moral values among the young people', she wrote on reading Hindus's *Red Bread*:

> both races are concentrating their energies on the production of material wealth ... the American intent on making *himself* rich and the Soviet citizen obsessed with the desire to enrich the community even if he himself has to starve. It seems likely that given the survival of this strange creed Russia will become the richest country in the world. What then? Communal riches will do little more for the *good life* than personal riches ... But the disinterested work by which alone communal riches can be obtained is a big moral asset. The method of attaining the Purpose is finer than the Purpose itself, whereas in the USA, the Purpose is amoral and the method immoral.[102]

The collapse of American prosperity at the end of the 1920s was consequently greeted by Beatrice with unmistakeable *Schadenfreude*.[103] At the same time, she continued to regard Europe as little more than the field of battle between these younger powers. Britain, with its peculiar air of deadness, was just a 'pawn in the struggle'.[104]

By the end of 1931 Sidney belatedly came to the same conclusion. In a Fabian lecture of 1927, the journalist S.K. Ratcliffe challenged the Webbs' notion of capitalist decay with the image of a capitalist America itself 'creating a new type of civilisation'. Sidney would hardly have demurred, for with his 'American' attributes of efficiency and philistinism he showed little of the hostility and condescension towards the new world of many other British socialist intellectuals. 'And even if Europe fails', he had countered one of Beatrice's jeremiads in 1926, 'there is always the USA – a self-confident and overwhelmingly prosperous race'.[105] Five years later, however, the 'American way' of the 1920s was failing even on its own terms. In the Fabian Society's autumn lectures for 1931, 'The American collapse' now provided Harold Laski with much scope for satire, while a chastened Ratcliffe was saddled with the theme of 'The Russian experiment'.[106]

Meanwhile, though the 1931 general election was being fought out as if the future of civilisation depended on it, Beatrice commented in her diary on its basic irrelevance, as the fundamental issues of society were settled in the contest between these 'two great laboratories of social organisation'.[107] Twelve days later, Sidney, himself now a convert to such an outlook, made the point in almost identical terms in his own contribution to the Fabian lecture series.[108] The title of his lecture was

'Capitalism in dissolution'. Though arriving there by different routes and timetables, the Webbs at last were ready for their trip to Russia.

## NOTES

1. BWD 9 September 1915.
2. Herbert Tracey, 'Makers of the British labour movement. Socialism as common sense', *Labour Magazine*, June 1923, pp. 51-3.
3. SW, 'Fabianism justified'; BWD, 25 May and 30 August 1924, 16 September 1925; Passfield papers 4/18, SW, typescript on first MacDonald government, c.1924-5 ('whilst fresh in memory').
4. Hamilton, *Sidney and Beatrice Webb*, pp. 269-70; Jones, *Whitehall Diary. Volume 1: 1916-1925*, Oxford: OUP, 1969, p. 269.
5. Tillett cited Citrine papers 1/1, diary entry for 29 December 1924: 'Sidney Webb and the Trades Union Congress'.
6. Strachey, *What Are We To Do?*, Gollancz, 1938, esp. ch. 8, 'The three inevitabilities'.
7. See for example Trevelyan papers, CPT 144, Philips Price to Trevelyan, 26 November 1931.
8. Liebman, 'Les Webb', p. 414; M. Cole in *Beatrice Webb's Diaries 1924-1932*, p. xvi; Clarke, 'Liberals', pp. 261-2.
9. BWD 3 October 1917.
10. BWD 29 February, 10 July and 30 August 1924 .
11. BW to Sally Fairchild, n.d. but January 1900, Mackenzie, *Letters*, vol. 2, p. 124.
12. Shaw to C.P. Trevelyan, 14 March 1918 in Laurence, *Letters 1911-1925*, pp. 538-43.
13. Murray papers, MSS Gilbert Murray 25/36-7, SW to Murray, 21 September; BWD 16 April 1915*; SW to Shaw, 18 August 1915, Mackenzie, *Letters*, vol. 3, p. 61. For one of Sidney's strongest post-war statements, see Passfield papers 2/4/F/7, 'England and the war', n.d.
14. E.g. Harrison, 'Sidney', pp. 65-9.
15. Brockway, *Inside*, p. 123.
16. BWD 5 August 1914 and 16 April 1915*; Passfield papers 2/4/F/7, Beatrice to Gilbert Murray, 14 October 1914.
17. BWD 7 December 1916*, also 3 January 1915.
18. Morgan, 'The Webbs', p. 58; BW to Gilbert Murray, 14 October 1914; MSS Gilbert Murray 26/27, BW to Murray, 19 December 1914.
19. *CSC*, pp. 274-5; *DCC*. ch. 6.
20. BWD 8-9 December 1903, *MA*, pp. 32-3; BWD 25 September 1900 and 22 February 1906, *OP*, pp. 170, 333-4; BWD Whitsun 1904, Mackenzie vol. 2, p. 322; BWD 10 July 1924.
21. BWD 2 January 1901 and September 1902, Mackenzie, vol. 2, pp. 197 and 255, 16 July 1921
22. *MA*, pp. 15-19, 76.
23. BWD 29 October 1925.
24. BWD 12 August 1914, 4 April 1916. For the dualism of Beatrice's beliefs, and its resolution in the USSR, see her contribution to *I Believe. The personal philosophies of twenty-three eminent men and women of our time*, Allen & Unwin, 1940, pp. 323-48.

25. For further 'war socialism' arguments, see *CSC*, pp. 324-5, *DCC*, pp. 119-21, 131-3.
26. BWD 16 April 1915.
27. BWD 9 December 1916, 19 and 22 February, 15 May and 18 July 1917.
28. For Labour and the coalition see BWD 8 and 9* December 1916 and 4 November 1918.
29. BWD 5 October and 11 December 1917.
30. *Labour and the New Social Order. A report on reconstruction*, Labour Party, 1918, pp. 3-4 and passim.
31. BWD 24 June and 25 December 1919, 23 October 1920. Other testimonies of relevant personal contentment include BWD 12 March 1919, 29 November 1920*, 16 July 1921.
32. Passfield papers, 2/4/H, Laski to Beatrice, 15 June 1926.
33. On eugenics see Richard A. Soloway, *Demography and Degeneration. Eugenics and the declining birthrate in twentieth century Britain*, Chapel Hill & London: University of North Carolina Press, 1995 edn, pp. 226-58.
34. Wyndham Lewis, *Blasting and Bombardiering, Autobiography (1914-1926)*, Eyre & Spottiswood, 1937, p. 1.
35. Wyndham Lewis, 'Paleface' in *The Enemy*, 2, 1927, pp. 15-16, 35, 91-3.
36. BWD 14 November 1927*.
37. Lewis, 'Paleface', p. 51.
38. BWD 5 December 1925, 26 October 1928*, 12 September 1929, 5 May 1931*, 30 October 1932.
39. Lewis, *Hitler* (1931), cited Tom Normand, *Wyndham Lewis the artist: holding the mirror up to politics*, Cambridge: CUP, 1992, pp. 155-6.
40. BWD 12 March 1919; also 18 November 1919.
41. 'Paleface', pp. 87-8.
42. Lewis cited Richard Griffiths, *Fellow Travellers of the Right. British enthusiasts for Nazi Germany 1933-39*, Oxford: OUP, 1983 edn, p. 178.
43. BWD 1 October and 14 November 1927, 24* and 25* March and 7 September 1934.
44. Lewis, 'Paleface', p. 44.
45. SW, 'Is civilisation decaying?' (lecture), *Fabian News*, November 1923, p. 41; 'Voluntary internationalism' (lecture), *Fabian News*, December 1926, pp. 66-7. Conventional eugenicist sentiments will also be found in *DCC*, pp. 43-4.
46. Leo Chiozza Money, *The Peril of the White*, Collins, 1925.
47. Harris, *William Beveridge*, pp. 259-60, 279-82, 331.
48. BWD 10* and 11* March, 11 May* and 6 December* 1937.
49. BWD 20 July 1920*; see also e.g. BWD 17 October 1922.
50. BWD 7 September and 18 October 1937*.
51. BWD, 6 March 1923*, 18 May 1926 and 11 October 1937*.
52. S. Webb, 'Fabianism justified'.
53. E.g. BWD 22 August 1927; see also George Moore, *Spring Days*, Vizetelly, 1888.
54. See BWD 17 October 1922; Woolf papers, Beatrice to Woolf, 29 May 1919.
55. 'In pursuit of the limitless natural wealth of new and slightly peopled lands the profit-maker proceeds with his destructive process from conti-

nent to continent. ... fur-bearing and food animals are killed ... to the point of extermination of the species; primeval forests are levelled to the ground; natural pastures are denuded; virgin soils are defertilised; coal and metals, oils and gases ... are wasted and exhausted; the rivers are dried up, and the very climate is impaired'. See *DCC*, pp. 92-7, 139-41.

56. Philip M. Williams, *Hugh Gaitskell*, Oxford: OUP, 1982 edn, p. 32.
57. *DCC*, pp. 159-77; also pp. 83-4 where the same theme is developed historically.
58. BWD 18 June 1926.
59. *HTU*, pp. 663-73.
60. BWD 10 and 24* September 1926.
61. Passfield papers 7/4/H, SW to Shaw, 13 May 1926.
62. BWD 4 May, 30 June, 21 August 1926, 1 and 24* September 1926 , 9* and 24 October 1926, 10 November 1926*.
63. BWD 25 March 1929, 5 February* and 16 April* 1930; Hamilton, *Remembering*, p. 257.
64. Sydney R. Elliott, *Co-operation and Socialism*, ILP, c. 1926, p. 3.
65. A. Emil Davies, 'Protecting the consumer' in Herbert Tracey, ed., *The Book of the Labour Party*, Caxton, 3 vols, c. 1925, vol. 2, pp. 47-69.
66. Leonard Woolf papers III, Beatrice to Woolf, 8 December 1921; M. Cole, *Story*, p. 201.
67. Leonard Woolf papers III, Davies to Woolf, n.d., late 1921; *The Producer*, December 1921, pp. 38-9; *Co-operative News*, editorial, 10 December 1921; review by Fred Hall, 24 and 31 December 1921 and 7 January 1922
68. Percy Redfern, *Journey to Understanding*, Allen & Unwin, 1946, p. 164; BWD 21 September 1930*.
69. Employing very much the same rationale as lay behind the Webbs' social parliament, George Lansbury had advanced similar proposals some six years earlier; see John Shepherd, *George Lansbury. At the heart of old Labour*, Oxford: OUP, 2002, p. 220.
70. Passfield papers, 4/24, 'A scheme for devolution', c. March 1930; 6/83, 'Can we make our parliamentary institutions equal to their task?', typescript talk for BBC, 2 April 1930; BWD 15 November 1929; 23 January*, 7 March, 3 April 1930
71. Cole, *The Next Ten Years in British Social and Economic Policy*, Macmillan, 1929, ch. 15.
72. BWD 25 November* and 1 December* 1930.
73. Harris, *Unemployment and Politics*, pp. 42-3.
74. See e.g. Jonathan Schneer, *George Lansbury*, Manchester: MUP, 1990, pp. 60-7.
75. *DCC*, pp. 130-1.
76. See the Webbs' *English Poor Law Policy* [*EPLP*], Longman, 3 vols, 1927-9, and for illuminating diary references, BWD 20 June*, 10 November* and 31 December 1926*; 14 February and 7 July 1927; 2 February and 20 June* 1929; 23 November 1930*; 24 August 1931.
77. See Beatrice's comments, BWD 1 August 1938.
78. BWD 16 April* and 25 November* 1930, 4 January* and 18 April* 1931, MSS Gilbert Murray 543/30, BW to Lady Mary Murray, 6 September 1930; Lloyd George papers G/11/4, Lansbury to Lloyd George, 16 February 1931.

79. BWD 31 May 1930.
80. *EPLP*, pp. 1006-7, 1023.
81. BWD 22 June, 16 September 1925; 18 and 30 June, 19 October 1926, 25 March, 30 May and 9 June 1929.
82. Hansard 160 HC Deb 5s., cols 937-50, 20 March 1923.
83. Hamilton, *Sidney and Beatrice Webb*, pp. 259-60.
84. BWD 19 September 1925.
85. BWD 16 April 1930*, 4 February and 18 April* 1931.
86. BWD 23 September 1931; also e.g. 14 May and 4 August* 1932 for entries indicating Beatrice's earlier and greater enthusiasm for the USSR.
87. Harben, *Diary Written During a Visit to Russia in September and October 1930*, privately printed 1930, pp. 16, 22-3. Harben was to become a 'devoted admirer' of *Soviet Communism* (BWD 30 May 1937) and its influence can be detected in his own later commentaries such as *Russian Quiz*, British-Soviet Society, 1947.
88. BWD 28 December 1930*.
89. Hindus, *Humanity Uprooted*, Cape, 1929, pp. 120, 224 and passim.
90. BWD 3 January and 3 April 1924.
91. BWD 4* and 15 March and 12 April 1924; 5 April 1927.
92. BWD 12 February, 18 August, 16 September and 27 December* 1925, 11 October 1928.
93. Passfield papers 2/4/F/6, BW to Betty Balfour, 22 August 1913.
94. BWD 3 January 1924.
95. BWD 6 March 1924; Colin Cross, *Philip Snowden*, Barrie & Rockliff, 1966, p. 200; Hamilton, *Sidney and Beatrice Webb*, p. 268. M. Cole, *Story*, pp. 198 ff, presents the conventional view without a single relevant reference.
96. BWD 15 and 18 January, 7 and 15 February, 3 and 16 March 1924, 19 September 1925.
97. SW, typescript commentary on first Labour government, c.1924-5.
98. BWD 20 June and 12 July 1929, 23 August 1931.
99. BWD 14 February 1934.
100. BWD 20 February, 9 March* and 12 November 1930, 1* and 13 July 1931.
101. BWD 4 June 1933*.
102. BWD 18 August* and 19 November* 1930, 6* and 30 June, 28 July and 10 October* 1931. For Herzen see Franco Venturi, *Roots of Revolution. A history of the populist and socialist movements in nineteenth century Russia*, Weidenfeld & Nicolson, 1960, pp. 26, 33.
103. BWD 19 November 1930* and 4 January 1932.
104. BWD 28 December 1930, 6 June and 23 September* 1931.
105. BWD 18 May 1926; *Fabian News*, December 1927, pp. 62-3. It is indicative of the perceptions of America otherwise prevailing on the British left that the title Ratcliffe was given – and evidently thought little of – was 'Industrial feudalism – the capitalist autocracy'.
106. *Fabian News*, January 1932, 1-4; February 1933, pp. 7-8.
107. BWD 10 October 1931.
108. *Fabian News*, November 1931, p. 41.

## *Chapter seven*

# Roads to Russia (1) workers' dictatorship

### I

Soviet Russia between the wars provided a political terminus or resting place for countless British socialists. Easily mistaken as a single destination, its discovery at different times and by different routes suggests both commonalities and complications eluding straightforward tabulation. Simple lines of causation, tautologically sufficient to the individual case, invariably break down when confronted with the multiple trajectories which themselves defined the range of possibilities open to any one of them. Of nobody is this truer than of the Webbs. Perhaps it is for this reason that some of the most insightful observations on *Soviet Communism* have been made in approaching it from a wider perspective in which distinctive and generic features alike are more readily perceived.[1] In this as at every other stage of their careers, the Webbs saw themselves as very much part of a movement of opinion; and for information, moral support, the assurance of a readership and a purpose in addressing it, they depended on the broad progressive constituency to which, by the 1930s, they were offering virtual open house at Passfield Corner. *Soviet Communism*, despite its singularity, was thus a work of synthesis. Its unfamiliar subject matter meant that it could not have embodied the independent researches employed for the Webbs' genuinely investigative projects. Rather, it is the echo of countless half-remembered lectures, newspaper articles, conversations and political tracts that helps explain its gestation and gives the work much of its wider interest. Putting aside the zoom lens of biography, its exegesis calls for a wider cast of actors whose movements helped block or open up the spaces that the Webbs themselves occupied

For many historians, attempting to differentiate between the disparate admirers of Soviet power, timing has been the key to separating revolutionary wheat from bureaucratic chaff. For the Webbs, self-evidently chaff, it has thus assumed some significance that throughout the 1920s theirs is supposed to have been an unremitting hostility to Bolshevism. Sidney is described as urging armed intervention in the early years of the revolution, while Beatrice, as late as 1927, is notorious for having described Bolshevism as a disaster without parallel for the British labour movement.[2] Unfettered by direct citation, Royden Harrison described their ambition as one of 'putting Lenin down by fire and sword', and suggested that prior to 1932 they declined all invitations to visit the country for fear of being taken hostage. This is presumably a reference to the highly apocryphal story that Bukharin had invited them over in that barren year for visiting social investigators, 1918.[3] As we shall see, the Webbs were not nearly as hostile to Bolshevism as such accounts suggest. Even Sidney's initial support for Allied intervention was avowedly based on strategic rather than ideological grounds, and not sustained after the ending of the war with Germany.[4] Moreover, that very year of 1918, Beatrice approvingly recorded Labour's indictment of Allied intervention. She also expressed the hope that even the British military establishment – which, she observed, would 'unhesitatingly shoot down every nationalist in Ireland, every striker in Great Britain, and blow from the cannon mouth every Indian rebel' – would think twice 'before committing itself to maintaining order in Russia against the will of the mass of Russian peasants and town workmen'.[5] That was putting them down by fire and sword.

As well as the notion of a 'conversion', generally dated from around 1930, what such accounts usually stress is the degenerated form of communism to which alone the Webbs can be imagined as having converted. According to Marcel Liebman, what drew them to Russia was not the early proletarian upsurge they identified with anarcho-syndicalism but the Stalinist affectation of technocratic rationality.[6] To this Harrison added a cruder dichotomy between a revolutionary Trotsky and 'pedestrian' Stalin, placidly conforming to the demands of Webbian insularity.[7] Peter Clarke, from a rather different perspective, described how 'their mechanical reformism inoculated them against any sympathy for the Russian experiment in the 1920s', but how they warmed to Stalin's consolidation of power on the basis of a centralised bureaucracy.[8] Crosland in *The Future of Socialism* even portrayed them as being won over by the suppression of workers' control and abortion respectively, though these suppressions occurred some fifteen years apart.[9] Quite apart from their accuracy as regards the Webbs, such interpretations often depend upon the counter-mythology of a revolutionary innocence betrayed, which is itself unequal to what was a notably involuted pattern of engagement. In Liebman's writings, the interdependence of these storylines is especially evident, with the Webbs' delayed conversion providing confirmation of the 'absolute' distinction that Liebman upheld between a basically healthy Leninism and its regressive and bureaucratic Stalinist sequel.[10] Whatever its merits or otherwise in a Soviet context, so stark a periodisation is inadequate to the complexities of western fellow-travelling, and not even the much-abused Webbs can be made to serve as its ideal types. That much is apparent even on the most cursory reading. Not only reformism but democratic and associationist elements were mixed up in the Webbs' initial resistance to Bolshevism, while their succumbing to the latter's hypercollectivism involved the sublimation of older social projects and the stifling of a nagging liberal conscience. Moreover, set in a broader context, similar tensions can sometimes be discerned through widely differing patterns of timing and intensity of commitment.

Briefly, as Liebman rightly indicated, the Webbs did identify Bolshevism with syndicalism and guild socialism. However, they did so not as common creeds of emancipation but as further expressions of the impulse to violence and irrationalism that they believed had given such destructive force to international rivalries.[11] Far from Bolshevism maintaining the ultra-democratic impetus of syndicalism, for the Webbs it merely confirmed the hollowness and deceit they had previously detected behind such rhetoric. 'When the syndicalist movement did announce a prescription by the average sensual worker of his own remedies, the Webbs … raised the spectre of "small minorities" of workers with special needs being "swamped" by the "mass" of the workers who exert a majoritarian tyranny', comments Tony Wright.[12] Though Wright does not indicate a specific reference, such a summary fails to recognse other sentiments expressed by the Webbs, when, rightly or wrongly, they contested precisely this purported identification of syndicalism with the ordinary worker. 'We uphold the authority of the mass of the people and object to any defiance of it or any tricks of evasion', Beatrice had written in 1913. 'The minority must submit until they have succeeded … in persuading their fellow men to accept their aims or their methods of reaching those aims'.[13] Beatrice at least read Michels's *Political Parties* on its translation into English in 1915, and she must have endorsed its view of the oligarchical character of syndicalism, 'not … in the dominion of the leaders over the masses, but in the dominion of a small fraction of the masses over the whole'.[14] Thus, when old assailants like William Mellor – whom Beatrice had been amused to find thought Michels 'a new and wonderful revelation' – acclaimed the Bolsheviks' 'total disregard for the ordinary canons of bourgeois morality', the latent authoritarianism uniting the two programmes must have seemed confirmed.[15] Even Cole, while never joining the communist party, justified the dictatorship of the proletariat, at least as something 'infinitely better' than a parliamentary system, and did so on explicit grounds of the unfitness of the 'stunted' masses for majority rule. 'For a long time to come, a minority will continue to govern, and the test of the social system will be whether it is weighted so as to bring the right minority to the top', he wrote in 1920.[16] If, as Cole rightly averred, the Webbs would have felt uneasy in the Russia of 1920, it was not, as Harrison conceded, because they regarded the regime as an unleashing of democracy.[17]

In any case, long before Lenin's death or Trotsky's banishment, Bolshevism had lost for the Webbs its initial syndicalist colouring. As early as February 1920, Beatrice described the regime as '"government from above" with a vengeance', a 'bureaucratic administration exercising far-reaching coercive power'. Later that year she again recorded the abandonment of workers' control for a 'rigid consumers' collectivism', wryly describing it as the 'Servile State' that the new regime's devotees had once so fiercely denounced.[18] At the same year's Fabian summer school, Leonid Krasin of the Russian Trade Delegation spelt out the full creed of Soviet collectivism with spellbinding eloquence. It was, Beatrice wrote to Wells, 'the most rigid form of state socialism; the dominant note being "Working to a Plan" conceived by scientific men and applied without any regard for personal freedom or group autonomy'. Not only was producer to be subordinated to the consumer, but the consumer in turn to what sounded like an all-powerful expert reified in the 'plan'.

> Every expedient of modern industrialism designed to increase the output of the individual worker, whether new mechanical inventions, new forms of power, new methods of remuneration – piecework, premium bonus, the concentration of business in the best equipped factories – were to be introduced ... Even consumption was to be organised. Payment in kind, with a small balance of money for 'supplementary needs', was to supersede the ordinary wage system so that the consumption of commodities by individuals might lead to the maximum mental and physical development of the race.

This was the Servile State indeed, so 'admirably conceived and delivered' as to bring even a Fabian audience to its feet.[19] As his biographer points out, Krasin has some claim to be regarded as one of the first of the Soviet planners, and the episode anticipated some of the attractions of the Stalin era.[20]

Beatrice too was impressed; but her reservations were stronger. Twelve months later, she reviewed Philips Price's *Reminiscences of the Russian Revolution*, the fullest yet study of its subject in English, and derived from it not a picture of proletarian revolt but one of party dictatorship, economic centralisation and the suppression of workers' rights. Nor, even on the most positive reading, could she regard the cost worth paying 'of famine, disease, civil war and the rapid decay of urban life, in order to come out at what Mr Price, somewhat unkindly, believes to be the programme of the Fabian Society'. The suggestion, in any case, was a libel. 'However highly Fabians may value the efficiency brought about by scientific expertness and reasonable discipline', Beatrice went on, 'they value even more highly the consciousness of consent dependent on a free democracy, political and industrial'.[21] To Charles Sarolea, when he later drew the same analogy between Webbism and Leninism, she insisted that they had 'never been State Socialists' but favoured instead municipal and co-operative organisation.[22]

**II**

The implication that the Webbs objected to Bolshevism purely as an affront to their sense of order thus requires a credulous conception of Bolshevism itself as well as a lack of interest in what Beatrice at least actually had to say about it. Nevertheless, it is not some special hybridity of the Webbs which belies the simple opposition of bottom-up and top-down forms of socialism, let alone their tidy affixture to different phases of the Russian Revolution. Thrown together in different strengths and permutations, shared beliefs and experiences produced in other individuals variations quite as resistant to flow-chart interpretations, and intersecting with the Webbs' own trajectories in unpredictable ways. Among these variations, the Soviet enthusiasms of co-operators, which were already widespread, and would-be planners, which very largely did coincide with the Russian plans, stand out as suggesting possible connections with the Webbs' own thinking. Each is therefore considered here in a separate chapter.

First, though, even at this early stage, among those drawn to Bolshevism precisely as a workers' dictatorship there is one case which had a special personal resonance for Beatrice and yet has never been remarked upon by her biographers. This was the husband-and-wife team of Eden and Cedar Paul, authors, translators and proselytisers for workers' revolt, who seemed to occupy the very opposite end of labour's spectrum to the Webbs. As such, they have sometimes been taken to represent the youthful insurgency of the 1920s.[23] With regard to Cedar Paul, whom Beatrice was to describe as 'a clever linguist friend of Rosa Luxemburg and Clara Zetkin', there is indeed no reason to believe that she had not always been associated with the revolutionary left.[24] Eden Paul, however, was a near-contemporary of Beatrice's, born in 1866, who had shared with her some of her most formative experiences. Politically the more productive of the couple, like Beatrice he leaves a trail in which the embrace of workers' power begins with the discovery of social guilt and responsibility by the Victorian middle class.[25]

Paul, unlike Beatrice, could be said to have been born into this 'consciousness of sin'. His father was the publisher Kegan Paul, an Anglican clergyman and Christian socialist who was influenced to take orders by Charles Kingsley before successively embracing positivism and the Roman Catholic church. Whether as 'a call from God', or from Auguste Comte, Kegan Paul described the desire to help others as the ruling passion in his life. In even tones of paternal sympathy, he recounted the benign and gratifying influence he exercised over the boys at Eton, where for a number of years he was a master, and over the labouring poor of his country parishes.[26] Acquired or inherited, these characteristics were transmuted and even replicated by Eden Paul, whose earliest childhood memories were of his father's efforts on behalf of Joseph Arch's Agricultural Labourers' Union.[27] First encountering Beatrice in 1884, the younger Paul was still at this time known as Maurice, presumably having been named after his father's friend, the Christian socialist F.D. Maurice. A medical student who had led a 'low fast life' since arriving in London, Paul had then undergone what he called a 'Conversion', inexplicable by ordinary processes of reasoning, which Beatrice summed up as 'a sudden desire to do right and walk by the light that was in him'. In his remaining true to this inner light, Beatrice according to her own account played no inconsiderable part. 'I remember telling him it was just a toss up whether he went to the dogs or became a useful member of society', she recalled with wondrous complacency, and had her reward as Paul spurned 'low pleasures' to run the boys' club and reading room at the Whitechapel tenement she then co-managed with her friend Ella Pycroft.[28] Paul's father, whose 'great delight' had been 'trying to raise boys who come under my influence in the social scale', must surely have approved.[29]

In this period Beatrice counted Paul an intimate friend, 'intellectually among my most intimate'. Long before the more durable intimacy with Sidney, he encouraged her reading of history, directed her to Milton as a model of literary expression and led her fatefully in joining Charles Booth's pioneering social survey at its inception in 1886. These were significant contributions to Beatrice's apprenticeship, and the survey work in particular was to prove her making as a social investigator. Nevertheless, by Beatrice's somewhat monastic criteria, Paul's renunciation proved less than total. Instead, it was with disillusionment mixed with jealousy and injured self-esteem that Beatrice observed his subtle sensuality, which she compared to the strange sexual magnetism of the priest, redirected from herself towards Ella Pycroft, some twelve years his elder. 'I have done my best to brace him up to a more manly life', she commented as their 'triple partnership' foundered. 'If other friends had been as kind as me.'[30] A few years later Paul jilted Ella for another woman, and for decades thereafter his and Beatrice's paths seem hardly to have crossed.[31]

Paul's life in these intervening years has not been properly documented, but he crops up – first as M. Eden Paul, eventually as plain Eden Paul – as variously a medical practitioner, eugenicist, Japanese high-school teacher, Poor Law guardian and ILP socialist.[32] Though not conspicuously identified with the Fabian Society, his political philosophy was a quintessentially Fabian one, which by the Edwardian years stressed the paramountcy of state action, the guiding role of 'trained experts' in effecting social change and the incapacity of the trade union movement for such purposes.[33] In 1909 he described the attraction to socialism of those, like himself, with a scientific training as being the search for order and an antipathy to the chaos of competitive society. Since 'the man of science cannot find the order he desires', he wrote, 'his next step is to endeavour to create it'. Socialism was thus the 'organisation of society', as science was the organisation of knowledge, and in this period only the political action of the Labour Party offered the prospect of such a project of social order being undertaken: 'Our proletariat has had little or no scientific training, and is apt to be hostile to what it does not understand.'[34]

Paul's instantaneous conversion to communism thus seems to exemplify the correspondence stressed by Harrison 'between the value system of certain late-Victorian professional people and the "strange syndrome of Soviet Marxism under Stalin"'.[35] Indeed, the Pauls' book *Creative Revolution* (1920) might be taken as the first major document of that 'correspondence', were it not that Stalin was all but unheard of – the volume was inscribed instead to Lenin – and that what might be thought its Fabian tone of superciliousness towards the wider working class was expressed in terms of the labour and intellectual revolt of the early 1900s. Among the volume's stated influences, apart from Lenin, were Freud's 'determinism', Bergson's 'indeterminism' and Michels's 'iron law of oligarchy', the English translation of which was the work of the Pauls themselves.[36] They also acknowledged a debt to Trotter's *Instinct of the Herd in Peace and War*, with its 'biological' explanations of man's political suggestibility.[37] Curiously enough, while drawing from it very different political conclusions, their fellow ILPer Ramsay MacDonald simultaneously found in Trotter confirmation of his pronounced pessimism as to the capacities of the new mass electorate. In a surprisingly friendly notice of *Creative Revolution*, MacDonald even conceded opaquely that 'those of us … content to call ourselves democrats and Parliamentarians are by no means fired by some dogma so that we do not accommodate ourselves to new facts'.[38]

Most striking of all was the Pauls' debt to that classic Edwardian text, H.G. Wells's *Modern Utopia*. Often linked with the Webbs' *Soviet Communism*, Wells's device of a Samurai caste was explicitly invoked by the Pauls to justify the dictatorship of the educated worker which they described as 'ergatocracy'. Commending the Bolsheviks for having found 'a supremely congenial mode of self-expression in … large-scale manipulation of man the social being', they did not suggest that such opportunities were peculiar to Russia or specific to any putative transitional period. On the contrary, encoded in human nature itself they perceived a Wellsian distinction between those with a taste for ruling – the 'intellectual aristocracy', or what Wells called a 'voluntary nobility' – and those incapable of rising above quotidian tasks and amusements. 'For Lenin was reserved the privilege of exercising his genius upon the plastic material of living humanity', the Pauls wrote, as if describing a G.D.H. Cole of the deed. In Britain, moreover, if as yet such an authority could be exercised only on paper, so profoundly moulded by capitalism were the country's many 'recalcitrant' elements that they would need 'governing' not less 'strenuously' than elsewhere but more. 'The hand of revolutionary authority', they wrote, 'will weigh heavily upon ... the disorderly elements of proletarian society'.

> The dictatorship of the proletariat does not mean a dictatorship exercised by the *Lumpenproletariat*. Nor does it mean a dictatorship exercised by those members of the proletariat (the majority under capitalism) whose mentality, whose ideology, remains more or less distinctively bourgeois.

This, the Pauls continued, would bring not 'ergatocracy' but 'ochlocracy', or mob rule, and through ochlocracy, chaos.[39]

In many respects, it is the hidden continuities apparent in the work which now appear most striking. A decade earlier, Paul had used almost identical words in defending the Webbs' Poor Law minority report, conceding the desirability of democracy but only once 'Demos' had attained sufficient intelligence to practise it. 'Failing this intelligence, we should have, not democracy, but ochlocracy – mob-rule – worse than oligarchy ... worse even than bureaucracy'.[40] In this earlier period, Paul envisaged the gradualist advance of socialism as itself providing the opportunity for Demos 'to cultivate his intelligence', exactly as the Webbs described the overcoming of destitution as the precondition of a 'self-supporting citizen life'.[41] So too in their communist writings the Pauls continued to uphold the 'remoter goal' of 'freedom through self-discipline', while looking in the meantime to the 'absolute dominion' of the 'more intelligent over the less intelligent members of the proletariat'. They did not, they wrote, advocate the rule of 'proletarians who have not yet attained to class-consciousness, of the ragged-trousered philanthropists', but the dictatorship of that 'rival oligarchy' which – arousing the scientist in them – would 'save the world from chaos' by 'revolutionary mass psychology'.[42]

This heavy emphasis on order and the continuing adherence to a Wellsian scheme of basic human types suggested that even the remoter goal of freedom was to be attained more by discipline than self. Precisely in the manner of Sidney Webb's *Works Manager Today*, the prophets of ergatocracy were again among those invoking the analogy of the orchestra, whose 'harmonious self-discipline' was only ever to be achieved through 'the guiding will and inspiration of a competent orchestral conductor'. Labour discipline, they stressed, had been 'one of the first demands of the bolsheviks', and they invoked William Morris to demonstrate that it was inherent in any scheme of 'social production'.[43] More than just an argument for revolutionary elitism, theirs was a frank exposition of the 'iron law of oligarchy' and a denial of the possibility of democracy in any human order.[44] It is no surprise to discover that the book provided an introduction to communist ideas for that most Wellsian of communists, J.D. Bernal, who had converted to socialism as a student on the second anniversary of the Russian revolution.[45]

Of course, there were major discontinuities too. Primarily these concerned the tempo and agencies of change, for in Britain, in contrast to Russia, the revolutionary oligarchy was to be based on the 'new proletarian intelligentsia': that is, the working-class militants with whom the Pauls were associated through the Plebs League, and for whom they abandoned both the ILP and BSP even before the formation of the British communist party.[46] Intellectuals were implicitly co-opted into the ergatocracy, and actual workers disinherited, by the distinction they drew between proletarians 'by status merely' and those so defined 'by revolutionary conviction'. Nevertheless, there was also a genuine identification with the working-class activist, militant, secular and independent, to whose superior virtues the Wellsian eternals of the 'dull' and 'base' were to be emphatically subordinated.[47] 'We have no Lenin here, nor need of one', they wrote. 'Here the working-class movement is fashioning its own intellectuals in the labour colleges and Marxist classes ...' On the other hand, this was not incompatible with a certain contempt for the average feckless man, whose plebeian amusements and pseudo-culture were dismissed in their second book *Proletcult* (1921) as 'dope' diverting the 'inert mass' from the 'class war'.[48] Similar attitudes found expression in Eden Paul's eugenicist writings spanning a period of some two decades.

In respect of this basic distinction, connections can be made, not only with the different phases of Paul's political evolution, but with currents of contemporary socialist opinion which were formally quite distinct or even opposed to each other. Simultaneously in 1920, for example, the syndicalist Tom Mann also contrasted the 'Mass of Workmen' with the 'small thinking minority' and acclaiming the Bolsheviks for rejecting 'frittering opinions' about 'the democratisation of government'.[49] Beatrice Webb, though her earlier sympathies with both Paul and Mann were now largely dissipated, expressed the same dichotomy in its reformist variant almost the same week. Visiting Seaham for the first time as the candidate's wife, she discoursed like a true Fabian on the lack of any intellectual or spiritual life. Instead, she noted the domination of drink, gambling, the 'pictures' and, for the constituency's sole corporate identity, 'a dingy and commercialised co-operation' and 'mechanically blackleg-proof union'. There was, however, as the one redeeming feature, a gentler version of the Pauls' revolutionary intelligentsia: the 'bookish miner, usually a secularist, with quite a large bookcase filled with the well known poets and classics – a little philosophy and more economics'. Hardly representative of their 'rough and stupid' workmates, it was nevertheless on these bookish miners that Sidney's candidature, like Mann's workers' control, the Pauls' workers' dictatorship and Cole's national guilds, was to depend.[50] It was Cole's later judgement that the idea of workers' control, while too exacting ever to have become a mass movement, embodied the aspirations of that 'small minority of skilled, intelligent workmen who wanted to be given a chance of putting their intelligence to social use'. If his assessment was correct that it was the defeat of the movement in industry that caused the same intelligent minority to transfer their attention to 'the basic problem of politico-economic power', then the link between these movements is more obvious still.[51]

## III

A modernist credo rooted in Victorian 'respectability', the Pauls' 'ergatocracy' suggests that, even for their middle-class advocates, the espousal of respectable values represented more than just a crude ideological control mechanism. Never wholly disinterested, but irreducible to terms of vulgar self-regard, its values were internalised and projected onto upstart social movements promising their fullest realisation by the overturning of bourgeois society. Confused and ambivalent these affiliations certainly were, but they cannot be regarded simply as another, distinctly convoluted attempt at social subordination. For the Webbs, it is true, they provided not the bookish miner but Sidney himself with a parliamentary seat; and yet the Pauls' blend of vicarious authority with its simultaneous relinquishment to organised labour provided an undercurrent in their own thinking which at last was given comprehensive expression in *Soviet Communism*. Among that volume's admirers, appropriately, were Eden and Cedar Paul. Active for several years in the CPGB, for a time the couple ran the communist childrens' sections in St Pancras, recalling the earlier paternalist endeavours of both Eden and his father. Party meetings in the district were either treated or subjected – audience responses have not yet been traced – to Cedar's renderings of revolutionary song.[52] Like her a steadfast supporter of the Soviet Union, Eden at last renewed his acquaintance with Beatrice in the dark days of the Nazi-Soviet pact.[53]

More directly than the Webbs themselves, Paul shows the possible affinities between the technocratic collectivism of the Edwardian years and a later relish for Soviet power. Like some other middle-class commentators, including the lecturer and journalist William T. Goode, who actually visited Russia in 1919, he also shows that even at this stage perceptions of Bolshevism as a force for order and constructive reform were perfectly possible even without any obvious predisposition towards revolution.[54] There is no evidence, on the other hand, that the Webbs were attracted by or even interested in the Pauls' notions of ergatocracy.[55] Indeed, the circumstantial evidence suggests that they were not. Although the Webbs remained on terms of personal intimacy with Shaw, Beatrice was repelled by his ever more provocative apologias for dictatorship, whether exercised by a Lenin, a Stalin or a

Mussolini. Shaw too in 1920 was already boosting Bolshevism for its efficiency and cult of 'getting things done', suggesting that the future lay with men of action like Lenin – and Winston Churchill. 'They did not worry about such trifles as democracy ... The future ... would be decided by people who had the strength and the will to do what they wanted'.[56] These claims, however, had little or no resonance for the Webbs and the suggestion that they were Shaw's 'converts' to Soviet communism is misconceived.[57] When Shaw eventually visited Russia in 1931, what Beatrice took from his pronouncements was the already congenial notion of the Webbian 'threefold state', while somewhat discounting his larger claims, on account of his 'equally demonstrative admiration of Italian Fascism'. What Shaw admired in the two regimes, she added, was 'not their several social ideals (seeing that they are diametrically opposite...), but their common political constitution – the dictatorship of a creed oligarchy'. What Beatrice, on the other hand, admired in Soviet Russia was – with qualifications to be noted in due course – the social ideal that in her view distinguished it from fascism.[58] The very month that *Soviet Communism* was completed with Shaw's assistance, she contrasted his fascination with 'the *will to power* over other mortals' with the 'essentially democrat[ic]' philosophy of the Webbs themselves.[59]

Instead, it is from the rather different experience she shared with Paul of the Victorian moral reformer that her first signs of sympathy to Bolshevism can be traced. Already clearly evident in the 1920s, in both timing and character this trajectory set Beatrice apart from mainstream Labour thinking far less than is usually indicated. Though immune to any real enthusiasm for the regime, the Webbs did not so much display the strenuous anti-Bolshevik sentiments suggested by Liebman and Harrison as show a Fabian instinct for avoiding controversy on what appeared to be peripheral issues. At the founding congress of the LSI in 1923, Beatrice actually spoke out against the representation of Mensheviks and Socialist Revolutionaries.[60] The following year, as her attitude further softened along with that of the wider labour movement, the liberal journalist H.W. Nevinson was apparently snubbed by her because of his criticisms of Labour's stance over Georgia.[61] By the same token Beatrice shared emphatically in the greater antagonism evident after 1926, though on the whole what little she had to say on the subject tended towards conventional restatements of democratic values offset by mild extenuations on grounds of historic legacy, good intentions and misrepresentation. In a constituency letter of 1925, while she simply recapitulated Sidney's views on current domestic political issues, Beatrice interpolated a long Russian digression of her own in which already she commended the 'knowledge, faith, and self-devotion to their cause' of the Bolsheviks. 'Lenin and his friends honestly believed that they had to make the world better for the workers and that they even had to sacrifice themselves in order to do so', she wrote. 'Of course in their attempt to change the whole order of society suddenly and simultaneously they made some tragic mistakes; but so far as I can judge from all the books I have read on Russia and all the conversations I have had with Russians and with those who know Russia, this autocratic view of social organisation and this ignorance of administration is gradually changing as the Soviet Government gains experience of human nature and the organisation of industry.'[62]

It is in 1928 – and not, as is universally suggested, after the launching of the plans – that the possibility of a more dramatic change of heart can be discerned. In that year Beatrice contributed a foreword to Alexander Wicksteed's *Life Under the Soviets*. Ostensibly this was in remembrance of the author's father, Philip Wicksteed, a Unitarian minister, Toynbee Hall lecturer, anti-marxist economist and inspiration behind the Labour Church movement of the 1890s.[63] A sympathetic account by a Quaker, *Life Under the Soviets*, nevertheless aroused in Beatrice moral sentiments of a character which the elder Wicksteed, and no doubt the elder Paul too, would have recognised. Conceding that the revolution could hardly yet be judged a material advance even on Tsarism, she heralded instead the discovery of a new 'Scale of Values' which was replacing pecuniary self-interest by the 'nobler motive of public service'. Like most Labour intellectuals of the 1920s, she conceded what she called the 'amazing ruthlessness' of the dictatorship, but set against this the greater freedom and dignity of the ordinary Russian and the opportunity now provided for education and a higher cultural life. 'Music, the drama, art and literature, philosophy and science – all that is rare and distinguished in the world – is today in Russia as effectively open to the unskilled labourer as it is to the highly placed official or busy professional', she wrote. 'The new rulers of Russia, professing a crude scientific materialism, have done more for the soul than the body.' Order, discipline and authority were only mentioned in a negative sense.[64]

In general terms, this resembled the balance sheet of any number of British observers of the 1920s. One of them, the MP Susan Lawrence, took over the larger part of the Webbs' London home in 1928; and though it is nowhere mentioned in the standard accounts, Lawrence was already at this early date helping the Webbs to plan their own Russian trip.[65] Possibly it was Sidney's return to office the following year that caused it to be postponed. In any case, it is only from the spring of 1930 that one can trace the development of a more continuous interest, while as late as June 1931 a plan of future work in Beatrice's diary includes no mention of Russia.[66] It is clear from the same source that Beatrice took the initiative with the project, and to a greater extent than any other of their collaborations the major themes of *Soviet Communism* can be found rehearsed and refined in her diary as the work took shape.[67] Nevertheless, it was Sidney as usual who did most of the actual writing and whose release from active politics was practically speaking a precondition for the project being undertaken. At the same time, Sidney's greater susceptibility to Shaw's views and the shock of the collapse of the second Labour government meant that their interest in the Soviet exemplar – though still more conditional on his part – was literally redoubled. The longer intellectual gestation was crucial, but so too was the crisis of the early 1930s that drew so many eastwards.

Among the steady flow of pilgrims, two visiting parties suggest particular lines of analogy with the Webbs. One was a group of active co-operators, such as had been drawn to Bolshevism almost since the revolution, again attesting the attraction of Soviet power for Britain's non-statist movements of social reform. This phenomenon will be considered in a later chapter. The other party was an 'expert' delegation of Cole's New Fabian Research Bureau (NFRB), reflecting the technocratic allure of economic planning and a general reorientation to the state for which the Soviet experiment now provided a reinforcement if not the actual cause. Though such a reorientation may be thought a precondition of the larger claims of *Soviet Communism*, particularly in the sphere of economic planning, the tracing of this further lineage also suggests how something more than Fabianism was needed to produce a work of such utopian fervency. This too requires some closer attention in its own right.

## NOTES

1. See for example Barker, 'The Fabian state' and Beilharz, *Labour's Utopias*.
2. Passfield papers, 4/15, BW letter to Seaham women, 1 July 1927
3. Harrison, 'Sidney', pp. 68-9, 73; M. Cole, *Beatrice Webb*, p. 165.
4. Liebman, 'Les Webb', p. 409. The text of the interventionist resolution supported by Sidney can be found in Stephen R. Graubard, *British Labour and the Russian Revolution 1917–24*, Oxford: OUP, 1956, pp. 60-2.
5. BWD 22 December 1918. Very characteristically, this very passage is excised from the relevant entry in the Cole edition of the diaries, though this purports to give full entries except in cases of personal sensitivity or where Beatrice 'had got her facts so wrong that extensive rewriting would be necessary to correct them' – which itself appears to refer mainly to passages about Cole and the guild socialists!
6. Liebman, 'Les Webb', p. 410.
7. Harrison. 'Sidney and Beatrice', p. 72.
8. Clarke, *Liberals and Social Democrats*, p. 262.
9. Crosland, *Future*, p. 356.
10. Liebman, *Leninism Under Lenin*, Merlin edn, 1980, pp. 433-42 and passim.
11. BWD 19 February 1918 and 14 November 1915.
12. Wright, 'Fabianism', p. 229.
13. BWD 8 December 1913.
14. Robert Michels, *Political Parties. A sociological study of the oligarchical tendencies of modern democracy* (1915), New York: Transaction Publishers edn, 1999, pp. 222-3; for Beatrice's comments, on Michels see Woolf papers III a, BW to L. Woolf, 1 April 1916.

15. BW to Woolf, 1 April 1916; Mellor, *Direct Action*, p. 61.
16. Cole papers, A1/49, NGL lectures, Kingsway Hall, 4 March and 6 May 1920.
17. Harrison, 'Sidney', p. 68.
18. BWD 25 February and 1 July 1920.
19. BWD 4 September 1920; BW to Wells, 8 September 1920 in Mackenzie, *Letters*, vol. 3, p. 141.
20. Timothy Edward O'Connor, *The Engineer of Revolution. L.B. Krasin and the Bolsheviks 1870-1926*, Boulder, Cal.: Westview Press, 1992, p. 172.
21. *Fabian News*, June 1921, pp. 27-8.
22. BW to Sarolea, 16 June 1924 in Mackenzie, *Letters*, vol. 3, p. 207.
23. See e.g. Stuart Macintyre, *A Proletarian Science. Marxism in Britain, 1917-1933*, Cambridge: CUP, 1980, p. 93.
24. BWD 23 June 1940*.
25. See *MA*, pp. 154-5.
26. C. Kegan Paul, *Memories* (1889), Routledge and Kegan Paul edn, 1971, esp. pp. 163-4, 187-8, 209-10.
27. M. Eden Paul, 'Tolpuddle', *Socialist Review*, September 1909, p. 34.
28. BWD 15 October 1885, 12 April* and 20 August* 1886.
29. Kegan Paul, *Memories*, p. 247.
30. BWD 12 April*, 20 August*, 28 September* (with inserted letter from Maurice Paul dated 23 September 1886), 7 November* and 10 December 1886, 29 April 1888*, 26 April 1890*.
31. BWD 5 May 1890*, 5 May 1939*, 23 June 1940*.
32. For incidental biographical details see also Eden Paul, *Chronos: or the future of the family*, Kegan Paul, Trench, Trubner, 1930, pp. 26, 49.
33. M. Eden Paul, 'Tolpuddle', pp. 33, 37; Paul, 'Socialism and science', *New Leader*, 28 January and 4 and 11 February 1910;
34. M. Eden Paul, 'Socialism and science', *Socialist Review*, April 1909, pp.103, 105-6.
35. See above p. 15.
36. Eden and Cedar Paul, *Creative Revolution. A study of communist ergatocracy* (1920), Plebs League edn, 1921.
37. W. Trotter, *Instinct of the Herd in Peace and War*, Fisher Unwin, 1916, pp. 32-3 and passim.
38. J.R. MacDonald, *A Policy for the Labour Party*, Leonard Parsons, 1920, pp. 47, 67; *Socialist Review*, October-December 1920, p. 379.
39. Paul, *Creative Revolution*, pp. 14, 131-4, 147-61.
40. *Labour Leader*, 8 July 1910.
41. See *PD*, pp. 81-2
42. Paul, *Creative Revolution*, pp. 132, 143; Eden and Cedar Paul, *Communism*, Labour Publishing Co, 1921, p. 18.
43. Paul, *Communism*, p. 15.
44. Paul, *Creative Revolution*, pp. 147-61.
45. Fred Steward, 'Political formation' in Brenda Swann and Francis Aprahamian, *J.D. Bernal. A life in science and politics*, Verso, 1999, pp. 42-3.
46. ILP archives 6/12/10, Eden and Cedar Paul, letter of resignation from ILP and BSP, 28 April 1919.
47. Paul, *Creative Revolution*, pp. 63-79, 118, 143.

48. Eden and Cedar Paul, *Proletcult*, Leonard Parsons, 1921, pp. 25-6.
49. The *Call*, 27 May 1920.
50. BWD 8 June 1920; for Cole see e.g. *Self-Government*, p. 81.
51. Cole papers A1/52/12, typescript article for the *Observer*, dated 21 August 1942.
52. The Pauls were CPGB members at least as late as 1928; see RGASPI 495/100/489, Bell to Krebs, 20 November 1928; also Pollard papers, box 4, CPGB St Pancras LPC minutes 12 November and 28 December 1923.
53. BW to SW, c. 20 June 1940 in Mackenzie, *Letters*, vol. 3,pp. 441-2.
54. See William T. Goode, *Bolshevism at Work*, Allen & Unwin, 1920, pp. 119-42.
55. In *MA*, p. 231 Beatrice recorded the existence of these works without comment.
56. 'Bernard Shaw on Bolshevism', *Call*, 12 February 1920.
57. Michael Holroyd, *Bernard Shaw. Volume 3: 1918-1950. The lure of fantasy*, Penguin edn, 1993, pp. 248-52.
58. BWD 28 July and 8 August 1931, 2 July 1934.
59. BWD 1 July 1935.
60. Bruno Naarden, *Socialist Europe and Revolutionary Russia. Perception and prejudice, 1848-1923*, Cambridge: CUP, 1992, p. 511.
61. Nevinson papers, MS Eng. misc. e. 623/4, diary entries for 18 September and 7 October 1924; Passfield papers 4/15, BW's letters to Seaham women, 2 October 1924.
62. Passfield papers 4/15, BW to Seaham women, 25 January 1925; also 1 July 1927 for more hostile (and familiar) observations.
63. See K.S. Inglis, *Churches and the Working Class in Victorian England*, Routledge & Kegan Paul, 1974 edn, pp. 218 ff; Pelling, *Origins*, pp. 132-8; McBriar, *Fabian Socialism*, pp. 31-5; H.W. Nevinson, *Changes and Chances*, Nisbet, 1923, p. 83.
64. BW, 'Introduction' to Alexander Wicksteed, *Life Under the Soviets*, John Lane: the Bodley Head, n.d. but 1928, pp. vii-xiv.
65. Sidney to Beatrice, 25 April 1928, Mackenzie, *Letters*, vol 3, p. 298, BWD 7 February and 11 September 1928*. See also Lawrence, 'Russia. Some impressions and some guesses', *Labour Magazine*, November 1925, pp. 293-5 and December 1925, pp. 351-3.
66. BWD 19 June 1931*.
67. BWD 27 March, 25 April*, 11 May, 21 September*, 16 October* and 24 November 1933, 19 February*, 27 April, 18 October* and 13* and 27* November 1934.

## *Chapter eight*

# Roads to Russia (2) Planning

## I

Although tentatively prefigured in the 1920s, the Webbs' trip to Russia in 1932 belongs inextricably with the new wave of pilgrims and sight-seers prompted by the deepening crisis of western capitalism and sheer audacity of the Five Year Plans. Even the delay of a year or two, while Sidney sat in MacDonald's cabinet, made for significant adjustments of both expectations and perceptions. To its British sympathisers, NEP Russia was like a huge and far-flung left-wing Labour council, politically somewhat outré but enjoining solidarity by its social initiatives and the attacks to which it was subjected by Labour's enemies. Already a few admirers, like the Cambridge economist Maurice Dobb, dwelt on the marvels of planning and industrial organisation which they discerned even in the 1920s.[1] In Britain, however, Dobb was very much the exception, both as an academic expert embracing communism and as a communist embracing highly technocratic lines of argument. Like Beatrice in her preface to Wicksteed's book, it was overwhelmingly to its social ideals and not its economic achievements that British sympathisers with the revolution were attracted.

With the onset of the Five Year Plans, the social patina remained, but the Soviet experiment also acquired a technocratic and productivist dynamic, making for more grandiloquent claims: not just of a workers' citadel or social laboratory, but of the 'future' (singular) which the American journalist Lincoln Steffens had prematurely heralded in 1920. Moreover, the dissemination of such images was itself subjected to the same systematising logic, colouring and to some extent supplanting travellers' commentaries through the agency, either direct or indirect, of the Soviet state. First in the field was the Soviet organisation VOKS – the All-Union Society for Cultural Relations with Foreign Countries – which interestingly was founded a year *after* its British counterpart and satellite, in August 1925.[2] While VOKS was aimed mainly at intellectuals, the more plebeian Friends of the Soviet Union (FOSU) was launched internationally in November 1927, with an illustrated monthly *Russia Today* following in Britain three years later. Again, both the FOSU's founding Moscow congress and the conference of national sections it convened in Cologne in May 1928 took place at least ostensibly on the initiative of its British supporters.[3] Also established at this time were the state travel company Intourist, founded in 1929 and only gradually achieving an effective monopoly of the tourist route, and the foreign languages' publishing house (initially Co-operative Publishing Society of Foreign Workers in the USSR), which produced a stream of books detailing Soviet achievements in disparate fields of activity.[4] Also dating from 1931 was the *Moscow Daily News*, founded primarily for the benefit of foreign specialists in the USSR but circulating internationally and providing a major source for *Soviet Communism*. Edited by Borodin, the Comintern agent arrested in Britain in 1922, the head of its foreign section was Rose Cohen, formerly one of the LRD rebels, who solicited contributions from the Webbs themselves.[5] The larger project which the latter had now undertaken was inconceivable except on the basis of these new channels of information.

Among the hundreds of British socialists who availed themselves of the same facilities, different traditions and generational groupings, though rarely existing in pristine forms, are clearly distinguishable. One was the emerging cohort of rebels for whom communism now exercised a decisive formative influence, moulding and sometimes embodying their aspirations for change as they took shape against a backdrop of capitalist crisis. 'All the clever younger men are going communist', Harold Laski announced in 1933 from the Webbs' own nursery of the LSE; and as Liberal associates like the Simons and Toynbees told of their own children having actually joining the CPGB, the sense of engagement with the young brought Beatrice in particular the reassurance of continuing vitality and political relevance.[6] In 1933, while unblushingly dismissing the 'aged females' of the Fabian Society, she took a wry satisfaction when the young and 'fanatically' pro-Soviet scientist Patrick Blackett described as 'dead souls' such rivals or contemporaries as Wells, Shaw and Leonard Woolf. Perhaps, she pondered hopefully, the Webbs themselves might find themselves enshrined as the 'John the Baptist of the world revolution in western Europe'.[7]

While undoubtedly they drew sustenance from this new generation, influencing it in turn in a communist direction, the Webbs themselves need to be located within the general reorientation to the state which had been so marked a feature of British socialism over the previous decade. In some ways, it was like a revival of the Edwardian Webbs. Already in 1921, Beatrice had noted that younger intellectuals, emerging 'not on our left, but on our right', had retreated to where she and Sidney had been 'in 1899-1910'.[8] The archetype among them was Hugh Dalton, successively or concurrently a Cambridge Fabian, LSE lecturer, peripatetic Labour candidate and major contributor to the party's economic thinking – in several of which roles he had the moral and practical support of the Webbs.[9] Dalton himself was a member of the NFRB's 1932 Russian party, and according to his biographer Ben Pimlott the experience was of considerable significance in instilling in him a belief in the virtues of planning.[10] Nevertheless, though Dalton's form of a moderate bureaucratic collectivism might draw upon Russian lessons, it rarely gave rise to the sort of visceral identification with the Soviets of qualitative socialists. In Beatrice's rather damning assessment, Dalton himself was little more than a collectivist Liberal, drawn to Labour out of careerist motivations.[11] With his watchword of 'practical socialism', explicitly disavowing considerations of the ideal society, Dalton provides a useful context for the Webbs, but not the additional insight of analogy.[12]

A more instructive parallel is provided by G.D.H. Cole and the wreckage of the guilds tradition. By the end of the 1920s Cole's underlying affinity for the Fabian tradition had been formalised by his return to the Fabian Society and his development of schemes so bureaucratic in conception that even Beatrice demurred. Briefly, it seems, he even gave sign of fascist sympathies. In 1924, the year that he broke with the LRD and abandoned his struggling guilds journal *New Standards*, he had struck Beatrice as a 'lost soul' politically. When the following year he returned to his academic career, it was as if in escape from this 'mental isolation'.[13] Politically the move proved a fateful one, as Cole recovered his political impetus as mentor to a rising generation of academic socialists whose technocratic instincts already prefigured Labour's post-war revisionism. In Beatrice's view, they simply resurrected the now 'reactionary' collectivism of the Edwardian years.[14] Meanwhile, the rout of Labour's democratic utopias, more starkly represented by Cole even than the Webbs, suggests the possible attraction of Stalinism as corollary and compensation. The cordiality with which the Coles themselves succumbed to that attraction only underlines the interpenetration of what were only seemingly opposites.

**II**

In a European context, it is widely recognised that the corporate state had an appeal for many 'ideological' syndicalists.[15] In Britain, characteristically, the broader phenomenon had only a pallid reflection. This thread is best pursued not through Cole himself – though he was, as we shall see, at one time highly ambivalent about fascism – but through another of those awkward trajectories that have been almost completely discarded in the interests of linear narratives. The name of Emily Townshend, far from illuminating these questions, has been all but razed from the historical record. Nevertheless Townshend's personal and symbolic significance in the history of guild socialism was anything but negligible. Born in 1849 and one of the first enrolment of students at Girton College, Townshend was a suffragist, an educationalist and a disciple of William Morris from the days of the original Socialist League.[16] Subsequently she acted as a vehicle, perhaps the main vehicle, for Morris's ideas within the Fabian Society. Expressed with robust iconoclasm during the pre-war unrest, her challenge to Fabian collectivism thus helped kindle the passion for Morris of his later devotees among the guild socialists. In 1912 she wrote a Fabian tract, *William Morris and the Communist Ideal*, reaffirming Morris's repugnance for State Socialism and the 'Fabian yoke' and vigorously claiming him for 'the Syndicalist camp'.[17] These timely and congenial sentiments gave Townshend a considerable influence with the younger Fabian rebels, Cole to the fore, who gathered at her Earls Court flat for meetings and study circles. According to fellow guildsman Maurice Reckitt, she was 'the doyenne of the movement', acting 'in some degree as a mother to us all, but [as] a strong intellectual force too ... serving as a link with the ideas of William Morris ...' Among other activities, she helped draw up the FRD's constitution, and she was the one other member of the Fabian executive to resign in solidarity with Cole in 1915. Though their paths thereafter began to diverge, she remained an active participant in the NGL until, with Tawney, Reckitt and Penty, she resigned over its attitude to communism in 1920.[18]

That so generous and tangible an influence should later have gone all but unacknowledged is presumably to be explained by the embarrassment of Townshend's later leanings to fascism, abetted as these initially were by Cole himself.[19] Possibly the seed was sown even before the war, when Townshend stayed in Milan to observe Italian syndicalism at first hand.[20] Subsequently she translated two books by Odon Por, *Fascism* and *Guilds and Co-operatives in Italy* (both 1923), which provided the chief expression in Britain of the supposed realisation of guild ideals in fascism.[21] Both Townshend and the Anglophile Por leant heavily on Cole's writings, and they must have had his agreement to reproduce one of them as a postscript to *Fascism*. Possibly it was also through Cole's good offices that the two volumes received the unlikely imprint of the Labour Publishing Company, as well as an unqualified welcome in *New Standards*.[22] If, as one of his proteges indicated, the lost Cole of the mid-1920s entertained a degree of definite optimism about fascism, then these books must have been one of the sources of that optimism.[23]

Less idiosyncratic than she at first appears, Townshend reflected the general exhaustion of the democratic-utopian strand in guild socialism which had been grounded in the claims of manual labour. Usually, if acknowledged at all, the reactionary possibilities of the guilds philosophy have been associated with the pre-industrial trappings of figures like Penty, whose own fascist proclivities were rooted in a medievalist cult of craft. Even within Mosleyite fascism, generally regarded as a more obviously 'modernist' creed, claims were made to the William Morris who stood for the rejection of industrial society. Soaked in the Middle Ages, wrote a contributor to the *British Union Quarterly*, 'he would have felt particular interest in all those aspects of National Socialism which call to mind the medieval crafts' guilds. That the Corporate State should have citizenship not merely on a territorial foundation but on an active membership of a great guild of workmen, would have seemed to him the highest common sense.'[24] Townshend, arguably, was a more distinctive figure, seeking to embrace the 'new' mass production while remaining profuse in her genuflections to the Morris tradition. In 1924 she published a book, *Creative Socialism* – the title, like the Pauls' *Creative Evolution*, has obvious Bergsonian echoes – in which she argued that the 'new type of industry' then emerging demanded qualities of deftness, speed, social partnership and a new corporate discipline which were incompatible with the 'master and servant' relations of capitalism.[25] This attunement to industrial modernity, which we shall see compares intriguingly with Cole's and possibly helped set a precedent for it, was later to provide her career with a final ironic twist. In the last year of her life, as the Webbs toiled indefatigably over *Soviet Communism*, Townshend turned abruptly from fascism, whose crueller face had now been displayed in Germany. Like the Webbs themselves, she now vested her dying hopes in Soviet Russia.[26]

## III

According to John Parker's recollections, Cole himself expressed pro-fascist sentiments after his return to Oxford in 1925. If this is so, it must have post-dated what for most of the left was the final outrage of the murder by the fascists of the socialist deputy Giacomo Matteotti in 1924. Nevertheless, this should be taken as a mark of disorientation rather than active commitment. Though Cole was to propose a rethinking of past assumptions even more radical than Townshend's, it was not only more considered and comprehensive but self-consciously formulated as a contribution to mainstream labour thinking. Nevertheless, this programme too was conceived as a response to the 'new' capitalism, and in it Cole's old directive tendencies now resurfaced in the technocratic guise of 'statecraft and science'.[27] As Neil Riddell has argued, this conversion from pluralism to state socialism was 'deeply symbolic of the ideological predominance of the latter in Labour's thought thereafter', while also attesting the limitations and hidden ambiguities of Cole's own disappointed pluralism.[28]

Its defining statement was Cole's major programmatic survey of 1929, *The Next Ten Years in British Social and Economic Policy*. Intended as a 'mental spring-cleaning', the book seemed to herald Cole's return from the wilderness – the wilderness perhaps of Por, Townshend and Cole's first serious historical writings – to sustained contemporary analysis. Its vision, like the Webbs', was benevolent, bourgeois and bureaucratic – 'a text book for Labour Party administrators', Beatrice called it – and the only William Morris it mentioned made not men but cars, flourished by Cole as Oxford's authentic response to Henry Ford. [29] More profoundly than his later dallying with emergency powers, *The Next Ten Years* attested Cole's deep disillusionment with democratic methods. Although not to be equated with support for Stalin's Russia, or Mussolini's Italy, it expressed and reinforced a growing disposition to conceive of social advance centrifugally; as if in tacit corroboration of the Intourist brochures, socialism was presented as a matter of plans, planners, audits and efficiency. The volume therefore has a significance in the development of British socialist thought that, until the appearance of Riddell's useful discussion in the mid-1990s, had largely gone unrecognised. As a document of the post-war closure, the volume merits close consideration as the sequel and repudiation of Cole's guild socialism.

Cole, needless to say, did not speak of closure. He did however state as his central concern the exposition of a 'new' politics that would register the profoundly different circumstances confronting a 'new' generation demarcated by the war. Retrospectively, the years of revolt seemed to him ones of such stability that even rebels like himself had taken it for granted, spinning out social panaceas as a leisurely exercise in fantasy. With the shattering of this world, the depth of Britain's economic malaise and the urgency of its social problems now imposed on them more compelling responsibilities. More positively tending in the same direction, the prospect of a Labour government also demanded the elaboration of a realisable politics within a set term and inherited institutional framework. Given both the necessity and possibility of state action, 'post-war Socialism' needed redefining with a view to 'results'.[30]

This theme of a 'new generation' ran throughout the book. One obvious explanation was that Oxford's brightest hopes of the new era were, during its gestation, meeting regularly in Cole's rooms to discuss these issues with him. Among this so-called 'Cole group' were such future Fabian luminaries as Evan Durbin, John Parker, Colin Clark and above all Hugh Gaitskell, who provided Cole with a London pied-a-terre and a fascination which was only partly cerebral. Subsequently these younger associates were to claim substantial credit for Cole's relinquishment of guild ways of thinking.[31] Dedicating his efforts 'in spirit' to Gaitskell, Cole had written to him of how his mind 'insists on arguing with you instead of the world at large'.[32] Nevertheless, none of these figures was then even close to producing any significant work of socialist thought, and Gaitskell struck conventionally left-wing postures until the mid-1930s.[33] *The Next Ten Years* was thus a work which only Cole could have written, and from this unlikely source it provides what may be regarded as a founding text of revisionism. Several of its key arguments pointed that way: the rejection of wholesale nationalisation, even of coal and transport; the concern instead with control, investment and effective public management; the harnessing and stimulation of the greater technical development of the 'new capitalism'; the encouragement of its tendencies to industrial concentration; and the use of taxation, not public ownership, as the most effective instrument of redistribution.[34] Through the development of such ideas by the New Fabian Research Bureau, in its origins a more public and expansive version of the Cole group, this revisionism *avant la lettre* was to lead directly to its more famous sequel of the 1950s.[35]

Amid the inevitable expediencies of a short-term programme, what was more remarkable was the appearance of a fundamental transmutation of Cole's socialist values in ways also anticipating revisionism.[36] The key word in this regard was 'pleasure', to which Cole now gave his full, utilitarian endorsement, with an unexpected nod to Bentham himself.[37] Disregarding Mill's rationalisation of the qualitative differentiation of pleasures, Cole insisted that happiness was to be determined by the actual tastes and dispositions of 'ordinary people'; this alone, and not the strenuous mutuality he had once thought the essence of a free citizenship, provided the one legitimate purpose and justification of politics. If that were not sufficient self-criticism, Cole also took pains to demarcate this new realm of pleasure from the workplace, whose more numbing and arduous disciplines were to provide the greater income and leisure required for the joys of personal consumption. Cole now referred to this approvingly as 'paddling [one's] own private canoe'. Those so inclined could continue to find their satisfactions in public affairs; but no social structure was imaginable or desirable which required the active and continuous participation of the average, one might almost add sensual, citizen.[38]

To this 'substantial recantation', as Cole himself described it, a number of possible influences may have contributed. To its *Times* reviewer, the book showed that British socialists were at last heeding lessons long since absorbed by their continental equivalents.[39] Alternatively, it could be seen as succumbing to a Fordist symbiosis of efficiency and prosperity: that 'American ideal' to which, as Margaret Cole was arguing at this time, 'almost everyone instinctively subscribes'.[40] Closer to home, the cause and counterpart of Labour's shrunken ambitions was the resilience of a Conservative tradition which, as a chastened Cole conceded, had 'never made the mistake of supposing man to be continuously an active political animal'.[41] In a word, the issue between capitalism and socialism was that of 'outbidding' the other in the provision of a 'fuller' life understood in identical terms.[42] Responding, exactly as the revisionists later did, to the stimuli and challenges of Americanism, Conservatism and European social democracy, it is not surprising that Cole should appear as one of their forerunners. In words that Bentham might have used, and Dalton actually did, socialism in Cole's latest presentation was a 'quantitative thing; and his thrusts at moralising or even priggish political postures directly anticipated Crosland's later swipes at the Fabian tradition, also in the name of ordinary pleasures. In its obvious corollary, that of power conceived as a minority vocation, Cole was likewise echoed almost to the letter by Gaitskell and Crosland. 'The vast majority find their happiness in the family or personal relations, and why on earth shouldn't they?', Gaitskell insisted in the 1950s. 'There will always be a minority who are genuinely interested in social activity and social work. They can get on with the job.'[43]

That confusion of pronouns – the 'they' which really meant 'we' – served as a rhetorical link between mass contentment and the more energetic aspirations of a directive minority, whose holograph manifestoes these authentically were. In Sidney-Webbian fashion, Cole blithely assumed the narrative posture of the 'statesman', a device taken further in the role-playing of the Cole group, whose fresh-faced graduates were allocated fantasy cabinet portfolios and a country to govern.[44] That may be compared instructively with the workers', forces' and women's parliaments by which more plebeian movements periodically acted out their aspirations. Like a pendant to Modern Greats – the vocational degree for a ruling bureaucracy which most of the Cole group had taken – the method inculcated an assumption of leadership functions and the perception of society as an agenda of problems to be solved. Though the beneficiaries of Cole's revisionism were the many, its active agents were the few: the 'enlightened' employer, the disinterested colonial official, above all the 'expert' administrator to whom the transformation of British industry was to be entrusted.[45] In this, like the Webbs, Cole was very much abreast of the times. Appearing almost simultaneously with Bernal's *The Flesh, the World and the Devil*, that remarkable exposition of the hubris of the scientist, he expressed more modestly its demand that the expert intelligence be given scope to work its transformative powers. 'Within the limits of the broad control of policy by the State, it is indispensable to give the expert a wider discretionary power, and a liberal freedom to experiment in new methods', he wrote. The summary of his Fabian Society lecture captured it more pithily: 'One must give power to the expert ...'[46]

In disavowing effective self-government as his 'peculiar form of cant', Cole gave up more on behalf the movements with which he had identified than he did for himself.[47] After a phase of frankly disregarding the workers' disinclination to self-government – they would, he argued, 'learn to control, and to want control, by having to control'[48] – he now deferred to that seeming apathy the more readily since that in turn meant deferring to someone looking very like himself. Disentitled by the new politics was not so much the socialist intellectual, whose directive function Cole so deftly reformulated, but the union activist whose concerns with control had been rooted not just in theory but in daily work practices and the realities of exploitation. To these, Cole offered not a choice of values but the sterner logic of historical necessity. Not the employer or the state, but the inexorable dynamic of the 'new' machine production was overriding the 'vested claims and traditions' of manual labour. Though Cole retained a semantic attachment to some of his older turns of phrase, these now conveyed little more than the efficiency arguments of welfare capitalism and the industrial psychologist. Not just the old craft unions but the ideals with which they had shaped the labour movement were dismissed by the new Cole as wholly obsolete.

Like others of this time, Cole spoke of generations when he really meant class. This has been a recurrent theme in Labour Party history, in which the 'old' has routinely been identified with the working class, and its codes of seniority scorned by those enjoying a fast-track apprenticeship of birth and educational advantage.[49] Sometimes, as with the precocious dogmatism of the guild socialists, it had a radical hue. Nevertheless, because its underlying assumptions were so entirely traditional, it could equally take on more familiar guises, and Cole himself effected an easy transition between the two. This was nowhere clearer than in his proposals for the unemployed, on which the post-war Cole lavished a pre-war Webbian vocabulary of waste and degeneration, while acknowledging that his favoured rationalisation schemes could not but temporarily increase their numbers.[50]

Cole's solution, that of a National Labour Corps, was literally modelled on the teams of navvies who had built the capitalist world's transport systems. The particular example he cited, the Panama Canal, suggests intriguing continuities, for it had been advertised as an embryonic form of guilds organisation in the founding charter of guild socialism, S.G. Hobson's *National Guilds*. Though constructed by the US army under the strictest martial law – Sidney Webb in a review called it 'the crudest and most authoritarian State Socialism that the world has yet seen'[51] – this amazing feat of engineering suggested to Hobson the enlarged scope and status the guilds would provide for 'brains'. '[E]xecutive and administrative brains are hampered and restricted by the limitations and false economic conceptions of private capitalism', he wrote. 'The new era will inevitably develop a finer type of executive and administrative brains'; so ordered, indeed, as to make an economically useful life 'an occupation fit for gentlemen'.[52] Idiosyncratic that may seem; but with its explicit model of military organisation and early reminder of the ultimate authority of 'the nation', the parallel is hard to miss with Trotsky's 'labour armies' which a few years later provided what Orlando Figes has described as 'the prototype of the Stalinist command economy'.[53]

As for Cole's National Labour Corps, this was professedly no more militaristic than the Boy Scouts, after whose example its members were 'to take light-heartedly a certain amount of "roughing it" under somewhat primitive conditions'. Nevertheless, this, like the Bolsheviks' militarisation of labour, was explicitly set in opposition to traditional trade union practices. Indeed, by focusing specifically on the building industry, where his scout-like battalions were to 'run up' even the controversial Weir steel houses, Cole showed a readiness to confront this issue which not even Oswald Mosley was to equal.[54] 'The objection ... will come mainly from older men imbued with individualist ideas of the right to a craft', he observed loftily. These should be told to 'go to the devil'. Chronic oppositionists, having fought all their lives against conscription for private profit, they had come to see the enemy in discipline itself.

> Here is one of those Socialist attitudes, useful in days when Socialists were in permanent opposition, that have to be scrapped if Socialists are

> to make use of the opportunities of power ... The older Socialists will be wise, on all such points, to take the advice ... of their juniors.

With Bellamy cited in the place of Morris, Cole looked even beyond his ten-year plan to the permanent inauguration of a period of labour service for the youth of his socialist community. 'The younger generation has no such horror of discipline as afflicts a good many of its elders', he wrote complacently; and nowhere was that truer than of the 'gay, frivolous, stimulating' Oxford of the Cole group, that never for a minute imagined encountering that discipline from the receiving end.[55]

In describing craft unionism as 'played out', and its precepts and philosophy as politically 'obsolete', Cole threw into question both the underlying ethos and the social basis of the early Labour Party. Both in industry and within the labour movement, he envisaged the unions performing far more restricted functions, such as the previously unsaluted American unions had pioneered. Insultingly, he referred to chronic oppositionists like A.J. Cook, doggedly opposed to rationalisation, as 'barely articulate'; in reality though, it was Cook's very articulacy as a 'mere delegate mouthpiece' of the miners that Cole had come to find 'destructive of sound generalship in the class war'.[56] More fundamentally, the 'obsolescence' of the unions' wider functions did not, in Cole's view, require the development in their place of alternative democratic agencies. On the contrary, he queried the very principle of representation, suggesting that a society whose representative bodies had 'withered away as redundant' was, if expertly administered, the more content for not having to be concerned with such questions. 'The art of living is, in itself, so much more worth while.'[57] Like any statesman, actual or vicarious, Cole spoke as one wanting to live, when living for him meant administering and directing. Unblushingly he prefaced his four-hundred page exposition of the minutiae of Labour policy with the averral that 'many of us will welcome the successful establishment of a Socialist system mainly because it will at last put these highly uninteresting affairs in the proper place'.[58]

It was in this spirit that Durbin and Gaitskell, as mainstays of the NFRB's wages committee, and subsequently of the Labour Party's finance and trade sub-committee, disregarded trade unionists and discounted their possible contribution to a more equitable social order.[59] Though seemingly foursquare in the Fabian tradition, that may be contrasted with the genuine interaction promoted through Webbian precursors like the Control of Industry committee. As for Cole, though he soon veered back to the left, finding something of his 'post-war Socialism' even in Stalin's Russia, the theoretical rationale for his reinvigorated elitism remained. In 1933, while stressing that the labour movement itself provided the 'instruments' with which to achieve socialism, he argued that the wielding of these instruments required the direction of a 'keen and closely knit body of active Socialists, each prepared to put in a considerable amount of hard thinking and hard work on behalf of Socialism'. More exclusive than the ILP or Socialist League, Cole's 'New Fabian' research bureau, like its old Fabian prototype, was to disdain mere numbers in the interests of 'personal quality', meaning, for the few, that not a Benthamite pleasure principle but 'the furtherance of constructive Socialism' should provide their 'primary object in life'.[60] The same year Cole spelt out as his four principles of government: 'the organisation of the human will to serve the community'; 'the Benthamite principle of the greatest happiness of the greatest number'; 'the liberty of the majority' (to be distinguished from 'the liberty of the intelligentsia'); and 'efficiency in getting the world's work done'.[61] By this time he was a convinced supporter of Soviet communism as well as British social democracy. As far as one tell, he supported them precisely because they were creeds of centralisation and bureaucracy. The dualism which undoubtedly existed in Cole's thought can only be traced over time.

**IV**

Though it has a special resonance for the Webbs, Cole's 'new politics' was only one manifestation of the technocratic approach which was coming to dominate Labour thinking even before the stimulus provided by the debacle of the second Labour government. Other prominent examples were the ILP's *Living Wage*, adopted in 1926, and the *Revolution by Reason* of Oswald Mosley and John Strachey, perhaps the most conspicuously plutocratic of the Labour Party's new intellectual adherents. Still, it seems, Passfield Corner provided a hub of political communications, and apparently it was there that Mosley and Strachey made their first acquaintance.[62] Though the veteran underconsumptionist J.A. Hobson made a major contribution to the *Living Wage*, the programmes were essentially the work of what Beatrice called Labour's 'Frank Wise-Wheatley-Greenwood-Shinwell-Alexander-Mosley' generation of 'brain working' recruits.[63] Like the new Cole, neither programme recognised what Hobson described as 'proletarian economics', that is, the elevation of the claims of organised labour so characteristic of the immediately preceding period. *The Living Wage* in particular provoked opposition as seeming to threaten the displacement of union functions by the state.[64]

The Webbs themselves, while sharing in the general reorientation to the state, showed the continuing concern for the rights of workers' organisations that was to be reflected in their distinctive conception of Soviet communism. Indeed, it is suggestive of the intricacies of these questions that it was they whom in 1925 Hobson singled out as an example of 'proletarian economics'.[65] Even Cole, whom with gentle depreciation she accredited with 'the pure word of Webbian Fabianism', Beatrice thought at once too tentative towards capitalism and too dismissive of the aspiration to self-government. 'What one fears is that the swing away from workers' control ... may go too far', she noted privately. Chairing one of Cole's lectures, she good-humouredly chided him for his 'apparent sneers at Democracy'.[66] The Mosley group, whom she took less seriously, she described as young and gifted but nevertheless a 'foreign substance in the Labour Movement ... intruders into the world of manual workers'.[67]

As to *The Living Wage*, Beatrice was invited to provide comments on the draft version and these are especially illuminating. Presumably they were solicited because of the strong case made for such a concept in *Industrial Democracy*, where the Living Wage was preferred to the rival union doctrines of customary rights ('Vested Interest') and collective bargaining ('Supply and Demand'). 'The Match Girls had no vested interests to appeal to, and Supply and Demand, to the crowd of hungry laborers struggling at the dock gates, meant earnings absolutely inconsistent with industrial efficiency', they had written; and the arguments of efficiency and social equity, along with the deft linking of collectivism and the new unionism, must have appealed directly to a committee comprising an economist (Hobson), financial expert (Frank Wise) and TGWU research officer (Arthur Creech Jones).[68] Nevertheless, when the last of these, like Cole, put a case for industrial modernisation on American precedents, involving the unemployment, redeployment or emigration of skilled and other workers, Beatrice took strong exception to his highhandedness. She also questioned, as Ernest Bevin would, whether he or the ILP were 'quite qualified ... to lay down a strategy and tactic for the Trade Union Movement about wages and other conditions of employment'.[69] Privately, she described the document more forcefully as 'a monument of ... conceit and ignorance', assuming the right of 'The Elect' to pronounce on all ethical or scientific issues for the rank and file.[70] This was hardly a revolutionary analysis, involving as it did the defence of some of the most conservative trade unions; exactly as Beatrice counterposed to Mosley, Wise and Brockway 'the Arthur Hendersons, the Herbert Morrisons, the Alexanders, the Citrines and the Bevins, who are the natural leaders of the great organised communities of the proletariat'.[71] Nevertheless, the acceptance of the legitimate functions of labour movement bodies and their leaders continued to offset the cult of state power even in *Soviet Communism*.

The links with that volume should not be overstated. Extolling the Panama Canal did not have to mean doing the same for the White Sea Canal, the GPU's forced labour showpiece; and it took a good deal more than *dirigisme* to produce the sustained identification with the USSR with which we are concerned here. Nevertheless, the drift to bureaucratic collectivism did provide the language for translations from the Russian, while simultaneously its *realpolitik* left aspirations unexpressed to which the visionary rhetoric of the plans provided a possible outlet. Cole and Strachey, representing two of the major *dirigiste* programmes of the 1920s, virtually competed with each other in commending Soviet planning at those later extravaganzas of fellow travelling, the Congresses of Peace and Friendship with the USSR. Cole, who at the height of the terror saw developing in Russia 'a new and higher kind of liberty, hitherto unknown in the world', described the development of Soviet planning since the late 1920s as entirely the work of an enlightened leadership; indeed, he did not so much as mention any issue of workers' or consumers' representation.[72] As for the third of these programmes, the *Living Wage*, we shall see that one of its primary architects, Frank Wise, was already in the 1920s a friend, employee and ardent supporter of the Soviets.

In any case, it happened that almost simultaneously with the Webbs' Russian trip, Cole's New Fabian Research Bureau, founded to follow up the suggestions made in his *Next Ten Years*, undertook as its first major project the sending of an 'expert commission of enquiry' to Russia in the summer of 1932.[73] Cole himself was an absentee on grounds of health, and perhaps of his general disinclination to foreign travel. Margaret Cole, however, acted as the party's organiser and editor, and its credentials as socialists and specialists were such that even the Webbs considered foregoing their own visit to help with expenses.[74] According to its preamble, the party's object was to elucidate for the benefit of Labour policy the one available example of economic life being conducted 'on scientific and up to date lines'.

> While it is recognised that conditions in this country would require a policy very different from that at present pursued by the Soviets, it is obvious that over a very large range of subjects, particularly as regards the organised planning of economic and social life, valuable lessons can be learnt from the Russian experiment. It is indeed essential if the Bureau's work is to be on modern lines ...[75]

It was in this spirit that Dalton, politically the party's most significant member, digested the lessons of Soviet planning, without, it appears, even temporarily losing his head. Margaret Cole called it his 'Daltonesque sit-on-the-fence attitude', and over the next ten-to-fifteen years he was not the only Labour politician who found that the most comfortable and politic place to be.[76]

The same could not be said of every member of the delegation. D.N. Pritt, a Labour candidate and leading lawyer, was reported by Margaret Cole as being helpless in the Russians' hands: 'the eminent KC swallows it *all*'. Perhaps because his political outlook, like that of the younger generation, was as yet barely formed, the ideas of socialism and the USSR were ever after to be inextricably confused in Pritt's mind, and Cole's prediction that he would end up as 'some Communist before he's done' was amply confirmed.[77] More suggestive in the present context are the communications of a wondrous ingenuousness which Cole herself addressed to her husband. As a glimpse of a socialist future, the letters reflected the fads and phobias of inter-war Britain, with whom every Russian wonder invited its unflattering comparison, as surely as they did the attentive hospitality of the delegation's hosts. Naked bathers are described splashing straight out of a canvas by Gauguin, their bodies so taut and beautiful that Pritt's seemed the only paunch left in a sixth of the world. Perhaps, Cole conceded with a sudden flash of insight, this was due to 'rather short commons'. Sated with naturism, her eyes rested on hoardings free of sales devices, the dream of every 1930s planner and amenity group. '[T]hink what it would be like in England', she enthused. 'There are *no* advertisements – because there's nothing to advertise.' All that is lacking is a Webbian exclamation mark. The same letter even contains an echo of the Victorian slum visitor, for not only did Russian women hold down jobs; unlike their 'sluttish' English counterparts, they also managed to keep their homes 'surprisingly' clean. 'The only slut I've seen', Cole added gratuitously, 'is the working-class woman from England ...'[78] Doubtless that betrayed the special alertness to sluttishness that comes of having servants. In preparing her reflections for publication, Cole even got round to an exclamation mark: 'The lack of thick carpets and curtains – even of cushions! – together with the absence of coal fires, makes a Russian one-room dwelling far less frowsty than a similar one in Sheffield or Liverpool.'[79] Forgotten in her wonderment were the Coles' William Morris hangings, William Morris chaircovers, William Morris bust – and attendant domestics to beat and dust them.[80]

Located in English imaginings as much as Russian realities, this was the news from nowhere at last becoming somewhere. 'Whatever criticisms & faults – & there are plenty, some against Communism, some against Russians', ran one of Margaret Cole's euphoric passages, 'it *is* like a dream coming true'.

> To meet & talk to civil servants, & heads of large hospitals, & they to talk like the Movement – one keeps forgetting to be surprised ... because it comes so natural. One has come home. And all the things being topsy-turvy, education first, children first, workers first. I sound excited, but I'm not really as much as I thought, because it's as simple as becoming a Socialist.

Again, the letters serve as a warning against facile dichotomies. Even for those seduced by the claim of technocratic rationality, it took something more than socialism as a 'quantitative thing' to bring forth the empathy, indulgence, extenuation and generally dreamlike qualities required to take the Soviet claim to modernity at face value. In one letter, Cole described waking up in tears having dreamt of the revolution going under; now she realised how she had been much more moved 'under the skin' than she thought. 'I feel a little envious of Jack Reed, whose grave is under the Kremlin Wall, that is the sort of sentiment it induces.'[81].

The Webbs, as we shall see, were also fascinated by the notion of the plan. Lack of direct personal testimony means that we have to be circumspect about Sidney's precise motivations. Nevertheless, it is plausible to imagine that the practical demonstration of 'organised planning' explains why his interest in Soviet communism can be dated contemporaneously with that of Dalton, the Coles and other disorientated Labour socialists. Moreover, in *Soviet Communism* itself, analogies can be found between Gosplan and the planning mechanisms of the American trust, along with references to the 'unavoidable' bureaucratic apparatus of 'any highly developed industrial community'. These suggested a traditional view of state collectivism as representing the rationality inherent in, but always tending to be thwarted by, the modern capitalist economy.[82]

On the other hand, when Beatrice circulated a summary of her first impressions on returning from Russia, it was not successful planning that she principally stressed but the 'moral uplift' and 'intellectual advancement' which she found so much more pronounced and obvious than any increase in material wealth and comfort. It was this 'reformation of manners and morals', already remarked upon by her in 1928, that underpinned the claim to represent 'a new civilisation and a new culture with a new outlook on life'.[83] Other things than planning went into *Soviet Communism*, and one of them was an echo of the co-operative ideal which had first drawn Beatrice towards socialism. Indeed, travelling out on the very same boat as the experts of the NFRB was a delegation of grassroots co-operators.[84] How and why they made the journey opens up a further set of trajectories interlocking in crucial ways with those of the Webbs.

## NOTES

1. See Dobb papers DD16, 'Report on Russian visit 1925'; Dobb, *Russian Economic Development Since the Revolution* (1928), Routledge, 1929 edn.
2. Sylvia R Margulies, *The Pilgrimage to Russia. The Soviet Union and the treatment of foreigners, 1924-1937*, Madison, Wisconsin: University of Wisconsin Press, 1968, pp. 58-9.
3. Margulies, *Pilgrimage*, pp. 42-3.
4. See Margulies, *Pilgrimage*, pp. 63, 120 (for Intourist) and passim.
5. LHASC CP/Ind/Mont/7/3, Cohen to Ivor Montagu, 3 August, early 1930s.
6. BWD 18 June 1933*, 28 January*, 11 May* and 29 September 1936.
7. BWD 24 August 1933 and 30 March 1935*.
8. BWD 24 December 1921.
9. Dalton, *Call Back Yesterday. Memoirs 1887-1931*, Frederick Muller, 1953, pp. 124, 139, 198; BWD 24 December 1921.
10. Pimlott, *Hugh Dalton*, pp. 208-12.
11. BWD 15 October 1926, 20 June 1927 and 20 October 1936*.
12. Dalton, *Practical Socialism for Britain*, Routledge, 1935, pp. 26-7.
13. BWD 17 May 1924*.
14. BWD 24 August 1935* and 15 February 1936.
15. See for example Zeev Sterhell, *Neither Right nor Left. Fascist Ideology in*

*France*, Princeton, N.J.: Princeton University Press, 1994 edn; David D. Roberts, *The Syndicalist Tradition and Italian Fascism*, Manchester: MUP, 1979.

16. Biographical details have been taken from 'Foreword' and G.R. Stirling Taylor in *Emily Townshend 1849-1934: some memories from her friends*, Curwen Press, pp. 4 and 86-7; *Girton College Register, 1869-1946*, 1948.
17. Townshend, *William Morris and the Communist Ideal*, Fabian Society, 1912, pp. 17-20
18. M. Cole papers, MIC/C1/79, Arnot to M. Cole, 3 July 1975; LRD, Fabian Society Control of Industry committee minutes, 26 September 1913; Reckitt, *As it Happened*, p. 147; Cole, *Story*, p. 154; Cole papers, GDHC/D3/5, NGL special conference report, 11-12 December 1920.
19. W.G. Taylor comments directly on this omission, Margaret Cole papers, MIC/A1/5, Taylor to M. Cole, 1 December 1949.
20. *Emily Townshend*, pp. 71-5.
21. Odon Por, *Fascism*, Labour Publishing Co., 1923 and *Guilds and Co-operatives in Italy*, Labour Publishing Co., 1923.
22. Parker cited Wright, 'G.D.H. Cole', 109-10; *New Standards*, October 1923, pp. 23-4 (Rowland Kenney). For Cole and the LPC, see Pat Francis, 'The Labour Publishing Company 1920-9', *History Workshop*, 18, 1984, pp. 115-23.
23. John Parker cited Wright, *G.D.H. Cole*, pp. 109-10.
24. Arthur Reade, 'William Morris, National Socialist', *British Union Quarterly*, 2, 3, July-September 1938, pp. 61-8; also Thomas Linehan, *British Fascism 1918-39. Parties, ideology and culture*, MUP, 2000, pp. 31-2. Bearing the same (and not at all common) name as one of the CPGB's first political defectors, who is said to have flirted with Mosley at the time of the New Party, the mystery of Reade's identity has yet to be settled. See the entry by John McIlroy in Keith Gildart, David Howell and Neville Kirk, eds, *Dictionary of Labour Biography*, vol. 11, Basingstoke: Palgrave, 2003.
25. Emily Townshend, *Creative Socialism*, Dent, 1924, pp. 74-5, 82 and passim.
26. Taylor in *Emily Townshend*, pp. 86-8.
27. G.D.H. Cole, *The Next Ten Years in British Social and Economic Policy*, Macmillan, 1929, p. 17.
28. Neil Riddell, '"The age of Cole"? G.D.H. Cole and the British labour movement 1929-1933', *Historical Journal*, 38, 4, 1995, p. 379.
29. Cole, *Next Ten*, pp. 98 and passim; BWD 11 September 1928*.
30. Cole, *Next Ten*, pp. vii-viii, 7, 14.
31. Parker cited Elizabeth Durbin, *New Jerusalems. The Labour Party and the economics of democratic socialism*, Routledge & Kegan Paul, p. 95; Clark cited Williams, *Hugh Gaitskell*, p. 25.
32. Gaitskell papers F1, Cole to Gaitskell, n.d., c. 1928; Gaitskell, 'At Oxford in the twenties' in Asa Briggs and John Saville, *Essays in Labour History*, Macmillan, 1967 edn, pp. 13-14. Gaitskell recalled a 'moving reference' in Cole's preface to a 'tremendous argument' after which Cole ceded Gaitskell's case for the happiness of the individual. Apparently he was confusing Cole's published preface with the private note he sent him.
33. E.g. on coal nationalisation, which Cole's 'revisionism' disavowed; see Williams, *Gaitskell*, pp. 32, 46-51.
34. See Cole, *Next Ten*, esp. ch. 7, 'Socialisation'.

35. Durbin, *New Jerusalems*, pp. 97, 120; M. Cole, *Story*, pp. 225 ff.
36. Wright, *G.D.H. Cole*, p. 119, argues the opposite but does not really succeed in demonstrating the point.
37. *Next Ten*, pp. 19-20.
38. Cole, *Next Ten*, p. 103; Cole, *Fabian News*, December 1929, p. 46.
39. *Times*, 3 May 1929.
40. *Lansbury's Labour Weekly*, 17 July 1927.
41. Cole, *Next Ten*, p. 18.
42. Cole, *Next Ten*, pp. 103-4.
43. Dalton, *Practical Socialism*, p. 26; Williams, *Hugh Gaitskell*, p. 258.
44. Durbin, *New Jerusalems*, pp. 93-6, 113-14; also Cole, *Next Ten*, e.g. pp. 17-18.
45. Cole, *Next Ten*, e.g. pp. 18, 136-7, 242-3.
46. Cole, *Next Ten*, pp. 136-7, *Fabian News*, May 1929, p. 18; also Bernal, *The World, the Flesh and the Devil. An enquiry into the future of the three enemies of the rational soul*, Kegan Paul, Trench & Trubner, 1929. Immediately after his conversion to socialism in 1919, Bernal had been reassured to hear Cole himself point out 'the need for educated people in the labour movement'; see Steward, 'Political formation', p. 42.
47. This paragraph drawn from Cole, *Next Ten*, pp. 98 ff.
48. Cole, 'About nationalisation', *New Standards*, July 1924, pp. 258-60, an adaptation of the older formula of learning to control through experience of control, see *Self-Government*, pp. 99-100.
49. See for example *Bolshevism and the British Left*, volume 1, ch. 5.
50. Cole, *Next Ten*, pp. 48-67.
51. *New Statesman*, 6 June 1914, pp. 267-9.
52. Hobson, *National Guilds*, pp. 206-8 and ch.10 passim
53. Orlando Figes, *A People's Tragedy. The Russian Revolution 1891-1924*, Cape, 1996, p. 722; also L. Trotsky, *The Defence of Terrorism*, Labour Publishing Co/Allen & Unwin, 1921, pp. 118 ff.
54. Though the need for slum clearance initially struck Mosley as a way of absorbing unemployment, his 'Mosley memorandum' of 1930 envisaged only a road-building programme for its proposed 'mobile labour corps' and thus avoided inviting confrontation with strong union interests. Subsequently, as a popular front communist, Mosley's then PPS, John Strachey, did draw on this experience to propose like Cole a national housing scheme to absorb unemployment; see Robert Skidelsky, *Oswald Mosley*, Macmillan, 1981 edn, p. 136 and ch. 10 passim; Crossman papers, 154/3/AU/1/90, Strachey to Crossman, 23 March 1938; John Strachey, *What Are We To Do?*, pp. 346 ff. For the Weir house, see Kevin Morgan, 'The other future. The British left and America in the 1920s', *Socialist History*, 16, 2000, pp. 71-8.
55. Cole, *Next Ten*, pp. 48-67; also Gaitskell, 'Oxford', p. 6.
56. Cole, *Next Ten*, pp. 109, 114; Cole, *Lansbury's Labour Weekly*, 15 January 1927.
57. Cole, *Next Ten*, pp. 170-3.
58. *Next Ten*, p. 19.
59. Durbin, *New Jerusalems*, pp. 120 ff; Riddell, 'Age of Cole', p. 956.
60. Cole, 'If socialism is to come', *Adelphi*, March 1933, pp. 122, 127-8 and June 1933, p. 198.

61. *Fabian News*, November 1933, p. 42.
62. Skidelsky, *Oswald Mosley*, p. 137.
63. BWD 12 April 1924.
64. J.A. Hobson, *Free-thought in the Social Sciences*, Allen & Unwin, 1925, pp. 146-66.
65. Hobson, *Free-thought*, p. 162.
66. BWD 11 September 1928*; *Fabian News*, December 1929, p. 46.
67. BWD 29 May 1930; also 25 Febuary and 1 March 1931.
68. *ID*, pp. 559-99. The fourth member of the committee was H.N. Brailsford.
69. Passfield papers 4/19, Brailsford to BW, 8 April 1926, and BW to Brailsford, 17 April 1926; Cole, *A History of the Labour Party from 1914*, Routledge & Kegan Paul, 1948, p. 205.
70. BWD 16 April 1926. In the published version of *The Living Wage*, ILP, 1926, the section on 'industrial policy' which Beatrice had criticised has been replaced and Beatrice apparently thought more highly of the amended version; see e.g. BW to J.M. Keynes, 3 October 1926 in Mackenzie, *Letters*, vol. 3, p. 271.
71. BWD 29 May 1930.
72. *For Peace and Friendship. Proceedings of the Second National Congress of Peace and Friendship with the USSR*, Gollancz, 1937, pp. 150-66. Cole's attitude to the USSR, regarded by Beatrice as essentially at one with the Webbs' own (BWD 13 July 1934, 5 July 1938*), was moderated after the Nazi-Soviet Pact when as 'a bourgeois English intellectual' Cole proclaimed himself 'a liberal in my inmost being'. It is significant that he did not as yet take guild socialism as a reference point in adopting a moderately more critical position (Cole, *War Aims*, *New Statesman* pamphlet, 1939, p. 27).
73. See Cole, *Story*, pp. 225 ff.
74. BWD 22 February 1932*.
75. Cole papers, GDHC/D1/59/9, NFRB, 'Proposed mission of enquiry to Russia 1932', March 1932.
76. Dalton, 'A general view of the Soviet economy: with special reference to planning', in Margaret I. Cole, ed., *Twelve Studies in Soviet Russia*, Gollancz, 1933, pp. 16-34; Pimlott, *Hugh Dalton*, pp. 210-12; Margaret Cole papers, MIC/B1/14, Russian letters to G.D.H. Cole, July 1932, 'Saturday'.
77. Margaret Cole, Russian letters to G.D.H. Cole, 'Monday'.
78. Margaret Cole, Russian letters to G.D.H. Cole, 'Saturday'.
79. M. Cole 'Women and children' in Cole, *Twelve Studies*, p. 203, paraphrasing her Russian letters, 'Saturday'.
80. See M. Cole, *Life*, pp. 96-7; Virginia Woolf, diary entry for 24 April 1919 in Bell, ed., vol. 1., p. 268.
81. Margaret Cole, Russian letters to G.D.H. Cole, 'Wednesday', 'Saturday'.
82. *SCANC*, pp. 111, 1212.
83. BWD, 'Some of our conclusions about Soviet Russia and its relation to the world we live in', privately circulated, August 1932.
84. M. Cole papers, MIC/B1/14, M. Cole to G.D.H. Cole, 'Monday', July 1932.

*Chapter nine*

# Roads to Russia (3) co-operation

## I

For the well-disposed co-operator, Soviet Russia was not so much an experiment as a fulfilment. For some, even amidst the chaos of its founding civil war, the framework of a society based on co-operation could already be discerned. Predating the planners' route by as much as a decade, the co-operator's discovery of Russia thus had a starting point and topography that were rather different in character. Of course, the routes were not mutually exclusive: on the co-operative delegation that travelled out with the NFRB, the presence of E.F. Wise, a major figure in the development of a serious economic policy for the Labour Party, serves as a reminder that experts were also sometimes co-operators and could subscribe to many of the same values. Nevertheless, the key issues for co-operators, and the ones that link them with the Webbs, were distinctive. Foremost among them were a susceptibility to institutional indices of well-being, identified with the co-operative movement itself, and a profound ambiguity as to the ends of co-operation that proved especially vulnerable to the Soviet symbiosis of state and society. Predating and ill-subordinated to politics, and seemingly unconcerned with the apparatus of the state, this was precisely the environment in which Russophilia seemed to flourish. Though such sentiments were not peculiar to British co-operators, they do appear to have been more prevalent beyond the communists' ranks than in many other countries – which perhaps only means that they were less likely to lead to active communist commitments. Because co-operators, no less than socialists and trade unionists, conceived of their movement in international terms, the tensions between these different attitudes can be clearly traced through the International Co-operative Alliance (ICA), initially set up in 1895.[1] Indeed, the adoption of pro-Soviet positions by the ICA's British officials suggests unmistakeable parallels with the similar controversies provoked by A.A. Purcell's presidency in the mid-1920s of the International Federation of Trade Unions.[2] More pertinently in the present context, unlike the former communist Purcell, the ICA's British secretary, Henry May, based his positive view of the Soviets on arguments of explicitly Webbian derivation.

Wise, May and the sorts of current they represented within the co-operative movement therefore represent a further crucial context for the

Webbs. Whereas the initial attraction of the planners was very much a 1930s phenomenon, co-operative sympathies were expressed in such very different periods as that of War Communism (1918-21), when the co-operatives became virtually indistinguishable from the state; the New Economic Policy (NEP), when a degree of economic independence was restored and they emerged as plausible vehicles of socialisation; and the Five Year Plans, launched in December 1927, when the co-operatives were once more reduced to a clearly subordinated status. Due to the relatively undeveloped state of the relevant secondary literature, the account presented here is of a provisional character. Though necessarily based largely on primary sources, these do not include the ICA archives in Geneva, which would certainly have made possible greater precision in the mapping out of political relationships and alignments at the international level. Nevertheless, even a preliminary survey confirms the affinity which socialistic co-operators in Britain often felt for the USSR. Differences within the ICA over the recognition of the Bolshevised Russian co-operatives were clearly articulated; and these can be linked with varying relationships between national co-operative movements and their respective labour or socialist parties and with the different conceptions of a non-capitalist future to which these gave rise. The distinctive phenomenon is thereby identified of a moralistic, predominantly non-statist idealisation of Soviet Russia, to which the Webbs' own writings on co-operation inadvertently contributed, and which in turn left its mark on the Webbs themselves.

## II

The co-operative movements of Europe were if anything even more diverse in origin, function and social vision than their union counterparts. Homogeneous to the extent that by the 1920s the ICA was essentially a movement of consumers' co-operatives, the relations that these established with political organisations of the left conformed to no standard pattern. In 1921, the British movement's *People's Year Book* commissioned an international survey of these relationships. Despite traditional claims of political neutrality and open membership, it revealed that the trend in many countries was towards closer personal and institutional links between co-operation and social democracy, often at the cost of replicating wider political or confessional divisions. The variations which resulted helped give rise to quite marked differences of attitude towards Soviet Russia.

A special case was Belgium. Here, the working-class co-operative movement had actually been founded by the socialist party, the Belgian Workers' Party, and provided its main financial basis. Members and leaders alike had a dual and virtually indivisible allegiance to the two movements, and no fewer than twenty-eight of the socialists' seventy parliamentary representatives were directors or administrators of co-operative societies. Among them were four ministerial co-operators, including the country's leading social democrat, Emile Vandervelde. Moreover, the director of the Belgian co-operative union, Victor Serwy, had first come to prominence as secretary of the Second International when it located its International Socialist Bureau in Brussels at the turn of the century.[3] Although Serwy and the Belgian union were alone in formally rejecting political neutrality, the interlocking of socialist and co-operative personnel, and sometimes the establishment of rival non-socialist co-operatives, had a wider tendency to undermine the formal political commitment to universalism and the refusal of confessional or sectarian divisions. In Czechoslovakia, for example, the main co-operative union had also been founded at the instigation of the social democrats and was largely run by them.[4] In Finland, by contrast, the formation of an avowedly socialist co-operative union in 1917 represented a minority breakaway movement.[5] In Austria, where the new republic's first president, Karl Renner, had formerly been president of the main co-operative union, Renner's ideals of neutrality were jeopardised by the political weight and ambition of the social democrats.[6] Nevertheless, there was nothing like a uniform pattern providing a backdrop to a supposed British exceptionalism. In France in particular, the separate role and objectives of co-operation were far more distinctly articulated. In the north of the country, as in Holland, the Belgian federation admittedly provided an influential exemplar. Nevertheless, when after some seventeen years of controversy and internal division, the issue of political affiliations was finally settled in 1912, it was in favour of independence.[7] Prefiguring later tensions cutting across national boundaries, the following year Vandervelde used a French publisher to restate the socialist case against political neutrality.[8] Nevertheless, in France, as also perhaps in Germany, the very seriousness of the subsequent split on the left served paradoxically to validate a universalist basis of organisation that now seemed under threat even from within the working-class movement.[9]

To the extent that there was overlap between co-operation and the parties of the Second International, or where the latter provided the bulk of co-operative personnel, party-political perspectives tended to have priority. Though it was conceded that co-operation illustrated some of the features of the future society, generally it was dismissed as a means of attaining it. In Vandervelde's exposition of the socialist case, included with Ramsay MacDonald's endorsement in the ILP's pre-war 'Socialist Library', its transformative potential was explicitly rejected as a delusion, and the cause of socialism identified exclusively with state collectivism.[10] Even Serwy as the leading Belgian co-operative official described the movement as 'a means, and … not an end', and even as a means one subordinate to other agencies.[11] In the words of Charles Gide, the pre-eminent French co-operative theorist, the co-operative societies were often regarded simply as 'milch cows' for socialism or 'subordinate cogs' in the machinery of the workers' party.[12]

Nevertheless, Gide himself serves as a reminder of the diversity of positions taken up by European co-operators, reflecting on a wider scale the complexity of generational, ideological and organisational alignments evident within Britain. Most influentially, Gide's own very different conception of the 'Co-operative Republic' envisaged co-operation itself as providing the embryo of a new social order. Born even earlier than the Webbs, in 1847, Gide was far from disavowing socialism. On the contrary, he described the future co-operative order as the truest expression of socialist ideals as understood by Owen, Fourier and their followers – among whom he may in some respects he counted.[13] At the same time, Gide acknowledged an important but separate role for political action; and his ideal of the Co-operative Republic could thus be combined with active socialist commitments by his younger protégé, Ernest Poisson, born in 1882. Even so, as Poisson came to take on major responsibilities within the co-operative movement, he did so on a basis of jealously guarded co-operative neutrality and a recognition of the distinct but complementary functions which the two movements performed.[14] Superficially Poisson was Serwy's direct counterpart as a leading socialist co-operator. Nevertheless, their shared commitments concealed very different conceptions of the proper relationship between the two affiliations.

Though they long predated the Russian Revolution, these differences of emphasis help make sense of the divergent attitudes that were taken up towards it. As shall see, it was Serwy who was most actively opposed to any Bolshevik presence within the ICA, while Poisson and Gide, though rejecting the close identification of co-operation and communism, were much readier to look sympathetically upon the Bolsheviks. Perhaps the possibility of such a stance was already implicit in an aspiration summed up for Poisson's English readers as 'the extension of co-operation to the limits of the population and a similar augmentation of the powers of the community to control all [its] principal activities ...'[15] Even within the still unregimented ranks of the early French communist party, the main body of co-operators, led by Henri Sellier, were alleged to be working closely with Poisson and to share his 'neutralist' view that co-operation was not a party concern. According to Claude Pennetier, Sellier's initial adhesion to the PCF was more a matter of discipline than conviction and he broke with the party as early as October 1922.[16] Nevertheless, though he achieved more enduring fame as a socialist politician and housing reformer, Sellier was also briefly prominent in the French Friends of Soviet Russia, which he twice visited in 1936-7, and his initial adhesion to the PCF remains suggestive. Internationally as within Britain, one again encounters the paradox that it was not necessarily state or party orientated socialists who saw their ideals reflected in the Bolshevik party-state; Sellier himself indeed had been a strong partisan of the trade unions' political neutrality as well as that of the co-operatives. One may even conjecture that it was precisely those who had more developed conceptions of the state who could find these difficult to reconcile with the notion of Soviet power.

In respect of these diverse configurations of co-operation and party politics, the British movement epitomised the traditional co-operative values of inclusiveness and independence. Birthplace to the Rochdale principles and described by Vandervelde as a 'promised land' of co-operation, Britain was home to the oldest, the largest and most venerable of consumers' co-operative movements. Pre-empting dependence on any political formation by its very longevity, it was therefore unlikely to take its direction from the relative infant that was the Labour Party. If nothing else, the sheer scale of the movement's commercial interests imposed a pragmatic logic that drew it only falteringly into the political arena. Even then, it adopted the distinctive expedient of a Co-operative Party, which met with the doubtful allegiance or open scepticism of many co-operators.[17] Only one society of any size, the south-east London-based Royal Arsenal (RACS), affiliated directly to the Labour Party. Even A.V. Alexander, Labour's first co-operative cabinet minister, was aptly described by Beatrice as co-operator more than socialist.[18] The same could not have been said of his Belgian counterparts.

As a corollary of that relative detachment from party disciplines, British co-operation also provided spaces for more obviously ideological commitments that were irreducible to the terms of parliamentary socialism, still less the rival political creed of communism. Certainly, the radicalism of a section of British co-operators owed almost nothing to the CPGB, which did not recruit a single well-known co-operator, never established an effective co-operative department, and almost alone of the major European countries failed to send a delegate to the first international conference of communist co-operators in November 1922.[19] Instead, a lineage dating back to Owen and the Christian socialists was maintained in the attraction to the movement of varied idealists and utopians united if at all only by a rhetoric of mutuality. To nurture these ideals there existed a set of parallel institutions ministering to what the Webbs called 'the spiritual side of the movement', without themselves directly practising either producers' or consumers' co-operation.[20] Foremost among them were the Co-operative Union and the Women's Co-operative Guild, with the ICA fulfilling complementary functions on the international plane.

That it did so was particularly significant in a British context. With its central office located in London, and a broader 'central committee' which until 1921 was combined with an executive that was wholly British, the ICA was more obviously dependent on its British affiliates than the LSI or IFTU. Already before the war, this led to tensions regarding the relations between co-operation and social democracy, in which the British were strongly identified with the cause of autonomy. In 1910, French and Russian ICA delegates are said to have opposed a German move to have the association's office removed from Britain to

Hamburg, an episode that Gide recalled with dark mutterings of Teutonic discipline and uniforms 'of military cut'.[21] At the same congress a knot of socialist co-operators arrived direct from the previous week's congress of the Second International, strongly propounding the policy of an 'ever-increasing intimacy' between the two bodies.[22] From Austria, the call came to hold the 1913 ICA congress not in Glasgow but in Vienna, where it would have coincided with the next scheduled congress of the Second International.[23] In Gide's view, the intention was to reduce the ICA to an 'appendage' of international socialism.[24]

Instead, it was Henry May who in 1913 was appointed the ICA's secretary, and he remained so until his death in 1939. One immediate consequence was that the ICA avoided the dislocation of its socialist counterpart after 1914. Instead, it was May's achievement to hold the ICA together while very largely keeping faith with its internationalist precepts. Immediately on the outbreak of war, he led his executive in proposing an international peace manifesto on the lines of the ICA's pre-war declarations. Whether apologetically or defiantly, this was rejected by nearly all of his respondents.[25] Nevertheless, May successfully maintained the *International Co-operative Bulletin* as a comparative voice of sanity, discreetly censoring bellicose contributions, whether from France or Germany, and giving a prominence to those upholding internationalism. He also maintained continuous if sometimes prickly contacts with 'enemy' co-operators, including, after a brief hiatus, the printing of a German edition of the *Bulletin* from Hamburg.[26] As his opponents put it at a wartime by-election, a vote for May, in the best sense of the phrase, was 'a vote for the Hun!'[27]

Evidently, the ideal of co-operative neutrality did not imply the abjuration of politics in the wider sense. Instead, the ICA's lack of continuous forms of accountability provided scope for the sorts of unofficial socialism that remained embedded in corners of the British labour movement, giving rise to possible tensions with movements at once more disciplined and more closely aligned with social democracy. Already in his forties when he took on the ICA's secretaryship, May himself was no stranger to either the commercial or the party-political side of co-operation. A former official of the RACS, born in 1867, by 1918 he had completed several years as secretary of the Co-operative Parliamentary Committee. He had also, as we have seen, stood on two occasions for parliament. Nevertheless, the post-war years witnessed neither his absorption into Labour politics nor his subordination to it of co-operative interests. Rather, one can trace his growing identification with a co-operative world-view owing much to both Poisson and the Webbs. Like Poisson, whose *Co-operative Republic* he introduced to British readers in 1925, May regarded himself as a 'militant co-operator' who saw in co-operation itself a 'direct route' to the new organisation of society.[28] On the other hand, he also shared Poisson's appreciation of complementary forms of social progress, exemplified by his earlier union activities while an engineer at Woolwich Arsenal and his later active involvement with the Fabians.[29] It was this that brought him into direct contact with the Webbs. Already before the war May was a consultative member of Beatrice's Control of Industry committee; and in 1921 he travelled back with the Webbs from a co-operative congress in Lyons while they were preparing their *Consumers' Co-operative Movement*. Together with them he addressed a meeting of Parisian co-operators in which Gide, Poisson and Serwy also took part. Afterwards, Sidney wrote of how French and Belgian co-operators seemed 'much less imbued with the conception of furnishing *an alternative form* of industrial administration to Capitalism than our own Movement'. Presumably that reflected May's own dilation on the theme 'that the future of the world lay in co-operation'. It is interesting to speculate how far the Webbs' own exposition of co-operative ideals may have been influenced by it.[30]

If Fred Bramley was the most Webbian of trade union leaders, May was thus his co-operative counterpart; deriving, from their writings, conclusions that the Webbs themselves reached only several years afterwards. Long before 1921 he had come to regard Beatrice's original book on the subject as the 'keenest, clearest, and soundest' ever written; and now he acclaimed its successor as 'instinct with life from cover to cover', fearless and impartial as 'only the genius, intimate knowledge and enthusiasm of the authors could attain'. Moreover, he already drew from such writings, as the Webbs did not, a pro-Bolshevik moral. When, even before the Paris meeting, Poisson urged the incompatibility of Soviet communism and co-operation, May invoked the Webbs' *Constitution of a Socialist Commonwealth of Great Britain* to prove their fundamental identity as democracies of consumers. If communism was merely collectivism, he argued, then the same was obviously true of the Rochdale principles, while both, conversely, could be regarded as merely different forms of co-operation. 'The essential point of comparison is not the voluntary or obligatory constitution of the organisation but whether, in fact, the Communes of Russia or elsewhere are organisation of consumers freely open to the whole community in which to exercise democratic rights ... [and] supply the common needs without ... any other profit maker than the collectivity'.[31] Given May's international responsibilities, such an outlook was to prove hardly less controversial than Purcell's tumultuous presidency of the IFTU.

## III

The issue immediately reared its head with the post-war reconstitution of the ICA, formally effected at the Basle congress of August 1921. The issue at stake was the admission of delegates from Centrosoyus, the central union of Russian co-operatives, whose unbroken existence concealed its effective takeover by the Bolsheviks. Already at Basle the broader ICA central committee moved, against the British-dominated executive, that its delegates be refused credentials. When he spoke against the committee's position, May himself was strongly reproved by Albert Thomas, a leading French socialist co-operator henceforth to be associated with the International Labour Office. May, however, had the support of British co-operators, who controlled around a quarter of the congress votes, and it was largely due to them that Centrosoyus now held unbroken such international affiliations as were denied, or else rejected, by almost every other Soviet institution.[32]

The delegates' motivations were mixed. Just as Britain functioned as an *entrepôt* for movements and ideas as well as commerce, attitudes to Centrosoyus mixed elements of idealism and internationalism with not wholly disinterested practical considerations. For many years, the presence in Britain of Tsarist refugees had spiced metropolitan radicalism in particular with a seasoning of revolutionary sacrifice and adventure. May himself recalled hearing from the lips of exiles tales of oppression 'which fired us with an enthusiasm, only second to their own, for the liberation of a great nation'.[33] An especially memorable occasion, almost certainly with May in attendance, saw the then Menshevik Alexandra Kollontai address the southern sectional conference of the women's guild, along with Finnish and Polish speakers also bringing stories of their oppression by Tsarism. The guild's general secretary, Margaret Llewellyn Davies, found Kollontai's speech 'glorious' and its fluency and fine gesture irresistible. 'I am very sorry she has had to leave – she says her life is not her own – & she has to go where Russian friends send her', she reported of this humbling world of self-abnegation. She was not alone in succumbing to Kollontai's charm and eloquence. Seven years later, the memory added its further lustre to a glowing report in the *Co-operative News* on Kollontai's more recent achievements as the Bolsheviks' Commissar for Social Welfare.[34]

With the consolidation of the Bolshevik regime, the moral standing of the exiles was appropriated by state-sponsored bodies nominally bearing co-operative credentials. Despite certain personal and institutional continuities, this succession was a contested one, achieved by force. As such, it posed challenges in which co-operative sentiment meshed with issues of trade and great-power politics in ways barely discernible from standard diplomatic or co-operative histories. Even the Soviet trade delegation, the Bolsheviks' first real step to British diplomatic recognition, originated under the formal auspices of Centrosoyus, and from the beginning engaged the active sympathies of British co-operators. Though some were quickly undeceived, this legacy of pro-Soviet sentiment was to survive as one of the sources feeding into *Soviet Communism*.

A key actor in this process, and subsequently in Anglo-Russian co-operative relations, was E.F. Wise. More familiar as Frank Wise, the ILP financial expert and first chairman of the Socialist League, Wise was a significant political influence and linking figure whose biography remains somewhat sketchily delineated.[35] A Cambridge-educated lawyer and a civil servant from 1913, by 1920 Wise held the key position of British representative to the Permanent Committee of the Allies' Supreme Economic Council (SEC). He may thus be counted among the British state officials whose wartime experiences produced a lasting identification with the aims of Labour precisely at the moment when these seemed inextricably mixed with the cause of Soviet Russia. Similar figures, resigning from the service of the Foreign Office and Admiralty respectively, were George Young and Harold Grenfell, both of whom acted as advisers to the TUC's Russian delegation in 1924. Wise had also spent four years as a Toynbee Hall resident, and in 1918 he took the unusual step of returning to the settlement. This, one must imagine, represented some sort of renewal of the somewhat paternalist vision of social reform with which the settlement was associated. Other famous Labour residents included Clement Attlee, who also returned to the settlement just a few months after Wise, and R.H. Tawney Nevertheless, it is curious to reflect that Wise should have been based at Toynbee Hall at the time that he successfully concluded the Russian trade negotiations in 1920.[36]

Already Wise shared Russian links with figures like Young and Grenfell, having at one time been a member of the Anglo-Russian Supply Committee. His employment at the Ministry of Food also meant that co-operation entered early into his field of vision, and according to Cole he showed himself to be a 'good friend' of the movement in his three years at the ministry.[37] It was to these associations that Wise turned in 1919 to find a way through the impasse in Anglo-Russian relations. Supported by James O'Grady, the NAFTA-sponsored MP then leading negotiations with Litvinov in Copenhagen, Wise made a strong case for the ending of the Russian blockade and the re-establishment of trade through the agency of the Russian co-operatives.[38] When in January 1920 these positions were endorsed by the SEC and British government respectively, he was acclaimed in the co-operative press as the architect this breakthrough – 'the greatest triumph', according to Frederick Rockell of the Russo-British Co-operative Information Bureau, 'which co-operation has won in all its history'.[39] To Wise, who now chaired the committee charged with seeing through this policy, there fell the responsibility of not disappointing such expectations.

This proved more difficult than anybody anticipated. Initially, the aim was to exploit the relative autonomy and dislocation of Centrosoyus officials abroad, lukewarm or hostile towards the Bolsheviks and seeing in international trade a chance to reassert an independent role for the co-operatives. In this they were rapidly to be undeceived. Within a fortnight of the SEC announcement, all Russian co-operatives, including the key credit and producers' organisations, were merged by state decree; and in April all elected members of the Centrosoyus board were unseated and where possible arrested, leaving Soviet nominees in effective control of the movement. This was

Bolshevisation with a vengeance. Although the delegation that reached London in May bore nominal co-operative credentials, its members were such barely camouflaged political veterans as Litvinov, Krasin, Nogin and Klishko, all former leading figures in the RSDLP, and the last of them a veteran of several years on the London committee. In 1932 Margaret Cole was to encounter him in Russia as a general in charge of munitions. Berkenheim, the Centrosoyus vice-president who had worked closely with Wise to establish these negotiations, immediately disavowed the delegation, and with his fellow officials refused to entrust it with the movement's overseas business and assets. It was in these circumstances that Arcos, the All-Russian Co-operative Society, was registered as a British company to rebuild that business under the new regime's auspices. Among its first responsibilities, overseen by Klishko, was the transfer of funds to the British communist party.[40]

As to whether to recognise the Bolshevised Centrosoyus, described by its former officials as 'a purely state and bureaucratic organisation', Wise at least gave no hint of a dilemma. As late as April he described Berkenheim as his 'intermediary', but promptly on their arrival established the same cordial relations with Krasin and Klishko.[41] Possible common ground was the belief he appears to have shared with them in the softening effect of trade on Bolshevism. Quite explicitly, he banked on separating the Bolshevik right and centre – the former including Krasin, the latter such 'moderates' as Lenin and Trotsky – from 'out and out Eastern propagandists' whose guiding assumption was the imminence of European revolution. In exactly that spirit, he conveyed to Lloyd George Klishko's reassurance that the Kronstadt mutiny of March 1921 would rapidly be subdued. 'It is obvious that he thought the signature of the Trade Agreement would not be without some immediate political advantage to the moderate elements of the Soviet Government in connection with it.'[42] More constructively, the whole approach can be regarded as a direct precursor of the NEP, in which the new Centrosoyus was briefly to flourish, and which prompted Lenin himself to a lapidary re-evaluation of the role of co-operatives in the construction of socialism.[43] In these developments, Wise could take a certain satisfaction, not least when the unseated Centrosoyus officials accorded a grudging recognition to its continuing activities, if not to the Soviet regime itself.[44] Wise himself made clear his own attitude to Eastern propagandists when he joined not the British communist party but the ILP, which from 1923 he combined with salaried employment for Centrosoyus itself.[45]

For co-operators, it was a more delicate matter to accede in what its ousted officials described as the 'forcible annihilation and mutilation' of a sister movement.[46] Commercial motivations obviously played a part: it is difficult to see why otherwise so stolid and moderate a figure as Sir Thomas Allen, director of the Co-operative Wholesale Society, should have abandoned his stand for voluntary principles to support May's position on Centrosoyus. Allen at least made no secret of his concerns with the proper recognition of commercial liabilities, and in due course the same pragmatic instincts would be demonstrated by CWS delegations to NEP Russia and joint ventures like the Russian British Grain Export Company.[47] That British delegates to the ICA should simultaneously have tabled motions of concern at Soviet-inspired propaganda was thus in no way inconsistent with these underlying principles of inclusiveness, neutrality and the independence of co-operation from political ties.[48] It was not a political position but the reluctance to adopt one that allowed in such circles a certain lenity towards Bolshevism.

These concerns with trading relations were not solely the prerogative of what May called co-operators 'of a materialistic tendency'. Linking all co-operators was some perception of co-operative trade not just as a matter of turnover – for by this criterion, links with Russia were of relatively limited significance – but as a form of equitable interdependence abating the force of national rivalries. May described it as 'a co-operative lifeboat that will go out and save the world for humanity'.[49] Invited to address the ICA in Geneva, Wise even expounded a mutualist version of Cobdenite themes that saw in the development of peaceful trading relations the development of a new international order, and in the ICA itself the transcendence of the national divisions that so marked inter-governmental relations.[50] 'International co-operative commerce could do more to bind nations together than any other force', said Women's Co-operative Guild secretary Margaret Llewellyn Davies, moving a resolution of welcome to Krasin in April 1920. At the guild's congress that August, the possibility of trade with Centrosoyus was similarly seen as 'lay[ing] the foundation of a world-wide Co-operative Commonwealth'.[51] May, who as yet remained concerned for the Russian movement's autonomy, and dismayed at Krasin's neglect of co-operative contacts while pursued by 'shoals of harpies and undesirable traders', advanced a gloomier variant of the same argument. 'If co-operators ... [maintain] that the undoubted interference with the Co-operative Societies' operations is to be completely redressed before we ... grapple with the greater problems of economic restoration', he wrote in October 1920, 'it will be at the cost of demonstrating to the world the power and influence of the people's own Movement to achieve the only peace worth having'. The 'pooling or fusion of Europe's co-operative resources' was the only alternative to economic devastation.[52]

## IV

In setting such a premium on unity, co-operative ideals thus contained an inherent propensity to compromise and extenuation, and these would later confront honourable figures like May with comparable dilemmas in dealing with regimes of the authoritarian right.[53] Nevertheless, it took something more than just a generalised liberality to produce a positive identification with Soviet rule. This something more was the dream of the co-operative commonwealth or 'republic'. May, as we shall see, was to be seduced by it, but preceding him in making this connection was the Women's Co-operative Guild (WCG), an organisation jealous of its independence and often regarded as the movement's conscience.[54] Almost since the guild's formation in the 1880s, its moving spirit and undisputed leader had been the Cambridge-educated Margaret Llewellyn Davies, a marvellously gifted activist of Christian socialist antecedents, whose godfather was F.D. Maurice and who was profoundly influenced by the visionary socialism of the late Victorian years. 'W[illiam] M[orris] always excites me so much', she wrote in 1913 of the most pervasive of these influences. 'I get started off on all sorts of glorious possibilities – to be brought up in despair against the way everything seems so fairly *set* – in our wretched civilis[ation].'[55] Though far from regarding herself as a Fabian, Davies also regarded Beatrice's original book on the co-operative movement as 'rather an epoch in Cooperation' and, against her initial expectations, found the more expansive chapters of its post-war sequel 'extremely good'.[56] Again, what are sometimes constructed as discrete movements and traditions – Fabian collectivism and the working-class feminism of the WCG – can obscure the complexities of political identity and belief evidenced by their points of interconnection.

Evidently the Bolsheviks provided the same sort of free play for the imagination. Even in the early years of war communism, Davies betrayed that confusion of state and non-state forms which alone could render its desperate expediencies familiar. Whether out of necessity or ideological fanaticism, war communism was the ultimate command economy.[57] Davies, however, claimed to see in it the logic of mutuality. 'The whole idea of Soviet Russia has been to rebuild the industrial system on the most fundamental co-operative principle – that production should be carried on for use and not for profit', she wrote at the beginning of 1921. 'In Russia, co-operation having become co-extensive with the population, it has necessarily ceased to be voluntary, because trading for private profit is no longer recognised as legitimate ...' While for Britain she envisaged a less statist approach to the control of industry, the common objective of both movements was the 'abolition of profit-making capitalism', varying only according to national circumstances and traditions.[58] Once again, the conventional chronology of fellow-travelling seems hopelessly oversimplified. A whole-hearted supporter of the Russians, from its establishment in 1924 Davies was chairman of the Soviet-instigated Society of the Cultural Relations between the USSR and Britain. She resigned in 1928 on grounds of ill-health.[59]

Though revived under the stimulus of the Russian Revolution, the roots of Davies's arguments can be traced at least as far back as the 1890 Co-operative Congress. There, in a paper which incidentally was commended by Beatrice Webb, she looked beyond the co-existence of different forms of enterprise to that time 'when all industry will be carried on on a co-operative basis'.[60] In the glimpse of this future commonwealth, now purportedly being realised in Russia, there seemed little to distinguish the statist and mutualist approaches. Thus the Labour politician Lansbury, visiting Russia at the height of war communism, also claimed that co-operation, socialism and Bolshevism were alike synonymous with the principle of universal service, which itself carried forward the basic principles of the Rochdale pioneers.[61] The congress of the women's guild, implicitly holding to the same opinion, asserted more directly that 'in Russia … Capitalism has been replaced by Co-operation'.[62] Even the *Co-operative News*, on the pragmatic grounds that only time would settle the issue, argued for the toleration of different currents within the movement and thus, as its apparent subtext, for the continued recognition of Centrosoyus.[63] It may be noted that in the *People's Year Book* survey of co-operation and politics, the Russian point of view was contributed by Arcos.[64]

Within Britain, the intense opposition that such views aroused was expressed by the veteran Liberal co-operator E.O. Greening, a long-standing opponent of socialism who also took the opportunity to liken the Bolsheviks to the ILP.[65] Even for those without Greening's doctrinal objections, the fate of dissenting Russian co-operators posed as awkward a question as to the proper objects of solidarity as did the suppression of free trade unions for trade unionists. In allaying such concerns, while skilfully tapping into the vein of co-operative idealism, a crucial legitimising role was played by V.N. Polovtsev, first representative of the reorganised Centrosoyus to the ICA. A pre-Bolshevisation co-operator whose 'handsome, stately presence' was already familiar at co-operative congresses, Polovtsev was credited with having played a major role in maintaining communications between the two movements. Remaining in London as Centrosoyus director of information, her fluency in the higher language of co-operative idealism made for especially cordial relations with Davies and the women's guild. 'It was very difficult to get Dr Polovtsev to talk about herself – her whole interest is so engrossed in the movement for which she is working', commented a reporter for the guild's magazine *Woman's Outlook*, as if describing another Kollontai. May also paid tribute to Polovtsev at the 1922 Co-operative congress, when again she spoke of Russian co-operation having 'developed its machinery so as practically to embrace the whole population of the country'.[66] Despite his initial reservations, May himself had by this time become an outspoken advocate of such views within the ICA. It was this espousal of the Soviet cause that, at the moment of decision, set him at loggerheads with his continental rivals.

As so often, the contest took as one of its guises that of rival travel itineraries. The first of these, in March 1922, was undertaken by one of the first international delegations to Soviet Russia, an ICA party headed by May. The majority of its members were British, including Sir Thomas Allen, and they were accompanied for Centrosoyus by the communist and former war resister, F.L. Kerran, whose first Russian contacts had been made with Georgi Chicherin, now Soviet minister for Foreign Affairs, in Brixton prison.[67] On May as the party's leader the glimpse of a long-imagined future made exactly the sort of impression which Margaret Cole was to describe as 'coming home'. The ubiquitous appellation *comrade*, like the 'obvious exuberant joy' with which the visitors were everywhere welcomed, seemed a proof in every speech and handshake of Morris's vision of fellowship – always, it seems, it was Morris who was thought of at such times. Already a 'heaven' compared with Tsarism, the restoration of co-operative rights and property under the NEP nurtured further hopes of a 'co-operated Russia', distantly fulfilling British dreams as well as Russian ones. 'It is the realisation at one stroke of the ideals of co-operation and labour which we set out to achieve by peaceful evolution', wrote May. 'We are startled and shocked because our perorations have come true':

> the economic life of Moscow is comprised in one word – co-operation … economically, co-operation is the State, and the State is co-operation. This has been the consummation to be wished for. Let us not, therefore, shrink from its realisation.
>
> Co-operation, independent and voluntary as to the main part of its activities, has behind it in Russia the resources of the richest country in the world, the facilities which only a People's Government could afford, the organisation of a movement instinct with life and energy …[68]

The very words, instinct with life, were those he had used of the Webbs' book on co-operation. More directly, Lenin himself, in his last writings, was to describe co-operation as utopian no longer, but rather, in conditions of Soviet power, as 'identical with the growth of Socialism'. Seen as representing a 'profound change' in Lenin's thinking, depending on one's point of view its further elaboration could either promise or threaten the reclaiming of the revolution by co-operation. 'Even in Soviet Russia it is possible to have a certain deviation in the direction of Rochdale principles and complicity with petty bourgeois elements', declared the French communist co-operator Henriet, for whom Poisson's endorsement represented a danger even within Russia itself.[69] These differing evaluations of co-operation were to figure prominently in Russian party debates over NEP.

Among the non-British members of the party, the object of dispelling continental suspicions of the Russians was satisfactorily achieved in the case of Poisson, who now encouraged Mensheviks and SRs to work through official co-operative channels. However, if Poisson was reassured, his Belgian colleague Serwy emphatically was not. Unable to prevent the adoption of its report, Serwy pushed ahead instead with an ICA delegation to Georgia as requested by the association's Georgian representative Gugushvili.[70] There could indeed have been no clearer riposte. Following the imposition of a Bolshevik government on Georgia the previous year, the proscription of the country's Menshevik-dominated co-operative movement posed the same quandaries of internationalist ethics and protocol as bedevilled the issue of Russian representation. Moreover, the movement in Georgia had closely conformed to what might be called the Belgian model, with a membership reportedly covering three-quarters of the population, closely aligned with the Mensheviks and moved by a 'socialistic method and spirit'. 'It has not been influenced by bourgeois ideology', Gugushvili had noted stiffly; 'it has not had endless disputes about the political neutrality of co-operation, and has always taken an active part in all phases of social life, hand in hand with the Socialist Parties'.[71] With its social, cultural and educational ambitions, its growth and suppression therefore provided social democrats with both a potent counter-attraction to Bolshevism and a devastating indictment of its oppressions. All this was conveyed in sober tones by the truncated delegation of Serwy and Gugushvili alone that visited in May-June 1922. Twenty years earlier, Serwy had worked closely with Vandervelde, when they were respectively secretary and president of the International Socialist Bureau of the Second International. Hence one may be certain that Serwy would again have taken soundings with him following Vandervelde's participation with Ramsay MacDonald on an LSI delegation to Georgia the previous year. Serwy's report was adopted by the ICA only after 'lengthy and animated discussion', through lack of any reasonable grounds for repudiating it; the dissemination of its findings, including an English edition, had to be undertaken by the Belgians themselves.[72] Nevertheless, the message percolated through. Vandervelde's friend Louis De Brouckere, another leading socialist co-operator, took Serwy's revelations up at the League of Nations and moved a resolution for the recognition of Georgian independence. Even in the British co-operative press, Serwy's findings were given full publicity, and favourable comment on Bolshevism was henceforth tempered by reports of the 'communist nightmare' in Georgia.[73]

May, for the time being, was immovable. In due course he would react bitterly to the betrayal of his hopes for a co-operated Russia, but for the moment he was uninhibited in his support for communist causes. Until January 1925 he served as first British chairman of Workers' International Relief, and in November 1923 he revisited Russia to celebrate the twenty-fifth anniversary of Centrosoyus and the sixth of Soviet power. At the Moscow Central Co-operative Club, a Russian witness later recorded with mild derision, he 'gave us from this red rostrum the benefit of the whole of his Russian vocabulary in the two words "Tovarischy Kooperatory"'. Accompanying him was Gide, who from the same rostrum announced his thesis of the 'new Rochdale', and together they relayed without demur the reassurances of pro-Bolshevik Georgian co-operators as to the well-being of their movement.[74] 'It is futile to talk, as the journalists and some politicians do, of the small minority imposing its will upon the mass', May observed in the *Labour Magazine*. 'It is the active minority in most countries, as in all parties, that dominates the situation.'[75]

Gide put forward similar views in a much fuller account, which, among other things, noted May's considerable enthusiasm for the Red Army parade on the anniversary of the revolution.[76] Characterising the regime as a dictatorship, not of, nor over, but for the proletariat, Gide admitted its character as a 'proletarian aristocracy' while invoking the disinterested and often heroic qualities of the Bolsheviks who had ventured so much for the revolution. How different, he observed of these young lives of exile and uncertainty, from his own experience as an ageing professor – almost like one of Beatrice's own future diary entries.[77] Just as she would, Gide also described the Bolshevik party as a sort of religious order, enjoining the strictest poverty and obedience, while at the same he saluted the intellectual culture and thirst for knowledge that was increasingly extending from these Bolshevik exemplars to the wider population.[78] Gide also described how the workers in the factories had a new sense of being in their own place ('*se sentir chez eux*'), not only because exploitation by another class had given way to a sense of their own sovereignty, but because the factory with its varied cultural activities was itself like a sort of family home to them.[79] While disavowing any need for such a revolution in the west, it was a notably sympathetic account, and Gide even justified its failure to mention any atrocities by the fact that he had not personally seen or heard any reference made to them.[80] Presumably, only the relatively early date of such an account that can have led so hostile a commentator as Fred Kupferman to describe it as 'measured'.[81]

## V

Although this suggests obvious parallels with Webbs, throughout this period the Webbs themselves seem to have been more or less oblivious to co-operative glosses on Soviet power. Though Beatrice's earlier book on co-operation had had its largest circulation in Russia, where it was said to have provided a text book for the infant co-operative movement, its sequel failed even to mention the controversy over Centrosoyus which was then at its height.[82] Perhaps the Webbs' understanding of co-operation as intrinsically a voluntary form of association meant that they were less readily susceptible to Bolshevik claims than some of their associates. For the time being, it was therefore from other pens that the positive balance sheets were drawn up which they were to make use of in *Soviet Communism*. Encouraged by the greater autonomy allowed the co-operatives under NEP, friendly observers now accredited them with a distinct and even pre-eminent role in Soviet construction. Naturally, Gide devoted the longest chapter of his report to the subject and described co-operation as the most important factor in the Soviet economy 'and even its national life'. While conceding its departure from the Rochdale principles, particularly in the early years of the revolution, he also drew attention to the recovery of its independent character and frankly described it as the realisation of his own ideal of the Co-operative Republic.[83] Six years later, his protégé Poisson, who at one time had been so sceptical, led a French delegation which was reported not only to have approved the Russian movement's legitimacy in the western sense but congratulated it on the 'decided victory [it] has won over Communism in Russia, a victory in which even the Communists themselves have been forced to acquiesce'.[84] Should a similar upheaval in the west prove unavoidable, Gide even saw co-operation as the force which would temper its rigours and set about the task of reconstruction.[85] There is considerable scope here for the much fuller development of these transnational lines of comparison..

Within Britain, Wise was perhaps foremost in presenting a similarly buoyant picture based on co-operative values. Although employed by Centrosoyus in a commercial capacity, he assisted with deft propaganda efforts in which he described the social, cultural and educational aspirations of co-operators as at last being achieved in Russia. Taking as his reference points the co-operative pioneers and the later pronouncements of Lenin, he depicted co-operation as a 'humanising and democratic' influence on the Russian people and a 'great school' for its working-class administrators and business organisers. He laid particular stress on the contrast between the period of war communism, when even the children forgot how to laugh, and the new social tissue – 'high-spirited, healthy, athletic' – that had grown up since:

> A whole generation has now grown up since the Revolution ... Their philosophy of life, their standards of value are those of the Soviet. Its teaching and ideals are the basis of their intellectual and moral outlook, and ... neither in intellect nor in character is the young Russian inferior to the rest of the world.[86]

Both the language and the aspirations expressed are strikingly evocative of the Webbs, but transferred to a new Russian context. Echoing the role of 'moral reformers' which Beatrice had long ago sketched out for British co-operators, Wise seems to have seen in Centrosoyus, and in the NEP more generally, the moderating influence on Bolshevism that he had first sought to encourage as a British civil servant. He died in 1934, and, like many such figures, the Soviet dimension to his career has been consistently underplayed. 'Frank Wise buzzed loudest', Hugh Dalton noted of his unabashed pro-Soviet lobbying as a Labour MP, but the buzzing has since been largely forgotten. Only at the Society for Cultural Relations, the Soviet sponsored 'friendship' organisation, was his contribution properly recognised, by the naming in his honour of the 'Frank Wise Club-room and Library'.[87]

By the time of the Webbs' visit, interest in Russia had quickened again. In 1929, the year in which Wise entered parliament and the agitation over Anglo-Soviet relations was reignited by the formation of a second Labour government, there commenced a series of annual visits by British co-operators, whose impressions were published under the auspices of the Co-operative Union. The inspiration behind the visits was Joseph Reeves, a successor to May as RACS educational officer and a stalwart of pro-Soviet causes from the time of his first Russian visit as a guest of Centrosoyus in 1927.[88] Initiatives of this type had never been entirely spontaneous, and they were becoming less so. Special care had been taken by the Comintern when A. Honora Enfield, Davies's successor as secretary of the WCG, took part in a WIR delegation to Russia in 1925; and the following year the Comintern proposed to the CPGB exactly such a grassroots delegation of co-operators as Reeves was to organise.[89] Perhaps it helped that the RACS was the one society in which the communists had established a limited presence, while the FOSU from 1927 provided a means of organising such delegations in which communist fractions were usually active.[90]

Nevertheless, Reeves, at least this time, was a fellow-traveller, not a surrogate communist. Already in 1920 he had taken a party of co-operators to what he continued to regard as the 'mecca' of 'Socialist Co-operation', namely Belgium. Strongly committed to the Labour Party, which he later represented in parliament, in 1926 Reeves sat on an ILP committee on the role of co-operation in the achievement of socialism, and by his own later account was already persuaded of the limitations of the voluntary tradition.[91] This, however, is far from self-evident from his contemporary writings. In 1927 he was part of the large British delegation in Moscow attending the tenth anniversary celebrations of the revolution and the first International Congress of Friends of the Soviet Union. In the reports which he published on his return he described how, thanks to the genius of Lenin, the idea of 'a complicated system of State Socialism' had been discarded in favour of building socialism 'from beneath' through the medium of a 'purely voluntary' co-operative movement organised on Rochdale principles. 'Thus one hears the slogan "Socialism through Co-operation" repeated on all hands throughout the USSR', he wrote.

> The more I saw of the Co-operative Movement in the USSR the more I realised that Socialism can only be achieved by the proletariat, for the reasons that it cannot be super-imposed upon people from above, but must be built by the collective efforts of the whole working class through their many and varied co-operative organisations.[92]

Many years later, Reeves complained of how co-operative resolutions at the Moscow congress were amended almost beyond recognition. In the official report of the British delegation, his allusions to the movement's voluntary character have disappeared and any hint of a comparison unfavourable to the Russian co-operatives – for example, in the preponderance of male members – has been vigorously corrected. Even so, Reeves's franker impressions were published in Dutt's *Labour Monthly*.[93]

Reeves was a former Christian socialist and disciple of H.G. Wells, who might almost have been modelled on one of the latter's plebeian counter-heroes. Combining the higher rhetoric of co-operation with the Edwardian autodidact's belief in the possibilities of science, he was also an early and an enthusiastic patron of the Woodcraft Folk, whose moots, pow-wows and Robin Hood jerkins he provided with their first official encouragement in the peripheries of outer London. According to Leslie Paul, originator and 'Headman' of the 'Folk', he was of an immediately recognisable type. 'All those for whom ... the problem of faith had been jettisoned in favour of the act of service, had been transformed into a secular priesthood', Paul reminisced. 'They were marked by an ardent look, a firm step, a conviction of vocation' – marked, one might almost say, by that 'vocation of leadership' which the Webbs were to find in Soviet Russia.[94] Paul himself, whose half-Wellsian, half-Whitmanesque imprint the Woodcraft Folk bore, was at this time another vigorous co-operative partisan for the Russians. In 1931 he edited the report for one of Reeves's Russian parties and afterwards produced a survey of Soviet co-operation which again provided one of the Webbs' sources.[95]

Most nearly coinciding with the Webbs' visit as well as the NFRB's, the co-operative parties of 1932, with their combination of moral fervency and institutional fetishism, provide a fitting point of comparison. In a familiar conflation of state and social movement, the achievement of a co-operative trading monopoly was presented in their report both as 'the ultimate aim of Soviet State Policy' and as 'being attained naturally ... without any form of economic restriction or oppression'. Despite the acknowledged hardships and shortages, it provided a 'perfect example of the free development of individuals to a co-operative and communistic society without State oppression or dictation'. Moreover, with the eradication of all that was tawdry and exploitative in Soviet society, a new moral world was seen to be unfolding in conformity to values already held by its admirers in the west. For May the attraction had been the high cultural standards achieved by an enlightened censorship and prohibition of 'sensational films'. For Lansbury it had been the hours retrieved from gambling and prize-fighting for the pursuit of useful knowledge. For the visiting co-operators, in much the same spirit, it was the 'sense of order and discipline' of Russians at their leisure; for it seems they did not witness the sorts of hooliganism which Sheila Fitzpatrick tells us were actually so common at the time.

> In the streets progress is orderly and self-disciplined. The crowds of loungers, often ready for horseplay, one finds on English street corners on Sunday nights, have no counterpart in Russia. There is no jostling on the pavements, extremely little drunkenness, no dress parades, and no promiscuous seeking of acquaintances. In Rostov ... from 7 to 12 p.m.

> [there] was a constant throng of people, out for their evening walk; in twos, threes, or larger groups, they happily promenade without rowdiness, loud noise, or any rough behaviour.

Beatrice had no need to have gone to Russia to have made her famous observation that there was no 'spooning' to be seen in Russian parks. Indeed, the Civil Service union leader W.J. Brown used the very same expression, in the very same context, in 1928. As for the co-operators, only the goldfish in the illuminated stream were described, without censure, as 'lively'. The flower beds were 'beautifully massed'.[96]

Neither dictatorship, planning or co-operation was precisely the route to Russia taken by the Webbs. More even than Wise, Eden Paul or the Coles, the couple's bifocalism, longevity and latitudinarianism make them more than usually ill-suited to attempts at typological reductionism. On the other hand, it has become apparent that throughout their careers they were intellectually gregarious and abnormally attuned to changing movements of opinion. Often it is rightly stressed how fatal was the reliance of *Soviet Communism* on official communist sources. What the footnotes to that work also reveal is how far Russian sources were prefigured or validated by outside commentaries, themselves not free from Soviet insinuations but appearing through the intermediacy of the Webbs' own world of associations. Their very travel arrangements drew on these connections, with Centrosoyus guides providing the same zealous attentions as had helped win round May and Poisson, though with the significant difference that they were now made to feel not so much like comrades as 'a new type of royalty'.[97] In such personal matters, however, the Webbs were neither credulous nor particularly vain. For the endorsements they gave, not to the heaven but the hell of Stalin's Russia, there are no such easy explanations as *amour propre* or old age.

## NOTES

1. For the ICA, see Rita Rhodes, *The International Co-operative Alliance in Peace and War 1910-1950*, Geneva: ICA, 1995.
2. See *Bolshevism and the British Left*, vol. 3.
3. Victor Serwy, 'Co-operation and politics in Belgium', *The People's Year Book*, 1921, pp. 165-8; Serwy, *Le mouvement coopératif en Belgique: aperçu historique*, Brussels: Les Propagateurs de la Coopération, c. 1938, pp. 13 ff. and 45-6; Janet Polasky, *The Democratic Socialism of Emile Vandervelde. Between reform and revolution*, Oxford: Berg, 1995, pp. 96, 98-9.
4. Vojtech Fiser, 'The co-operative movement in the Czecho-Slovak republic and its relation to political parties', *The People's Year Book*, 1921, pp. 169-77.
5. E. Linna, 'The Finnish co-operative movement. Its attitude towards the labour movement and political life', *The People's Year Book*, 1921, pp. 178-81.

6. Olgar Misar, 'The co-operative movement and politics in Austria', *The People's Year Book*, 1921, pp. 159-64.
7. Charles Gide, 'The relations of the co-operative movement in France to political parties and trade unionism', *The People's Year Book*, 1921, pp. 182-6; Georges Lefranc, *Le Mouvement socialiste sous la troisième république*, Paris: Payot, 1963, pp. 155 ff; G.J.D.C. Goedhart, 'The co-operative movement in Holland', *The People's Year Book*, 1921, pp. 194-7.
8. Emile Vandervelde, *La coopération neutre et la coopération socialiste*, Paris: Felix Alcan, 1913.
9. Heinrich Kaufmann, 'Co-operation and political parties in Germany', *The People's Year Book*, 1921, pp. 187-93.
10. Emile Vandervelde, *Collectivism and Industrial Evolution*, ILP, 1907, pp. 163-5, 193 ff, 206. J.R. MacDonald, *The Socialist Movement*, Williams & Norgate, 1911, p. 249.
11. Serwy, 'Co-operation and politics', p. 166.
12. Gide, *Consumers' Co-operative Societies*, p. 262.
13. See for example his chapters on these 'associative socialists' in Charles Gide and Charles Rist, *A History of Economic Doctrines from the Time of the Physiocrats to the Present Day*, Harraps, 1917, pp. 231-55.
14. Lefranc, *Mouvement socialiste*; H.J. May, preface to Poisson, *Co-operative Republic*; Gide, *Consumers' Co-operative Societies*, New York: Alfred A. Knopf, 1922, ch. 17: 'Co-operation and socialism'; see also the entry on Poisson in the *Dictionnaire biographique du mouvement ouvrier français*, vol. 14, pp.284-6.
15. Charles Gide, *The International Co-operative Alliance*, ICA, c. 1920, p. 7; Poisson, 'Voluntary co-operation and consumers' communes', *International Co-operative Bulletin*, March 1921, pp. 61-4; May, preface to Poisson, p. x.
16. RGASPI 506/1/28 pp. 29 ff and 111 ff, French delegate Henriet, First International Conference of Communist Co-operators, November 1922; Pennetier, entry on Sellier in *Dictionnaire biographique du mouvement ouvrier français*, vol. 41, pp. 219-25.
17. See Sidney Pollard, 'The foundation of the Co-operative Party' in Briggs and Saville, *Essays in Labour History 1886-1923*, pp. 185-210
18. BWD 14 September and 21 September* 1930. .
19. The other exception was Finland. For typical Comintern complaints about the CPGB's co-operative department, see e.g. RGASPI 495/100/213, ECCI to CPGB co-operative department, 8 May 1925.
20. *CCM*, pp. 134 ff.
21. Gide, *International Co-operative Alliance*, p. 7. The issue appears to have been raised only informally, and the contemporary record (*International Co-operative Bulletin*, November 1910, pp. 169-70) suggests that Gide was more concerned about the relative representation of the French and Germans on the central committee.
22. ICA, Eighth Congress *Report* (September 1910), ICA, 1911, pp. 72 ff.
23. Dr Karpeler, *International Co-operative Bulletin*, December 1910, pp. 191-2
24. Gide, *International Co-operative Bulletin*, January 1911, pp. 4-7 and *International Co-operative Alliance*, pp. 6-7.
25. The letter and responses will be found in *International Co-operative Bulletin*, August-October 1914.

26. Among other anti-war contributions, note May's own, more delphic contribution, 'The co-operative press', February 1915, pp. 17-20, where he reasserts the internationalist principles of the working-class movement as 'the best guarantee of a lasting peace and new order of society'. See also *International Co-operative Bulletin*, August 1915, pp. 145-50 for May's editorial policy; Rhodes, *International Co-operative Alliance*, pp. 77 ff.
27. *Co-operative News*, 25 November 1939.
28. May in Poisson, *Co-operative*, p. ix; see also the tributes to May in *Review of International Co-operation*, December 1939 and *Co-operative News*, 25 November 1939.
29. May occasionally reviewed for *Fabian News*, e.g. January and July 1926.
30. *Co-operative News*, 4 June 1921; SW to Leonard Woolf, 16 May 1921; see also LRD archives, Fabian Society Control of Industry committee minutes, 24 October 1912.
31. *International Co-operative Bulletin*, March 1921, pp. 65-6 and January 1922, p. 22.
32. *Co-operative News*, 30 April 1921; ICA Tenth Congress *Report* (August 1921), 45-55.
33. May, 'Soviet Russia as I saw it', *Labour Magazine*, March 1924, pp. 496-9.
34. Woolf papers, Davies to Woolf, n.d. but 1913; P. Eyre, 'What the Russian "barbarians" are doing for women and children', *Co-operative News*, 14 February 1920.
35. There is a useful entry on Wise by Noel Thompson in the *Oxford Dictionary of National Biography*, Oxford; OUP, 2004, which cogently summarises his role in Labour's developing economic thinking but has less to say about his Russian and co-operative associations.
36. J.A.R. Pimlott, *Toynbee Hall. Fifty years of social progress*, Dent, 1935, p. 290 where Wise's dates as a resident are given as October 1908-November 1912 and October 1918-October 1920. Attlee returned to the settlement on his demobilisation in January 1919.
37. G.D.H. Cole, *A Century of Co-operation*, Allen & Unwin, 1945, pp. 269-70.
38. W.P. and Zelda K. Coates, *A History of Anglo-Soviet Relations*, Lawrence & Wishart/Pilot Press, 1943, p. 152; Davidson papers, file 108, Wise, 'Memorandum on economic aspects of British policy covering Russia', 6 January 1920 and 'Report of committee appointed to consider the reopening of certain trading relations with the Russian people', presented to SEC (with Wise as co-signatory), 16 January 1920.
39. *Co-operative News*, 24 January 1920. J.M. Kenworthy, *Sailors*, pp. 184-5, claimed to have initiated the approach to Centrosoyus but it was Wise who had the official leverage and co-operative contacts. His role is not mentioned in a standard account like Stephen White, *Britain and the Bolshevik Revolution. A study in the politics of diplomacy 1920-1924*, Macmillan, 1979.
40. W. Selheim and H. Stencil-Lenskaya, 'On relations with Russia' (memorandum to ICA Central Committee), and 'The co-operative movement under the Soviets', submitted by Arcos, both in *International Co-operative Bulletin*, October-November 1920, pp. 306-19; Lloyd George papers F/58/1/10, Klishko to Chicherin (decrypt), 23 and 24 May 1920, and

F/48/3/3, Berkenheim and Morossoff for Centrosoyus to Wise, 1 March 1920. For biographical details of the delegation members see NA FO 371 N3179/3179/38, 'Who's who in Soviet Russia' compiled by British commercial mission, April 1923; also Margaret Cole, Russian letters to G.D.H. Cole, 'Wednesday'. For Bolshevik policy towards co-operatives, see E.H. Carr, *The Bolshevik Revolution 1917-1923*, vol. 2, Harmondsworth: Penguin edn, 1966, pp. 124-30, 236-9, 336-8.

41. Lloyd George papers, F/202/3, memorandum by Wise on 'Negotiations for re-opening trade with Soviet Russia', 18 April 1920; *Fifty Second Annual Co-operative Congress* (May 1920), pp. 574-5.
42. Lloyd George papers, F/48/3, Wise to Philip Kerr (Lloyd George's secretary), 5 and 7 January 1921, memo to Kerr, n.d. but c. March 1921. For Krasin's opposition to Russian 'extremists' see also Lloyd George papers F/202/3/19, conversation between Krasin and Lloyd George, 16 June 1920.
43. See Lenin, *On Co-operation* (January 1923), various Soviet editions; first available in English, *Labour Monthly*, September 1923, pp. 137-43; see also Robert C. Tucker, *Stalin in Power. The revolution from above, 1928-1941*, New York & London: Norton, 1992 edn, p. 31; Stephen F. Cohen, *Bukharin and the Bolshevik Revolution. A political biography 1888-1938*, Oxford: OUP, 1980 edn, pp. 134-8.
44. RGASPI 506/1/28/57 ff, Russian delegate Kantor, First International Conference of Communist Co-operators.
45. Thompson in the *Oxford DNB* refers to Wise's pre-war membership of the ILP, though he is described in 1923 as a recent recruit to Labour who has placed himself at the service of the ILP (*Catholic Herald*, 1 December 1923).
46. Selheim and Stencil-Lenskaya, 'Relations with Russia', pp. 309, 311.
47. *Fifty Third Annual Co-operative Congress* (May 1921), pp. 473-4; ICA Tenth Congress *Report*, pp. 50-1; Rhodes, *International Co-operative Alliance*, pp. 52-3; *Labour Magazine*, February 1926, p. 479.
48. *Labour Magazine*, September 1927, p. 239.
49. May, *Fifty Third Annual Co-operative Congress* (May 1921), p. 477.
50. Wise. 'The economic situation in Europe', *International Co-operative Bulletin*, June 1920, pp. 158-61.
51. Davies, *Co-operative News*, 3 April 1920; WCG congress resolution, *International Co-operative Bulletin*, August 1920, p. 230.
52. May, *International Co-operative Bulletin*, September 1920, pp. 245-6 and October-November 1920, pp. 292-3.
53. See Rhodes, *International Co-operative Alliance*, pp. 178-92. See also for example the views of Charles Gide, another strong supporter of co-operative internationalism, expressed in his *La Russie Soviétique*, Paris: Les Publications de la Conciliation, 1924, p. 44: 'Social institutions, like animals and plants, take the character and sometimes the colour of the milieux where they exist. If the bear if brown in the Pyrenees and white in the polar regions, it is natural that the co-operatives should be red in Moscow – and that in Italy they should wear the black shirt of the fascists.' Gide's views of Soviet Russia are discussed below.
54. See Jean Gaffin and David Thoms, *Caring and Sharing. The centenary history of the Co-operative Women's Guild*, Manchester: Co-operative Union, 1983, pp. 25-53 and passim.

55. Woolf papers, Davies to Woolf, October 1913; for Davies see also *Millgate Monthly*, June 1922, pp. 507-12.
56. Woolf papers, Davies to Woolf, 18 November (1920?), 6 July 1921 and n.d., late 1921.
57. Figes, *People's Tragedy*, pp. 612-15.
58. *Co-operative News*, 1 and 29 January 1921.
59. Entry by Joyce Bellamy, H.F. Bing and John Saville in Bellamy and Saville, eds, *The Dictionary of Labour Biography*, vol. 1, Macmillan, 1972, p. 98.
60. Davies, *The Relations Between Co-operation and Socialistic Aspirations*, Co-operative Union, 1890, p. 5; BWD 24 May 1890, Mackenzie vol. 1, p. 332.
61. Lansbury, *What I Saw in Russia*, Leonard Parsons, 1920, ch. 4, also reported *Co-operative News*, 28 February 1920.
62. WCG resolution August 1920.
63. *Co-operative News* editorial, 29 January 1921.
64. 'Co-operative movement under the Soviets', *The People's Year Book*, 1921, pp. 215-21.
65. *Co-operative News*, 1 January 1921.
66. *Co-operative News*, 24 January 1920, 10 June 1922; 'Co-operation wins the hearts of Russian women', *Woman's Outlook*, January 1922, pp. 66-7; *International Co-operative Bulletin*, May-June 1922, pp. 122-3; *Fifty Fourth Annual Co-operative Congress* (June 1922), p. 289. Subsequently Polovstev remained in Britain for the Russian Red Cross and was an executive member of the British WIR.
67. Lloyd George papers, F/203/1/11, Chicherin to Kamenev (decrypt), 31 August 1920. The non-British members of the delegation were Poisson, Serwy and a Swiss co-operator, Huber.
68. May, *Co-operative News*, 1, 8 and 15 April 1922.
69. Khinchuk and Henriet, Conference of Communist Co-operators, November 1922; also Lenin, *On Co-operation*; Cohen, *Bukharin*, pp. 195 ff; E.H. Carr, *Socialism in One Country, 1924-1926. Volume 1*, Harmondsworth: Penguin ed, 1970, p. 279.
70. *Co-operative News*, 28 May 1921.
71. Gugushvili, 'The co-operative movement of the republic of Georgia', *International Co-operative Bulletin*, February 1921, pp. 42-4; Catherine Tcherkesi-shvili, interviewed *Woman's Outlook*, August 1922, pp. 293-7.
72. Serwy, *Co-operative Georgia under Bolshevik Rule*, Brussels: Co-operative Society Lucifer, 1922.
73. *Co-operative News*, 19 August, 23 September and 4 November 1922.
74. RGASPI 495/100/213, R. Vilian, circulated article, 'Russian co-operators at their post', 2 September 1925.
75. May, 'Soviet Russia'.
76. Gide, *La Russie Soviétique*, p. 56.
77. Gide, *La Russie Soviétique*, ch. 1 and pp. 53-5.
78. Gide, *La Russie Soviétique*, pp. 10-11, 54.
79. Gide, *La Russie Soviétique*, pp. 21-3.
80. Gide, *La Russie Soviétique*, p. 12.
81. Fred Kupferman, *Au pays des Soviets. Le voyage français en Union soviétique*, Paris: Gallimard, 1979.
82. *MA*, p. 334.

83. Gide, *La Russie Soviétique*, ch. 4.
84. John Downie, 'Soviet co-operation', *Co-operative Review*, May 1930, pp. 104-9. In his *Co-operative Republic*, pp. 98-9, Poisson had argued that only co-operation in Russia 'really makes socialism actual and gives the revolution a material embodiment'.
85. Gide, *La Russie Soviétique*, p. 48.
86. Wise, 'The growth of the Consumers' Co-operation in Russia', *Labour Magazine*, April 1923, pp. 541-4; Wise, *Consumers' Co-operation in Soviet Russia*, Manchester: Co-operative Union, 1929; Wise, 'Russia revisited. Neighbourly marketing; Britain's opportunity', *New Leader*, 22 October 1926.
87. SCR headed notepaper in MRC 157/3/RU/1; Dalton, *Call Back Yesterday*, p. 230.
88. Rita Rhodes, *An Arsenal for Labour*, Manchester: Holyoake Books, 1998, pp. 43 ff.
89. RGASPI 495/100/281, Helen Crawfurd to E.N. Brown, 27 April, 21 July and 20 August 1925; 495/100/304, ECCI to CPGB central committee, 16 August 1926
90. RGASPI 495/100/339, Murphy to CPGB politburo, 14 August 1926; also e.g. 495/100/738, Arnot to Pollitt, 15 May 1931.
91. Reeves, *A Century of Rochdale Co-operation*, Lawrence & Wishart, 1944, pp. 108 ff, 118-22, 176-7.
92. Joseph Reeves, 'Co-operation in the USSR', *Labour Monthly*, February 1928, pp. 95-100.
93. Margulies, *Pilgrimage to Russia*, p. 40; *Soviet Russia Today. Report of the British workers' delegation, 1927*, LRD, 1927, pp. 63-70.
94. Leslie Paul, *Angry Young Man*, Faber, 1951, pp. 125-6, 155-95
95. *Russia 1931: report of two groups of co-operators*, Manchester: Co-operative Union, 1932; Leslie Paul, 'The Woodcraft Folk. A new orientation to co-operative education', *Co-operative Review*, September 1930, pp. 196-9; Paul, *Consumers' Co-operation in the USSR*, Gollancz, 1934.
96. *Soviet Russia 1932. Reports of two groups of co-operators on a visit to the USSR in the summer of 1932*, Manchester: CU, 1933, pp. 31, 44. See also May, *Co-operative News*, 8 April 1922; Lansbury, 'Russia revisited', *Socialist Review*, November 1926, p. 16; Sheila Fitzpatrick, *Everyday Stalinism. Ordinary life in extraordinary times: Soviet Russia in the 1930s*, New York: OUP, 1999, p. 53; W.J. Brown, *Three Months in Russia*, Labour Publishing Co, 1928, p. 47.
97. BWD 23 May 1932*.

# *Chapter ten*

# 'A big gamble of the intellect'

I

When the Webbs, as Beatrice put it, 'hobbled over' to the new civilisation, they were already committed to reaching a favourable verdict upon it. Perhaps they were not quite so eager as that other veteran of progressive causes, Charlotte Despard, who recorded having 'come at last into a true democracy' – 'no class, no separation of interests, no superiorities' – the day her Russian boat left London.[1] Nevertheless, it was obvious to contemporaries that the Webbs went to Russia seeking confirmation of the image they had already formed of the subject. If in this sense *Soviet Communism* was 'a big gamble of the intellect', as Beatrice put it, it was also a palpably Webbian construction, including passages taken literally word-for-word from their previous writings.[2] At the same time, however, in identifying their *Weltanschauung* with the claims or realities of Soviet Russia, they also submitted it to profound though often unacknowledged modifications. While they remained what Beatrice once called 'non-party communists', or what we might call 'fellow-travellers', their adhesion was akin to an act of joining whereby their own ideas were realigned in significant ways with the system in which they now found solace and inspiration.[3] To this extent, they can be grouped with those for whom the Soviet elevation of state and party exerted a formative influence, and yet even state and party were understood by them more in Webbian than in Bolshevik terms. Their book is thus a veritable compendium of Webbian doctrine in which strands from their different periods and personalities are rediscovered in the unsettling context of this Stalinist behemoth. If ever there was a multi-layered text, this is it.

In its ambitions it was far more than a work of reportage, just as in its achievements it was far less. S.P. Turin, an LSE lecturer who helped the Webbs with Russian sources, chaffed Beatrice with having '*invented*' a constitution for the USSR, adding bluntly: 'Are you now going to *invent* the meaning of their activities?'[4] Though she would not have put it like that, this was precisely what Beatrice intended doing. Not by invention but induction, the Webbs' aim was to articulate the ideology they held to be implicit in the practice of Soviet communism, but only imperfectly expressed or understood by the Soviets themselves. The approach was thus exactly akin to that which they had taken to the British trade union and co-operative movements, and, like the precepts of Industrial Democracy or the co-operators' state within the state, they described the Soviet constitution as 'one which has never been enacted or proclaimed, but which has arisen, as it were, spontaneously'.[5] This claim was the more audacious in that the Bolsheviks themselves are usually regarded as anything but reticent as to their guiding aims and principles. What they nevertheless lacked, as the Webbs saw it, was a science of society and human behaviour commensurate with the scale of the experiment being undertaken. Soviet marxism they judged wholly inadequate for this purpose, frankly disregarding it in favour of their time-honoured research methods, 'examining the methods of thinking, and the aim and purpose, of Soviet Communism as these are exhibited, not so much in the words of the philosophic writers, as in the policy and actions of the Soviet Government'.[6] Thus the Webbs claimed the Soviet plans for Fabianism, exactly as they previously claimed unwitting collectivists of left, right and centre in their own country. Ivan Maisky, the Soviet ambassador in London from around the time of their visit, knew exactly how to rub them up the right way. 'Teachers of Lenin', he would call them, and retail how on reading their *History of Trade Unionism* he 'forthwith became a political revolutionary'. With similar cajoling intent, he also assured them that nothing to compare with their text had been produced even by the Soviets themselves.[7] Beatrice, independently, had already come to the same conclusion. She believed their exposition of Soviet planning 'far more persuasive than any Soviet publication'.[8]

If there was much they had to learn from Russia, there was also much to teach it. Their book was therefore intended for the improvement as well as the advertisement of Soviet communism. That was the point of its criticisms of the 'disease of orthodoxy', properly described as dysfunctional as well as barbarous, and, as well as the task of western proselytisation, the volume was expressly intended for a Russian readership. Above all Beatrice wanted it in the hands of the new generation of Konsomols, or Communist Youth, the virgin soil on which the prospect of a new civilisation ultimately depended.[9] Repeatedly Maisky and other Soviet officials assured them that a promised Russian translation was actually in progress; a more reliable augury was the refusal into the country even of its English edition. Conceivably Maisky himself was not being disingenuous: he had been particularly keen that the Webbs' criticisms of the Comintern appear in the book, and, like Krasin and Wise in a different context, may have hoped through western levers to exert a small moderating influence within Russia.[10] The very possibility of such an idea, in 1936-7, would be enough to explain why the translation never appeared.

Although it was conceived on the pattern of earlier texts, cultural distance imprinted on *Soviet Communism* defining differences of both design and execution. At a relatively superficial level, mention has often been made of the Webbs' reliance on Soviet sources for support and information. Beatrice herself described Passfield Corner as a virtual 'holiday resort' for visiting Soviet officials, conceding that they seemed to speak more freely there than in the atmosphere prevailing in Moscow. Undeterred by such insights, the couple submitted their drafts to a variety of Soviet functionaries and even expressed a special debt to Julius Hecker, whom they were warned off by Wicksteed as a GPU agent.[11] To the Webbs these were tried and tested practices, and they acknowledged no difference in principle between consulting the head of Gosplan or an official from the Co-operative Union. Nevertheless, Beatrice in her more lucid moments did concede that what they were offering was a paper constitution, definitive as to the anatomy of its different parts but powerless to describe the 'living relations between them':

> we do not really *know* how the business works; we can't picture the daily comings and goings … as we could those of the trade union world, or of parliament and Whitehall and municipal administration in Great Britain.[12]

It is this peculiarly disembodied character that makes the book seem closer to the system building of their socialist *Constitution* than any of their other investigative works. In one extraordinary section they described the role of a 'universal audit' in promoting efficiency and accountability in Soviet industry. 'Tovarischi' ('*Comrades*'), an official is described as opening a works' meeting, before beginning a long disquisition illustrative of the virtues of 'measurement and publicity'. 'Gentlemen', his exact counterpart in the *Constitution* had begun fifteen years earlier, and apart from such concessions to the vernacular, the entire section of several paragraphs is reproduced verbatim from the earlier volume.[13] A sly reminder of their own powers of precognition, this was also a tacit admission of the volume's descriptive limitations. 'Will our record turn out to be a mere mechanical and inaccurate recital or summary of the bare formal facts of the soviet … together with a misunderstanding of the CP, its metaphysics and ethics?', Beatrice wrote in a moment of misgiving.[14] Of course, it turned out to be exactly that.

## II

It is a truism of Webbian commentaries that institutional preoccupations were a feature of all their major writings. Nevertheless, whatever the limitations of such an approach, the Webbs had not regarded institutions as abstracted from time and agency, but as forms of human association, historically located and always in a process of development. The abandonment of such an approach in *Soviet Communism* thus betrayed a more fundamental departure from Webbian precedent, for this, unlike any of their previous investigative projects, was a work virtually bereft of history. The moral and intellectual significance of such an omission is incalculable. When, in 1918, Lenin proclaimed the construction of the 'towering edifice of socialist society' on a 'space cleared of historical rubbish', nothing could have been more foreign to the spirit of Fabian gradualism.[15] Now, however, it was precisely the slash and burn of Bolshevism that allowed the Webbs their crowning literary edifice. To William Gillies, of the Labour Party's international department, Sidney declared that they were not interested in reading anything from 'before 1927'.[16] Certainly the revolution itself provided them with a *tabula rasa*. Though initially intending an opening section on the Tsarist period, in an inversion of their usual methods they put back its writing until the rest of the book was completed.[17] Finally they abandoned it entirely, simply interpolating a potted history of the regime itself at the start of volume two. Like any good system-builders, they began, as for five hundred pages the book itself did, with the constitution.

In approaching the Russians as a people without a history, the Webbs denied them those 'habits and established expectations' – the phrase Sidney had used in his 'inevitability of gradualness' speech – which were the nearest they ever came to a language of rights. In refusing them a history, in other words – in discounting or failing to register the accretion of customs, institutions and relationships that for the Webbs was synonymous with the word – they also refused them their basic humanity. Behind the glorification of Soviet power there thus survived attitudes to the Russian people that were nothing short of inhuman. In 1922 Beatrice had pondered and rejected the claims of Russian famine relief. 'The always present doubt whether by saving a Chinese or Russian child from dying this year, you will prevent it from dying the next year, together with the larger question of whether those races are desirable inhabitants, compared to other races, paralyses the charitable impulse', she wrote. 'Obviously one would not spend one's available income in saving a Central African Negro from starving or dying from disease ...'[18] The denial of famine relief prefigured the verbal denial a decade later of Russian famine itself, and the attribution of such scarcities as were acknowledged to the recalcitrance of its victims.[19]

Rooted in their own version of modernisation theory, the Webbs thus assumed the existence of a racial hierarchy whose one redeeming feature was that it was not innate or immutable.[20] As they abandoned the investigator's craft for a sweeping cultural prejudice, this was the clue to their utter incapacity as foreign observers. Understandably, the editors of Beatrice's American and Australian diaries regard her as too parochial and 'British' to have understood her hosts.[21] Beyond the English-speaking world, the gulf was wider still, and in thinking of *Soviet Communism* one cannot but recall by analogy their description in 1911 of the Japanese occupation of Korea, writing as virtual guests of the occupying forces.

> [We were] met at each railway station by bevies of bowing officials in gorgeous uniforms; taken out in the Governor's State Carriage, the only one in Seoul; and shown palaces and schools and prisons and hospitals and tombs etc. The Koreans are 12 millions of dirty, degraded, sullen, lazy, and religionless savages, who slouch about in dirty *white* garments of the most inept kind, and who live in filthy mudhuts.

Such judgements, on a mere six days' trip, insulated by language, show how little equipped the Webbs were for the vaulting of cultural, linguistic and geographical distance. An arrogant insularity – Beatrice in her long skirts deploring the Koreans' 'absurd little senseless black hats' – permitted a gross political relativism, as a declared unfitness or immaturity to sustain self-government provided a clinching case for authority.[22] Though it was acknowledged in *Soviet Communism* that the sufferings of forced collectivisation were 'beyond all computation', it is difficult not to feel that accepting the Bolsheviks' civilising mission, as they had Japan's, concealed a fundamental contempt for peasant cultures as incapable of developing their own social tissue. Russia, like Korea, was judged a 'low type of society ... its masses illiterate, superstitious, exceptionally diseased, and in places actually barbarous; its governing classes ... degenerate, and in more than one sense corrupt ...'[23] As such, they provided fit material for the Bolsheviks to 'test their assumptions by observation and experiment', with other nations able to follow in their stead 'without the suffering and oppression the Russian people have had to endure'.[24] Here, it seems, the axiom of legitimate expectations did not apply, least of all to the Russian peasant.

Formally the Webbs presented the new civilisation in cyclical terms, encouraged by the appearance the previous year of Arnold Toynbee's 'brilliant and erudite' *Study of History*. From another aspect, however, it appeared more like a westernising process bringing Fabian-style improvements to a population whose 'remaking' by socialism needed to be more than usually energetic.[25] Perhaps that transferred to the international plane the Webbs' deep-seated ambivalence as to whether social progress depended on unforced development from below or directive action from above. *Soviet Communism*, while verbally reconciling the two, effectively resolved the issue in the latter sense. That may explain why Sidney, once having made his commitment to it, never wavered under the impact of merely ephemeral atrocities, as Beatrice did.

The same resolution, again suggesting a basically linear conception of development, can be inferred from the parallel the Webbs drew between Bolshevism and Britain's own traumas of modernisation. In this they were fed simultaneously by the news from Russia and the 'pessimist' or 'catastrophic' reading of the British industrial revolution that had been expounded so eloquently by J.L. and Barbara Hammond.[26] Already in the early 1920s the Webbs noted the similar remorselessness, the pitiless 'smashing up' of existing social arrangements, displayed alike in ascendant capitalism and the Bolshevik dictatorship. To the labourers of Cobbett's time, Beatrice wrote in *My Apprenticeship*, the tyranny of the factory, economic dislocation of the family and 'summary abrogation of immemorial customs' must have appeared 'not only as artificial and unnatural, but also as a gigantic and cruel experiment, which, in so far it was affecting their homes, their health, their subsistence and their pleasure, was proving a calamitous failure'.[27] On the other hand, torn like the marxists between the indictment of capital and acceptance of its historic rationale, the Webbs could not but concede that this giant experiment had *not* proved a failure. All social transformation depended on 'experimenting in the lives of other people', and the point of the analogy could in that sense be turned on its head. 'Much is subsequently forgiven to a revolution which succeeds', they wrote already in *The Decay of Capitalist Civilisation*, echoing their mentor Spencer who had discerned 'a large, far-seeing benevolence' in the myriad individual sufferings of the industrial revolution.[28] Already the hint was there of extenuation for the Bolsheviks should their experiment too appear destined for success, and thus it came to pass. With the chancier wisdom, not of hindsight but of the crystal ball, the Webbs conjured up the 'future generations' who would judge such upheavals 'not so much by the temporary misery that they inevitably create, but largely according to the relative social value, in each case, of the new order in comparison with the old'. With the building up of 'new social tissue', the cutting away of the old could be regarded with something like equanimity.[29]

**III**

As far back as the 1880s Sidney, like most British radicals, had allowed that the special predicament of the Russian autocracy might necessitate revolution. Nevertheless, in describing Soviet communism as a new civilisation, the Webbs claimed for it more than superiority merely to the system it replaced. On the contrary, Russia to them now represented the future of social organisation. If its methods were vernacular, its achievements were of universal application, whether disseminated – and again one notes the old ambivalence – by revolution, penetration or imitation. Combining diversity with universalism, democracy with authority and science with a new communist ethics, two achievements in particular fed the Webbs' millenarianism: that of 'planned production for community consumption', which they regarded as the realisation of 'Fabian consumer's economics'; and that of a multiform democracy, whose intricate polyphony seemed to balance differentiation and integration with Spencerian comprehensiveness.[30] With the further attraction of the sort of religious order that Beatrice had yearned for since at least the turn of the century, the impression created was of a utopia largely conceived in Webbian categories; not 'emotional' or 'libertarian', but seemingly well-regulated rather than autocratic.[31]

It was to the first of these claims – planned production for community consumption – that the Webbs attributed their initial decision to investigate the subject. In Beatrice's words, it provided its motive-force and the 'axle' on which the whole work turned.[32] Of the numerous incongruities in which the book abounds, this at first sight seems the most extraordinary. The year that they visited Russia, famine gripped whole swathes of the country. Even in the cities there were chronic shortages of the most basic commodities and a perilous decline in living standards. Ideologically and iconographically, it was not consumption that inspired Soviet novels and films, or the vertiginous bar charts synonymous with the plans, but the output of steel, cement, tractors, the proverbial pig iron. To the country's rulers distribution was a detail neither valued nor understood, and the very year the Webbs visited it the Soviet premier Molotov warned against any notions that 'socialism is production for consumption's sake'.[33] Never perhaps has a society been at once so enraptured with production and indifferent to popular consumption.

Despite their professed consumers' economics, the Webbs seemed to add their own voice to the exaltation of work and producer identities. Complacently they described the relocation of the private sphere to the factory, seen by the Soviet worker as 'very largely the centre of his life' and the provider of nursery facilities, technical classes, clubs, amusements, excursions, even, such as it was, his very home.[34] In the work process itself, thanks to socialist emulation, the old demarcations of toil and recreation were eroded in fantastical ways. 'It was not at first realised', the Webbs commented, 'that there may be just as much pleasurable excitement in trying which team can lay the most bricks, or the greatest length of railway track ... as in the game of knocking little balls into holes, or in forcing a larger ball against all defences into an enemy's goal'. The same throaty partisanship was even to be aroused by less obviously visual and competitive activities, such as securing the best balance sheet on the Volga steamboats. This was a sublimation indeed of the sporting instinct, and guarantee that, as the Webbs put it, there would be 'no pleasurable excitement for the mere spectator!' Relocated to the sphere of production, this once again recalls their co-operative utopia, in which reports of the relative achievements of the co-operative societies were imagined thrilling readers like the cup final or latest test match. Voluntary shifts ('subbotniks') and shock brigades were similarly idealised, lifting workers to 'a higher and nobler motive for work than merely the wage that it yields', even when this involved 'hard manual labour for hours at a stretch'. Obligatory in such a context was their paean to the further 'pleasurable excitement' – again, their actual words – of the GPU's White Sea Canal project.[35]

Manifested here in conditions of acknowledged scarcity, consumers' economics seem exposed as a mere euphemism for industrial discipline, or at best the cannier incentives of the progressive employer. Not the state rendered toothless as an association of consumers, but the consumer as a pretext for a tyrannous authority: thus were the warnings of a servile state now vindicated in the most exemplary fashion.[36] Nevertheless, the Webbs, however paradoxically, did not quite lose sight of their consumerist utopia. Philosophically, the Soviets stood in their view for the aim of a 'fuller and richer human existence', which Beatrice counterposed to asceticism and the 'denial of desire'.[37] 'In the USSR, even more obviously than in countries of a more mature civilisation, it is in the nature of human desire to be literally insatiable', they wrote in *Soviet Communism*. Ambitious as was their benchmark of western bourgeois consumption patterns, for the Webbs this was only the beginning.

> When that degree of satiety has been reached – indeed long before it has been even approached – there will arise new and competing desires for greater leisure, for larger and more frequent vacations, and for new opportunities of travel. If every material want has been supplied and every desire satisfied ... the ultimate remedy for over-production is always at hand in a reduction of the working day of the entire population – at last, by the then universal machine, freed from insistent toil – from eight hours a day to seven, to four or even to two.

Utopian enough when called forth by the CWS, in the Russia of the early 1930s such a vision recalls the fairy-tale 'magic tablecloth' to which Sheila Fitzpatrick likens the consoling vision of Soviet abundance. The Webbs themselves described the *Pyatiletka* as a 'Self Denial Plan'. It was as if they regarded its frenetic concentration on production as a societal 'price to pay' by which not hours but a whole future of compensatory pleasures was being secured.[38]

Giddily hypothetical though it was, the expanded realm of consumption did not resolve Webbian dilemmas through the legerdemain of utopia, but revealed their intractability even in a world of the imagination. Described by the Webbs in familiar categories, the issue was a defining one for any socialist. If consumption was a realm of empowerment, as they eloquently propounded, who then was to exercise that power, and to what human ends? Was socialism to be regarded simply as the continuous, insatiable enlargement of this faculty, extending that 'presence of opportunity' – the 'doing as one chooses' – which the Webbs offered as their definition of freedom?[39] Or was it also visionary, prescriptive and reformatory, a new moral order requiring the improvement as well as the liberation of humankind? In November 1933, Beatrice recalled how the issue had already been posed by her study of the British co-operative movement some four decades previously.

> The crux lies in the question, are the *needs* of the community to be tested by the free and spontaneous appetites and 'desires' whether these be good, bad or indifferent, of each individual or by a science of consumption devised and administered by experts with the object of improving mankind? ... Must consumption be planned: how far must this planning go? Man as a producer ... has to obey orders. But it is argued the same man as a consumer gives orders as to what he requires for his subsistence and enjoyment. That seems to assume that he will have ... freedom to choose what services and commodities he prefers to consume ... Are all these to be determined by experts' decision as to which form of recreation is good for the community and which is indifferently or wholly bad?

Though the categories employed are Webbian ones, the tension between 'needs' and 'appetites', deliverance and control, were as old as socialism itself.[40]

Nor, in this case, did the Webbs resolve it. In theory, Beatrice was drawn to the prospect of individual autonomy within an expanding private sphere, with the future Soviet citizen 'free to develop his personality, by loneliness, contemplation, exploration of external nature, music, art and even meditation, religion and metaphyics'.[41] This was the strain in 'multiformity' that Stephen Spender drew upon for the conclusion to his book *Forward from Liberalism*, depicting communism as successor to the liberal tradition and guarantor of an equitable individualism.[42] Nevertheless, Beatrice's vision, like Spender's, was a highly subjective one. Underpinned by a powerful sense of human development from lower pleasures, or 'appetites', to higher ones, it implied a clear agenda as to the legitimate uses of socialist leisure. Partly that registered the wider repercussions of personal conduct, so that even domestic hygiene and a well-ordered diet and sexual life assumed the 'dignity of social obligation'.[43] More basically, socialism was not agnostic as to the hours it freed from production. Rather, it embodied normative claims to a fuller life that discountenanced idle or pernicious pursuits contributing nothing to the development of 'personality'. 'Work productively, rest culturally', the Konsomol leader Kosarev pronounced, and resting culturally required what seemed a form of cultural conscription to overcome the indifferent human legacy of Tsarism. As a monument to this endeavour, Beatrice reworked their chapter on 'the social services', which she considered the book's weakest, into a more portentous and visionary effort, 'The remaking of man'. In this chapter the development of human potential was depicted as anything but a spontaneous process:

'The Soviet Government ... made it a fundamental purpose of its policy not merely to benefit the people whom it served but actually to transform them', the chapter began. 'Far from believing that human nature could not be changed, Lenin and his colleagues thought that the principal object and duty of a government should be to change drastically the human nature with which it dealt.'[44]

*Soviet Communism* thus tapped easily into images of purposeful leisure suggesting a sort of hyper-collectivism of the hours of rest. In the factory club, sports field, conducted tour and parks of culture, the private sphere seemed swallowed up in 'rational' and 'organised' amusements. For the meditative person of Beatrice's daydreams, the invasion of time and space they described was the stuff of nightmare. 'Daily physical exercises become a social obligation, the fulfilment of which is urged every morning throughout the land by the innumerable loud speakers of the state radio service', the couple effused; it was as if Mr 'Callisthenes' Webb had finally come into his own, and his wife now acquired an entire population to rouse to salubrious exertion.[45] In the Soviet press, crime, sex, fashion and gossip gave way, not so much to music, art and religion, as to relentless 'public affairs'. 'Exciting stories, full of statistics', the Webbs enthused without irony, as they once had for the cup-tie excitements of the Department for Co-operative Progress.[46] At the resort of Kislovodsk, Beatrice recorded a formidable list of activities not taking place, including drunkenness, shouting, bawling, staying up after 11 p.m., spooning (for the most part), litter, merry-go-rounds, cockshies, shooting galleries, and exhibitions of monstrosities. On the other hand, she went on, there were 'endless lectures in the rest-houses on Marxism', to say nothing of concerts, opera and ballet performances, organised sports and a little 'mild mountaineering'.[47] The Konsomols, whom Beatrice particularly admired, practised what even she admitted was an 'almost terrifying puritanism', mixed with priggishness, hypocrisy, lack of humour and contempt for their elders. But if she did not expect a whole people to accept this 'subordination of man's appetites to his reason and moral purposes', it was in the Spartan virtues of the Communist youth that she discerned the brightest augury for Russia's future transformation.[48]

No doubt, as she promised, the 'private part of the individual life' would in time increase, exactly as the sterner demands of socialist production were regarded by the Webbs as transitional.[49] Nevertheless, the admitted congeniality of the transitional stage of exertion reveals the ambiguity that lay at the very heart of the Webbs' consumers' economics. It was with the discovery that use and not labour created value that Beatrice had accredited the Rochdale pioneers. This idea, of production for use and not for any 'vested' or producer interest, was arguably far more significant for the Webbs' basic social philosophy than the familiar Fabian theory of 'rent', and links them with a Ruskinian tradition opposed to classical political economy.[50] Turned inside out, however, the correlation of value with use made it difficult for the Webbs to conceptualise any scale of values except as the product of 'use' or 'utility'. Though they scorned the Bloomsbury-type intellectuals whose higher virtues were based on the unseen but compulsory labour of others, their unease with idle pleasures went beyond any particular class connotations. Rather, in rejecting the conventional associations of culture with the 'absence of any use-value in the pursuit or practice of the cultured life', they implicitly postulated their own 'use-value', not according to an 'economic calculus' but a moral or 'utilitarian' one reflected in the level of personal conduct and 'the valuation of what conduces to the permanent well-being of the human race'.[51] In this calculus, 'service' functioned as the moral equivalent of work. 'Men will be taught that an existence of play ... is a good existence for gnats and sucking fish; but not for men', Ruskin had preached; 'that the best prayer at the beginning of a day is that we may not lose its moments; and the best grace before meal, the consciousness that we have justly earned our dinner'.[52] Exactly this sensibility was reflected in the Webbs' view of consumption divorced from work or service as parisitic or 'functionless', culminating in their 'new' communist ethic of 'the subordination of the life of the individual to the service of the community'.[53] The attainment of the Purpose, Beatrice had written of communism, was finer than the Purpose itself; and in attaining it, the ethics of construction remained disciplined, collective and avowedly puritanical, with the 'licence' of upheaval giving way to 'the modern essentials of the good life, notably in improvement of one's qualifications and character, in the fulfilment of family duties, and in a personal behaviour useful to society and considerate of the comfort of others'.[54] These, of course, were not such modern essentials that Ruskin himself would not immediately have recognised them sixty years earlier.

## IV

The same confusion of public and private spheres underlay the Webbs' second major claim for the new civilisation: that it practised the sort of 'multiform democracy' that Beatrice regarded as their distinctive contribution to the Fabian tradition. Underlying its guiding notions of diversity and participation was a denial of the absolute separation of public authority and the private citizen of Wells's 'Fabian-Fascist' blueprints or Shaw's parodic version of Fordism. In Shaw's imaginings, the more obvious point of comparison, the control of all public affairs was to be surrendered to the capable few as the price of private opportunity. '[N]ot Fraternity but Privacy, and not Liberty in the old sense but Leisure', Shaw wrote to Beatrice in 1928, adding that liberty in the new sense – the sense of a Lenin or a Mussolini – began and ended with the hours of 'free' time.[55] Expounded in Shaw's *Intelligent Woman's Guide to Socialism and Fascism*, published the same year and probably the most widely read socialist text in inter-war Britain, the idea that liberty 'was' leisure and vice versa was recognisably congeneric with the Webbs' 'price to pay'. Its utter repudiation of democracy rested on a Fabian basis of specialisation in the skills of government; no doubt taken to the point of a Shavian *reductio ad absurdum*, it still impressed Sidney as an 'amazing piece of work'.[56] Even Beatrice, though more sceptical, toyed with the idea of a 'new governing class' assuming all collective responsibilities in return for 'short hours, long holidays [and] free services' at the disposal of the individual. On one occasion, though apparently only one, she even speculated on the possible adoption of Soviet social goals by Mussolini.[57] Fundamentally, though, the Webbs' utopia was very different from Shaw's, and with its lack of personal or political freedom and its compulsory work and equality Beatrice had even found the latter 'weird'.[58] Its stark opposition of government and people was not to find much support in *Soviet Communism*.

On the contrary: in resisting this categorical trade-off, the Webbs upheld not only the democratic accountability of public institutions, but also the accountability of the private citizen for the proper functioning of those institutions. Democracy itself was part of the price to pay, an obligation as much as a right, and promoted in similar ways: through efforts 'to incite, persuade and press the apathetic toiling masses' to take an interest in public affairs'. 'This determination to make every labourer or cook ... take part in the work of government and social endeavour ... is perhaps the finest trend in Soviet Communism', Beatrice commented, echoing the famous sentiments of Lenin.[59] The text of *Soviet Communism* is peppered with encomiums to this ideal of universal participation. Described with Webbian earnestness, the 'almost inconceivable amount of political discussion' has one hankering for a Shavian breathing space. By the easy linking of 'government' and 'social endeavour', not only such constant volubility but subbotniks – working on one's free day – and shock brigades were treated equally as an exercise in citizenship; and tasks elsewhere performed by a salaried bureaucracy were imagined as voluntarily performed.[60] With its ideal of the 'activist' citizen, this was less Shaw's imagined future than Cole's; or rather it resembled that 'politically minded person's Utopia' which Cole himself – with a Shavian line of reasoning, just a year after the appearance of the *Intelligent Woman's Guide* – had come to reject.[61] It was Beatrice, conversely, who held that 'all that was good and feasible' in guild socialism had been put into practice by the Russians.[62]

While hardly doing justice to the strengths of this tradition, *Soviet Communism* undoubtedly exposed some of its weaknesses. In particular, through aversion to politics and woolly-mindedness about the state, it lacked any theoretical safeguards against accepting the purported identification of state, party and people in terms that negated its pretended multiformity. 'The Union of Soviet Socialist

Republics does not consist of a government and a people confronting each other, as all other great societies have hitherto been', they wrote. 'It is a highly integrated social organisation in which ... the people themselves ... unite to realise the good life'.

> This is in fact not a state in the old sense of the word, but an organised plan for living which the people as whole adopt ... a highly elaborate and extremely varied texture of many kinds of collective organisation, by the universal membership of which the *interests and desires of all the different sections of the population will be fulfilled in a manner and to a degree never yet attained in any other community*.[63]

It was thus that the Webbs not only failed to celebrate Stalin's dictatorship, but tortuously denied its existence, or else sought to accommodate it to a vision of a continuously animated democracy.[64] Held in a miracle of equilibrium, the appearance of teeming diversity nevertheless masked the lack of effective mechanisms for the resolution, articulation or even recognition of conflict. Commenting approvingly on the lack of conventional political parties, Sidney observed that 'the whole population so far as English terminology is used, is and remains politically unorganised'.[65] Beatrice expressed it very differently. 'Once class conflict ... has ceased to trouble humanity ... I foresee a rise of infinite varieties in the grouping of men and women for different but not inconsistent purposes', she wrote in a new wartime introduction to *Soviet Communism*. What nevertheless held two such contrasting statements together was not just the disallowance of political parties – 'One, Two or Many' – but any crystallisation of disharmonious interests.[66]

It is true that party competition had never counted for much in Webbian thinking, and an electoral process denying faction for principles of enlightenment and accountability was entirely in the spirit of their own socialist *Constitution* of a decade earlier. In other respects, however, the surface continuities were more deceptive. Notably this was the case with the social movements that figured so prominently in the Webbs' multiform conception of democracy. For over forty years, the priority that the Webbs accorded to the co-operative and trade union movements had constantly fluctuated in line with the shifts in their thinking between state collectivism and a more libertarian 'Co-operative Commonwealth'. Nevertheless, however minimal their attention to these movements sometimes was, when outflanked by more ambitious theorists like Woolf and Cole they had always argued for the limited but unnegotiable functions they performed, and their incompatibility with the compulsory powers the Webbs identified with the state. As Tony Wright has commented, while 'Guild Socialist man' appeared to have a 'natural' tendency to fellowship, thwarted only by a 'divisive social environment', his Webbian counterparts needed 'protecting from each other' on the assumption that some such divisions were ultimately ineradicable.[67] More exactly, 'Fabian men' needed protecting, not so much from each other as from their functionally other selves. This was simply a more conflictual and realistic version of Cole's own insight that man 'as a whole' could not be represented. In *Soviet Communism*, however, as the multiplicity of function gave way to the commonality of class and the overriding claims of the 'citizen', producer and consumer were explicitly subordinated to man the citizen and hence the brute reality of the state.[68] With the denial and suppression of a divisive social environment, the abandonment of Fabian-style protections served to legitimise a social and political catastrophe.

Co-operation was the most obvious victim. Though 'man as a consumer' figured prominently in the Webbs' early comments on Soviet Russia, already in January 1932, when approached regarding a 'Society for Promoting Co-operative Economics' instigated by the émigré Russian co-operator Nikolai Barou, the Webbs asserted their 'decided' preference for compulsory forms of association.[69] In due course, this apparent conflation of the citizen and consumer allowed the virtual erasure of voluntary co-operation from the picture they developed of Soviet communism. The clarification of this issue was one of the objects of Sidney's second Russian visit in 1934; and by the time *Soviet Communism* appeared, a remarkably summary chapter described co-operation as essentially a distributive mechanism, practically coterminous with its potential membership and offering little distinction in principle from the state itself.[70] Even this modest emphasis was undermined by Stalin's arbitrary dissolution of Russia's urban co-operatives as the book was about to appear. For some of the regime's former sympathisers, this was the crowning disillusionment. New demands were heard for the Russians' exclusion from the ICA, and Henry May, in a series of bitter ruminations, described the Soviets' attitude as indistinguishable from that of Nazi Germany. Though in earlier years, he recalled, the vision of 'at least some of the rulers in Russia' was of 'a new civilisation ... broadly based upon the free institutions which are the essence of the Co-operative System', now these institutions had been commandeered as a mere appendage of Stalin's 'super Socialist State'. Anywhere else but in Russia, such a regime would have been universally denounced by co-operators as 'an enemy of the people'.[71] Gide by this time was dead, but his nephew André Gide revisited many of the themes that his uncle had in producing his famous record of disillusionment, *Retour de l'URSS*.[72]

Grimmer lessons still were provided by the testimony of the Centrosoyus president, Isaac Zelensky, at the third Moscow show trial in March 1938. What, in those fevered times, could have offered a more obvious object of suspicion than this sole Soviet institution bearing unbroken links with a non-communist world? The very building it worked from, the first large project of the Swiss-French architectural modernist Le Corbusier, breathed the heterodoxy and cosmopolitanism of more expansive times, now the subject not of celebration but of grotesque paranoia.[73] Paraded before Vyshinsky, Zelensky confessed to having used the Centrosoyus foreign bureau to spread 'tendentious and false information ... [s]tressing the independent character of the co-operative movement and exaggerating its economic significance'. He even cited the Webbs' friend A.V. Alexander as having pledged his support should Stalin be overthrown: an obviously specious claim to which Beatrice did not record her reaction.[74]

Leslie Paul, who did, became an avowed opponent of the USSR as a result of the trial.[75] Other pro-Soviet co-operators, Cole among them, concluded instead that the voluntary Rochdale principles were better suited to the capitalist societies in which they originated than a planned economy whose inherent logic was universality. Indeed, Cole claimed by the 1940s never to have regarded the voluntary principle as fundamental to co-operation, which in the 1920s he had nevertheless described as 'of its essence a voluntary movement'. Once again, one notes the possibility of easy and even unconscious transitions from one emphasis to the other.[76] Joseph Reeves, though conceding the dismay felt by co-operators at the confounding of the Webbs' earliest reports on the Russian movement, confronted May directly with such arguments.[77] By the 1940s Reeves too was stating bluntly that 'socialism cannot tolerate the existence of voluntary co-operation', and in Labour Britain and Soviet Russia alike celebrated the ascendancy of the state.[78] The Webbs for their part, in the second edition of *Soviet Communism*, limply attempted to bring out the expanding role for Centrosoyus among the country's rural majority.[79] Paradoxically, it was May who, having cited the Webbs in defence of the Soviets, now proved truer to the spirit of their co-operative writings, in upholding the voluntary principle and reacting outspokenly to its abrogation.

Something similar can be traced in the case of the unions. The Webbs had always held that even under socialism free trade unions were indispensable, both to defend groups of producers against the generality of consumers and to affirm the vocational identities by which personality was expressed in the field of production.[80] Of these dual functions, so basic to Webbian social theory, practically nothing remained in *Soviet Communism*. Instead, the disparate claims of actual workers were lost in a single class interest straddling both sides of industry and its sectoral, occupational and geographical subdivisions. On the one hand, this was held to justify the atrophy of established union functions, on the grounds that workers needed no defence against themselves: there was, the Webbs said, 'no enemy left to fight'. On the other, it meant that the vestiges of vocational organisation were lost in vast 'employment' unions, organised around the productive unit and functioning to all intents and purposes as company unions.[81] Soviet practice was in each case preferred to Webbian theory, and the ousting of officials upholding traditional union rights and functions was endorsed. 'He ... is reported to have said that the government must indeed be hard up if it wanted "socialist competition" among the workers to increase output!', the Webbs related incredulously in relation to the fall of the Russian trade union president Tomsky in 1928. They also discoursed ingenuously on the self-flagellation of speed-up, socialist competition and a sometimes humiliating labour discipline, which only the assumption of a common purpose could distinguish from the oppressions of an enemy.[82] Threatened with a worse fate, Tomsky committed suicide in 1937. However, the impulses of the trade unionist survived without persecution among the Webbs' own readers. It was hardly to be expected that such a system would be approved by older union stalwarts, Arthur Henderson warned them. Ellen Wilkinson stated plainly of a workers' movement thus compromised, 'Then what's the good of it?'[83] Older or simply timeless, these were attitudes that for decades had been shared and even inculcated by the Webbs themselves.

Thus once more one encounters the paradox of Webbian precepts surviving in those influenced by them to reproach the Webbs themselves with their abandonment. This was notably the case with the TUC secretary Walter Citrine, a figure who like his predecessor Fred Bramley was very much cast in a Webbian mould. As a young union activist, Citrine had studied *Industrial Democracy* 'from cover to cover'. Regarding it as his 'bible', he had then explicitly drawn upon it for the trade union philosophy he expounded as TUC secretary from 1925-6.[84] Conciliatory and corporatist-minded though he was, Citrine's anglicised version of 'functional decentralisation' maintained a clearly demarcated sphere of influence for the unions. Not so far removed from the stalwarts invoked by Arthur Henderson, he was described by Beatrice in 1933 as 'dead against any deviation from the old old way of British trade unionists, of increasing the weekly earnings and diminishing the daily effort of each section of the workers, separately, at all times, and at any cost and by any method ...'[85] 'At any cost' in the 1930s meant not general strikes but a willingness to court advantage with Conservative employers and politicians, while preserving room for manoeuvre also meant remaining at arm's length from the Labour Party. Accordingly, Beatrice also criticised Citrine's leadership in leftist terms, for remaining 'closeted with the leading capitalists ... to extract slightly better terms for some sections of the workers' instead of frankly declaring 'heart and soul for the liquidation of the landlord and the capitalist'.[86] Nevertheless, this had nothing to do with the old, old union functions so elaborately codified in the Webbs' own writings.

The distinction was much clearer in a Soviet context. On first visiting the country in 1925, Citrine had already advanced arguments for union autonomy of unmistakeably Webbian derivation. Describing the unions as the workers' 'protective instrument ... against the State', he upheld the right to strike on the analogy of workers' disputes with co-operative societies in which the strikers themselves often held membership. 'I said that often the position of an individual as a producer and his position as a consumer were in conflict', Citrine recalled, and, unlike the Webbs, he did not abandon this position when he revisited the USSR in the 1930s.[87] On the contrary, his travelogue *I Search for Truth in Russia* (1936) seems intended as a Webbian antidote to the Webbs themselves: debunking Stakhanovism, rejecting the assimilation of the unions to the state, and disputing the very possibility of an identity of interests within industry. Supplementing as it did his rasping reviews of *Soviet Communism* in the official Labour press, Citrine's hostility must have played its part in the thwarting of hopes for a TUC edition of *Soviet Communism*. No doubt it also contributed to the exasperation Beatrice now expressed with the 'nit wits and boozers of Transport House'.[88] Proclaiming freedom of association and independent action as the foundations of legitimate trade unionism, Citrine's thoroughgoing scepticism showed how far the British and Russian unions had diverged since the days of the Anglo-Russian committee of the 1920s. Convinced supporters like George Hicks and A.A. Purcell, until his death in 1935, remained steadfast.[89] As to the former TUC secretary Fred Bramley, one can only speculate as to whether he would have shared the disillusionment – in the Webbs, perhaps, as much as in the Soviets – of May and Citrine.

What is certain is that the perversion of trade union principles in *Soviet Communism* was picked up, not by moderates or class-collaborators, but by maximalists of the left. In the communist *Labour Monthly*, the demolition of Citrine's arguments was entrusted to T.A. Jackson, sometimes depicted as the most impish and heterodox of communists. On this issue, however, he freely plundered the Webbs down to their ludicrous exclamation marks. 'It doesn't occur to him that Stalin ... instead of being the master of the people of the USSR, is literally their chief servant – carrying out the people's bidding!', he taunted Citrine; 'any "criticism" of Stalin must also and more primarily be a self-criticism of the people by themselves!' Jackson was another 'Victorian', born in 1879, who converted to socialism at the beginning of the century and rapidly passed through the majority of socialist parties then available. In contesting the conventional categories of 'government' and 'people', describing the state as simply '*the People, collectively, doing things for themselves*', he located the phantasm of Soviet democracy in the old socialist dream of unmediated self-government.[90] The Webbs, who had seen through the dream, could not see through the supposed reality. If Beatrice became uncharacteristically venomous towards Citrine – 'you don't come here again', she muttered on his final visit to them – perhaps that was before he reminded her of her own better judgement.[91]

## V

What the Webbs provided in *Soviet Communism* was thus only a simulacrum of multiformity, held together by a homogeneous class interest itself linked indissolubly to the party-state. 'All the diversity of participation in the universal multiformity of organisation', they noted in their 'epilogue' of 1937, 'makes more than usually indispensable that leadership without which democracy, in any of its forms, is but a mob'.[92] It was this element of leadership, largely identified with the Soviet communist party, that provided the fourth and decisive component of the Soviet quadrilateral. It was also the one which, superficially, was least anticipated in the Webbs' own attempts at system-building. Beatrice herself described it as providing the 'soul' that was missing from their own socialist constitution; and as they completed their book she acknowledged the party's growing supremacy – the 'special contribution' of the 'quondam priest' Stalin – as marking the decisive change in Soviet communism since she had first become interested in it.[93] Nevertheless there were also hidden continuities behind this new 'steel frame' of a ruling party, for fundamentally the Webbs did not regard the CPSU as a political party at all, but as a 'companionship', an 'order', a 'united confraternity' merely 'termed the Communist Party' and hence avoiding the negative connotations they had previously attached to such forms of organisation.[94] Instead, they described it as a phenomenon hitherto unknown to political science which they felicitously designated the 'Vocation of Leadership'. 'The soviet, trade union and co-operative movements', Beatrice commented, with just a hint of concern at the implications for Soviet democracy, 'are all alike gripped tight by the Vocation of Leadership'.[95]

The connotations of the phrase were deliberately ambiguous. In functionalist terms, it signified the Webbian ideal of specialisation as applied to the practice of government. Hence the party was likened to the professional bodies whose several competencies had underpinned previous Webbian schemes of social advancement. As what Beatrice called 'the authorised profession of the leaders of men', and Sidney more prosaically 'a vocational association of persons engaged in public administration', it was seen as a repository of specialised knowledge and proficiency demanding of its members the attainment and continuous practice of appropriate levels of conduct and expertise.[96] Applied to the exercise of power, this seemed to imply not only a vocation but almost 'a new governing class', with the danger of it degenerating into a mere 'privileged and self-seeking caste' with all its attendant vices.[97] It was thus a crucial feature of the new elite that its members were not 'abstracted' from society in the manner of a professional political class, but on the contrary could be found in 'ubiquitous personal intercourse' with their fellow citizens, working at the bench or in the mine, 'continuously educating, inspiring, guiding and leading the whole people among whom they live and work'.[98] Fewer than half of Russia's communists held administrative positions, and none, the Webbs claimed, enjoyed living standards higher than those of the average skilled worker. Indeed, far from enjoying a privileged existence, they were called upon to show exceptional qualities of discipline and self-sacrifice. Distantly this resembled a sort of augmented and diversified shop steward's role, linked to competence and exemplarity in the performance of constructive tasks of leadership. It was as a means of maintaining these standards of conduct, rather than as a form of political control, that the Webbs explained the periodic purging of the party.[99] As Beatrice confessed to Harold Laski, they had found it 'extraordinarily difficult' to obtain accurate information as to how the organisation actually worked.[100]

Equally important were the religious connotations of vocation. Indeed, these alone are alluded to in Beatrice's early diary entries on the subject, and it is only with Sidney's *Political Quarterly* article of 1933, 'The steel frame', that the analogy with professional organisation appears to take shape. Beatrice, on the other hand, remained drawn by the idea of a secular theocracy or what she actually described as a 'Spiritual Power over and above the ostensible government'.[101] As she wrote before their visit: 'It is the invention of the religious order, as the determining factor in the life of a great nation, which is the magnet that attracts me to Russia.' To some extent, this represented a reaction against the moral corruption and lack of any driving faith of the leaders of social democracy, and more generally against the post-war degradation of public values against which she fulminated in the same diary entry. Hence she laid great stress on the austerity and self-abnegation of communism – 'the exact opposite of D.H. Lawrence's cult of sex which I happen to detest'.[102] On the other hand, Beatrice admitted to having always hankered after a spiritual authority, and in likening communism to Comte's Religion of Humanity took up a thread dating as far back as the 1880s.[103] Freed of any specific sectarian associations, the theme can be traced in particular in those periods of relative political pessimism when Beatrice was least persuaded of the democratic possibilities of reformation. 'Oh! for a church that would weld into one living force all who hold this faith, with the discipline and the consolations fitted to sustain their endeavours', she had confided in 1906 of her own belief in the subordination of man's physical desires to 'the intellectual and spiritual side of his nature'.[104] Twenty years later, in a diary entry dwelling on the absence of any ethical code or scale of values in writers like Lawrence and Huxley, she had commented on the inadequacy of mere changes of social machinery to curb the 'evil' impulses in man. 'No amount of knowledge or science will be of any avail unless we can catch the bad impulse and set free the good. Can this be done without the authoritative ethics associated with faith in a spirit of love at work in the universe?'[105]

Sidney was somewhat sceptical of such ideas. He never understood his wife's belief in the power of prayer, and although he even more than she had been saturated in the mental atmosphere of Comtism, the Fabians were never converts to its religious aspects. Sidney even expressed regret at the surrounding of Comte's social theories by 'a dense mass of other doctrines which have impeded its progress'; as Willard Wolfe observes, 'it was because Comte had rejected democracy and had trusted ... to the sanctions of an organised religious cult that "Comtism" could be no more than the "metaphysical stage of Collectivism"'.[106] In this, at least, the two typewriters beat to different rhythms. Though Sidney was also prepared to link the communist party with the Jesuits, and with the 'strictly disciplined officer-corps' of the Salvation Army, on this aspect of the new civilisation Beatrice recorded that the couple had 'slightly divergent views'.[107] After Sidney had a stroke in January 1938 – 'The end of our partnership?', Beatrice asked – his incapacity for further work meant that at last there was a sort of resolution. 'In fact', the published text of *Soviet Communism* has it, 'in the nature of its mentality, as in the direction of its activities, the Communist Party reminds us less of a religious order than of the organisation of the learned professions of Western Europe, such as those of the lawyers and doctors, engineers and public accountants'. Evidently the formulation did not meet with Beatrice's approval, and in *The Truth About Soviet Russia*, published after Sidney's stroke, she simply reversed it: 'In fact, in the nature of its mentality, as in the code of personal conduct, the Communist Party resembles *more* a religious order than the organisation of the learned professions of Western Europe, such as those of lawyers and doctors, engineers and public accountants.'[108]

Sidney was not the only sceptic. Originally, the Webbs' chapter on the communist party was to have had the title 'Man as a believer', complementing their chapters on man the consumer, the producer and the citizen. Nevertheless, the proposal met with little favour on the part of their Soviet confidants. Though their suggested alternative of 'Man as an organiser' was also rejected, the 'vocation of leadership' incorporated both desired accents while allowing the liberal use of religious metaphors lifted straight from Beatrice's diaries.[109] Even then, the implications were ambiguous. Though the communists had their own canonisations, holy writ and 'collective confessional' in the form of self-criticism, for Beatrice, as she made note of these phenomena, they remained objects of suspicion rather than attraction. Indeed, in their corollaries of a 'scholastic metaphysic' and 'fanatical repression of heresy', they even recalled the 'barbarities and pedantries of the middle ages'.[110] Hence, just as the ideal of a vocation of leadership had explicit religious connotations, so too, in a negative sense, had the 'disease of orthodoxy' which the Webbs identified as the single greatest blight on the new civilisation. What attracted them instead was the underlying gospel of the Service of Man, practically manifested in 'vows of obedience and poverty ... intensity of faith ... self-sacrifice and even martyrdom', and yet based not on religious faith but on 'the newest and most up-to-date science, meaning man's ever expanding knowledge of the universe, which it eagerly adopts and confidently applies to every task or problem'.[111] It was from the combination of alternative meanings that the Vocation of Leadership derived such potency while accommodating the different emphases of its authors.

Similarly, it was by a mixture of religious and bureaucratic impulses that the Webbs explained the motivations of those prepared to submit themselves to so exacting and even hazardous a code of living. For the religious impulse, it provided 'not only a sure and certain conviction of absolute truth, but ... the consciousness of a special mission for the improvement of humanity'.[112] Back in 1907, at the 'First Public Conference on Mr H.G. Wells's "Samurai"', Beatrice had spoken up, not so much for the Samurai, but for the 'priest' and 'prig', defined as those self-selected to guide the world who were responsible for all the good that was done within it. 'Socialists would not succeed till they had become practical mystics', she explained, and the same curious combination of qualities was evident in her later descriptions of the Konsomols.[113]

On the other hand, the Webbs had also long ago appreciated that the 'magic' of democracy lay in its 'enlargement of human personality', so that 'the newly enfranchised human being ... feels that he has grown in moral and intellectual stature – he has lost a sense of inferiority – he has gained new interests, new responsibilities, new powers of making the world more as he wishes it to be'.[114] It was the psychological need for this sense of empowerment that underlay their emphasis on the 'consciousness of consent', and the ductility that they believed paradoxically resulted from it. If this were true of the ordinary citizen, then for what they called the 'Super-citizen engaged in the Vocation of Leadership' the prospect existed of a further enlargement of personality by what the Webbs might have called the consciousness of authority – and what they did expressly acknowledge to be 'the craving, even of the ordinary man or woman, for power'. In relation to public affairs, they thus combined a longstanding emphasis on the satisfaction derived by 'every person of ability and character ... in the successful exercise of his vocation' with the 'sense of achievement, which some may call the sense of success or the sense of power, in directing or influencing the actions of others'. Moreover, in a more material sense they did not overlook the fact that, with the accumulation of personal wealth banned, party membership provided the vast majority of Soviet citizens with their one possibility of '"rising in the world"'.[115] Multiformity was not in contradiction with such a conception, but on the contrary provided the condition for its realisation. Like Wells, if less systematically, Beatrice had a tendency to speculate in terms of human 'types', like the famous Webbian 'A's (anarchist, aristocratic and artistic) and 'B's (benevolent, bourgeois and bureaucratic, like the Webbs themselves). On one occasion, at the end of the First World War, she had tried to match these types to the possible societies of the future. The rebel and fanatic, naturally, were to find self-realisation in 'sheer chaotic anarchy', and 'the common herd of apathetic citizens' in the 'efficient equalitarian bureaucratic collectivist state'. However, for a 'self-reliant, intelligent and good tempered race', the maximum of free activity would be achieved in 'a community of highly organised circles or groups, multiform and multifarious in character'.[116] Systematised in the Vocation of Leadership, it was precisely this benign, public-spirited and ubiquitous authority that the Webbs, against all probability, believed they discerned in the USSR.

**VI**

With the Vocation of Leadership, particularly in its bureaucratic aspects, we come at last to the full institutional expression of the yearnings for status and authority traditionally regarded as the key to the Webbs' socialism and the link connecting their Fabianism and their communism. 'All the diversity of participation in the universal multiformity of organisation which distinguishes the USSR from every other country', they wrote in 1937 in their 'epilogue' to *Soviet Communism*, 'makes more than usually indispensable that leadership without which democracy, in any of its forms, is but a mob'.[117] As eulogists of the Stalinist bureaucracy, they thus appear as harbingers of the 'managerial revolution', elevating the *nouvelle couche sociale* of *fin-de-siècle* Fabianism into the 'new class' delineated by Milovan Djilas and a host of other critics of Stalinism emerging from the 1930s. The most famous British anti-Stalinist, George Orwell, ascribed British 'russophilia' precisely to the hunger for power of this 'managerial' class of bureaucrats, technicians, scientists, journalists and educators. 'These people look towards the USSR and see in it, or think they see, a system which eliminates the upper class, keeps the working class in its place, and hands unlimited power to people very similar to themselves', Orwell wrote in his classic essay on Burnham's *Managerial Revolution*. 'It was only *after* the Soviet regime became unmistakably totalitarian that English intellectuals, in large numbers, began to show an interest in it.'[118] As noted at the outset, the prevalent interpretation of *Soviet Communism* has been of exactly this vicarious exercise in super-citizenship, emancipating and empowering social planners 'like the Webbs' or superior people 'like themselves'.[119] Without singling out the Webbs' particular responsibility, Orwell described it as the intellectual's 'secret wish ... to destroy the old, equalitarian version of Socialism and usher in a hierarchical society where the intellectual can at last get his hands on the whip'.[120]

Whether this was really what the Webbs saw, or thought they saw, is actually far from self-evident. Though they were captivated by the formal intricacies of an ordered society and inspired by its discovery of a new scale of values, it is impossible not to be struck by the otherness of the Webbs' new ruling order; the sense that, not only in respect of its youth and fanaticism but also of social class, it was not in the hands of people like the Webbs. In crude social terms, what they depicted was, if not a working-class revolution, at least the emergence of a working-class elite. It was not, in any direct or obvious way, a dictatorship of the intellectuals. Politically, the Webbs noted the deliberate preponderance in the communist party of manual workers, only offset by the advance of working-class recruits to positions of administrative responsibility.[121] Educationally, they heralded the advance of polytechnicalisation as narrowing the gulf between brain-worker and manual worker. In the world of work itself they looked to the 'intermixture of manual work' with even the most cerebral employments to complement the rising cultural horizons of the shopfloor worker. In both status or remuneration they thus envisaged the obliteration of the distinction between the worker by hand and by brain, 'other than in their respective functional proficiency'. Armed with the 'proletarian faith' that 'they were conquering the world for themselves', the industrial workers were depicted both as beneficiaries of the revolution and a proof of what it had already achieved.[122] On the other hand, it was what the Webbs themselves described as their 'strangely ironic conclusion' that it was precisely the intermediate category of managers and technicians – those whom Lenin referred to as the 'bureaucracy' and the 'old technical intelligentsia' – that seemed to them to represent the greatest failure of the revolution, whether in the matter of honesty, disinterestedness or sheer basic competence.[123] In respect of its salariat, as of almost nothing else, the Webbs declared unequivocally for the superiority of the old civilisation, and for this alone met with the disapproval of the Arcos official to whom they sent the relevant chapter of their book.[124]

For a few groups of brainworkers claims could no doubt be entertained of a superiority of circumstance under Soviet rule. Of these, by far the most significant were the scientists. Indeed, in *Soviet Communism* the Webbs' account of the greater opportunity and rationality of Soviet intellectual life focused primarily on the natural sciences and was given the overall title 'Science the salvation of mankind'.[125] On these matters, the Webbs were greatly influenced by the Cambridge physicist Patrick Blackett, a convinced and even 'fanatical' supporter of the USSR and the 'most accomplished and ... most personally attractive' of their younger acquaintances. Better known politically as one of the moving spirits behind the 'white heat' rhetoric of the Wilson era, Blackett visited the Webbs on several occasions in 1934-5. In between strengthening Beatrice's prejudice against homosexuality, Blackett persuaded her of the USSR's reputation among younger scientists as being unmatched in its facilities and provision of a creed and purpose.[126] 'What attracts the young *physical scientist* in Soviet Communism is that they would have a good deal to gain and nothing to lose if they were born and bred in the USSR', Beatrice recorded.

> One of the main attractions ... to scientific workers is the greater respect paid them under Soviet Communism than under capitalism. In Great

> Britain the scientist has a bare living not comparable to that of the lawyer, the tradesman, the business manager. In the USSR he is relatively well paid. Moreover the Soviet scientist has unlimited equipment and a very generous allotment of assistants.[127]

Even these arguments were somewhat dented in September 1934, when the Russian-born physicist Peter Kapitza, a colleague of Blackett's at Rutherford's Cavendish laboratory, was forcibly prevented from returning from his annual trip to the USSR. Though quickly forgotten, this was a case that briefly exercised the Cambridge left and even provoked demurrals from the CPGB.[128] Nevertheless, for scientists it remained a powerful attraction that they were to enjoy 'more power and more responsibility' under communism, indeed that the leading Soviet commissars, controlling industries compared to which ICI was 'small fry', were already often 'business executives, mostly trained as engineers'.[129]

Beyond the ranks of scientists, however, even the Webbs were under few illusions as to the standing of Soviet intellectuals. Quite apart from the considerable body of critical literature that they read, even sympathetic observers like Hindus referred without dissimulation to a virtual 'holocaust' of the intelligentsia. Hindus's accounts, as we have seen, had a considerable impact upon Beatrice, and in his *Humanity Uprooted* he strongly contrasted the new dignity and self-respect of the worker and peasant with the 'trial and turbulence ... self-denial and even self-abasement' that was the lot of the Russian intellectual.[130] Henry Harben, whose account Beatrice read the same year, pointed a similar contrast in a section on the terror, emphasising the special vulnerability of intellectuals and party functionaries whom, he noted mildly, might be 'shot out of hand' for wrongdoing.[131] Precisely like Harben, the Webbs in *Soviet Communism* described how the Cheka and its successors met with little disapproval from the populace at large, and in her diary Beatrice described the regime's 'nasty terrorism' as satisfying 'the suspicions and hatred of its proletariat'. 'In the USSR today the mass are uplifted: the exceptionally gifted are held down if they dare to question the Holy Writ', Beatrice observed in 1934. This, she went on, was 'contrary to "Science the Salvation of Man"'.[132] It certainly does not sound like the rule of 'superior people like themselves'.

More generally it was true in Britain that, among those with any genuine expertise in political questions, technocratic instincts rarely gave rise to an extreme idealisation of Stalinism except where combined with the prior or simultaneous idealisation of the real or potential capacities of working-class organisation. John Strachey, conceivably, was an exception. But in visitors like Gaitskell, described by Beatrice as an 'orthodox Fabian of the old pre war school', a lack of interest in the USSR seemed linked to the disparagement of the unions, and exclusive preoccupation with 'political action of a reformist character'. 'What is wrong about this group of clever and well meaning intellectuals, politicians, professors of economics and philosophy, or economists', Beatrice noted, contrasting the younger Fabians with their scientific *confrères*, 'is the comfort and freedom of their own lives; they have everything to gain and nothing to lose by the peaceful continuation of capitalist civilisation'.[133] H.G. Wells, in whom one might reasonably expect to find a recognition of his own Samurai conception, was also unattracted by Stalinism. Like Eden Paul he seemed to identify the Samurai with Lenin – the 'intensely practical and intensely middle-class' Lenin, who had invented the communist party to rule over the 'nominally sovereign masses', precisely on the lines of Plato's Guardians – only for such striking 'modernity' to succumb to the 'heavy load of democratic and equalitarian cant' expounded by Lenin's successors. 'In its attempts to modernize, it refused the assistance of just the most characteristically modern types in the community', Wells wrote of the USSR's treatment of its managers and technicians in *The Shape of Things to Come* (1933); and of course, when things accordingly went wrong, it shot or imprisoned them.[134] As Beatrice noted impatiently, 'throughout the book he asserts, in angry tones, that it is a stinking mess!'[135]

Nevertheless, even for the Webbs the denial of intellectual freedoms was the 'dark spot' that from the beginning provided an undercurrent of doubt about the new civilisation. It troubled them as much by its obvious dysfunctionality as by its human costs. As Beatrice noted privately in December 1934, the 'obstinate refusal of security ... against arbitrary and apparently unjustifiable punishment' negated the commitment to 'scientific ethics' and impeded the progress to 'higher levels of thought and feeling'[136] In *Soviet Communism* itself, they appended to their chapter on 'Science – the salvation' their rather mildly formulated strictures on the 'disease of orthodoxy', along with a curious plea for the social scientific investigations to which their own lives had so largely been dedicated. Partly disguised in reflections about fascism, as if hoping to bypass the Glavlit and reach the Konsomols, the Webbian device of the list of pros and cons was not ineffective in its understatement. 'What, for instance, is the effect upon productive efficiency of the emotion of fear?', they asked.

> How is initiative affected ... by apprehension that lack of success in departures from routine may lead to reprimand or dismissal? What is the effect of 'terrorist' measures, taken in order to deter counter-revolutionaries, upon members of the intelligentsia who, though not communist in opinion, are yet loyally serving the community ... ?

What indeed, they continued, of the counter-revolutionaries themselves, and the emotions of hatred deliberately inculcated against them?

> Why is it that in the USSR, as in other countries, the Communist Party is distinguished from all other controversialists by the peculiar virulence of the hatred that it concentrates on the bourgeoisie, leading to hatred of the various religious denominations, hatred of the other parties created by different factions among the wage-earners, hatred even of those in its own ranks who are thought to be deviating ...? Is there any truth in the assertions that in some of the Ogpu's concentration camps, and even in some of its closed places of detention for 'political' offenders ... there has prevailed not only very unscientific insanitation and overcrowding, with an unnecessary amount of disease and mortality, but also bad cases of deliberate cruelty and torture, possibly only by subordinate officials, equal to the worst that is alleged against the fascist dictatorships?

And finally, what was the effect, 'alike on "the leader" and on the mass of the people', of the 'extreme adulation now given in one country or another to the chosen head of the community for the time being?'

> Is this adulation of one citizen ... in harmony with the spirit of equalitarian comradeship? How far is the exaggeration and repetition, which seem to be inherent in this national habit, detrimental to veracity in the adulator, and to his own resistance of the temptation to hypocrisy? What other evils are suggested by the contemporary experience of leadership in Italy and the German Reich?[137]

In a book of a thousand pages, this was hardly the dominant motif. Implicitly it raised the question of why the Webbs themselves had not done a good deal more to explore such questions. Nevertheless, it does suggest that their critical faculties had not entirely been abandoned when it came to discussing the USSR.

## VII

One of the limitations of *Soviet Communism* was that it applied research methods developed in the context of British gradualism to the study of a society undergoing convulsions of change without precedent in European history. Defying historical clichés as to the continuing opposition between the ILP's 'passionate', 'evangelical', 'nonconformist' socialist 'morality' and the 'antiseptic', 'elitist' 'positivism' of the Webbs, the book's reviewer in the ILP's *New Leader* simply ran through superlatives for their 'genius for sorting, assimilating, classifying and clarifying' the Soviet experience.[138] Nevertheless, these were not the skills primarily required to understand a society in which rules and conventions were daily abrogated, extemporised or simply disregarded on the most massive scale. Already dated on its publication, in many respects the book presented a picture more appropriate to the early 1930s or even the 1920s; for example, its account of political differences within the CPSU was true, if at all, only of the 1920s, and was almost entirely based on sources for that decade. By the time of the book's second edition in 1937, its central thesis of a new civilisation seemed, even to sympathetic observers, to have been confounded by the gathering momentum of repression and the shock of the Moscow show trials. Troubled by events without an obvious rationale, Beatrice in her diary toyed with a variety of explanations. These ranged from the lingering effects of civil war, to the legacy of backwardness manifested in the 'savage pursuit of the heretic', through to the mysteries of revolutionary psychology and 'the peculiarly Russian characteristic of a liking for confessions!' Nevertheless, despite the implausibility of the conspiracies revealed, Beatrice found the behaviour of both prosecutors and accused unfathomable except on the assumption that the confessions must be true.[139] The result was that, in the second edition of *Soviet Communism*, the Webbs provided what Harold Laski justly described as an apology for the trials, 'reasoned', 'careful', but ultimately tortuous.[140] Notoriously, the question posed in the original edition – *Soviet Communism: a new civilisation?* – was now perfunctorily settled by the dropping of the question mark from the title.

The impact of the purges was not just to heighten the scale of the repression but also to bring it almost to the doorstep of Passfield Corner. Even before the completion of *Soviet Communism*, the Webbs' standing as a major public intellectuals meant that several individual cases of repression were brought to their notice. Some were members of the old intelligentsia, including essentially non-political figures like Kapitza. 'Believe me that I cannot sleep at night when I think of all the hardships, humiliation and prosecution of so many of my friends and hundreds of the Russian scholars!', wrote one of these correspondents in 1933, though the Webbs at this point do not appear to have been personally acquainted with any such cases.[141] This, however, was to change dramatically with the purges. Already in the second show trial of January 1937, one of the principal accused was the same Grigorii Sokolnikov whom Beatrice had so admired during his London ambassadorship. More than once Sokolnikov had actually stayed at the Webbs' home. Another acquaintance, who like A.V. Alexander was implicated in the third trial of March 1938, was the then recently deceased Michael Farbman, a Russian-born journalist whose insights were commended in *Soviet Communism*, but who was cited as a British agent in Rakovsky's confession.[142] Finally there was Rose Cohen, one of the 'youths and maidens' of the wartime FRD, who as a communist had married the Ukrainian Petrovsky and settled in Moscow. Invited to Passfield on one of her British visits in the early 1930s, Cohen's arrest, though not the fact that she had already been shot, became known to Beatrice in December 1937.[143]

The plight of superior people like themselves could hardly have been more clearly demonstrated. Discreetly, the Webbs appear to have made representations on behalf of both Sokolnikov and Cohen; and when Farbman's widow and daughter were sacked by Arcos, Beatrice sent them money and tried to find them work as translators.[144] In Sokolnikov's case, she consoled herself that their interventions may have contributed to his receiving not the death penalty but ten years' penal servitude; meaning, she said, 'useful work with adequate detention'. In reality, Sokolnikov, like Cohen, was shot without ceremony.[145] As Beatrice said, it was a horrible thought that those with whom one had been friendly might be 'shot at dawn'.[146] On the other hand, the Webbs' failure to make any clear public statement on such cases reflected, not only their profounder emotional commitment to the new civilisation, but a personal quality of disengagement and even callousness which was merely the uglier side of the coin to their equanimity and lack of rancour. 'One wants to be friendly and helpful to the men and women one meets', Beatrice wrote in connection with the Turins, disillusioned Russian emigres who were helping them with *Soviet Communism*, 'but neither Sidney nor I like emotional relationships: we do not want either to love or to hate, to flatter or be flattered, to give or accept favours from fellow travellers – it all means ties which it is horrid to ignore or to break, but which it may be onerous and tiresome to keep intact to the end of the road'. Comparing Turin with the 'self-complacent' Stalinist Julius Hecker, she even wrote unpleasantly that Turin had '[taken] the wrong road and knows it. Hecker can visit England but Turin cannot return to Russia.'[147] Like the Coles, the Webbs did not sign a moderately worded public protest about Cohen's plight; in fact it attracted only nine signatures. Moreover, despite the assistance she gave to Farbman's widow, she described her dismissal as not only justified but necessitated by 'her present "disillusionment' coupled with her "*private information*" on the rotten state of the Soviet Union'.[148] In Kapitza's case, though she signed a petition on his behalf, she also speculated as to whether the indebtedness of the individual to society actually legitimised a government's refusal to a citizen of permission to leave the 'community'. She showed no concern about the fact that his correspondence was liable to be opened and read by the authorities.[149]

Back in 1927, when Shaw was boosting Mussolini, Beatrice had indicted him for his indifference to the 'agony' of the best and wisest Italians and the mental degradation that resulted from suppressing basic liberties.[150] If she allowed herself to overrule such instincts in the case of Stalin's Russia, it was not under any illusion that the best and wisest Russians held the whip. Rather than the crude projection of interests implied by such interpretations, the Webbs' road to Russia shows how values and aspirations that were both complex and contingent were translated into a political trajectory always responsive to associations and events. Finally, like the revolution itself, these accommodations destroyed the very conditions of well-being – intellectual enquiry, expert administration, industrial and consumers' democracy –

that they were meant to have upheld. Like other fellow-travellers, the Webbs were prepared to offset the constraints on an 'intellectual elite' with the 'presence of opportunity' purportedly being established for the Soviet people as a whole.[151] In reality, of course, if 'Science the Salvation of Man' meant anything at all, then the implication of an inverse correlation between workers' and intellectual interests was, except in the most basic material sense, untenable even in theory.

The whole episode is a sobering one. The American journalist Eugene Lyons, in many respects an unreliable commentator on the Webbs, described them accurately as having tortured their aspirations into shape 'to make them coincide with a Russia which, in their hearts, they could not possibly accept'. He continued:

> If people like the Webbs desert, who then shall speak up for the revolutionists in Soviet 'isolators', for the victims of punitive famines, for a population denied freedom of press, thought, and movement, for the million-fold victims of organized terror? When people like the Webbs are able, for any reason, to join the fanatic executioners and liquidators ... then there is a danger that the very memory of decency and humaneness is fading out.[152]

Harold Laski, so warm and yet finally equivocal an admirer of *Soviet Communism*, both the book and the system, put it differently. 'Tolerance will come [in Russia], as elsewhere', he wrote in reviewing the second edition, with its dropped question mark, 'because those who believe in the immense service that the Soviet Union can render ... are militant about the urgency of its coming. It will not come unless people with the authority of Mr and Mrs Webb urgently protest against any action that is arbitrary and unexplained ... The more I reflect upon Mr and Mrs Webb's argument, the more inclined I am to suspect that a new and long dark age lies before us through which we have to pass before a recovery of tolerance becomes again a possible adventure.'[153]

## NOTES

1. BWD 17 July 1934*; Charlotte Despard, Russian diary, 8 August 1930.
2. BWD 5 April 1932.
3. BW to R. Palme Dutt, 28 May 1942 in Mackenzie, *Letters*, vol. 3, p. 458.
4. BWD 29 November 1933.
5. Passfield papers 6/86, broadcast talk by Beatrice, 22 September 1932.
6. *SCANC*, pp. 944-5.
7. BWD 24 July*, 20 December 1935 and 27 June 1942*.
8. BWD 3 January 1934*.
9. BWD 10 September 1935*.
10. BWD 28 July 1934*, 25 November* and 12 December* 1936. Interviewed by Royden Harrison in 1966, Maisky claimed to have had a major hand in the Webbs' chapter on 'The liquidation of the landlord and

the capitalist'. This does not however appear to be corroborated by Beatrice's diaries, although mention is made of Maisky's approval of their section on foreign affairs, with its criticisms of the Comintern, and his discomfort with, but not objection to, their criticisms of the disease of orthodoxy; see Harrison, 'Sidney', p. 88 n. 68, BWD 8 April 1934* and 24 July 1935*.

11. BWD 13 June*, 21 October* and 16 December* 1933, 22 August 1934*, 15 September 1936*.
12. BWD 9 June 1933*.
13. *SCANC*, pp. 1078-82.
14. BWD 4 July 1933*.
15. Lenin, cited Marcel Liebman, *Leninism*, p. 213.
16. LHASC WG/RUS/13, Gillies to F. Adler, 22 April 1932.
17. BWD 4 January 1933* and 27 March 1933*.
18. BWD 7 February 1922.
19. *SCANC*, 258-72.
20. Thus they celebrated the USSR's invention of the 'unnational state' and rejection of all doctrines of racial superiority, while, on criteria of social development, themselves continuing to refer to the country's 'lower races': *SCANC*, pp. 153 ff.
21. See e.g. David A. Shannon (ed.), *Beatrice Webb's American Diary*, University of Wisconsin Press, 1963, pp. xii-xiii.
22. SW to Bernard Shaw, 29 October 1911 and BW to Kate Courtney, 18 October 1911, Mackenzie, *Letters*, vol. 2, pp. 374-8
23. *SCANC*, p. 807.
24. BWD 25 March 1931*.
25. *SCANC*, pp. 807, 1119-22. The first three volumes of Toynbee's *Study of History* appeared in 1934.
26. See e.g. Clarke, *Liberals and Social Democrats*, pp. 243-52; E.P. Thompson, *The Making of the English Working Class*, Gollancz, 1963, pp. 195-7.
27. *MA*, pp. 293-6.
28. *DCC*, pp. 75-8; Spencer, *Social Statics* (1851) cited Zygmaunt Bauman, *Between Class and Elite. The evolution of the British labour movement: a sociological study*, Manchester; MUP, 1972, p. 3; also *MA*, pp. 291-2.
29. *SCANC*, pp. 595-601.
30. See *SCANC*, pp. 1119-43; also BWD 20 November 1933* and 3 May 1934*.
31. BWD 3 May 1934*.
32. *SCANC*, p. 602; BWD 29 November 1933*; Laski papers (IISH) 27/2, Beatrice to Laski, 12 March 1935.
33. Fitzpatrick, *Everyday Stalinism*, ch. 2; Molotov cited Tucker, *Stalin in Power*, p. 214.
34. *SCANC*, p. 188.
35. *SCANC*, pp. 734 ff; also *CCM*, p. 373.
36. See *SCANC*, pp. 604-8 for the Webbs' dismissal of workers' control on grounds of the inevitable subordination of the producer to the will of the consumer.
37. BWD 21 May 1936*.
38. *SCANC*, pp. 655, 682-3, 691 ff; Fitzpatrick, *Everyday Stalinism*, ch. 4.

39. *SCANC*, p. 1033.
40. BWD 5 November 1933*, also 17 May 1932 and 27 November 1934*.
41. BWD 24 January 1934*.
42. Stephen Spender, *Forward from Liberalism*, Gollancz, 1937, pp. 263 ff.
43. *SCANC*, p. 1053.
44. *SCANC*, pp. 805 ff; Kosarev cited Fitzpatrick, *Everyday Stalinism*, p. 92.
45. *SCANC*, pp. 909-11.
46. *SCANC*, pp. 912-14; compare *CCM*, pp. 411-13.
47. *SCANC*, p. 1047.
48. 'Some of our conclusions about Soviet Russia and its relation to the world we live in' in BWD, August 1932.
49. For earlier discussions, see pp. 107-13 above.
50. *MA*, pp. 325-8; see McBriar, *Fabian Socialism*, pp. 29-47 for the Fabian theory of rent; also John Ruskin, *Muna Pulveris* (1872), George Allen, 1904 edn, e.g. pp. 27-8.
51. *SCANC*, p. 1216.
52. John Ruskin, 'Work' (1865) in *The Crown of Wild Olive*, Routledge edn, nd, p. 14.
53. BWD 1 March 1932.
54. *SCANC*, pp. 923-4, 1070.
55. Shaw to BW 5 July 1928, copied into BWD; also BWD 11 February 1939* re Wells's *Holy Terror* .
56. G.B. Shaw, *The Intelligent Woman's Guide to Socialism and Capitalism* (1928); Pelican edn, 1937, p. 305 and passim; BWD 9 June 1928*; also Shaw to Augustin Hamon 9 April 1927 and to Friedrich Adler 2, 11 and 14 October 1927 in Laurence, *Collected Letters 1926-1950*, pp. 51-2, 67-74.
57. BWD 17 August 1932* and 13 June 1933.
58. BWD 2 December 1927.
59. BWD 5 January 1934* and 5 June 1939*.
60. *SCANC*, pp. 427 ff.
61. Cole, *Next Ten*, p. 161.
62. BWD 17 January 1941*.
63. *SCANC*, p. 450, 1071-2.
64. *SCANC*, pp. 427-9, 438-40.
65. SW, 'The steel frame of Soviet society', *Political Quarterly*, January-March 1933, p. 7.
66. Sidney and Beatrice Webb, *The Truth about Soviet Russia* (henceforth *TASR*) (1942), Longmans, 1944 edn, p. 30; also BWD 19 February* and 19 August* 1934.
67. Wright, 'Fabianism and guild socialism', p. 231.
68. *TASR*, p. 34.
69. BWD 21 September 1930*; BWD 17 January 1932. Barou had recently been dismissed from the Moscow Narodny Bank, to which emigre Russian co-operators had gravitated after the Bolshevik grip on Centrosoyus had tightened (see RGASPI 506/1/28/57 ff, Russian delegate Kantor, First International Conference of Communist Co-operators). In the NEP period, that had not precluded collaborations between Barou and E.F. Wise.
70. BWD 16 December 1933* and 5 March 1934*; *SCANC*, pp. 304-38.

71. May, *Review of International Co-operation*, December 1935, pp. 441-2 and March 1936, pp. 82-6.
72. See André Gide, trans. Dorothy Bussy, *Back from the USSR* (1936), Secker & Warburg, 1937.
73. Jean-Louis Cohen, *Le Corbusier and the Mystique of the USSR. Theories and projects for Moscow 1928-1936*, Princeton University Press, 1992, ch. 4.
74. *Report of Court Proceedings in the case of the anti-Soviet 'Bloc of Rights and Trotskyites'* (March 1938), Moscow: People's Commissariat of Justice of the USSR, 1938, pp. 337-8.
75. Paul, *Angry Young Man*, pp. 192-5.
76. Cole, *Century*, p. 354; Cole, *Next Ten*, p. 281.
77. Reeves in *For Peace and Friendship*, pp. 176-84.
78. Reeves, *Century*, pp. 170ff.
79. *SCANC*, p. 1187.
80. See e.g. *CCM*, pp. 231-2 and 474-7.
81. *SCANC*, pp. 161 ff, 1162 ff.
82. *SCANC* pp. 169-70 for Tomsky and pp. 759-67 for their approval of 'public honour and shame'.
83. BWD 22 February* and 19 August *1934.
84. Citrine, *Men and Work*, pp. 47, 65, 267 ff; Citrine papers 1/1, memorandum on 'Trade union government', 10 February 1926 (citing *Industrial Democracy*); Ross M. Martin, *TUC: the growth of a pressure group 1868-1976*, Oxford: OUP, 1980, pp. 216-17.
85. BWD 2 October 1933*.
86. BWD 26 November 1934*.
87. Citrine, *Men and Work*, 95 ff. See also See Arthur Horner, *Incorrigible Rebel*, MacGibbon & Kee, 1960, pp. 107-8 for an intriguing account of conversation between Citrine and Horner about the need for trade union independence.
88. Citrine, *I Search for Truth in Russia*, Routledge, 1936, pp. 129, 158-9, 185, 353-4, 360-1; reviews in *Daily Herald*, 28 November 1935 and *Labour*, January 1936, pp. 106-7; also BWD 25 June 1934, 23 May 1936*; 10 March* and 25 May* 1937.
89. For Hicks, see *Labour Monthly*, November 1937, pp. 672-3; for Purcell *Bolshevism and the British Left*, vol. 3.
90. Jackson, 'A worm's eye view of Russia', *Labour Monthly*, September 1937, pp. 575-9. Jackson had held memberships of the SDF, the ILP and the Socialist Party of Great Britain as well as the CPGB. He was also closely identified with the Plebs League.
91. BWD 23 May 1936*.
92. *SCANC*, p. 1130.
93. BWD 4 January 1932 and 27 July 1935*; also BWD 22 August 1934.
94. *SCANC*, pp. 342, 1130; SW, 'Steel frame'.
95. BWD 27 July 1935*.
96. BWD 6 September 1933*; SW, 'Steel frame', p. 11; *SCANC*, pp. 339, 414-15; *TASR*, pp. 39-40.
97. BWD 13 June 1933* and 27 July 1935*.
98. *SCANC*, pp. 6-7, 417.
99. *SCANC* pp. 376 ff; BWD 6 September 1933*.

100. Laski papers (IISH) 27/2, BW to Laski 12 March 1935.
101. BWD 14 May 1932.
102. BWD 4 January 1932; also 4 June 1933*.
103. See *MA*, pp. 128-9.
104. BWD 30 November 1906, *OP*, p. 366.
105. BWD 22 November 1925.
106. Wolfe, *Radicalism to Socialism*, pp. 183, 185-92; also McBriar, *Fabian Socialism*, pp. 147-8.
107. SW, 'Steel frame', pp. 9-10; BWD 22 September 1932*.
108. *SCANC*, p. 415; *TASR*, p. 40 (emphasis added); see also BWD 25 January 1938.
109. E.g. 'vows of obedience and poverty', BWD 4 January 1932, *SCANC*, p. 414; see also BWD 4 December 1933*, and *SCANC*, p. 339 for the Webbs' observations on the dual meaning of vocation.
110. BWD 14 May 1932; 'Some of our conclusions'.
111. *SCANC*, pp. 413-18.
112. *SCANC*, pp. 373-4.
113. *New Age*, 2 May 1907, p. 11.
114. BW, 'Diseases of organised society' in Mary Adams, ed., *The Modern State*, Allen & Unwin, 1933, p. 184.
115. *SCANC*, pp. 63, 373-4.
116. BWD 30 December 1918*.
117. *SCANC*, p. 1130.
118. Orwell, 'James Burnham and the managerial revolution' in Sonia Orwell and Ian Angus, eds, *The Collected Essays, Journalism and Letters of George Orwell. Volume IV. In front of your nose 1945-1950*, Harmondsworth: Penguin edn, 1970, p. 212.
119. Jones, *Russia Complex*, pp. 21-2; Mackenzie, *Socialism and Society*, pp. 17-18, 24-5.
120. Orwell, 'James Burnham', p. 212.
121. *SCANC*, pp. 292, 346.
122. *SCANC*, pp. 905-7.
123. *SCANC*, pp. 795 ff.
124. BWD 28 July 1934*.
125. *SCANC*, pp. 944-88.
126. See David Horner, 'The road to Scarborough: Wilson, Labour and the scientific revolution' in Richard Coopey, Steven Fielding and Nick Tiratsoo, eds, *The Wilson Government 1964-70*, Pinter, 1993, pp. 48-71.
127. BWD 12 April* and 26 July* 1934, 30 July 1935* and 15 February 1936.
128. BWD 4* and 25* June 1935; RGASPI 495/100/754, Maurice Dobb to Harry Pollitt 22 October 1934, forwarded to Moscow by Pollitt, 24 October 1934.
129. J.B.S. Haldane, *Why Professional Workers Should Be Scientists*, CPGB, 1945, p. 4.
130. Hindus, *Humanity Uprooted*, pp. 224, 235.
131. Harben, *Diary*, pp. 95-8.
132. *SCANC*, p. 585; BWD 23 December 1934*.
133. BWD 12 April* and 26 July* 1934, 30 July 1935* and 15 February 1936.
134. H.G. Wells, *The Shape of Things to Come. The ultimate revolution*, Hutchinson, 1933, pp. 138-41.

135. BWD 6 September 1933.
136. BWD 10 October and 23 December* 1934.
137. *SCANC*, pp. 992-6.
138. James K. Hopkins, *Into the Heart of the Fire. The British in the Spanish Civil War*, Stanford University Press, 1998, pp. 56-7; Jon Evans, *New Leader*, 24 January 1936. These sympathies with Soviet Russia had previously been indicated by the 'New Russia' supplement which the *New Leader* had run at about the time that the Webbs' were making their own pilgrimage there (information courtesy of Gidon Cohen).
139. BWD 20 October* and 25 November 1936, 20 February 1937*.
140. Laski, review of *SCANC* (second edition), *Political Quarterly*, January-March 1938, pp. 130-3; similarly, for the changing attitudes of the ILP, see the protest about the trials of ILP MPs, published *New Leader*, 11 March 1938 (reference courtesy of Gidon Cohen).
141. Passfield papers II/4/J/2, Paul Haensel to SW n.d. but c. June 1933.
142. *Report of Court Proceedings*, p. 304; *SCANC*, p. 546.
143. BWD 13 December 1937*; Ivor Montagu papers (LHASC), Cohen to Montagu, 3 August, 1932 or 1933? For Cohen see Kevin Morgan and Gidon Cohen, 'Rose Cohen (1894-1937), communist' in Keith Gildart, David Howell and Neville Kirk, eds, *The Dictionary of Labour Biography. Volume 11*, Palgrave, 2004.
144. BWD 13 July 1938*.
145. BWD 1 February 1937*.
146. BWD 1 February 1937*.
147. BWD 25 May* and 22 August* 1934.
148. BWD13 July 1938*.
149. BWD 4* and 25* June 1935.
150. BWD 1 October and 14 November 1927, 24* and 25* March and 7 September 1934.
151. BWD 11 May 1937*.
152. MRC MSS 292/947/8, review cutting from *Mercury* (US), July 1936.
153. Laski, review of *SCANC* (second edition).

# *Epilogue*

# The temple of death

If Soviet communism was the new civilisation, the rival dictatorship of the Nazis represented its antithesis. Like a 'recession to the barbaric tribes of ancient times', the disaster which had befallen Germany preoccupied Beatrice even despite her absorption in Russia, and as she worked on *Soviet Communism* she described herself as 'devour[ing]' whatever she could find to read on the subject.[1] When the Spanish war broke out, she dreamt of the communists in Britain and Germany joining their respective armed forces so that they might 'fly over to the proletarian army' when the battle of the two civilisations, 'proletarian' and 'fascist', was inevitably joined.[2] In 1938 the same horror of Nazism led her to broadcast to Germany through the communist operated Freedom Station, calling upon its people to rise up and establish a classless society the moment the opportunity arose. With the 'sinister madness' of his persecution of the Jews, Hitler – 'the maddest of men' – was like the symptom of a civilisation gone to ruin.[3]

But instead of the issues clarifying themselves into Beatrice's 'class war', both in policy and diplomacy the lines between proletarian and fascist became confused. Laski's long dark age, it seemed, was already at hand. Though Beatrice continued to rationalise Stalin's persecutions in the presence of others, her diaries reveal a mounting disillusionment with the disease of orthodoxy, combined with anxieties over the threat of another great European conflagration. With the old working partnership now broken, as a result of Sidney's stroke, Beatrice succumbed once more to the despairing tone of some of her earlier diary entries. The day she first noted Rose Cohen's arrest she recorded the now ever-present suspicion that not just Hitler but Stalin and his clique '*may* have lost their heads!'; and with the news of the final pre-war show trial four months later, she gave vent to undisguised dismay. 'It is then that my poor old brain begins to whizz and ache and I feel worn out, too old to live', she wrote.

> It is clear that this trial is not a frame up ... but so many of the old leaders are involved ... that it darkens that great continent ... and gives it the features of hell rather than heaven ... The sickening vilification of all who differ from the policy of the governing clique, the perpetual fear of

> innocent citizens of being wrongly accused and convicted is a terrible social disease ... The poor Maiskys, what a life they must be leading![4]

'Oh! where? Oh! where? is the progress we all believed in half a century ago, and most of us continued to believe in up to the Great War?', she asked again in the aftermath of Munich.[5] In August 1939 she affirmed her belief in the professional rather than religious conception of the vocation of leadership, admitting that 'the disease of orthodoxy coupled by the idolisation of the leader, past and present, is a cause of disastrous developments ... insecurity, lack of initiative, the selection of individuals for important posts who are stupid or selfish or deceitful'. 'Let us hope', she concluded wanly, 'that the constitution of an active multiform democracy (unknown to the Fascist Italy or Nazi Germany) ... will eventually eliminate the human parrot and human herd from the Soviet Union'.[6]

Seven days later followed the 'holy horror' of the Nazi-Soviet Pact. Even Sidney was troubled; Beatrice was 'knocked almost senseless' by 'evil behaviour' apparently confirming the hidden affinity between the dictators. 'Satan has won hands down', she wrote as they carved up Poland, although 'the other one', still capable of following the news, assured her that it really would be all the same a hundred years hence: 'Sidney observes that, within a century, it may be "a forgotten episode".'[7] As the new year dawned, she looked back on 'the darkest Christmas in thoughts and feelings about the world we live in, that has happened since our marriage in 1892'.[8]

Not a hundred years hence, but less than two, Sidney was seemingly proved right. In June 1941 Hitler launched the German invasion of the USSR, and Beatrice's abhorrence for bloodshed and anxiety for the Soviets' achievements was outweighed at once by relief that at last the world had been set back on its axis. 'Bombarded' with requests for talks and messages, the couple received the biggest advertisement in their fifty years of collaboration, and as her last significant public pronouncement Beatrice counterposed to the Beveridge report of 1942 the communist principles of the Land Without Unemployment.[9] 'The aged intellectual lives on the horns of a dilemma: hurt if ignored, exhausted if appealed to', she had written in her diary earlier that year. 'H.G. Wells is more hurt than exhausted; and I am more exhausted than hurt.'[10] Quietly basking in this renewed esteem, Altiora Bailey at last had had the final word.

Wells was to survive into the nuclear age: his last book, published in 1945, was entitled *Mind at the End of its Tether*. Sidney, outliving him by a year, could never have entertained such an outlook, even had he not been debilitated by his stroke. Beatrice, who could have, was spared any further tests. Confident once more in her new civilisation, by the last year of her life she wanted for nothing more than the gentle dissolution of personal consciousness. For many years haunted by the dream of euthanasia, as early as 1926 she had pondered the possibility of 'managed deaths', exactly as health or the birth-rate might be 'managed'. Perhaps that betrayed the influence of her old friend Eden Paul, an advocate of 'death control' as well as birth control, and precisely on grounds of the parasitism of decrepitude such as Beatrice in her bleaker moments might have sympathised with.[11] In any event, the assurance that nobody under communism would be forced to use such facilities had provided one of the eeriest and most fantastical images of her new civilisation. There, in a 'perfected communist society', she wrote in 1936, 'there will rise up *Temples of Death*, where in an environment of peaceful charm and beauty of sight and sound, any human being who is weary of life, could fade out of existence without pain or distressing circumstances, and without discredit to surviving relatives'.[12]

Not for the first time, the reality was more attractive than the dream. Bound by affective relations so often forgotten in the Webbian social calculus, Beatrice felt unable to take her life in advance of Sidney's, and hoped instead that their simultaneous passing might make life easier for their trustees.[13] Thwarted by some unknown power, she breathed her last some four years before him, on 30 April 1943.

## NOTES

1. BWD 7 September 1934.
2. BWD 24 July 1936*.
3. BWD 27 September*, 13 November and 15 December* 1938.
4. BWD 16 December 1937*; BWD 8 March 1938.
5. BWD 13 November 1938*.
6. BWD 16 August 1939*.
7. BWD 18 September 1939.
8. BWD 1 January 1940.
9. *Co-operative News*, 19 December 1942; Laski papers (IISH) 27/2, BW to Laski, 7 January 1943.
10. BWD 14 March 1942*.
11. BWD 18 September 1926, 24 July 1928*; Eden Paul, 'Editorial summary and conclusion' in Eden and Cedar Paul, eds, *Population and Birth Control. A symposium*, New York: The Critic & Guide Co, 1917, pp. 296-7.
12. BWD 29 December 1934, 29 April 1936.
13. BWD 25 March and 19 April 1943.

# Bibliography

## A NOTE ON SOURCES

As in the first volume of *Bolshevism of the British Left*, I have listed here archival sources and such secondary accounts as are cited in the footnotes. By what can be a fairly arbitrary distinction, I have not usually included published diaries and autobiographies or contemporary printed materials generated from within the British left, whether in book, pamphlet or periodical form.The chapter footnotes provide full details where such items are directly cited. For most of the chapters, the main sources used are the writings and papers of the Webbs themselves, as detailed below.

## ORGANISATIONAL RECORDS

Comintern archives, RGASPI
Fabian Society archives, BLPES
ILP archives, BLPES
Labour Research Department archives, LRD, London
NAFTA, minutes and printed monthly and annual reports, WCML
TUC archives, MRC (MSS 292)
UCATT archives, MRC (MSS 78)

## PERSONAL PAPERS

Walter Citrine papers, BLPES
G.D.H. Cole papers, Nuffield College, Oxford
Margaret Cole papers, Nuffield College, Oxford
Richard Crossman papers, MRC
Margaret Llewellyn Davies papers, BLPES
Charlotte Despard, Russian diary, Fawcett Library
Maurice Dobb papers, Trinity College, Cambridge
Hugh Gaitskell papers, University College, London
Ivor Montagu papers, LHASC

Gilbert Murray papers, Bodleian Library, Oxford
H.W. Nevinson papers, Bodleian Library, Oxford
Graham Pollard papers, Bodleian Library, Oxford
Ernest Simon papers, Manchester Central Library
R.H. Tawney papers, BLPES
C.P. Trevelyan papers, University of Newcastle Library
Sidney and Beatrice Webb (Passfield) papers, BLPES
Leonard Woolf papers, University of Sussex

**WRITINGS AND PAPERS OF THE WEBBS**

The Passfield papers at the BLPES include personal and working papers of the Webbs and the full manuscript of Beatrice's diaries. Reference is also made to the following published editions (listed in order of publication) drawing extensively on these materials. Abbreviations as used in the footnotes are provided in parenthesis.

Beatrice Webb, *My Apprenticeship*, Longmans, 2nd edn, n.d. (*MA*)
Beatrice Webb, ed. Barbara Drake and Margaret Cole, *Our Partnership*, Longmans, 1948 (*OP*)
Margaret Cole, ed., *Beatrice Webb's Diaries, 1912-1924*, Longmans, Green & Co, 1952 (Cole edn)
Margaret Cole, ed., *Beatrice Webb's Diaries, 1924-1932*, Longmans, Green & Co, 1956 (Cole edn)
David A. Shannon (ed.), *Beatrice Webb's American Diary*, University of Wisconsin Press, 1963
Norman Mackenzie, ed., *The Letters of Sidney and Beatrice Webb*, 3 vols, Cambridge: CUP, 1978 (Mackenzie, *Letters*)
Norman and Jeanne Mackenzie, eds, *The Diary of Beatrice Webb. Volume One, 1873-1892: 'Glitter around and darkness within'*, Virago, 1982 (Mackenzie edn)
Norman and Jeanne Mackenzie, eds, *The Diary of Beatrice Webb. Volume Two, 1892-1905: 'All the good things of life'*, Virago, 1983 (Mackenzie edn)
Norman and Jeanne Mackenzie, eds, *The Diary of Beatrice Webb. Volume Three, 1905-1924: 'The power to alter things'*, Virago, 1984 (Mackenzie edn)
Norman and Jeanne Mackenzie, eds, *The Diary of Beatrice Webb. Volume Four, 1924-1943: 'The wheel of life'*, Virago, 1985 (Mackenzie edn)

For the present account, diaries, correspondence and other papers held by the BLPES were systematically consulted for the period from 1912 to the couple's deaths in the 1940s. Full references are provided for citations of original correspondence and manuscripts. Citations to

Beatrice's diary (BWD) without further bibliographic information refer to the original transcripts at the BLPES normally made available to researchers. According to Norman and Jeanne Mackenzie, this typescript version is largely faithful to Beatrice's original manuscript and the alterations she made are, with a very few exceptions, cosmetic ones. I have not myself checked the typescript against the manuscript; and like both Beatrice and her editors I have occasionally tidied up punctuation, capitalisation or obvious typographical errors. Here, as more generally, I have also followed conventional English spellings (e.g. labour, not labor) in citing Fabian texts. In a few cases there are small discrepancies between the dates of entries provided in published editions (presumably taken from the original handwritten version) and the typescript version at the LSE; none are of great significance.

*Asterisked* references indicate passages or entries which do not appear in either the Mackenzie edition, the Cole edition or Beatrice's own autobiographies. It will be seen that these are especially common in relation to *Soviet Communism*. The Cole edition simply stopped in 1932; and, despite the excellence of the Mackenzie edition, the extracts are necessarily highly selective; and for this period in particular exclude a good many passages which, as the Mackenzies put it, 'summarize her reading, current events or outdated gossip with or about acquaintances' (*The Diary of Beatrice Webb, Volume Four*, p. xv). For better or for worse, such materials are used extensively in the study that follows.

For the period to 1912, the text relies heavily on the published editions of the diaries, including the two volumes of autobiography in which Beatrice herself reproduced extensive passages. Particular themes and references have been followed up selectively, but except in certain details (e.g. the drafting of *Industrial Democracy* and the link with Eden Paul) the account of this period draws mainly on published materials including the extensive secondary literature for this period.

The volume also draws heavily on the Webbs' published writings and the following abbreviations have been used for the most frequently cited books.

*CCM* S. & B. Webb, *The Consumers' Co-operative Movement*, Longmans, 1921

*CMGB* B. Potter (Webb), *The Co-operative Movement in Great Britain*, Allen & Unwin, 1930 edn

*CSCGB* S. & B. Webb, *A Constitution for the Socialist Commonwealth of Great Britain*, Longmans, 1920

*DCC* S. &. B. Webb, *The Decay of Capitalist Civilisation*, Fabian Society and Allen & Unwin, 1923 (written c. 1919-20)

*EPLP* S. &. B. Webb, *English Poor Law Policy*, Longmans, 3 vols, 1927-9

*HTU* S. &. B. Webb, *The History of Trade Unionism 1866-1920*, Longmans, 1920 edn

*ID* S. &. B. Webb, *Industrial Democracy*, Longmans, 1920 edn
*PD* S. & B. Webb, *The Prevention of Destitution*, Longmans, 1911
*SCANC* S. & B. Webb, *Soviet Communism. A new civilisation*, Longmans, 1937 edn
*TASR* S. & B. Webb, *The Truth about Soviet Russia*, Longmans, 1944 edn
*WMT* S. Webb, *The Works Manager Today. An address prepared for a series of private gatherings of works managers*, Longmans, 1917

**SECONDARY SOURCES (BOOKS AND ARTICLES)**

Rodney Barker, 'The Fabian state' in Pimlott, *Fabian Essays in Socialism*, 1984

Logie Barrow and Ian Bullock, *Democratic Ideas and the British Labour Movement 1880-1914*, Cambridge: CUP, 1996

Zygmunt Bauman, *Between Class and Elite. The evolution of the British labour movement: a sociological study*, Manchester; MUP, 1972

Peter Beilharz, *Labour's Utopias. Bolshevism, Fabianism, Social Democracy*, Routledge, 1992

Peter Beilharz and Chris Nyland, eds, *The Webbs, Fabianism and Feminism. Fabianism and the political economy of everyday life*, Aldershot: Ashgate, 1998

Anne Olivier Bell, ed., *The Diary of Virginia Woolf. Volume 1: 1915-1919*, Hogarth Press, 1977

Anne Oliver Bell, ed, *The Diary of Virginia Woolf. Volume 2: 1920-1924*, Hogarth Press, 1978

Stefan Berger, *The British Labour Party and the German Social Democrats. A comparative study 1900-1931*, Oxford: OUP, 1994

Asa Briggs and John Saville, eds, *Essays in Labour History*, Macmillan, 1967 edn

Asa Briggs and John Saville, eds, *Essays in Labour History 1886-1923*, Macmillan, 1971

Barbara Caine, *Destined to be Wives. The sisters of Beatrice Webb*, Oxford: OUP, 1988

Barbara Caine, *Victorian Feminists*, Oxford: OUP, 1993 edn

E.H. Carr, *The Bolshevik Revolution 1917-1923*, vol. 2, Harmondsworth: Penguin edn, 1966

E.H. Carr, *Socialism in One Country, 1924-1926. Volume 1*, Harmondsworth: Penguin ed, 1970

David Caute, *The Fellow Travellers: a postscript to the enlightenment*, Weidenfeld & Nicolson, 1973

Peter Clarke, *Liberals and Social Democrats*, Cambridge: CUP, 1978

Jean-Louis Cohen, *Le Corbusier and the Mystique of the USSR. Theories and projects for Moscow 1928-1936*, Princeton, N.J.: Princeton University Press, 1992

Stephen F. Cohen, *Bukharin and the Bolshevik Revolution. A political biography 1888-1938*, Oxford: OUP, 1980 edn

G.D.H. Cole, *A Century of Co-operation*, Allen & Unwin, 1945

G.D.H. Cole, *A History of the British Labour Party from 1914*, Routledge & Kegan Paul, 1948

Margaret Cole, *Beatrice Webb*, Longmans, 1945

Margaret Cole, 'Guild Socialism and the Labour Research Department' in Briggs and Saville, *Essays in Labour History 1886-1923*

Margaret Cole, *The Life of G.D.H. Cole*, Macmillan, 1971

Margaret Cole, *The Story of Fabian Socialism*, Mercury Books edn, 1963

Margaret Cole, ed., *The Webbs and their Work*, Frederick Muller, 1949

Colin Cross, *Philip Snowden*, Barrie & Rockliff, 1966

H.M. Drucker, *Doctrine and Ethos in the Labour Party*, 1979

Elizabeth Durbin, *New Jerusalems. The Labour Party and the economics of democratic socialism*, Routledge & Kegan Paul, 1985

Nicholas Ellison, *Egalitarian Thought and Labour Politics. Retreating visions*, Routledge, 1994

Orlando Figes, *A People's Tragedy. The Russian Revolution 1891-1924*, Cape, 1996

Sheila Fitzpatrick, *Everyday Stalinism. Ordinary life in extraordinary times: Soviet Russia in the 1930s*, New York: OUP, 1999

Martin Francis, 'Economics and ethics. The nature of Labour's socialism, 1945-1951', *Twentieth Century British History*, 6, 2, 1995, pp. 233-42

Pat Francis, 'The Labour Publishing Company 1920-9', *History Workshop*, 18, 1984

Jean Gaffin and David Thoms, *Caring and Sharing. The centenary history of the Co-operative Women's Guild*, Manchester: Co-operative Union, 1983

Charles Gide and Charles Rist, *A History of Economic Doctrines from the Time of the Physiocrats to the Present Day*, Harraps, 1917

Martin Gilbert, *Plough My Own Furrow*, Longmans, 1965

J. Bruce Glasier, *William Morris and the Early Days of the Socialist Movement*, Longmans, 1921

Laurence Goldman, *Dons and Workers. Oxford and adult education since 1850*, Oxford: OUP, 1995

Maxim Gorky, *Untimely Thoughts. Essays on revolution, culture and the Bolsheviks 1917-1918*, Garnstone Press, 1968

W.H. Greenleaf, *The British Political Tradition. Volume two: the ideological heritage*, Methuen, 1983

Richard Griffiths, *Fellow Travellers of the Right. British enthusiasts for Nazi Germany 1933-39*, Oxford: OUP, 1983 edn

Helmut Gruber, *Red Vienna. Experiment in working-class culture 1919-1934*, New York: OUP, 1991

Mary Agnes Hamilton, *Sidney and Beatrice Webb. A study in contemporary biography*, Sampson Low, Marston & co, nd
Keith Harding, 'The "Co-operative Commonwealth"; Ireland, Larkin and the *Daily Herald*', with editorial note, in Yeo, *New Views*
Jose Harris, *Beatrice Webb. The ambivalent feminist*, LSE, 1984
Jose Harris, *Unemployment and Politics. A study in English social policy 1886-1914*, Oxford: OUP, 1972
Jose Harris, *William Beveridge. A biography*, Oxford: OUP
Royden Harrison, *The Life and Times of Sidney and Beatrice Webb. 1858-1905: the formative years*, Basingstoke: Palgrave, 2000
Royden Harrison, 'Sidney and Beatrice Webb' in Levy, *Socialism and the Intelligentsia*
R. Harrison, 'The War Emergency Workers' National Committee, 1914-1920' in Asa Briggs and John Saville, *Essays in Labour History 1886-1923*, Macmillan, 1971
Gertrude Himmelfarb, 'The intellectual in politics: the case of the Webbs', *Journal of Contemporary History*, 6, 3, 1971
E.J. Hobsbawm, 'The Fabians reconsidered' in *Labouring Men. Studies in the history of Labour*, Weidenfeld & Nicolson, 1968 edn
J.A. Hobson, *John Ruskin. Social reformer*, Nisbet & Co, 1898
Michael Holroyd, *Bernard Shaw. Volume 3; 1918-1950. The lure of fantasy*, Penguin edn
James K. Hopkins, *Into the Heart of the Fire. The British in the Spanish Civil War*, Stanford University Press, 1998
David Horner, 'The road to Scarborough: Wilson, Labour and the scientific revolution' in Richard Coopey, Steven Fielding and Nick Tiratsoo, eds, *The Wilson Government 1964-70*, Pinter, 1993
David Howell, *British Workers and the Independent Labour Party*, Manchester: MUP, 1983
H. Stuart Hughes, *Oswald Spengler: a critical estimate*, New York: Scribners, 1952
K.S. Inglis, *Churches and the Working Class in Victorian England*, Routledge & Kegan Paul, 1974 edn
Paul Barton Johnson, *Land Fit for Heroes. The planning of British reconstruction 1916-1919*, University of Chicago Press, 1968
Bill Jones, *The Russia Complex. The British Labour Party and the Soviet Union*, Manchester: MUP, 1977
Gareth Stedman Jones, *Outcast London*, Penguin edn, 1984
Thomas Jones, *Whitehall Diary. Volume 1: 1916-1925*, Oxford: OUP, 1969
Patrick Joyce, *Visions of the People. Industrial England and the question of class 1848-1914*, Cambridge: CUP, 1994 edn
Krishan Kumar, *Prophecy and Progress. The sociology of industrial and post-industrial society*, Penguin edn, 1978
Fred Kupferman, *Au pays des Soviets. Le voyage français en Union soviétique*, Paris: Gallimard, 1979

Harold Laski, *The Webbs and Soviet Communism* (Webb Memorial Lecture), Fabian Society, 1947
Dan H. Laurence, ed., *Bernard Shaw: collected letters 1911-1925*, Max Reinhardt, 1985
Dan H. Laurence, *Bernard Shaw. Collected letters 1926-1950*, Viking Penguin, 1988
Georges Lefranc, *Le Mouvement socialiste sous la troisième république*, Paris: Payot, 1963
Shirley Robin Letwin, *The Pursuit of Certainty*, Cambridge: CUP, 1965
Marcel Liebman, 'Fabianisme et communisme; les Webb et L'Union Soviétique', *International Review of Social History*, vol. 5, 1960, pp. 400-23 and vol. 6, 1961, pp. 49-73
Marcel Liebman, *Leninism Under Lenin*, Merlin edn, 1980
Thomas Linehan, *British Fascism 1918-39. Parties, ideology and culture*, Manchester: MUP, 2000
Alan McBriar, *An Edwardian Mixed Doubles. The Bosanquets versus the Webbs. A study in British social policy 1890-1929*, Oxford: OUP, 1987
Alan McBriar, *Fabian Socialism and English Politics 1884-1914*, Cambride: CUP, 1962
Alan McBriar, 'Sidney Webb and the LCC' in M. Cole, *The Webbs and their Work*
Stuart Macintyre, *A Proletarian Science. Marxism in Britain, 1917-1933*, Cambridge: CUP, 1980
Norman Mackenzie, *Socialism and Society: a new view of the Webb partnership*, London School of Economics, 1978
Norman and Jeanne Mackenzie, *The First Fabians*, Quartet edn, 1979
Ross McKibbin, 'Arthur Henderson as Labour leader' in Ross McKibbin, *The Ideologies of Class. Social relations in Britain 1880-1950*, Oxford: OUP, 1991
Paddy Maguire, 'Co-operation and crisis. Government, co-operation and politics, 1917-1922' in Yeo, *New Views of Co-operation*
Jane Marcus, ed., *The Young Rebecca. The writings of Rebecca West 1911-17*, Virago, 1992, p. 218
Sylvia R Margulies, *The Pilgrimage to Russia. The Soviet Union and the treatment of foreigners, 1924-1937*, Madison, Wisconsin: University of Wisconsin Press, 1968
Standish Meacham, *Toynbee Hall and Social Reform 1880-1914*, Yale University Press, 1987
Robert Michels, *Political Parties. A sociological study of the oligarchical tendencies of modern democracy* (1915), New York: Transaction Publishers edn, 1999
Kenneth O. Morgan, 'The Webbs' in *Labour People. Leaders and lieutenants from Hardie to Kinnock*, Oxford: OUP, 1987
Kevin Morgan, 'The other future. The British left and America in the 1920s', *Socialist History*, 16, 2000

Kevin Morgan and Gidon Cohen, 'Rose Cohen (1894-1937), communist' in Keith Gildart, David Howell and Neville Kirk, eds, *The Dictionary of Labour Biography. Volume 11*, Palgrave, 2004

Lloyd Morris, *William James. The message of a modern mind*, New York: Sribners, 1950

Margaret Morris, *The General Strike*, Penguin, 1976

A.L. Morton, *The English Utopia*, Lawrence & Wishart, 1952

A.L. Morton, ed., *Political Writings of William Morris*, Lawrence & Wishart, 1973

Robert Skidelsky, *Oswald Mosley*, Macmillan, 1981 edn

Kitty Muggeridge and Ruth Adam, *Beatrice Webb. A life 1858-1943*, Secker & Warburg, 1967

Michael Newman, *Harold Laski: a political biography*, Macmillan, 1993

Bruno Naarden, *Socialist Europe and Revolutionary Russia. Perception and prejudice, 1848-1923*, Cambridge: CUP, 1992

Nigel Nicolson, ed., *The Question of Things Happening. The letters of Virginia Woolf. Volume 2: 1917-1922*, Hogarth Press, 1976

Tom Normand, *Wyndham Lewis the artist: holding the mirror up to politics*, Cambridge: CUP, 1992

Chris Nyland and Gaby Ramia, 'The Webbs and the rights of women' in Beilharz and Nyland, eds, *The Webbs, Fabianism and Feminism*

Timothy Edward O'Connor, *The Engineer of Revolution. L.B. Krasin and the Bolsheviks 1870-1926*, Boulder, Cal.: Westview Press, 1992

Edward Pease, *The History of the Fabian Society*, A.C. Fifield, 1916

Henry Pelling, *America and the British Left*, A. &. C. Black, 1956

Henry Pelling, *Origins of the Labour Party*, Oxford: OUP edn, 1966

Ben Pimlott, *Hugh Dalton*, Macmillan edn, 1986

J.A.R. Pimlott, *Toynbee Hall. Fifty years of social progress*, Dent, 1935

A.J. Polan, *Lenin and the End of Politics*, Methuen, 1984

Janet Polasky, *The Democratic Socialism of Emile Vandervelde. Between reform and revolution*, Oxford: Berg, 1995

Sidney Pollard, 'The Foundation of the Co-operative Party' in Briggs and Saville, *Essays in Labour History 1886-1923*

Bernard Porter, *Critics of Empire. British radical attitudes to colonialism in Africa 1895-1914*, Macmillan, 1968

Rita Rhodes, *An Arsenal for Labour*, Manchester: Holyoake Books, 1998

Rita Rhodes, *The International Co-operative Alliance in Peace and War 1910-1950*, Geneva: ICA, 1995

Neil Riddell, '"The age of Cole"? G.D.H. Cole and the British labour movement 1929-1933', *Historical Journal*, 38, 4, 1995

David R. Roediger & Philip S. Foner, *Our Own Time. A history of American Labor and the working day*, Verso edn, 1989

Nicholas Salmon, ed., *William Morris. Political writings: contributions to Justice and Commonweal 1883-1890*, Bristol: Thoemmes Press, 1994

Jonathan Schneer, *George Lansbury*, Manchester: MUP, 1990
Jonathan Schneer, *Ben Tillett. Portrait of a Labour leader*, Croom Helm, 1982
Victor Serwy, *Le mouvement coopératif en Belgique: aperçu historique*, Brussels: Les Propagateurs de la Coopération, c. 1938
Carole Seymour-Jones, *Beatrice Webb. Woman of conflict*, Alison & Busby, 1993
Richard A. Soloway, *Demography and Degeneration. Eugenics and the declining birthrate in twentieth century Britain*, Chapel Hill & London: University of North Carolina Press, 1995 edn
Fred Steward, 'Political formation' in Swann and Aprahamian, eds, *J.D. Bernal*
Richard Stites, *Revolutionary Dreams. Utopian vision and experimental life in the Russian Revolution*, New York: OUP, 1989
Brenda Swann and Francis Aprahamian, eds, *J.D. Bernal. A life in science and politics*, Verso, 1999
J.L. Talmon, *The Origins of Totalitarian Democracy* (1952), New York: Norton Library edn, 1970
R.H. Tawney, *The Webbs and their Work*, Fabian Society, 1945
Anne Taylor, *Annie Besant. A biography*, Oxford: OUP, 1992
E.P. Thompson, *The Making of the English Working Class*, Gollancz, 1963
E.P. Thompson, 'Time, work-discipline and industrial capitalism' in his *Customs in Common*, Penguin edn, 1993
E.P. Thompson, *William Morris. Romantic to revolutionary*, Lawrence & Wishart, 1955
Noel Thompson, *Political Economy and the Labour Party. The economics of democratic socialism, 1884-1995*, UCL Press, 1996
Laurence Thompson, *The Enthusiasts*, Gollancz, 1971
Dona Torr, *Tom Mann and his Times. Volume one: 1856-1890*, Lawrence & Wishart, 1956
Robert C. Tucker, *Stalin in Power. The revolution from above, 1928-1941*, New York & London: Norton, 1992 edn
Franco Venturi, *Roots of Revolution. A history of the populist and socialist movements in nineteenth century Russia*, Weidenfeld & Nicolson, 1960
Betty D. Vernon, *Margaret Cole 1893-1980. A political biography*, Croom Helm, 1986
Martha S. Vogeler, *Frederic Harrison. The vocations of a positivist*, Oxford: OUP, 1984
Chris Waters, *British Socialists and the Politics of Popular Culture 1884-1914*, Manchester: MUP, 1990
Stanley Weintraub, ed., *Bernard Shaw: the diaries 1885-1897. With early autobiographical notebooks and diaries, and an abortive 1917 diary*, University Park and London: Pennsylvania State University Press, 1986

Anthony West, *H.G. Wells. Aspects of a life*, Penguin edn, 1985
Joseph White, *Tom Mann*, Manchester: MUP, 1991
Stephen White, *Britain and the Bolshevik Revolution. A study in the politics of diplomacy 1920-1924*, Macmillan, 1979
Andrew Williams, *Labour and Russia. The attitude of the Labour Party to the USSR, 1924-34*, Manchester: MUP, 1989
Philip M. Williams, *Hugh Gaitskell*, Oxford: OUP, 1982 edn
Raymond Williams, *Culture and Society 1780-1950*, Penguin edn, 1961
Raymond Williams, *Politics and Letters. Interviews with New Left Review*, Verso edn, 1981
Duncan Wilson, *Leonard Woolf. A political biography*, Hogarth Press, 1978
J.M. Winter, *Socialism and the Challenge of War. Ideas and politics in Britain 1912-1918*, Routledge & Kegan Paul, 1974
Willard Wolfe, *From Radicalism to Socialism: men and ideas in the formation of Fabian socialist doctrines 1881-1889*, New Haven: Yale University Press, 1975
Leonard Woolf, 'Political thought and the Webbs' in Cole, *The Webbs and their Work*
A.W. Wright, 'Fabianism and guild socialism: two views of democracy', *International Review of Social History*, 23, 1978
A.W. Wright, *G.D.H. Cole and Socialist Democracy*, Oxford: OUP, 1979
A.W. Wright 'Tawneyism revisited: equality, welfare and socialism' in Ben Pimlott, ed., *Fabian Essays in Socialist Thought*, Heinemann, 1984
Chris Wrigley, *Arthur Henderson*, Cardiff: GPC Books, 1990
Eileen Janes Yeo, *The Contest fot Social Science. Relations and representations of gender and class*, Rivers Oram Press, 1996
Eileen and Stephen Yeo, 'On the uses of "community": from Owenism to the present' in Stephen Yeo, ed., *New Views of Co-operation*, Routledge, 1988
Stephen Yeo, 'Notes on three socialisms – collectivism, statism and associationism – mainly in late-nineteenth- and early-twentieth-century Britain' in Carl Levy, ed., *Socialism and the Intelligentsia 1880-1914*, Routledge & Kegan Paul, 1987

# Index

## Bolshevism and the British left
## Other books in this series

### Part 1: Labour Legends and Russian Gold

As the opening of communist archives in Moscow has abundantly confirmed, for years after the Russian Revolution communist parties internationally were subsidised at levels sometimes far exceeding their domestic income. In Britain, the discrepancy was possibly greatest of all; Harry Pollitt himself described it as grotesque. Manifested in a distended party apparatus, a wide range of publishing activities and a constant to-ing and fro-ing, between Britain and Moscow, it was the biggest open secret of its time.

If the scandal never really caused the shockwaves that might have been expected, one possible reason was the general murkiness of British political finance between the wars. This first volume of *Bolshevism and the British Left* goes far beyond Russian gold to dig beneath a host of myths and misconceptions regarding the British left. Revisiting archives, not just in Moscow but in Britain, it suggests that Labour's parliamentary advance was itself inconceivable solely on the basis of the workers' and trade union 'pennies' with which it is usually identified. It also describes the brilliant cultivation of private benefactors, not excluding Russian ones, by which George Lansbury created the space both for his own political career and Labour's daily newspaper, the *Daily Herald*. A similar story is told of the Labour Research Department under G.D.H. Cole's direction. From this perspective, Russian gold is seen to have provided both an alternative to such compromising connections and the most compromising connection of all. Naturally, the funding of the British communist party, where its uneven flow and contested application gave rise to fierce controversy, is examined in detail.

Rather than the mass subscription basis of the 'modern' political party, the book shows how the left in Britain often depended on a combination of intense minority activism and private financial support, persisting even despite the subventions of the unions. Approached in this broader perspective, political resourcing throws new light on a wide cast of actors, from Hardie and MacDonald to Morrison and Pollitt. It also assists in understanding the social dynamics of the inter-war labour movement, and shows how tensions of gender, social class, professionalisation and metropolitan centralisation divided parties internally while helping define the cleavages between them.

*Contents list*



## Part 3: Workers of all countries? Syndicalism, internationalism and the lost world of A.A. Purcell

The British trade unionist and Labour MP A.A. Purcell (1872-1935) once enjoyed international notoriety. An outspoken champion of Soviet Russia who nevertheless performed the highest labour movement responsibilities, he was a member of the earliest British labour delegations to Russia and a leading figure in the TUC General Council. His succession to J.H. Thomas as president of the International Federation of Trade Unions in 1924 coincided with TUC's energetic promotion of the cause of Anglo-Russian trade union unity. The publication of a glowing TUC report on the Soviets in 1925 only added to the sense of scandal which Purcell's behaviour caused. However, as a leading TUC 'left' his credibility was badly dented by the failure of the General Strike in 1926, and the following year he lost his position with the IFTU. He ended his career in the relative obscurity of the Manchester and Salford Trades Council.

The third volume of *Bolshevism and the British Left* provides, in part, an extended biographical treatment of a sort that working-class militants like Purcell so rarely receive. However, it also approaches his life as those of the Webbs are approached in the preceding volume: as a way of exploring the disparate cultural and political fields in which Purcell was involved and trying to make sense of the transitions and connections between them. Concurrently or consecutively, Purcell was a marxist local councillor, a syndicalist, a trade union officer, a communist, guild socialist and Labour MP – as well as a publicist for Soviet Russia. From the Furnishing Workers' Guild to the Red International of Labour Unions, and from a neglected seam of trade union internationalism to the nemesis of Direct Action in 1926, the study recovers a tradition of indiscriminate militancy which looked on Bolshevism as merely its boldest manifestation. Critics of Purcell such as Friedrich Adler and Emma Goldman also figure prominently; and through the articulate anti-communism of TUC secretary Walter Citrine, a final chapter traces the hardening during the 1930s of a more familiar line of cleavage centring on the issue of communism.

*Provisional contents list*